This Book Belongs to...

Christmas

all through the house

©2011 by Gooseberry Patch
2500 Farmers Drive, #110, Columbus, OH 43235
1-800-854-6673, **gooseberrypatch.com**

©2011 by Time Home Entertainment Inc.
135 West 50th Street, New York, NY 10020

ISBN-13: 978-0-8487-3454-1
ISBN-10: 0-8487-3454-8
Printed in the United States of America
First Printing 2011

Oxmoor House
VP, Publishing Director: Jim Childs
Editorial Director: Susan Payne Dobbs
Brand Manger: Vanessa Tiongson
Senior Editor: Rebecca Brennan
Managing Editor: Laurie S. Herr

Gooseberry Patch Christmas All Through the House
Project Editors: Sarah H. Doss, Diane Rose
Director, Test Kitchens: Elizabeth Tyler Austin
Assistant Director, Test Kitchens: Julie Christopher
Test Kitchens Professionals: Jane Chambliss; Kathleen Royal
    Phillips; Catherine Crowell Steele; Ashley T. Strickland;
    Kate Wheeler, R.D.
Photography Director: Jim Bathie
Senior Photo Stylist: Kay E. Clarke
Associate Photo Stylist: Katherine Eckert Coyne
Senior Production Manager: Greg A. Amason
Production Manager: Tamara Nall Wilder

Contributors
Designer: Nancy Johnson
Assistant Designer: Allison Sperando Potter
Proofreader: Julie Bosche
Indexer: Mary Ann Laurens
Editors: Jasmine Hodges, Leah Van Deren
Editorial Assistant: Cory L. Bordonaro
Food Stylists: Ana Price Kelly, Debby Maugans
Photographer: Lee Harrelson
Photo Stylist: Leigh Anne Montgomery

Parts of this book were previously published as *Gooseberry Patch Christmas* Books 7, 8, and 9 and *Gooseberry Patch Very Merry Christmas*.

To order additional publications, call 1-800-765-6400 or
1-800-491-0551.
For more books to enrich your life, visit **oxmoorhouse.com**
To search, savor, and share thousands of recipes, visit
myrecipes.com

Cover: Sugar Cookies (page 258); Festive Cranberry Honey (page 42); plated Herb-Roasted Turkey (page 158), Fresh Cranberry Relish (page 159) and Feta & Walnut Salad (page 159); Chairback Wreath (page 14)

Christmas

all through the house

Dear Friend,

We love tradition as much as you do, and there's no time like Christmas to celebrate ways to make the holidays memorable. That's why all of us at **Gooseberry Patch** are so excited about our largest, best-ever book of holiday cheer, ***Gooseberry Patch Christmas All Through the House***.

Whether you love the excitement of the hustle and bustle of holiday activity or you're counting on quiet winter days at home, you'll find just what you need to make this Christmas heartfelt and magical. Choose your holiday fare from more than 400 recipes for meals, desserts, snacks, drinks and more. Over 200 craft ideas that include patterns and clear step-by-step instructions will allow you to stitch, glue, arrange and paint to your heart's content! Accompanied by over 400 see-and-do color photos, Country Friends® Kate, Holly & Mary Elizabeth will entertain you in whimsical illustrations throughout the book.

The first section of the book, "Home for the Holidays," will help you prepare for Christmas with creative decorations, ideas for themed gatherings, homemade gifts and recipes for make-ahead meals. "Christmas Creations" will have you crafting gifts so nifty you may not want to give them away! In "Memories of the Season," country friends from all over share their Christmas recipes and their special Christmas recollections. You'll also find bright ideas for gifts that let you cook and craft. Our definitive "Christmas Cookbook" will boost your cooking creativity as you peruse easy-to-prepare yet perfectly mouthwatering dishes. And our bonus "Holiday Guide" in the back of the book offers tips and hints for planning parties, special meals and more.

Thank you for inviting the **Gooseberry Patch** Family to be your companions as you make it Christmas All Through Your House!

Wishing you peace and joy this Christmas!

Vickie & JoAnn

How Did Gooseberry Patch Get Started?

You may know the story of Gooseberry Patch...the tale of two country friends who decided one day over the backyard fence to try their hands at the mail order business. Started in JoAnn's kitchen back in 1984, Vickie & JoAnn's dream of a "Country Store in Your Mailbox" has grown and grown to a 96-page catalog with over 400 products, including cookie cutters, Santas, snowmen, gift baskets, angels and our very own line of cookbooks! What an adventure for two country friends!

Through our catalogs and books, Gooseberry Patch has met country friends from all over the world. While sharing letters and phone calls, we found that our friends love to cook, decorate, garden and craft. We've created Kate, Holly & Mary Elizabeth to represent these devoted friends who live and love the country lifestyle the way we do. They're just like you & me... they're our "Country Friends®!"

Your friends at Gooseberry Patch

Mary Elizabeth ★ Holly ★ Kate ★ Spot

Table of Contents

Home for the Holidays 8

Welcome Home.................................... 10
Game Night 16
All the Creatures Were Stirring.................. 20
From Hand to Heart 24
Just-Right Gifts from the Kitchen............... 32
A Farmhouse Dinner 46
Cooking Ahead to the Holidays 52
Kate's Chocolate Cure-Alls...................... 58
A Club Christmas................................ 62

Christmas Creations 76

Keeping Christmas............................... 78
All Through the House 86
Christmas Is for Sharing........................ 124
Tasteful Offerings.............................. 140
Flavors of the Season 156

Memories of the Season 184

Years Gone By 186
12 Tags of Christmas...................194
Come Home for Christmas 198
Simple Pleasures to Share..............228
Gifts in the Nick of Time................244
Seasoned Greetings 252

Christmas Cookbook 286

Gooseberry Patch Family Holiday Favorites 288
Merry Christmas Menu....................298
Christmas Classics......................308
In a Wink of an Eye 320
Second Time Around.....................330
Potluck Pleasers 340
Christmas Open House...................352
Breakfasts & Brunches 364
Heartwarming Soups & Stews............374
For Kids Only 384
Cookie & Candy Exchange...............392
Giftable Goodies 404

Special Section: Holiday Guide.....414

Holiday Hints 414
12 Days of Christmas Menus............416
Party Planner 418
Favorite Recipes.....................420

General Instructions 422
Project Instructions 432
Patterns.................................464
Project Index.............................507
Recipe Index 509
Credits 512

Home for
the Holidays

Welcome Home

At Christmastime, "home" is the sweetest word of all! When friends & family arrive at your house, you'll want them to see decorations that are really special. Getting this charming look is as easy as folding a fat quarter of vintage fabric and displaying cherished ornaments. Try these festive ideas to see how fast your home can extend a warm & cozy welcome!

FAT QUARTER NAPKINS
(shown on page 11)

To make coordinating napkins, hem the sides of purchased fat quarters (or surprise your loved ones with some of their old favorite prints). Tie twill tape around each folded napkin and hot glue Christmas balls to the back of the knot.

PLACEMATS
(also shown on page 10)

These red & white placemats will conjure up sweet memories of Grandma's kitchen. Matching the short ends, fold a tea towel in half (our towel is 19"x28"). Sew a button at each corner...how simple!

TABLE CENTERPIECE
Never leave burning candles unattended.

For a centerpiece that will draw everyone to the table, knot twill tape around a pillar candle and place it in an oversized glass footed vase. Fill in around the candle with faux raspberries. Place fresh greenery around the vase and add red berry sprigs and glittered snowflakes to reflect the warm glow.

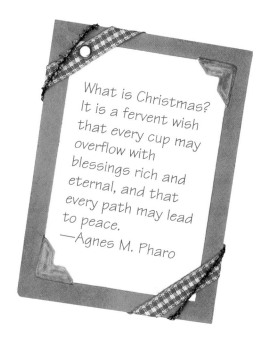

What is Christmas? It is a fervent wish that every cup may overflow with blessings rich and eternal, and that every path may lead to peace.
—Agnes M. Pharo

TIERED ORNAMENT DISPLAY
- floral wire
- fresh greenery
- tiered wooden display
- vintage ornaments
- assorted ribbons
- faux red berries
- glittered snowflakes

Just a handful of vintage ornaments will inspire a tree-full of memories with this clever display. Wire greenery sprigs together to form a wreath to fit around each tier. Wire ornaments to the wreaths and tie a few to the center post with ribbon. Fill in with faux berries and glittered snowflakes for added sparkle.

HANGING BASKET ARRANGEMENT

Everyone will feel like family when greeted with this welcoming arrangement. Faux red and green berries accent twigs and greenery in a whitewashed basket. Dangle a glittered snowflake from a brass label holder. Glue red and cream twill tape over the back of the holder and add a message with rub-on letters. Glue red twill tape around the basket, leaving a streamer at the front. Glue the label holder on top.

CHAIRBACK WREATHS
(shown on page 10)

To "spruce" up your wooden chairs, use red twill tape to tie wired greenery-sprig wreaths to the chairbacks. Hang glittered snowflakes from the tape and glue cream twill tape with rub-on messages to the snowflakes.

TEA TOWEL PILLOW

Matching right sides and leaving an opening for stuffing, sew two tea towels together; turn right side out. Stuff with fiberfill or a pillow form, sew the opening closed and add buttons at the corners for a charming accent pillow...in minutes!

VINTAGE PILLOW

For a pillow that's sure to add a cozy touch to your room, cut a 19" square from a vintage or reproduction tablecloth or quilt piece and a 19" square backing. Matching right sides and leaving the bottom open for stuffing, sew the squares together; turn right side out. Insert an 18" square pillow form and sew the bottom closed. Beginning at the center back of the pillow, insert a needle through a button, the pillow and a button at the front. Take the needle back through the front button, pillow and back button. Pull the thread tightly and tie at the back to tuft.

sweet dreams.

GAMe NiGHT

Bring out the snacks and warm up the cider...it's time for an evening of old-fashioned fun! Classic games such as checkers and backgammon are sure to bring smiles when played with buttons. Our reversible game board rolls up for easy storage, and playing pieces don't get lost when kept in easy-to-make bags. There's even a tray to hold playing cards and a felt cover to make the game table more inviting. Store everything in a large, lined basket, and you'll be ready for future matches in less than a minute!

Square Card Table Cover instructions are on page 18 and Game Board instructions are on page 69.

SQUARE CARD TABLE COVER

(shown on page 16)

- red felt
- square card table
- fabric glue
- green jumbo rickrack
- tracing paper
- green faux leather
- ⅛" dia. hole punch
- craft knife and cutting mat
- eight ⅞" dia. buttons

1. Cut a felt square 11" larger than the tabletop. Glue rickrack along the edges.
2. Center the square on the tabletop. Pinch the corners together to form pleats and pin in place.
3. Using the pattern on page 470, cut four faux leather strips. Cut the holes and slits as marked.
4. Fasten the strips to buttons sewn to each side of the pleats.

PLAYING CARD TRAY

Instructions are on page 66.

SCORE PAD

Stack score cards cut from white paper on a same-size cardstock backing. Fold a faux leather strip in half and punch two holes through both layers. Punch matching holes in the score pad. Fold the leather over the top of the score pad and tie twill tape through the holes. To complete, glue a wavy-edged cardstock strip to the back edge of a striped paper strip and glue to the back edge of the leather on the front of the pad. Add rub-on letters.

GAME-PIECE BAGS

For each of these quick bags, sew a felt tube; then, sew one end closed and turn. Tie the bag closed with twill tape or make a flap by cutting away the top edge at the front and the corners at the back of the bag. Fasten a faux leather closure (pattern on page 470) to buttons sewn to the bag and flap. Make a scrapbook paper tag and add rub-on letters. Tie the tag onto the bag with twill tape.

You can find the snack mix recipe on page 66.

SPICED CIDER
The aroma is fantastic!

2 qts. apple cider
1/4 c. brown sugar, packed
1/2 t. whole allspice
1 t. whole cloves
1 cinnamon stick

1/4 t. salt
dash nutmeg
1 orange, cut in wedges

Prepare cider using a large automatic coffee maker. Substitute apple cider for water. Place remaining ingredients in coffee basket with filter and brew. Makes two quarts.

— Pat Akers

BASKET LINER
- paper for pattern (newspaper or kraft or butcher paper work well)
- basket
- tape
- striped fabric
- 7/8"w fusible web tape

Fabric-lined baskets are handy for corralling your game-night entertainment. They make great gifts too!

1. To make a pattern, drape one length of paper over and into the basket horizontally, adding a 4" overhang to each end. Cut or fold the paper to fit inside the basket.
2. Repeat vertically across the first piece. Cut to fit. Tape the two pieces together to form a cross.
3. Arrange the pattern on the wrong side of the fabric. Adding 1/2" to each side for the seam allowance, cut out the fabric liner. Matching right sides, sew the corners together. Turn under and fuse a 1" hem along the top of the liner.

All the Creatures were Stirring

'Twas the night before Christmas, when all through the house, ALL the creatures were stirring, including the mouse! In the kitchen, a Spotty look-alike seems to play "tag" with a little gray mouse and a bewhiskered feline. From the dog dish tree stand to the mischievous kitty topper, pet-themed decorations fill the tree. Wouldn't your canine pal welcome the buckets of treats? Turn the page to find photo frames and framed ornaments that will show off your furry friends to perfection.

Spotty, Mouse, Kitty and Tabletop Tree Stand instructions are on pages 67-68.

MOUSE
Instructions are on page 68.

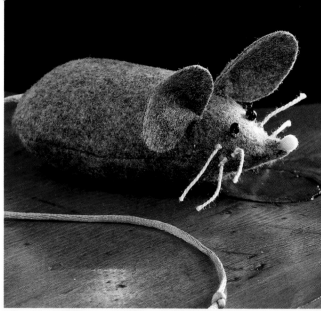

LUGGAGE TAG ORNAMENTS
Luggage tags are a quick & simple way to give your furry friends places of honor on the Christmas tree (they make fun package tie-ons too)…just slide photos inside and you're done. We removed the straps from our luggage tags and used them as mini collars for our Kitty I.D. Tag Ornaments, then replaced them with ball chain hangers.

DOG BONE ORNAMENTS
Fido won't be able to wait to get his paws on these ornaments when he finds out there's a surprise inside…they squeak! To make each ornament, use the pattern on page 469 and cut 2 bones from fabric. Tuck the ends of a ribbon or trim hanger between the right sides of the bones and sew them together, leaving an opening for stuffing. Turn right side out. Stuff with fiberfill, place a pet toy squeaker inside and sew the opening closed.

PET SILHOUETTE ORNAMENTS
These ornaments make the sweetest Christmas keepsakes for pet lovers. Use the patterns on page 469, or for silhouettes of your own pets, trace images from photos and transfer them onto cream ball ornaments. Paint the designs with black glass paint.

PET PHOTO FRAME

Personalize a display of your favorite four-legged friend. Glue pieces cut from a leather collar to a framed picture of your pet. Add a bell or metal tag to the collar. Stamp your pal's name on the tag with StazOn® ink.

KITTY I.D. TAG ORNAMENTS

• tracing paper
• craft knife and cutting mat
• mat board
• 1/16" dia. hole punch
• silver metallic acrylic paint
• paintbrush
• alphabet stamps
• black StazOn® ink pad
• clear dimensional glaze
• jump rings
• lanyard hooks
• jingle bells
• straps removed from luggage tags

These clever ornaments are oversized replicas of Kitty's metal I.D. tag. For each ornament, use the pattern on page 469 and cut a tag from mat board. Punch a hole at the top. Paint the tag silver. Stamp Kitty's name on the tag and paint the tag with glaze. Use a jump ring to attach the tag to a lanyard hook and add a bell. Attach the hook to a luggage tag strap.

from Hand to Heart

Nothing gets us in the Christmas spirit better than giving gifts! And doesn't the giving seem even more fun when you make the presents yourself? This assortment of ideas to share has something for everyone. Make an office organizer from felt that's sure to be appreciated. Play Santa's helper and cover clothes hangers with vintage linens or add ribbon to a boxed set of photo albums. Just turn the pages to see more of these thoughtful projects. They're so exciting, you may have trouble keeping your plans secret!

Motif Scrap Afghan instructions begin on page 71. Flocked Candle Box instructions are on page 69.

HINGED FRAME WITH ORNAMENT

- 2 same-size white photo frames with glass removed
- two 1" hinges
- screwdriver
- buttons
- craft glue
- adhesive foam dots
- patterned and solid scrapbook papers
- vellum tape
- vellum Christmas quote
- mica glitter
- papier-mâché ornament
- cream rickrack
- ⅛" dia. hole punch
- ribbon

Share a message of good tidings with this clever display. Connect the frames with the hinges. Adhere buttons to the frame corners with glue and foam dots. Cover one of the frame backings with patterned paper (discard the other backing). Tape the quote to solid paper and attach it to the frame backing with foam dots. Insert the backing in one frame.

Glue glitter on the top and bottom sections of the ornament and rickrack around the middle. Make a paper tag and add a button. Tie a ribbon hanger through the ornament and tag. Glue one ribbon end to the top back of the empty frame.

BOXED PHOTO ALBUMS

Make a purchased boxed photo album set a more personal gift by fusing layered ribbons onto the box and albums. Add album labels in metal holders. To get an album started, mat a few special photos with coordinating colors of cardstock, attach photo corners and adhere the photos to the pages along with vellum and cardstock labels.

EGG CUP PIN CUSHION

- green paint
- paintbrush
- egg cup
- brown embroidery floss
- 7½" tan wool felt square
- polyester fiberfill
- extra-strength craft glue
- 2" and 2½" dia. circle templates
- 3"x15" pink wool felt piece
- light blue rickrack
- tracing paper
- scrap of green wool felt
- sand

1. Paint the egg cup. Sew brown French Knots (page 422) at the center of the tan felt. Stuff the felt with fiberfill and tie closed with floss. Glue the bottom of the cushion in the cup.

2. For the inner row of petals, cut two 2" diameter pink felt circles in half. Cut four 2½" diameter circles in half for the remaining two rows. Overlapping for a rose petal look, glue the straight edge of the petals to the cushion, tucking the bottom row of petals in the cup. Glue rickrack around the cup.

3. For the needle sharpener, use the pattern on page 473 and cut two green felt leaves. Matching right sides and leaving an opening for turning, sew the leaves together. Turn right side out, fill with sand and sew the opening closed. Sew a vein along the center of the leaf and glue the leaf to the cup.

FLOWER BROOCH

This happy little flower would make a great gift for a teacher, friend or secret pal. Use the pattern on page 472 and cut an illustration board backing and a slightly larger dark green wool felt backing; glue together. Cut stem/leaf and flower pieces from scraps of wool felt. Sew or glue buttons on the flower. Glue the flower, stem/leaf and a pin back to the backing. For a friend who doesn't wear jewelry, make it a magnet instead. Simply substitute a round magnet for the pin back.

EMBELLISHED KNITTING NEEDLES

These colorful needles will add cheer to a friend's craft area and they're simple to make! Lightly sand the tops of bamboo knitting needles; then, paint them with acrylic paints, adding stripes, zigzags and dots. Brush clear dimensional glaze over the painted areas. Top off the needles with glued-on felt beads.

VELVET JEWELRY POUCH

- white waxed transfer paper
- blue-green velvet fat quarter
- red, green and ecru embroidery floss
- cotton fat quarter
- ⅛"w ecru silk ribbon

Any woman will feel pampered when given this timeless pouch. Refer to Embroidery Stitches on pages 422-423 before beginning.

1. Enlarge the pattern on page 464 to 160%. Slide a sheet of transfer paper between the pattern and the velvet, with the waxed side toward the velvet. Transfer the pattern to the velvet.
2. Follow the Stitching Diagram on page 464 to embroider the velvet. Cut out the circle along the drawn line. Cut a cotton circle the same size.
3. Matching right sides and leaving an opening for turning, sew the circles together. Turn right side out. Press, cotton side up; then, sew the opening closed. Topstitch around the edge.
4. Using the ribbon and beginning and ending on the velvet side, work a Running Stitch through both layers around the edge of the circle. Knot both ribbon ends. Pull the ribbon and tie in a bow to close the pouch.

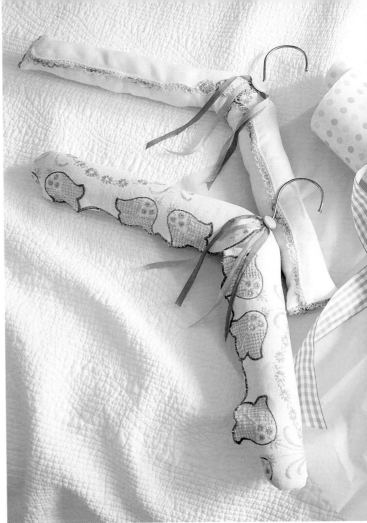

PADDED HANGERS

- fabric glue
- batting
- wooden hangers
- kraft paper
- linens with decorative edging
- ¼"w silk ribbons
- buttons

These hangers are so nice, no one will want to cover them up! Wrap and glue batting around each hanger. Draw around each half of the padded hanger separately (excluding the hook) on kraft paper to make patterns for the cover. Add enough of an allowance to the patterns for the decorative linen edges to overlap the raw edges and for the covers to overlap at the center of the hanger. Cut out the patterns and use them to cut the linens. Wrap and glue the covers around the hanger. (For the embroidered floral hanger, we matched right sides and sewed the rounded ends together, then turned the cover right side out before gluing to the hanger.) Add ribbons and buttons to make the hangers extra pretty.

APPLIQUÉD BAG

- hand-dyed wool felt
- red felt bag
- cranberry embroidery floss
- gold and pink glass beads

Add a whimsical touch with this beaded bouquet.

1. Enlarge the patterns on page 472 to 128%. Use the patterns and cut flowers and stems from felt.
2. Pin the shapes to the bag.
3. Work *Running Stitches* (page 423) to sew the stems and large flowers to the bag. Attach the small round flowers with *Straight Stitches*. Add gold and pink beaded highlights to the flower centers.

PAINTED GUEST TOWELS

Give guests an extra-special welcome...surprise them with their very own towels. Use a computer to print their initials; then, use transfer paper to transfer them onto purchased towels. Mix acrylic paint with textile medium and paint the letters. Add rickrack around the bottom with fabric glue and you're ready to show some hospitality.

Just Right Gifts from the Kitchen

CRANBERRY CIDER MIX

Find a nice blend of flavors in this mix.

12 cinnamon sticks, broken into pieces
½ c. sweetened, dried cranberries

1 T. whole allspice
1 T. nutmeg
½ t. ground cloves

Mix together all ingredients. Store in an airtight container. Include instructions with gift. Makes about 1½ cups mix. Instructions: In a large saucepan, combine 2 quarts apple cider, one quart water and cranberry cider mix; heat until warm. Add 2 sliced oranges. Makes 3 quarts. (Apple Bags instructions are on page 74.)

Gifts from the kitchen are twice as nice…you have fun cooking them up; the recipients have fun eating them up! Is there anything that could make this assortment of goodies even better? Yes! You'll find terrific tags, bow-tied boxes and plenty of other clever ways to present your Christmas treats. Just don't be surprised when these delicious gifts show up on next year's wish lists!

SEASONED RICE MIX

Here's a recipe that will make 5 quick gifts!

3 lbs. long-grain rice
2 c. dried celery flakes
2/3 c. dried, minced onion
1/2 c. dried parsley
2 T. dried chives
1 T. dried tarragon
1 T. dried oregano
1 T. salt
2 t. pepper

Combine all ingredients; mix well. Place 2 cups each in 5 plastic zipping bags. Include instructions with each gift. Makes 10 cups mix.

Instructions: In a saucepan over medium heat, bring 2 cups water and 2 tablespoons butter to a boil; add one cup rice mix. Reduce heat; cover and simmer for 20 minutes. Remove from heat; let stand for 5 minutes or until liquid is absorbed. Fluff with a fork. Makes 4 servings.

CHINESE TAKE-OUT BOX

- plastic zipping bag filled with Seasoned Rice Mix
- Chinese take-out box
- tracing paper
- white cardstock
- craft glue
- Christmas scrapbook paper
- scallop-edged scissors
- red chalk
- 1/4"w and 1 1/2"w ribbons
- black fine-point permanent pen
- white vellum
- rub-on letters
- 1/4" dia. hole punch
- twill tape
- faux greenery
- red mini ornaments

A Chinese take-out box is a nice break from traditional gift packaging. Place the rice mix in the box. Use the pattern on page 471 and cut a cardstock tag. Cover the tag with scrapbook paper, fold in half and scallop the bottom edge. Chalk the front and add a ribbon scrap. Write the mix instructions on the inside of the tag. Using half the pattern, make a vellum tag and tear away the bottom edge. Chalk the edges and spell "joy to you" with rub-ons. Knot narrow ribbon through holes punched in the tags. Tie wide ribbon and twill tape around the box. Tuck the tag ribbon ends and greenery under the wide ribbon and glue ornaments to the box lid.

PAPER CONES

- double-sided tape
- scrapbook papers
- clear icing bags
- Spicy Vanilla Pecans
- craft glue
- brown chalk
- 2³/₈"x4³/₄" shipping tags
- cream thread
- textured cardstock
- rub-on letters
- jingle bells
- ⅛" dia. brads
- embroidery floss
- assorted ribbons and fibers

For each cone, trimming as necessary, roll and tape scrapbook paper into a cone to fit inside an icing bag. Place the cone inside the bag and fill with pecans. Glue a scrapbook paper piece to a chalked shipping tag and zigzag the paper edges. Make a torn cardstock label, add rub-ons and glue the label to the tag. Tie bells to a brad with floss and attach the brad to the tag. Tie the tag onto the bag with ribbon and fibers.

SPICY VANILLA PECANS

When you give these pecans as gifts...be prepared to share the recipe too!

1 lb. pecan halves
6 c. water
½ c. sugar
3 T. butter, melted
1 T. corn syrup
1 T. vanilla extract

¼ t. salt
¼ t. cinnamon
¼ t. nutmeg
¼ t. allspice
⅛ t. pepper

Boil pecans in water for one minute; drain. Immediately toss pecans in a large bowl with sugar, butter, corn syrup and vanilla; mix well. Cover bowl and let sit 12 to 24 hours.

Place pecans on an ungreased jelly-roll pan. Bake at 325 degrees for 30 minutes, stirring every 5 minutes. While pecans are baking, combine remaining ingredients in a large bowl. After baking pecans, immediately toss them with spices until well coated. Spread pecans on jelly-roll pan in a single layer to allow to cool. Makes 5½ cups.

JO ANN'S WALNUT-OATMEAL COOKIE MIX

By giving most of the ingredients for these cookies in a decorated box, fresh-baked cookies will be ready in a snap.

2¼ c. quick-cooking oats,
   uncooked
1½ c. all-purpose flour
1 c. chopped walnuts
¾ c. brown sugar, packed
½ c. sugar
½ c. chocolate chips
1¼ t. cinnamon
¾ t. baking soda
¼ t. nutmeg

Combine all ingredients; place in Oatmeal Cookie Box. Attach instructions.

Instructions: Place mix in a large bowl. Stir in one cup softened butter, one egg and one teaspoon vanilla extract. Drop by tablespoonfuls onto ungreased baking sheets. Bake at 350 degrees for 10 minutes; cool. Makes 3 dozen.

Jo Ann

(Oatmeal Cookie Box instructions begin on page 74.)

CHOCOLATE-WRAPPED PEPPERMINT COOKIES

The two-tone dough and chocolate jimmies give these cookies a festive look!

1½ c. powdered sugar
1 c. butter, softened
1 egg
2¾ c. all-purpose flour
½ t. salt
¼ c. baking cocoa
1 T. milk
⅓ c. chocolate jimmies
¼ t. peppermint extract
4 drops red food coloring

Combine powdered sugar, butter and egg; mix in flour and salt. Divide dough in half; place each half in a separate mixing bowl. Add cocoa and milk to one half; mix well. Add chocolate jimmies, peppermint extract and food coloring to the remaining half; mix well. Roll out chocolate dough into a 12"x6" rectangle on wax paper; set aside.

Shape peppermint dough into a 12-inch long roll; place to fit on chocolate dough rectangle. Wrap chocolate dough around peppermint dough, using wax paper; seal seam. Keep dough wrapped in wax paper and refrigerate until firm, at least 2 hours.

Remove wax paper; cut dough into ¼-inch thick slices. Arrange on ungreased baking sheets; bake at 375 degrees for 8 to 10 minutes. Cool on a wire rack. Makes 4½ dozen.

(Holly Tag instructions are on page 75.)

CHOCOLATE-RASPBERRY TRUFFLES

A wonderful melt-in-your-mouth candy!

3 c. chocolate chips, divided
2 T. whipping cream
1 T. butter
2 T. seedless raspberry jam

Combine 1½ cups chocolate chips, whipping cream and butter in a double boiler over low heat; stir until melted and smooth. Add raspberry jam; remove from heat and cool. Cover with plastic wrap and freeze for 20 minutes. Shape into one-inch balls and freeze until firm.

Melt remaining 1½ cups chocolate chips in a double boiler over low heat; using a toothpick, dip balls into melted chocolate. Place on wire racks; chill until set. Makes about 3 dozen.

Virginia Garrelts
Salina, KS

(Truffle Box instructions are on page 75.)

GINGERBREAD COOKIE CANISTER

- scallop- and deckle-edged scissors
- red felt
- brown lightweight cardboard
- white acrylic paint
- paintbrush
- brown chalk and colored pencil
- craft glue
- ³⁄₈"w and 1¹⁄₂"w ribbons
- canister with lid
- scrapbook papers
- rub-on letters
- twine
- ¹⁄₈" dia. hole punch
- adhesive foam dot

Cut a 3¹⁄₂" diameter scalloped felt circle and a 3" diameter deckle-edged cardboard "cookie." Paint "gingerbread cookies" on the cardboard cookie and color with chalk and the pencil. Gluing the ends at the front, wrap the wide ribbon around the center of the canister. Glue the felt circle to the front. Wrap and glue the narrow ribbon around the canister and glue the cardboard cookie to the felt circle. Make a layered scrapbook paper tag and add a name with rub-ons. Knot twine through a hole punched in the top and adhere the tag to the lid with the foam dot.

DECORATED GINGERBREAD COOKIES

Nothing says "the holidays" like gingerbread, and these pretty cookies will make someone very happy!

1¹⁄₂ c. light molasses
1 c. brown sugar, packed
²⁄₃ c. cold water
¹⁄₃ c. shortening
6 c. all-purpose flour
2 t. baking soda
¹⁄₂ t. salt
1 t. allspice
1 t. ground ginger
1 t. ground cloves
1 t. cinnamon

Mix first four ingredients together until thoroughly combined. Sift together dry ingredients and stir into molasses mixture. Chill dough overnight.

When ready to bake, roll dough to ¹⁄₄-inch thickness and use a 3¹⁄₄-inch round cookie cutter to cut out cookies. Place on lightly greased baking sheets; bake at 350 degrees for 15 minutes. Decorate with icing. Makes 3 dozen.

Decorated Gingerbread Cookie Royal Icing:
2¹⁄₄ c. powdered sugar
1¹⁄₂ T. meringue powder
2 to 3 T. warm water
¹⁄₂ t. almond extract

Beat all ingredients with an electric mixer until stiff. Spoon icing into a pastry bag fitted with a small round tip. Pipe snowflake design onto tops of cookies.

CHOCOLATE-PEANUT BUTTER COOKIES

Two favorite flavors combine for a great-tasting cookie.

1/2 c. butter or margarine, softened
1/2 c. creamy peanut butter
1 c. powdered sugar
3/4 c. brown sugar, packed
1 egg
1 t. vanilla extract
1 c. all-purpose flour
1/2 c. baking cocoa
1/4 t. salt

In a large bowl, beat butter, peanut butter and sugars until fluffy. Add egg and vanilla; beat until smooth. In a small bowl, combine flour, cocoa and salt. Add dry ingredients to butter mixture; stir until a soft dough forms. Cover dough and chill 2 hours.

On a lightly floured surface, use a floured rolling pin to roll out dough to 1/4-inch thickness. Use 1 1/2-inch high cookie cutters or patterns on page 470 to cut out cookies. Place on greased baking sheets. Bake at 375 degrees for 7 to 9 minutes or until edges are firm. Transfer cookies to a wire rack to cool. Store in an airtight container. Makes about 11 dozen.

DIVIDED COOKIE BOX

• 4 3/8"x4 7/8" cookie box with flap lid (we found ours in the cake decorating section at a local craft store)
• craft glue
• scrapbook paper
• red and yellow textured cardstock
• tracing paper
• mat board
• craft knife and cutting mat
• sandpaper
• red chalk
• alphabet stamps
• brown ink pad
• ribbon
• Chocolate-Peanut Butter Cookies
• foil cupcake liners

1. Trimming and folding the edges to the inside, cover the box lid with scrapbook paper. Glue red cardstock to the inside of the lid.

2. Use the pattern on page 470 and cut a star from mat board. Cover the star with yellow cardstock. Sand and chalk the edges and stamp "Merry Christmas" on the star. Glue the star to the lid. Tie ribbon into a bow around the lid at the fold and secure with a dot of glue.

3. For the dividers, matching long edges, fold a 3 5/8"x4 1/2" red cardstock piece in half and cut a 5/8"-long slit in the center of the folded edge. Matching long edges, fold a 3 3/4"x4 1/8" red cardstock piece in half and cut a 1 1/8"-long slit in the center of the unfolded edges. Cross and connect the dividers and place them in the box.

4. Stack the cookies in the liners inside the box.

If you enjoy putting a personal touch on gift packages, your friends probably do too. Why not invite the gang over for a Christmas crafting party so everyone can make bags, tags and boxes for their own food gifts? Send out a few of these creative invitations, and gather plenty of crafting supplies. And be sure to prepare a few of these yummy recipes for everyone to enjoy while they work. What fun!

PARTY INVITATIONS

- 5$7/8$"x7$7/8$" white flat cards with envelopes
- craft glue
- scrapbook papers
- alphabet stickers
- rub-on letters
- deckle- and large scallop-edged scissors
- white vellum
- square brads
- lightweight cardboard
- corner rounder
- $3/8$" dia. silver jingle bells
- $1/4$"w red and $3/8$"w green ribbons
- white and red cardstock
- sandpaper
- twine
- eyelets and setter

These festive invitations are mailable, but be sure to have them hand-cancelled.

1. For each invitation, cover the card with scrapbook paper.
2. For the pocket, spell the message with stickers and rub-ons on a 4$7/8$"x5$1/8$" deckle-edged vellum piece. Attach the vellum to a 5$3/4$"x5$7/8$"

scrapbook paper piece with brads. Glue a scalloped cardboard border along the right edge of the pocket. Glue the pocket to the outer edges only on the left side of the card. Round the card corners. Threading bells onto the red ribbon, tie layered ribbons around the card along the scalloped border; secure with glue.
3. For the tags, cut three 1$3/4$"x6" white cardstock pieces. Glue torn scrapbook paper or sanded red cardstock to one end of each tag. Add the party information on the tags with rub-ons and round the corners. Knot ribbon and twine through eyelets attached to the tags.

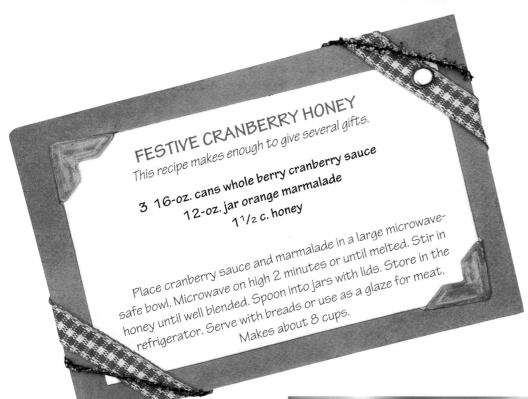

FESTIVE CRANBERRY HONEY
This recipe makes enough to give several gifts.

3 16-oz. cans whole berry cranberry sauce
12-oz. jar orange marmalade
1½ c. honey

Place cranberry sauce and marmalade in a large microwave-safe bowl. Microwave on high 2 minutes or until melted. Stir in honey until well blended. Spoon into jars with lids. Store in the refrigerator. Serve with breads or use as a glaze for meat. Makes about 8 cups.

HONEY JARS

Pick up small jelly jars by the boxful for party guests to fill and decorate for gift giving. Remove the ring and lid from each jar. Use double-sided tape to cover the lid with scrapbook paper. Replace the lid and ring on the jar. Fold and glue a green scrapbook paper piece in half. Cut holly leaves from the doubled paper (pattern on page 471). Pinch the bottoms of the leaves and connect them with a brad. Thread three red wooden beads onto green embroidery floss and tie onto the brad. Glue the leaves to the lid. Tie a ribbon bow around the jar neck.

CELLOPHANE BAG TOPPER

- scrapbook papers
- craft glue
- scallop-edged scissors
- assorted ribbons
- tracing paper
- cardstock scrap
- message rubber stamp
- ink pad
- twine
- embroidery floss
- $1/16$" dia. hole punch
- $1/8$" dia. brads
- 5"x11½" cellophane bag filled with Dipped & Drizzled Pretzels
- $3/8$" dia. jingle bell

For the topper, match short edges and fold a 5"x6" scrapbook paper piece in half. Glue a 1"-wide scalloped scrapbook paper strip along one short edge for the front. Glue ribbon over the paper seam. Use the patterns on page 471 and make cardstock and scrapbook paper tags. Stamp a message on the small tag. Layer the tags and knot ribbons, twine and floss through holes punched in the tops. Attach the tags to the topper with a brad. Fold the top of the bag to the back and sandwich it in the fold of the topper. Punch holes through all layers at each end of the ribbon on the topper front. Attach brads through the holes to close the bag. Tie the bell to one brad with floss.

DIPPED & DRIZZLED PRETZELS

A pretty and tasty gift!

18 oz. white melting chocolate, divided
4 c. small pretzel twists
pink paste food coloring

Melt 12 ounces white chocolate in a double boiler. Dip pretzels in melted chocolate and place on wax paper to harden. Melt remaining 6 ounces white chocolate in a small saucepan and tint pink; drizzle over pretzels. Allow to harden. Store in an airtight container. Makes 5 cups.

CHEWY GRAHAM POPCORN

Snacks are always a welcomed gift!

10 c. popped popcorn
1½ c. golden raisins
2½ c. graham cracker cereal
1 c. mini marshmallows
1 c. chopped, dried dates
¼ c. butter, melted
¼ c. brown sugar, packed
2 t. cinnamon
½ t. ground ginger
½ t. nutmeg

Toss together first 5 ingredients; stir well. In a small bowl, combine remaining ingredients; stir into popcorn mixture. Pour mixture in a jelly-roll pan; bake at 250 degrees for 20 minutes, stirring after 10 minutes. Cool. Makes about 3 quarts.

STAMPED BAGS

(also shown on page 41)

Your party guests will appreciate the simplicity of this make-ahead gift packaging idea. Decorate lunch-size paper bags with Christmas stamps, acrylic paints, glue and glitter. Trim the tops of the bags with scallop-edged scissors. For each tag, stamp a design on white cardstock, sprinkle with glitter and cut out. Add a silver cord hanger through a hole punched in the top of the tag. Make a ribbon loop bow for each bag; then, tie separate ribbon lengths around the center for ties. Glue the tag hanger and the bow to the bag front. Thread the tie ends through holes punched through both layers near the top of the bag and knot at the back.

RECIPE CARDS

Chewy Graham Popcorn is so tasty, everyone will want the recipe, so why not send a recipe card home with each guest? For each card, type and print the recipe onto white vellum and tear away the bottom edge. Use vellum tape to adhere the vellum to an index card covered with scrapbook paper. Trim the bottom edge with large scallop-edged scissors and punch a hole in each scallop. Glue a scrapbook paper strip along the top edge and tie ribbons around the card.

A Farmhouse Dinner

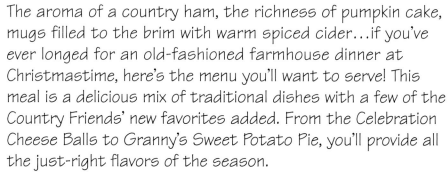

The aroma of a country ham, the richness of pumpkin cake, mugs filled to the brim with warm spiced cider...if you've ever longed for an old-fashioned farmhouse dinner at Christmastime, here's the menu you'll want to serve! This meal is a delicious mix of traditional dishes with a few of the Country Friends' new favorites added. From the Celebration Cheese Balls to Granny's Sweet Potato Pie, you'll provide all the just-right flavors of the season.

Celebration Cheese Balls

CELEBRATION CHEESE BALLS

This make-ahead snack is great when unexpected guests drop by. Keep one in the refrigerator...just in case.

2 8-oz. pkgs. cream cheese, softened
8-oz. pkg. shredded sharp Cheddar cheese
1 T. Worcestershire sauce
½ t. salt
¼ t. celery salt
1 c. chopped pecans, toasted

Blend together first 5 ingredients. Cover and chill 3 hours; then, shape into two balls. Roll in pecans. Keep refrigerated until serving. Makes 8 to 10 servings.

Cheri Emery
Quincy, IL

SPINACH-PECAN SALAD

The combination of flavors in this salad makes it a favorite!

1 T. butter or margarine
1 T. brown sugar, packed
½ c. pecan halves
7-oz. pkg. baby spinach, washed
1 Granny Smith apple, thinly sliced
½ c. crumbled blue cheese
3 T. olive oil
2 T. white vinegar
⅛ t. salt
⅛ t. pepper

Melt butter and sugar in a small skillet over low heat, stirring constantly. Add pecan halves; cook 2 to 3 minutes, turning to coat. Remove coated pecans from skillet and cool on wax paper.

Toss spinach, apple, cheese and pecans in a serving bowl. Whisk oil, vinegar, salt and pepper; drizzle over salad, tossing gently to coat. Serves 4.

Spinach-Pecan Salad

BUTTERNUT SQUASH SOUP

A creamy, flavorful soup that is perfect to start a holiday meal.

3-lb. butternut squash
8 carrots, peeled and cut
    into pieces
2½ c. chicken broth
¾ c. orange juice
½ t. salt
½ t. ground ginger
½ c. whipping cream
Garnish: 2 T. finely
    chopped, toasted
    pecans and nutmeg

Cut squash in half lengthwise; remove seeds. Place squash, cut sides down, in a shallow pan; add hot water to pan to depth of ¾ inch. Cover with aluminum foil and bake at 400 degrees for 40 minutes or until tender; drain. Scoop out pulp; mash. Discard shell.

Cook carrots in boiling water 25 minutes or until tender; drain and mash.

Combine squash, carrots, chicken broth and next 3 ingredients in a bowl. Process half of mixture in a food processor or blender until smooth. Repeat procedure with remaining half of squash mixture.

Place puréed mixture in a large saucepan; bring to a simmer. Stir in cream; return to a simmer. Remove from heat.

To serve, ladle into individual bowls. Sprinkle with pecans and nutmeg. Makes 8 cups.

MELT-IN-YOUR-MOUTH ROLLS

These rolls are the perfect accompaniment to any meal!

¾ c. plus 1 t. sugar, divided
½ c. warm water
2 T. active dry yeast
1 c. butter-flavored shortening
1 c. boiling water
1 c. cold water
4 eggs, beaten
2 t. salt
8 c. all-purpose flour, divided
non-stick vegetable spray

Dissolve one teaspoon sugar in warm water; sprinkle yeast over it and set aside. Blend shortening and remaining ¾ cup sugar; stir in boiling water. Add cold water, yeast mixture, eggs and salt; mix well. Add flour, 4 cups at a time; mix well. Let dough rise for one hour.

Divide dough into thirds. Roll each third into a circle; cut into 12 wedges. Roll each wedge up crescent-roll style. Cover with plastic wrap that has been sprayed with non-stick vegetable spray; let rise another hour. Bake on ungreased baking sheets at 350 degrees for 15 to 18 minutes. Makes 3 dozen.

Jerilyn Anderson
Provo, UT

HOMESTYLE GREEN BEANS

This is a tasty way to serve fresh green beans.

2 lbs. green beans, trimmed
2 c. water
1 t. salt
⅓ c. butter or margarine
1½ T. sugar
1 t. dried basil
½ t. garlic powder
¼ t. salt
¼ t. pepper
2 c. halved cherry or grape
    tomatoes

Place beans in a Dutch oven; add water and salt. Bring to a boil; cover, reduce heat and simmer 15 minutes or until tender. Drain; keep warm.

Melt butter in a saucepan over medium heat; stir in sugar and next 4 ingredients. Add tomatoes and cook, stirring gently until thoroughly heated.

Pour tomato mixture over beans, and toss gently. Serve hot. Makes 8 servings.

Homestyle Green Beans

CORN PUDDING

If you have it, try this dish using fresh sweet corn. Yum!

16-oz. can corn, drained
16-oz. can creamed corn
2 c. shredded Cheddar cheese
1 c. sour cream
8-oz. pkg. corn muffin mix
1/2 c. butter, melted
2 eggs, beaten

Combine all ingredients. Pour into a greased 11"x7" baking dish. Bake at 350 degrees for 20 to 25 minutes. Makes 6 servings.

ROASTED VEGETABLES

Easy to assemble and bake while you are finishing other items for dinner.

1 1/2 lbs. sweet potatoes, peeled
   and cut into 1 1/2-inch pieces
3/4 lb. turnips, peeled and cut into
   1 1/2-inch pieces
1 onion, peeled and cut into
   1 1/2-inch wedges
6 cloves garlic, peeled
3 T. olive oil
1 T. rosemary, chopped
1 T. oregano or marjoram,
   chopped
1 t. salt

Combine first 5 ingredients in a large bowl; toss well. Place vegetables in a single layer in a large roasting pan or broiler pan. Bake at 450 degrees for 25 to 30 minutes or until vegetables are tender, stirring gently every 10 minutes. Stir in herbs and salt just before serving. Makes 6 servings.

Cider-Baked Ham

CIDER-BAKED HAM

On Christmas Eve, I baked this ham and took it, along with all the trimmings, to Grandpa's house for a surprise dinner. We had a lovely day together and a white Christmas too!

12- to 14-lb. cooked ham
whole cloves
2 c. apple cider
1 stick cinnamon
1 t. whole cloves
1/2 t. allspice
1/2 c. brown sugar, packed
1/2 c. honey

Place ham in a shallow roasting pan. Score diagonal lines in fat with the tip of a knife to form diamond shapes, being careful not to cut into meat. Stud each diamond with a whole clove. Combine apple cider, cinnamon, 1 teaspoon cloves and allspice in a small saucepan; heat to boiling. Cover and simmer for 5 minutes; pour over ham. Bake, uncovered, at 325 degrees, basting every 30 minutes with cider sauce for about 3 hours.

Remove ham from oven. Increase oven temperature to 400 degrees. Combine brown sugar and honey in a small saucepan. Cook over low heat, stirring until sugar is melted. Brush over top of ham.

Return ham to 400-degree oven. Bake 30 additional minutes, brushing the ham every 10 minutes with remaining honey mixture until brown and glistening and meat thermometer registers 160 degrees.

Remove from oven. Let stand 20 minutes before slicing. Makes 24 to 26 servings.

Kelly Hall
Butler, MO

GRACE'S BOURBON BALLS

It doesn't take many ingredients to make this special treat.

1 1/4 c. pecans, finely chopped or ground
2 1/2 c. vanilla wafers, crushed (12-oz. box makes 3 c.)
2 T. baking cocoa
2 T. dark corn syrup
1/3 c. bourbon
powdered sugar
2 T. baking cocoa
1/4 c. powdered sugar

Combine first 5 ingredients and pinch together with hands. With powdered sugar on hands, roll into one-inch balls. Roll half the balls in powdered sugar again. Combine remaining 2 tablespoons cocoa and 1/4 cup powdered sugar; roll remaining balls in cocoa mixture. Store in tins lined with wax paper.

Do not serve for at least 2 weeks. Great if frozen a month ahead. Makes about 41.

Lee Charrier

HOLIDAY APPLE & CRANBERRY CASSEROLE

A fruit casserole is a nice addition to any meal.

3 c. apples, unpeeled and diced (hard or tart varieties)
2 c. cranberries
1 c. sugar
1 c. quick-cooking oats, uncooked
1 c. chopped pecans
1/2 c. brown sugar, packed
butter

Place the apples, cranberries and sugar in the bottom of a well-buttered 13"x9" casserole dish. Mix together the oats, pecans and brown sugar and sprinkle over the top of fruit. Dot the entire top with butter. Bake at 325 degrees for one hour. Makes about 8 servings.

Kathi Stein

MONTANA WINTER SPICED CIDER

It gets cold here in Montana…not just anything will warm you like this hug in a mug!

3/4 c. brown sugar, packed
1/2 c. vanilla ice cream, softened
2 T. butter, softened
1 t. cinnamon
1 1/2 gal. apple cider
Garnish: cinnamon

Combine the first 4 ingredients together in a blender; blend until smooth. Pour into a freezer-safe dish; cover and freeze several hours.

Heat apple cider thoroughly in a large saucepan; pour into serving mugs. Add one tablespoon frozen mixture to each mug; stir until melted. Sprinkle cinnamon on top. Makes 24 servings.

Linda Reynolds
Cut Bank, MT

FARMHOUSE PUNCH

A flavorful punch for any occasion.

46-oz. can apple juice
46-oz. can pineapple juice
12-oz. can frozen orange juice concentrate, thawed
2 qts. ginger ale

Combine apple juice, pineapple juice and orange juice until well blended. Add ginger ale and stir to mix. Makes 40 servings.

GRANNY'S SWEET POTATO PIE

It's just not the holidays without a sweet potato pie.

3 to 4 sweet potatoes
1 1/2 c. sugar
2 eggs
1 t. cinnamon
1 T. vanilla extract
12-oz. can evaporated milk
2 9-inch pie crusts

Place sweet potatoes in a large saucepan, cover with water and bring to a boil. Continue to boil potatoes until tender. Drain water and set potatoes aside to cool.

When potatoes are cool enough to handle, remove peel and discard. Place potatoes in a large mixing bowl and beat on high speed with an electric mixer until smooth. Add sugar, mixing well, then add eggs, cinnamon and vanilla, blending thoroughly after adding each ingredient. Reduce mixer speed to low and add milk. Divide equally into unbaked pie crusts and bake at 425 degrees for 30 to 45 minutes. Makes 12 to 16 servings.

Pumpkin Cake Roll

PUMPKIN CAKE ROLL

You will have people wanting another piece of this delicious dessert.

3/4 c. all-purpose flour
2 to 3 t. pumpkin pie spice
1 t. baking powder
1/2 t. salt
3 eggs
1 c. sugar
2/3 c. canned pumpkin
1 t. lemon juice
1 c. pecans or walnuts, finely
   chopped
powdered sugar

Combine flour, pumpkin pie spice, baking powder and salt. In a separate bowl, beat eggs on high speed with an electric mixer for 5 minutes. Gradually beat in sugar.

Stir in pumpkin and lemon juice. Stir in flour mixture. Spread in a greased and floured 15"x10"x1" pan. Sprinkle nuts on top. Bake at 375 degrees for 15 minutes.

Turn out on towel sprinkled with powdered sugar. Starting at narrow end, roll towel and cake together and let cool. Unroll. Spread Filling over cake and reroll. Chill.

Serve hot Nutmeg Sauce over pumpkin cake roll, if desired. Serves 8 to 10.

Filling:
1 c. powdered sugar
6 oz. cream cheese, softened
4 T. butter
1/2 t. vanilla extract

Combine powdered sugar, cream cheese, butter and vanilla. Beat until smooth.

Nutmeg Sauce:
1 c. sugar
2 T. all-purpose flour
1/2 t. nutmeg
2 c. water
1 T. butter
1 T. white or cider vinegar

Combine sugar, flour and nutmeg in 2-quart saucepan. Add water and stir while heating to a boil. Reduce heat and boil gently for 5 minutes. Stir frequently. Remove from heat and stir in butter and vinegar.

Lisa Murch

Cooking Ahead to the Holidays

Make it easy on yourself with Vickie & Jo Ann's fix-ahead dishes by freezing them before the holidays begin. The comfort-food casseroles and soups are complemented by the yummy breads and desserts. Prepare some ingredients ahead of time, like slicing veggies and cooking meat, so you can join in the fun instead of spending Christmas in the kitchen!

Turkey and Wild Rice Casserole

TURKEY AND WILD RICE CASSEROLE

Make this before the holidays and prepare it again with the turkey left after Christmas dinner.

6.2-oz. pkg. long-grain and
    wild rice mix, uncooked
½ lb. ground pork sausage
1 c. sliced mushrooms
½ c. celery, sliced
1 T. cornstarch
1 c. milk
1 T. Worcestershire sauce
3 c. cooked turkey, chopped
1 c. sweetened dried cranberries

Prepare rice mix according to package directions and set aside.

Cook sausage, mushrooms and celery in a large skillet until sausage is browned, stirring to crumble meat. Drain sausage mixture, reserving one tablespoon drippings in skillet. Set sausage mixture aside.

Add cornstarch to drippings in skillet, stirring until smooth. Cook one minute, stirring constantly. Gradually add milk and Worcestershire sauce; cook over medium heat, stirring constantly, until mixture is thickened.

Combine rice, sausage mixture, sauce, turkey and cranberries. Spoon mixture into a lightly greased 11"x7" baking dish.

To Store: Cover and refrigerate up to 2 days. Cover tightly and freeze up to 2 weeks.

To Serve: Thaw in refrigerator. Bake, uncovered, at 375 degrees for 40 to 45 minutes. Makes 6 to 8 servings.

Cheesy Sausage-and-Tomato Manicotti

CHEESY SAUSAGE-AND-TOMATO MANICOTTI

Use two 11"x7" baking dishes and take one to a neighbor to enjoy during the busy holidays. What a delicious gift!

8-oz. pkg. manicotti noodles, uncooked
15-oz. can tomato sauce
10-oz. can diced tomatoes and green chiles with garlic, oregano and basil
1 lb. Italian sausage
8-oz. pkg. cream cheese
1 c. ricotta cheese
4 c. shredded mozzarella cheese, divided

Cook pasta according to package directions; rinse with cold water. Drain.

Process tomato sauce and diced tomatoes in a blender 20 seconds or until smooth. Set aside.

Remove casings from sausage and discard. Cook sausage in a large skillet over medium-high heat, stirring until meat crumbles and is no longer pink. Stir in cream cheese, ricotta cheese and 2 cups mozzarella cheese. Spoon into manicotti shells; arrange stuffed shells in a lightly greased 13"x9" baking dish.

Pour tomato mixture over shells; sprinkle with remaining 2 cups mozzarella cheese.

Bake at 350 degrees for 20 minutes or until cheese is melted and bubbly. Let casserole stand 10 minutes before serving. Makes 6 servings.

To Store: Casserole can be assembled, tightly covered and frozen up to one month.

To Serve: Thaw in refrigerator overnight; bake, covered, at 350 degrees for 30 minutes. Uncover and bake 15 more minutes or until cheese is melted and bubbly.

Ground Beef-and-Tomato Manicotti: Substitute one pound lean ground beef for sausage. Stir in ½ teaspoon dried Italian seasoning, one teaspoon salt, one teaspoon pepper and one teaspoon fennel seed. Proceed as directed.

CHEESY CHICKEN CURRY CASSEROLE

Having guests during the holidays will be a breeze with this dish waiting in the freezer.

2 c. cooked chicken, chopped
2 c. cooked broccoli flowerets
10¾-oz. can cream of chicken soup
1 c. sour cream
1 c. shredded Cheddar cheese
¾ c. milk
1 t. curry powder
½ t. black pepper
¼ t. garlic powder
Optional: ⅛ t. red pepper
½ c. fine, dry breadcrumbs
2 T. butter or margarine, melted

Combine first 9 ingredients; add red pepper, if desired. Spoon into a lightly greased 11"x7" baking dish.

Bake at 350 degrees for 30 minutes or until hot and bubbly. Stir together breadcrumbs and melted butter; sprinkle over casserole and bake 10 more minutes. Let stand 5 minutes before serving. Makes 6 servings.

To Store: Freeze unbaked casserole, omitting breadcrumbs and butter, for up to one month.

To Serve: Allow to stand at room temperature one hour. Bake at 350 degrees for one hour and 30 minutes or until hot and bubbly. Stir together breadcrumbs and melted butter; sprinkle over casserole and bake 10 more minutes. Let stand 5 minutes before serving.

Smoky Red Beans and Rice

COUNTRY CORN CAKES

When you make these ahead, you won't be standing in the kitchen cooking when the family is ready to eat.

10-oz. pkg. frozen corn, thawed
2 T. onion, finely chopped
2 T. celery, finely chopped
2-oz. jar diced pimento, drained
1½ c. buttermilk
1 egg, lightly beaten
2 T. butter or margarine, melted
¼ t. salt
1¾ c. self-rising cornmeal
¼ c. vegetable oil, divided

Finely chop ½ cup corn. Combine chopped and unchopped corn, onion and next 6 ingredients in a medium bowl; stir well. Gradually add cornmeal, stirring just until moistened.

Heat 2 tablespoons oil in a large skillet over medium-high heat. Pour ¼ cup batter into skillet for each corn cake, cooking 3 to 4 cakes at a time. Cook 4 to 5 minutes on each side or until golden. Drain cakes on paper towels. Repeat procedure using remaining batter and adding oil to skillet, if necessary. Cool.

To Store: Refrigerate corn cakes in a tightly covered container up to 2 days. Freeze corn cakes in an airtight container up to one month.

To Serve: Place cakes on ungreased baking sheets. Bake at 350 degrees for 10 to 12 minutes or until thoroughly heated. Makes 14.

SMOKY RED BEANS AND RICE

Be sure and put the name of the dish and the date on a label before freezing.

½ lb. dried red beans
6 c. water, divided
¾ c. onion, chopped
½ c. celery, chopped
½ c. green pepper, chopped
2 cloves garlic, minced
2 T. parsley, chopped
1 bay leaf
½ t. salt
½ t. red pepper flakes
½ lb. smoked Polish sausage,
    cut into ¼-inch pieces
hot cooked rice

Combine dried red beans and 3 cups water in a large saucepan. Bring to a boil; reduce heat and simmer 2 minutes. Remove from heat; cover and let stand one hour. Drain well.

Return beans to saucepan. Add remaining 3 cups water, onion and next 7 ingredients. Bring to a boil; cover, reduce heat and simmer 2 hours or until beans are tender, stirring occasionally. Add sausage and simmer, uncovered, an additional 30 minutes. Remove and discard bay leaf. Cool.

To Store: Refrigerate bean mixture in a tightly covered container up to 3 days. Freeze in an airtight container up to 2 weeks.

To Serve: Thaw in refrigerator. Place bean mixture in a large saucepan. Cook over medium-low heat until thoroughly heated, stirring occasionally. Serve over rice. Makes 8 servings.

CREAMY OLIVE SPREAD

This recipe mixes up quickly for those friends who stop by to wish you a "Merry Christmas!"

2 8-oz. pkgs. cream cheese, softened
4¼-oz. can chopped ripe black olives
½ c. pimento-stuffed olives, chopped
1 clove garlic, minced
2 T. olive oil
2 T. lemon juice
Optional: ¼ t. salt
pita chips

Stir together first 6 ingredients; add salt, if desired. Serve with pita chips. Makes about 2¾ cups.

To Store: Refrigerate spread in an airtight container up to one week or freeze up to 2 weeks.

To Serve: Thaw in refrigerator. Let stand at room temperature 30 minutes and stir before serving.

CHUNKY BEEF CHILI

Pop this out of the freezer and enjoy a great family favorite.

4 lbs. boneless chuck roast, cut into ½-inch pieces
2 T. chili powder
2 6-oz. cans tomato paste
32-oz. can beef broth
2 8-oz. cans tomato sauce
2 t. granulated garlic
1 t. salt
1 t. oregano
1 t. ground cumin
1 t. paprika
1 t. onion powder
½ t. black pepper
¼ t. red pepper
Garnish: crushed tortilla chips, sour cream, shredded cheese, chopped onion

Brown meat in a Dutch oven over medium-high heat. Remove meat, reserving drippings in Dutch oven. Add chili powder to Dutch oven; cook, stirring constantly, 2 minutes. Stir in tomato paste; cook 5 minutes.

Return beef to Dutch oven. Stir in beef broth and next 9 ingredients; bring to a boil. Reduce heat to low and simmer, uncovered, stirring occasionally, 1½ hours or until beef is tender. Serve with desired garnishes. Makes 9 cups.

Note: See Smoky Red Beans and Rice, page 54, for storage and serving instructions, omitting rice.

CREAMY BEEF STROGANOFF

With this dish in the freezer, you and your family will be able to enjoy a great meal during the holidays.

1½ lbs. sirloin steak
2 T. vegetable oil
1½ c. sliced mushrooms
½ c. onion, chopped
1 clove garlic, minced
½ c. dry sherry or beef broth
½ c. beef broth
1 T. lemon zest
1 t. dried chervil
1 t. dried parsley
½ t. salt
pepper
3-oz. pkg. cream cheese
1 c. sour cream
hot cooked noodles or rice

Partially freeze steak; slice diagonally across grain into ¼-inch strips. Brown meat in hot oil in a large skillet; remove meat from skillet, reserving pan drippings. Sauté mushrooms, onions and garlic in reserved pan drippings until tender.

Return steak to skillet; add sherry or broth and next 6 ingredients. Cook over medium-low heat 10 to 12 minutes or until most of liquid evaporates. Remove from heat; add cream cheese, stirring until cheese melts. Cool.

To Store: Refrigerate beef mixture in a tightly covered container up to 2 days. Freeze mixture in an airtight container up to 2 weeks.

To Serve: Thaw in refrigerator. Cook in a large saucepan over medium heat until simmering, stirring frequently. Stir in sour cream; cook just until hot. (Do not boil.) Serve stroganoff over noodles or rice. Makes 4 to 6 servings.

Chunky Beef Chili

CHOCOLATE-PECAN BARS

These bars are so very rich and tasty. Make extras to give to teachers and friends!

1³/₄ c. all-purpose flour
1¹/₃ c. brown sugar, packed and divided
³/₄ c. butter or margarine, softened
4 eggs, lightly beaten
1 c. light corn syrup
3 T. butter or margarine, melted
1 t. vanilla extract
2 c. chopped pecans
6-oz. pkg. semi-sweet chocolate morsels

Combine flour and ¹/₃ cup brown sugar in a small bowl. Cut in ³/₄ cup butter with a pastry blender until mixture resembles coarse meal. Press mixture in the bottom of a greased 13"x9" baking pan. Bake at 350 degrees for 15 to 17 minutes.

Combine remaining one cup brown sugar, eggs, corn syrup, 3 tablespoons melted butter and vanilla, stirring well. Stir in pecans. Pour mixture over prepared crust. Bake at 350 degrees for 40 to 45 minutes or until firm. Remove from oven and sprinkle with chocolate morsels. Let stand 5 minutes or until morsels are softened; spread evenly. Cool completely and cut into bars. Makes 4 dozen.

To Store: Bars can be frozen up to one month.

To Serve: Thaw at room temperature.

CHOCOLATE-CARAMEL SHEET CAKE

A delicious mixture of two wonderful flavors…chocolate and caramel.

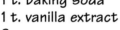

1 c. butter
1 c. water
¹/₄ c. baking cocoa
¹/₂ c. buttermilk
2 eggs
1 t. baking soda
1 t. vanilla extract
2 c. sugar
2 c. all-purpose flour
¹/₂ t. salt
1¹/₂ c. coarsely chopped pecans, toasted

Cook first 3 ingredients in a small saucepan over low heat, stirring constantly, until butter melts and mixture is smooth; remove from heat.

Beat buttermilk and next 3 ingredients at medium speed with an electric mixer until smooth; add cocoa mixture, beating until blended.

Combine sugar, flour and salt; gradually add to buttermilk mixture, beating just until blended. Batter will be thin. Line a 15"x10" jelly-roll pan with heavy-duty aluminum foil, allowing several inches to extend over sides. Grease and flour foil. Pour batter into pan.

Bake at 350 degrees for 20 to 25 minutes or until a wooden pick inserted in center comes out clean. Cool cake completely in pan on a wire rack.

Pour warm Quick Caramel Frosting over cake, spreading evenly to edges of pan. Sprinkle evenly with pecans. Makes 15 servings.

Quick Caramel Frosting:
¹/₂ c. butter or margarine
¹/₂ c. light brown sugar, packed
¹/₂ c. dark brown sugar, packed
¹/₄ c. milk
2 c. powdered sugar
1 t. vanilla extract

Bring first 3 ingredients to a boil in a 3¹/₂-quart saucepan over medium heat, whisking constantly, about 2 minutes.

Stir in milk and bring to a boil; remove from heat. Add powdered sugar and vanilla, stirring with a wooden spoon until smooth. Use immediately. Makes 3 cups.

To Store: After freezing several hours, lift frosted cake from pan using foil. Cut into serving pieces or cut cake in half and wrap pieces in foil. Freeze up to one month.

To Serve: Thaw at room temperature.

SOUR CREAM-STREUSEL POUND CAKE

A tried-&-true recipe that will become a holiday tradition in your family.

½ c. brown sugar, packed
¼ c. chopped pecans
2 T. butter or margarine, softened
2 T. all-purpose flour
1 t. cinnamon
1 c. butter or margarine, softened
3 c. sugar
6 eggs
3 c. all-purpose flour
¼ t. baking powder
¼ t. baking soda
¼ t. salt
1 c. sour cream
2 t. vanilla extract

Combine first 5 ingredients, stirring well. Set aside.

Beat one cup butter at medium speed with an electric mixer, gradually adding sugar. Add eggs, one at a time, beating well after each addition.

Combine 3 cups flour, baking powder, baking soda and salt; add to butter mixture alternately with sour cream, beginning and ending with flour mixture. Mix just until blended after each addition. Stir in vanilla.

Pour half of batter into a greased and floured 12-cup Bundt® pan. Sprinkle pecan mixture over batter; pour remaining batter over pecan mixture. Bake at 325 degrees for one hour and 15 minutes or until a wooden pick inserted in center comes out clean. Cool in pan 10 minutes; remove from pan and cool completely on a wire rack. Makes one 10" cake.

To Store: Cover and store at room temperature up to 3 days. Cover tightly and freeze up to one month.

To Serve: Thaw at room temperature.

LEMON-ORANGE ROLLS

These are so quick when you use a hot roll mix. Freeze several batches and give as gifts to your hairdresser, mail carrier and newspaper delivery person.

16-oz. pkg. hot roll mix
¼ c. butter, softened and divided
⅔ c. sugar
2 T. orange zest
1 T. lemon zest
2 c. powdered sugar
¼ c. orange juice

Prepare hot roll dough according to package directions.

Divide dough into 2 equal portions. Roll one portion of dough into a 12"x8" rectangle on a lightly floured surface. Spread with 2 tablespoons butter.

Stir together sugar and zests; sprinkle half of sugar mixture evenly over butter on dough. Roll up dough, jelly-roll style, starting at a long edge. Repeat procedure with remaining half of dough, 2 tablespoons butter and remaining half of sugar mixture.

Cut each roll into ½-inch thick slices and place in lightly greased miniature muffin pans.

Cover and let rise in a warm place (85 degrees), free from drafts, 20 minutes.

Bake at 375 degrees for 8 to 10 minutes or until golden. Remove from pans and place on wire racks.

Stir together powdered sugar and orange juice until smooth; spoon evenly over tops of rolls. Makes 4 dozen.

To Store: Glazed rolls can be baked up to one month ahead and frozen in plastic zipping bags.

To Serve: Thaw at room temperature. Reheat, uncovered, at 350 degrees for 3 to 5 minutes.

Lemon-Orange Rolls

KATE'S CHOCOLATE CURE-ALLS

The holidays are always a time of big events and exciting things to do, and you don't want to miss a single minute of the fun. To keep your get-up-and-go from getting away, why not treat yourself to one of Kate's chocolate cure-alls? Kate claims that eating chocolate helps her keep up with a busy schedule. And since peanut butter is also famous for its energy-boosting abilities, she says you ought to start with a rich and fudgy Buckeye Brownie. Feel like sharing this treasure trove of vitality enhancers? Make extras for gifts!

BUCKEYE BROWNIES

Chocolate and peanut butter...tastes just like buckeye candies.

19½-oz. pkg. brownie mix
2 c. powdered sugar
½ c. plus 6 T. butter, softened and divided
1 c. creamy peanut butter
6-oz. pkg. semi-sweet chocolate chips

Prepare and bake brownie mix in a greased 13"x9" baking pan according to package directions. Let cool.

Mix together powdered sugar, ½ cup butter and peanut butter; spread over cooled brownies. Chill for one hour.

Melt together chocolate chips and remaining 6 tablespoons butter in a saucepan over low heat, stirring occasionally. Spread over brownies. Let cool; cut into squares. Makes 2 to 3 dozen.

Heather Prentice
Mars, PA

Buckeye Brownies

PAN O' FUDGE

You will need to make more than one pan of this delicious fudge!

4½ c. sugar
12-oz. can evaporated milk
1½ c. butter
12-oz. pkg. semi-sweet chocolate
    chips
1 t. vanilla extract
½ c. chopped nuts

Combine sugar and milk in saucepan; boil for 6 minutes. Remove from heat. Add butter, chocolate chips and vanilla. Beat 10 minutes with mixer; stir in nuts. Pour into buttered 8"x8" pan. Makes about 1 pound.

Sue Utley
Papillion, NE

Chocolate Chip Cheesecake Squares

WHITE HOT CHOCOLATE

This hot chocolate will warm you head-to-toe.

12-oz. bar white chocolate, finely
    chopped
6 c. milk
2 c. whipping cream
1 t. vanilla extract
Garnish: milk chocolate shavings

Place white chocolate in a medium bowl; set aside.

Combine milk and cream in a saucepan; heat over medium heat until bubbles begin to form around edges, about 4 minutes. Do not boil. Pour over white chocolate. When chocolate begins to melt, gently stir to combine. Whisk in vanilla. Pour into mugs. Sprinkle with chocolate shavings and serve immediately. Makes 8 cups.

Dawn Brown
Vandenberg AFB, CA

TRIPLE CHOCOLATE CAKE

A chocolate lover's delight.

18¼-oz. pkg. devil's food cake mix
4½-oz. pkg. instant chocolate
    pudding mix
1¾ c. milk
12-oz. pkg. semi-sweet chocolate
    chips
2 eggs
Garnish: powdered sugar

Combine cake mix, pudding mix, milk, chocolate chips and eggs in a large bowl. Mix by hand until well blended, about 2 minutes. Pour batter into a greased and floured Bundt® pan. Bake at 350 degrees for 50 to 55 minutes or until cake springs back when touched. Do not overbake. Turn out onto a serving plate; sift powdered sugar on top before serving. Serves 10 to 12.

Jane Harm
Neenah, WI

CHOCOLATE CHIP CHEESECAKE SQUARES

As good as their name!

2 18-oz. tubes refrigerated
    chocolate chip cookie dough
non-stick vegetable spray
3 3-oz. pkgs. cream cheese,
    softened
3 eggs
1 t. vanilla extract

Press one tube of cookie dough into the bottom of a 13"x9" baking pan that has been sprayed with non-stick vegetable spray. Beat cream cheese, eggs and vanilla in a mixing bowl until smooth. Pour over cookie dough; crumble remaining cookie dough over top. Bake at 350 degrees for 30 minutes. Chill before serving. Makes 15 servings.

Jan Brown
Greenwood, AR

Hot Cocoa Cake

HOT COCOA CAKE

The warmth and coziness of hot chocolate on a plate!

½ c. shortening
¾ c. sugar
2 eggs
1½ c. all-purpose flour
2 t. baking powder
¾ t. salt
⅔ c. milk
4 T. or 1 env. instant hot cocoa
Optional: powdered sugar and
   chopped nuts

Beat shortening, sugar and eggs until mixture is fluffy. Add flour, baking powder and salt alternately with milk, beating well after each addition. Spoon half of batter into a well-greased 6-cup Bundt® pan. Sprinkle envelope of hot cocoa mix evenly over the batter. Top with the rest of the batter and spread evenly in pan.

Bake at 350 degrees for 35 minutes or until a toothpick comes out clean. Let stand 5 minutes and turn out onto serving plate. Delicious served warm as a coffee cake or let cool and dust with a little powdered sugar. If desired, add chopped nuts of any kind in the layer with the hot cocoa mix. Serves 10 to 12.

CHOCOLATE SILK PIE

Cut generous slices of this pie…everyone will love it!

1 c. sugar
½ c. baking cocoa
½ c. all-purpose flour
⅛ t. salt
2 c. milk
3 egg yolks
4 T. butter
1 t. vanilla extract
9-inch graham cracker crust
8-oz. container frozen whipped
   topping, thawed
½ c. chocolate chips
Garnish: fresh mint leaves

Combine sugar, cocoa, flour and salt in a saucepan over medium heat. Slowly pour in milk, stirring constantly. Stir in egg yolks, stirring well for 5 to 6 minutes. Remove saucepan from heat; stir in butter and vanilla. Pour mixture into crust. Refrigerate for 8 hours.

Top pie with whipped topping and sprinkle with chocolate chips. Garnish with fresh mint leaves. Serves 6 to 8.

Jamie Moffatt
French Lick, IN

HOLLY'S BROWNIE BLAST!

Serve with an explosion of whipped cream or chocolate chip ice cream!

½ c. butter, softened
1 c. sugar
16-oz. can chocolate syrup
4 eggs
1 c. all-purpose flour
Optional: 1 c. chopped nuts

Combine butter and sugar; blend in syrup, eggs and flour. Pour into a greased 13"x9" baking pan; bake at 350 degrees for 25 minutes. Frost while still warm and garnish with nuts, if desired. Makes 24 servings.

Frosting:
½ c. butter
1½ c. sugar
⅓ c. evaporated milk
½ c. semi-sweet chocolate chips
1 t. vanilla extract
⅛ t. salt

Combine butter, sugar and milk in a heavy saucepan; bring to a boil for one minute. Remove from heat; stir in chocolate chips, vanilla and salt until mixture is smooth.

Cheryl Duell
Marietta, OH

CHOCOLATE SNAPPERS

These won't stay in the cookie jar for long!

¾ c. shortening
1 c. sugar
1 egg
¼ c. corn syrup
2 oz. unsweetened baking
    chocolate, melted
1¾ c. all-purpose flour
2 t. baking soda
1 t. cinnamon
¼ t. salt
additional sugar

Combine shortening and one cup sugar; add egg. Blend in corn syrup and chocolate; add flour, baking soda, cinnamon and salt, mixing well. Shape dough by teaspoonfuls into walnut-size balls; roll in sugar. Place on ungreased baking sheets and bake at 350 degrees for 10 to 12 minutes. Makes about 3 dozen.

Debbi Baker
Green Springs, OH

FAVORITE CHOCOLATE PIE

This pie is delicious…so quick & easy to make, yet so elegant.

3.4-oz. pkg. cook-and-serve
    chocolate pudding mix
2 c. whipping cream, divided
1 c. milk
½ c. chocolate chips
9-inch chocolate cookie crust
Garnish: chocolate shavings

Mix together pudding mix, one cup whipping cream, milk and chocolate chips in a saucepan; cook over medium heat, stirring until thickened. Cool and pour into crust. Chill until set.

Whip remaining one cup whipping cream until stiff peaks form; spread over pie. Sprinkle with chocolate shavings. Keep refrigerated. Makes 6 to 8 servings.

Tanya Duke
Bethany, OK

FANTASY FUDGE COOKIES

Buttermilk and molasses give these cookies a great flavor.

2 c. all-purpose flour
½ c. baking cocoa
½ t. baking soda
¼ t. salt
¼ c. shortening
½ c. sugar
1 egg
½ c. buttermilk
½ c. molasses
1 t. vanilla extract
Optional: ¾ c. chopped walnuts

Combine flour, cocoa, baking soda and salt; set aside.

Beat shortening and sugar in a large mixing bowl; beat in egg, buttermilk and molasses. Stir in vanilla; gradually blend in flour mixture. Fold in walnuts, if desired. Drop by tablespoonfuls 1½ inches apart onto lightly greased baking sheets. Bake at 350 degrees for 12 to 15 minutes or until firm to the touch. Makes about 3 dozen.

Jen Vollmer
Bismarck, ND

Vickie's Chocolate Fondue

VICKIE'S CHOCOLATE FONDUE

Delicious dipping sauce for squares of pound cake, mandarin oranges, cherries and strawberries!

24-oz. pkg. semi-sweet chocolate
    chips
1 pt. whipping cream
6 T. corn syrup
6 T. orange extract

Melt chocolate chips in the top of a double boiler; add remaining ingredients and stir to blend. When fondue is warm, spoon into a fondue pot or small slow cooker on low heat to keep sauce warm. Makes 2½ cups.

Vickie

A Club Christmas

When it's time to share a cup of Christmas cheer, be sure to remember your book club, bowling team or knitting guild. These people brighten your life with their humor and friendship, so why not make a real event of the group's holiday get-together? This array of appetizers, snacks and beverages offers something tasty for every appetite. There's even a cheesecake that will satisfy the chocolate cravings of one and all. The menu is planned...now all you have to do is tell your garden society or bunko buddies that this year, the party's at your place!

NOT-YOUR-USUAL PARTY MIX

A tasty munchie no one can resist.

15.6-oz. pkg. crispy rice cereal squares
10-oz. pkg. oyster crackers
9.5-oz. pkg. mini cheese-filled sandwich crackers
6-oz. pkg. fish-shaped crackers
16-oz. pkg. mini pretzel twists
16-oz. pkg. peanuts
12-oz. bottle butter-flavored popcorn oil
1-oz. pkg. ranch salad dressing mix

Combine cereal, crackers, pretzels and peanuts in a large bowl. Combine oil and salad dressing mix in a small bowl; toss with cracker mixture until evenly coated. Store in an airtight container. Makes 20 servings.

Samantha Starks
Madison, WI

Not-Your-Usual Party Mix

HAM-CREAM CHEESE CROISSANTS

I like to top these with sour cream and salsa.

1½ c. cooked ham, cubed
8-oz. pkg. cream cheese, softened
12-oz. tube refrigerated croissants

In a medium mixing bowl, combine ham and cream cheese. Unroll and separate croissants; place a dollop of ham mixture on each croissant. Roll up and place on an ungreased baking sheet. Bake, uncovered, at 425 degrees for 15 to 18 minutes. Makes 8 servings.

Donna Vogel
The Colony, TX

VICTORIAN BLACKBERRY PUNCH

A pretty, rich color and delicious berry flavor.

1½ c. sugar
3 c. water
5 c. ice water
3 c. strongly brewed tea, cooled
2 c. grape juice
1 c. pineapple juice
1 c. blackberry juice
1 c. raspberry juice
juice of 6 lemons
juice of 4 oranges
ice mold
Garnish: lemon and orange slices

Dissolve sugar in 3 cups water in a saucepan. Boil for 5 minutes to make a sugar syrup. Cool.

Combine ice water, tea, sugar syrup and fruit juices in a large container. Pour over ice mold into a punch bowl. Garnish with lemon and orange slices. You may want to try this sometime with cranberry juice instead of blackberry juice. Makes 20 cups.

Herb-Marinated Shrimp

HERB-MARINATED SHRIMP

You will need to make this appetizer a day ahead to allow the great flavors to blend.

3 qts. water
1 lemon, sliced
4 lbs. large shrimp, unpeeled
2 c. vegetable oil
¼ c. hot pepper sauce
1 T. minced garlic
1 T. olive oil
1½ t. salt
1½ t. seafood seasoning
1½ t. dried basil
1½ t. dried oregano
1½ t. dried thyme
1½ t. parsley, minced

Bring water and lemon to a boil; add shrimp and cook 3 to 5 minutes or until shrimp turn pink. Drain well; rinse with cold water. Chill. Peel and devein shrimp. Place shrimp in a large heavy-duty plastic zipping bag.

Combine vegetable oil and remaining 9 ingredients; stir well and pour over shrimp. Seal bag; marinate in refrigerator 8 hours. Drain before serving. Makes about 18 appetizer servings.

Stuffed Strawberries

HERB-MARINATED CHEESE

Yummy with sourdough bread. Make this one to four days before serving.

4 to 6 oz. sharp Cheddar cheese, cubed
4 to 6 oz. Provolone cheese, cubed
½ c. olive oil
¼ c. herbal vinegar
3 to 4 cloves garlic, pressed
1 T. parsley, chopped
½ t. peppercorns
¼ t. fennel seed
1 bay leaf

Combine all ingredients in a bowl with a tight-fitting lid; refrigerate and marinate for one to 4 days, stirring and mixing each day.

Remove cheese from the bowl with a slotted spoon and serve with toothpicks.

Lynne Tharan
New Bethlehem, PA

HOT SEAFOOD & ARTICHOKE DIP

When company is expected, use a can of crabmeat and a can of shrimp; then double the amount of both the cream cheese and artichokes for an appetizer large enough to feed 'em all.

8-oz. pkg. cream cheese, softened
1 c. sour cream
1.4-oz. pkg. vegetable soup mix
6-oz. can crabmeat or shrimp, drained
6-oz. jar marinated artichoke hearts, drained and chopped
½ c. red pepper, chopped
Optional: ½ t. hot pepper sauce

Combine all ingredients and spread in a 13"x9" baking pan. Bake for 25 minutes at 375 degrees. Makes 4 cups.

Joely Flegler
Edmond, OK

ROASTED OLIVES

A sure hit at your next party!

3 c. assorted whole olives
¼ c. olive oil
4 cloves garlic, thinly sliced
2 T. rosemary, chopped
1 T. lemon zest
½ t. pepper
½ t. fennel seed, crushed
¼ t. red pepper flakes

Combine all ingredients in a large bowl. Let stand at room temperature at least 15 minutes or up to several hours to allow flavors to blend.

Place olives in a single layer on an aluminum foil-lined pan. Roast at 425 degrees for 10 to 12 minutes, stirring occasionally. Serve warm or let cool to room temperature. Makes 3 cups.

STUFFED STRAWBERRIES

Try using pecans in place of the walnuts for added variety.

20 strawberries, hulled and divided
8-oz. pkg. cream cheese, softened
¼ c. walnuts, finely chopped
1 T. powdered sugar

Dice 2 strawberries; set aside. Cut a thin layer from the stem end of the remaining strawberries, forming a base. Starting at opposite end of strawberry, slice into 4 wedges, being careful not to slice through the base; set aside.

Beat remaining ingredients together until fluffy; fold in diced strawberries. Spoon 1½ tablespoonfuls into the center of each strawberry. Refrigerate until ready to serve. Makes 18.

Barbara Parham Hyde
Manchester, TN

BROWN SUGAR PECANS

Seems I am forever making these throughout the holiday season. My family eats them before they're even cooled!

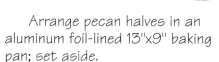

16-oz. pkg. pecan halves
½ c. butter
¾ c. brown sugar, packed
2 t. vanilla extract
¼ t. salt

Arrange pecan halves in an aluminum foil-lined 13"x9" baking pan; set aside.

Melt butter in a saucepan over medium heat; add brown sugar, vanilla and salt. Stir one minute; remove from heat. Continue stirring until sugar dissolves; pour over pecans, stirring to coat. Bake at 325 degrees for 25 to 35 minutes; stir every 10 to 15 minutes. Remove from oven; spread on wax paper to cool. Store in an airtight container. Makes 12 servings.

Nancy Wise
Little Rock, AR

THE GOVERNOR'S HOT BUTTERED COFFEE

Perfect for a dessert party!

¼ c. sweet, unsalted butter
2 c. brown sugar, packed
¼ t. cinnamon
¼ t. nutmeg
¼ t. allspice
¼ t. ground cloves
Optional: 1 oz. dark rum
2 T. whipping cream
freshly brewed coffee, strong and very hot
Garnish: whipped cream

Combine butter and sugar and blend in spices. Refrigerate in a jar until ready to use.

To serve, place a scant tablespoon of the spice mixture in a 10-ounce clear glass, heat-proof mug. Add rum, if desired, and whipping cream. Fill each mug with coffee. Garnish with a dollop of whipped cream. Makes 20 servings.

Governor's Inn
Ludlow, VT

CHOCOLATE-CAPPUCCINO CHEESECAKE

This makes an absolutely delicious cheesecake.

1½ c. pecans, finely chopped
1½ c. chocolate wafer cookies, crushed
⅓ c. butter, melted
2 c. chocolate chips, melted and divided
2 8-oz. pkgs. cream cheese, softened
1 c. brown sugar, packed
4 eggs
1 c. sour cream
⅓ c. cold coffee
2 t. vanilla extract
½ c. chocolate chips
⅓ c. whipping cream
2 T. powdered sugar

Mix pecans, cookies and butter together; press into the bottom of a greased 9" springform pan. Bake at 350 degrees for 8 minutes; cool in pan for 10 minutes. Drizzle crust with ½ cup melted chocolate; chill for 40 minutes.

Beat cream cheese with an electric mixer until creamy. Gradually add brown sugar, beating well. Add eggs, one at a time, beating after each addition. Add remaining 1½ cups melted chocolate, sour cream, coffee and vanilla; beat until smooth. Pour into pan; bake at 325 degrees for one hour and 5 minutes (center will not be completely set). Turn oven off and partially open oven door; leave cake in oven one hour. Cool completely. Cover and chill 8 hours.

Remove sides of pan. Heat ½ cup chocolate chips and whipping cream over low heat, stirring constantly. Stir in powdered sugar until smooth. Drizzle topping over cake. Makes 12 servings.

Sandy Stacy
Medway, OH

Chocolate-Cappuccino Cheesecake

PLAYING CARD TRAY
(also shown on page 18)
- mat board
- green felt
- spray adhesive
- scallop-edged scissors
- craft glue
- red rickrack
- clothespins
- buttons

1. For a standard-size card deck tray, cut and arrange mat board pieces on a 9"x10" felt piece as shown in Fig. 1. Working in a well-ventilated area and leaving 1/4" between pieces, use spray adhesive to glue the mat board pieces in place.

Fig. 1

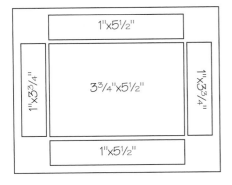

	1"x5½"	
1"x3¾"	3¾"x5½"	1"x3¾"
	1"x5½"	

2. Adhere a second felt piece to the other side of the mat board. Machine sew along the creases between the mat board pieces and around the outer edges close to the mat board. Cut away the excess felt and scallop the edges.
3. Fold the tray sides up and glue rickrack around the outside. Secure with clothespins until the glue dries. Add a button to each side.
4. For the divider, cut a 1"x5" mat board piece and a 3"x5" felt piece. Spray the felt with adhesive and fold it in half over the mat board. Cut the ends away at an angle to fit the tray. Sew along the top edge close to the mat board and scallop the edge. Glue the divider in place.

SANTA'S SNACK MIX
(also shown on page 19)
As far back as I can remember, we've enjoyed this crunchy snack mix...it just wouldn't be Christmas without it.

2 c. crispy corn cereal
2 c. crispy wheat cereal
2 c. crispy rice cereal
2 c. doughnut-shaped
   oat cereal
1 c. pretzel sticks
1 c. halved pecans
6 T. butter, melted
3½ T. Worcestershire sauce
1½ t. seasoned salt
¾ t. garlic powder
½ t. onion powder

In a gallon plastic zipping bag, mix together cereals, pretzels and pecans. To melted butter, add Worcestershire sauce and seasonings; stir to mix. Pour in plastic zipping bag, secure bag and shake to coat. Spoon mix onto a baking sheet and bake at 250 degrees for one hour, stirring every 15 minutes. Cool and store in an airtight container. Makes 10 cups.
Laurie Michael
Colorado Springs, CO

TABLETOP TREE STAND
(also shown on page 21)
- black acrylic paint
- paintbrushes
- 2" tall x 12¹/₂" dia. papier-mâché box without lid
- extra-strength glue
- 12¹/₂" dia. metal dog bowl with rubber base
- drill with hole saw or hammer, awl and metal snips
- 9¹/₂" length of 1¹/₂" dia. PVC pipe
- brown tape
- hot glue gun
- plaster of paris
- dog biscuits or toy dog bones

Spotty will have visions of dog bones dancing in his head when he sees this tempting tree stand. Use with a tabletop tree with a 1¹/₄" dia. trunk.

1. Paint the box. Glue the bowl to the bottom of the box. Make a hole in the bottom of the bowl and box for the pipe to fit through.
2. Wrap the pipe with tape and insert it in the hole. Seal around the pipe inside the bowl with hot glue.
3. Follow manufacturer's instructions to fill the bowl with plaster of paris. Allow the plaster to cure. Pile dog bones on top of the plaster.

SPOTTY
(also shown on page 20)
- tracing paper
- gray wool felt
- plaid fabric
- armature wire
- wire cutters
- polyester fiberfill
- ³/₈" dia. black shank buttons
- black and pink felt scraps
- brown embroidery floss
- ³/₄" dia. brown buttons
- alphabet stamps
- black StazOn® ink pad
- metal dog bone tag
- jump ring
- small red collar

This playful watchdog will gladly stand guard over the gifts around the tree. Match right sides and use a ¹/₄" seam allowance.

1. Use the patterns on pages 465-468 and cut these pieces from gray felt: 2 heads (1 in reverse), 2 bodies (1 in reverse), 3 ears, 4 front legs (2 in reverse), 4 back legs (2 in reverse) and 2 tails (1 in reverse). Cut 1 ear from plaid fabric.
2. Leaving openings for turning and openings in the body for attaching the head and tail, sew the parts together in pairs (pair one gray ear with the plaid ear). Turn right side out.

3. Bending the wire into a "J," insert one end of a 13" wire length into the tail. Stuff the head, body and tail. Turn the raw edges of the body ¹/₄" to the wrong side and sew the head and tail to the body. Sew the black buttons to the head for the eyes and add a black felt nose and pink felt tongue.
4. For each ear, curl one end of a 14¹/₂" wire length into a "P." Slide this end into the ear and lightly stuff the ear. Cut a small hole in the head and slide the other wire end into the head. Turn the raw edges ¹/₄" to the wrong side and *Whipstitch* (page 423) each ear to the head. Sew plaid spots on the dog.
5. Stuff the legs and sew the openings closed. Work brown *Straight Stitches* at the end of each paw to add toes. Adding a brown button on the outside of each, sew the legs to the body.
6. Stamp a name on the tag. Use the jump ring to attach the tag to the collar and fasten it around the dog's neck.

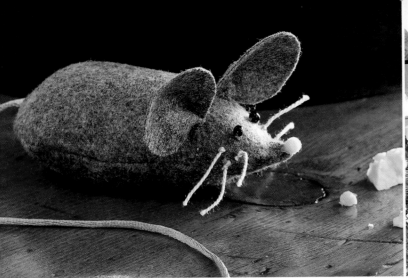

MOUSE
(also shown on page 22)
- tracing paper
- gray wool felt
- polyester fiberfill
- knotted tan cord length for the tail
- fabric glue
- 1/4" dia. pink pom-pom
- black E beads
- tan pearl cotton

While Kitty isn't looking, this little mouse sneaks out for a snack. Match right sides and use a 1/4" seam allowance.

1. Use the patterns on page 466 and cut 2 bodies and 2 ears from felt. Leaving an opening at the back for stuffing, sew the bodies together. Turn right side out, stuff and sew the opening closed, catching the tail.
2. Glue the pom-pom to the body for the nose. Sew the beads in place for the eyes. Knotting close to the face, sew pearl cotton whiskers to the face.
3. Pinch the bottom of the ears to pleat and sew them to the body.

KITTY
(also shown on page 20)
- tracing paper
- tan wool fabric
- polyester fiberfill
- blush or chalk and applicator
- 3/8" dia. black shank buttons
- pink and brown embroidery floss
- gold pearl cotton
- 3/4" dia. silver buttons

Kitty is poised to pounce at the first sight of presents. Match right sides and use a 1/4" seam allowance.

1. Use the patterns on pages 465-467 and cut these pieces from fabric: 2 heads, 2 bodies (1 in reverse), 4 ears, 4 front legs (2 in reverse), 4 back legs (2 in reverse) and 2 tails (1 in reverse).
2. Excluding the head and body and leaving openings for turning, sew the parts together in pairs. Turn right side out.
3. Stuff the tail and front legs and pin them in place between the body pieces. Leaving an opening for turning, sew the body together. Turn right side out, stuff and sew the opening closed.

4. Stuff the ears and sew 3/8" from the edges of each to form the inner ear. Sew about 1" up the center of the inner ear to make a slight fold. Blush the inner ear. Pin the ears in place between the head pieces. Leaving an opening for turning, sew the head together. Turn right side out, stuff and sew the opening closed.
5. For the eyes, sew the black buttons to the head through all layers. Add a pink *Satin Stitch* (page 423) nose and brown *Chain Stitch* (page 422) mouth. Knotting close to the face, sew pearl cotton whiskers to the face. Sew the head to the body.
6. Stuff the back legs and sew the openings closed. Work brown *Straight Stitches* at the end of each paw to add toes. Adding a silver button on the outside of each, sew the legs to the body.

FLOCKED CANDLE BOX

(also shown on page 25)
- acrylic paint (we used pink)
- paintbrushes
- papier-mâché box with lid (ours is 4½" square)
- tracing and transfer paper
- flocking kit (our kit includes flocking adhesive and assorted colors of flocking fibers)
- fabric glue
- wire-edged ribbon
- wood excelsior
- votive candles

Give this charming box to your favorite candle-lover. Never leave burning candles unattended.

Paint the box and lid. Transfer the pattern (page 473) onto the lid. Working on one small area at a time and following the manufacturer's instructions, flock the pattern. Glue ribbon around the sides of the box and lid and add a bow to the front. Arrange the excelsior and candles in the box.

GAME BOARD

(also shown on page 17)
- ⅜ yard brown felt
- ⅜ yard cream felt
- clear nylon thread
- spray adhesive
- ½ yard green felt
- tracing paper
- green faux leather
- three ⅞" dia. buttons
- ⅛" dia. hole punch

This clever roll-up game board has checkers on one side and backgammon on the other. Use spray adhesive in a well-ventilated area.

CHECKERBOARD

1. Cut a 13" brown felt square and thirty-two 1⅝" cream felt squares.
2. Zigzag the cream squares onto the brown square in a checkerboard pattern.
3. Adhere the brown square to one side of a 15½" green felt square.

BACKGAMMON BOARD

1. Cut a 12"x13½" brown felt piece and 12 each cream and green felt triangles (pattern on page 470).
2. Alternating colors, sew the triangles along the long edges of the brown piece.
3. Adhere the brown piece to the remaining side of the green felt square.

BAND

Round the corners of a 2"x8½" faux leather strip. Sew a button to one end. For the buttonhole, punch two holes, ⅞" apart, in the other end and cut a slit between the holes. Roll the game board and fasten the band around it.

TIP: If you don't have checkers, two different colors of buttons are fun alternatives.

Motif A

MOTIF SCRAP AFGHAN
Read Crochet on page 426 before beginning.

Finished Size: 37³/₄" x 61³/₄" (96 cm x 157 cm)

◗◖☐☐ EASY

Materials
Medium Weight Yarn
　[3¹/₂ ounces, 207 yards
　(100 grams, 188 meters)
　per skein]:
　Taupe - 3 skeins
Scrap colors
　39 ounces, 2,310 yards
　(1,110 grams, 2,113 meters)
　total (we used 7 colors)
Crochet hook, size G (4 mm) **or**
　size needed for gauge
Yarn needle

Gauge: Each Motif = 4³/₄"
(12 cm) (from straight edge to
straight edge)

Gauge Swatch: 2¹/₂" (6.25 cm)
(from straight edge to straight
edge). Work same as Motif A
through Rnd 2.

Note: Make 113 Motifs total, in
any combination.

Motif A

Rnd 1 (Right side): With first color,
ch 4, 11 dc in fourth ch from hook
(3 skipped chs count as first dc);
join with slip st to first dc, finish
off: 12 dc.

Note: Loop a short piece of yarn
around any stitch to mark Rnd 1
as **right** side.

Rnd 2: With **right** side facing, join
next color with slip st in same st
as joining; ch 3 **(counts as first dc,
now and throughout)**, dc in same
st, 2 dc in next dc, ch 1, (2 dc in
each of next 2 dc, ch 1) around; join
with slip st to first dc, finish off:
24 dc.

To work decrease (uses next 2 dc),
★ YO, insert hook in next dc, YO and
pull up a loop, YO and draw through
2 loops on hook; repeat from ★
once **more**, YO and draw through all
3 loops on hook.

Rnd 3: With **right** side facing, join
next color with slip st in same st
as joining; ch 3, dc in same st,
decrease, 2 dc in next dc, ch 2,
★ 2 dc in next dc, decrease, 2 dc
in next dc, ch 2; repeat from ★
around; join with slip st to first
dc, finish off: 30 sts.

*To work Front Post double treble
crochet (abbreviated FPdtr),* YO
3 times, insert hook from **front** to
back around post of dc indicated
(Fig. 3, page 426), YO and pull up a
loop (5 loops on hook), (YO and
draw through 2 loops on hook)
4 times.

Rnd 4: With **right** side facing, join
next color with slip st in same st as
joining; ch 3, dc in same st and in
next dc, work FPdtr around first dc
on Rnd 1, skip next decrease on
Rnd 3, dc in next dc, 2 dc in next
dc, ch 2, ★ 2 dc in next dc, dc in
next dc, skip next dc on Rnd 1, work
FPdtr around next dc, skip next
decrease on Rnd 3, dc in next dc,
2 dc in next dc, ch 2; repeat from ★
around; join with slip st to first dc,
finish off: 42 sts and 6 ch-2 sps.

Rnd 5: With **right** side facing, join
Taupe with sc in any st (see *Joining
with Sc, page 426*); sc in next st
and in each st around, working 3 sc
in each ch-2 sp; join with slip st to
first sc, finish off: 60 sc.

(continued on page 72)

Motif B

Motif C

Motif B
With first color, ch 4; join with slip st to form a ring.

To work Beginning Cluster (uses one sp), ch 2, ★ YO, insert hook in sp indicated, YO and pull up a loop, YO and draw through 2 loops on hook; repeat from ★ 2 times **more**, YO and draw through all 4 loops on hook.

To work Cluster (uses one sp), ★ YO, insert hook in sp indicated, YO and pull up a loop, YO and draw through 2 loops on hook; repeat from ★ 3 times **more**, YO and draw through all 5 loops on hook.

Rnd 1 (Right side): Work Beginning Cluster in ring, ch 2, (work Cluster in ring, ch 2) 5 times; join with slip st to top of Beginning Cluster, finish off: 6 ch-2 sps.

Note: Loop a short piece of yarn around any stitch to mark Rnd 1 as **right** side.

Rnd 2: With **right** side facing, join next color with slip st in any ch-2 sp; work (Beginning Cluster, ch 2, Cluster) in same sp, ch 2, (work Cluster, ch 2) twice in each ch-2 sp around; join with slip st to top of Beginning Cluster, finish off: 12 ch-2 sps.

Rnd 3: With **right** side facing, join next color with slip st in last ch-2 sp; work Beginning Cluster in same sp, ch 1, work (Cluster, ch 2, Cluster) in next ch-2 sp, ch 1, ★ work Cluster in next ch-2 sp, ch 1, work (Cluster, ch 2, Cluster) in next ch-2 sp, ch 1; repeat from ★ around; join with slip st to top of Beginning Cluster, finish off: 18 Clusters and 18 sps.

Rnd 4: With **right** side facing, join next color with slip st in any ch-2 sp; ch 1, 3 sc in same sp, sc in next Cluster, (sc in next ch-1 sp, sc in next Cluster) twice, ★ 3 sc in next ch-2 sp, sc in next Cluster, (sc in next ch-1 sp, sc in next Cluster) twice; repeat from ★ around; join with slip st to first sc, finish off: 48 sc.

Rnd 5: With **right** side facing, join Taupe with sc in any sc (see Joining with Sc, page 426); sc in next sc and in each sc around, working 3 sc in center sc of each 3-sc group; join with slip st to first sc, finish off: 60 sc.

Motif C
With first color, ch 5; join with slip st to form a ring.

Rnd 1 (Right side): Ch 1, 12 sc in ring; join with slip st to first sc, finish off.

Note: Loop a short piece of yarn around any st to mark Rnd 1 as **right** side.

To work Beginning Cluster (uses next 2 sc), ch 2, ★ YO, insert hook in next sc, YO and pull up a loop, YO and draw through 2 loops on hook; repeat from ★ once **more**, YO and draw through all 3 loops on hook.

To work Cluster (uses next 2 sc), YO, insert hook in same st, YO and pull up a loop, YO and draw through 2 loops on hook, ★ YO, insert hook in next sc, YO and pull up a loop, YO and draw through 2 loops on hook; repeat from ★ once **more**, YO and draw through all 4 loops on hook.

Rnd 2: With **right** side facing, join yarn with slip st in same st as joining; work Beginning Cluster, ch 4, (work Cluster, ch 4) around, working last leg of last Cluster in same st as Beginning Cluster; join with slip st to top of Beginning Cluster, finish off: 6 Clusters and 6 ch-4 sps.

Rnd 3: With **right** side facing, join next color with slip st in any ch-4 sp; ch 5 **(counts as first dc plus ch 2, now and throughout)**, 3 dc in same sp, ch 1, ★ (3 dc, ch 2, 3 dc) in next ch-4 sp, ch 1; repeat from ★ around, 2 dc in same sp as first dc; join with slip st to first dc, finish off: 36 dc and 12 sps.

Rnd 4: With **right** side facing, join next color with slip st in any ch-2 sp; ch 5, 3 dc in same sp, 3 dc in next ch-1 sp, ★ (3 dc, ch 2, 3 dc) in next ch-2 sp, 3 dc in next ch-1 sp; repeat from ★ around, 2 dc in same sp as first dc; join with slip st to first dc, finish off: 54 dc and 6 ch-2 sps.

Rnd 5: With **right** side facing, join Taupe with sc in any ch-2 sp (see Joining with Sc, page 426); 2 sc in same sp, skip next dc, sc in next 7 dc, ★ 3 sc in next ch-2 sp, skip next dc, sc in next 7 dc; repeat from ★ around; join with slip st to first sc, finish off: 60 sc.

Finishing

Using Placement Diagram as a guide, with Taupe, **wrong** sides together and working through inside loops, whipstitch Motifs together (Fig. 2, page 426), forming 5 vertical strips of 13 Motifs each and 4 vertical strips of 12 Motifs each, beginning in center sc of any corner 3-sc group and ending in center sc of next corner 3-sc group.
Join strips in same manner.

Placement Diagram

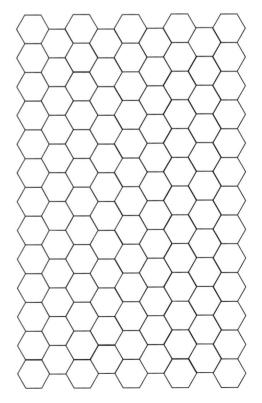

APPLE BAGS

(also shown on page 33)

- red print fabric
- ¼"w green ribbon
- plastic zipping bags filled with Cranberry Cider Mix (page 32)
- tracing paper
- green textured cardstock
- black fine-point permanent pen
- craft glue
- cinnamon sticks

Match right sides and use a ½" seam allowance unless otherwise indicated.

1. For each bag, cut a 6½"x12" fabric piece. For the casing, sew the short edges ¾" to the wrong side. Matching short edges, fold the fabric in half. Stopping at the casings, sew the sides together.

2. To form the bottom corners, match the side seams to the bottom fold. Sew across each corner 1½" from the point (Fig. 1).

Fig. 1

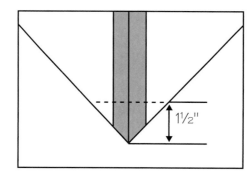

3. Knot the ends of a 22" ribbon length and thread the ribbon through the casing. Turn the bag right side out.
4. Place the mix in the bag. Pull the ribbon ends to gather the bag closed and tie into a bow.
5. Use the pattern on page 470 and cut cardstock leaves. Write a message on a leaf and glue the leaves to a cinnamon stick. Insert the stick in the bag opening.

OATMEAL COOKIE BOX

(also shown on page 36)

- empty oatmeal box with lid (ours measures 4" dia.x7⅛"h)
- craft glue
- green plaid and red print scrapbook paper
- white vellum
- deckle-edged scissors
- green textured cardstock
- square brads
- 1½"w sheer white ribbon
- tracing paper
- dark green and yellow cardstock scraps
- 3 yellow E-beads
- black fine-point permanent pen
- ⅛" dia. hole punch
- "To:" and "From:" stamps
- black ink pad
- Jo Ann's Walnut-Oatmeal Cookie Mix in a sealed cellophane bag (page 36)

1. Cover the box and lid inset with plaid paper.
2. For the label, use a computer to print the title on vellum and cut to 2¼"x4¼" with the deckle-edged scissors. Attach the corners of the vellum to a 3"x5" deckle-edged green cardstock piece with brads.

Glue the label to the box. Threading the ribbon between the label layers and gluing the ends at the back, wrap the ribbon around the box.

3. Use the patterns on page 471 and cut two large red paper flowers and one green cardstock leaf set for the box and a small red paper flower and green cardstock leaf set for the lid. Bending the petal ends up slightly and gluing at the centers only, layer and glue the large flower pieces to the box. Glue thin dark green cardstock strips and the beads to the flower center. Set aside the small flower pieces.

4. Matching short edges, fold a 3¾"x7" green cardstock piece in half and cut out a round card to fit the lid. Write the mix instructions inside. Glue the small flower and leaves and yellow cardstock circles to a plaid paper circle and stamp a message. Glue the circle to the card front and the card to the lid. Place the mix in the box.

TRUFFLE BOX
(also shown on page 37)
- double-sided tape
- Christmas scrapbook papers and sticker
- 2"x8" white jewelry gift box
- rub-on letters
- Chocolate-Raspberry Truffles (page 37)
- foil candy cups
- ³⁄₈"w ribbons
- textured cardstock
- ⅛" dia. hole punch
- twine

Tape scrapbook paper to the lid and the inside bottom of the box. Add a message on the lid with rub-ons and the sticker. Place truffles in candy cups inside the box. Replace the lid and knot ribbons around the box. Make a cardstock name tag and add rub-ons. Punch a hole in the tag and tie it onto the ribbons with twine.

HOLLY TAG
(also shown on page 37)

For the tag, scalloping the edge of the large circle, cut 2¾", 2⅜" and 2¼" diameter scrapbook paper circles. Layer and glue the circles together. Cut holly leaves from scrapbook paper (pattern on page 471). Spell "for you" on the leaves with rub-on letters. Adhere the leaves and ½" diameter scrapbook paper "berries" on the tag with glue and foam dots. Attach an eyelet to the tag. Stack Chocolate-Wrapped Peppermint Cookies (page 37) in a cellophane bag and tie the tag onto the bag with velvet ribbon.

Christmas Creations

Keeping CHRISTMAS

This year, do something truly special with your holiday photos and greeting cards…use them to make a Christmas calendar, a festive family tree and other fun mementos. You'll have a wonderful time displaying all your favorite memories. And any of these heartwarming creations would also make thoughtful gifts!

Celebrate Christmas with a scrapbook-style Family Calendar. Once it's completed, you can make copies to share with everyone on your gift list. Turn to page 432 to learn how easy it is to preserve your magical holiday memories.

The brightest ornaments on this Christmas tree will be the smiling faces of your loved ones! Your favorite snapshots get festive with scrapbook supplies and a minimum of work. How-to's for the Family Photo Tree are on page 432.

Christmas memories are some of the sweetest and fondest of those we carry through our lives. From our earliest childhood recollection, Christmas memories are stored in a special place in our hearts, to be recalled during quiet times of reminiscing. My family grew up in Pennsylvania where we enjoyed many Christmases together. In 1969, my parents secretly taped all four children opening presents as Dad pulled each gift from under the tree. Later that day, we added our own commentary to the celebration tape. Each Christmas thereafter, we gather to listen to and relive that special Christmas. Dad has since passed away, which makes the tape all the more precious and cherished. I hope to continue the tradition with our three children this Christmas.

—Cyndy Rogers
Upton, MA

A simple box of photos taken through the years makes the very best "coffee table" conversation starter.

Have you ever sent out all your greeting cards, only to discover that you've forgotten someone? Make your Christmas correspondence easier by converting an ordinary box into a Card Organizer. It will hold all the cards you receive this year, along with their envelopes. When you get ready to address next year's cards, you'll have all the information you need in one place. The instructions for this quick and memorable fix are on page 433.

God has given us our memories, that we might have roses in December.
—J.M. BARRIE—

Christmas is for the child in all of us, so who better to decorate this year's greeting cards than little ones? Get the kids busy on their merry masterpieces, then turn to page 433 to create the cheeriest greetings ever made!

A homemade checkerboard that will bring smiles, win or lose... decoupage a grandchild's picture over every other square of a pre-painted checkerboard. Copy and reduce photos, if necessary, on a color photocopier.

My favorite Christmas memory is putting up a small fireplace that was made of cardboard. We lived in a small house and Mom would make hot cocoa for my sister and me while we worked. We would then hang our stockings on our fireplace with shiny tacks. We would color in front of that lighted fireplace, sing carols and tell each other stories!

—Michelle Bagby
Templeton, CA

When my dad was a child in the 1940's, he and his siblings would write down their lists of wishes for Santa Claus on pieces of paper. They would then tear up the lists, sprinkle the pieces in the fireplace, then run outside quickly and watch as the smoke rose from the chimney, magically sending their Christmas lists on the way to Santa. This memory always makes me smile.

—Patricia Van Wyk
Newton, IA

I don't need to be rich; my children are my treasures.
~ MYRNA JEAN JOHNSON ~

Start a new tradition that involves everyone in your family! Kids big and little can add drawings, notes, photos and memories to your Christmas Journal. It's fun to see the pages fill up with sweet memories and fun stories. The easy instructions are on page 433.

remember all those toys baby loved?

Each year, my nieces and nephews come to decorate my Christmas tree. They each have to bring one homemade ornament and I make each of them an ornament. They each have a box that their ornaments go in. Every year, as we open the boxes, we fondly remember when they made this or that ornament. Soon we are traveling down memory lane 'til the last memory is hung. When they grow older and are on their own, I will give them their boxes for their own trees.

—Rita Wood
East Sparta, OH

Memory is the treasury and guardian of all things.
—MARCUS TULLIUS CICERO.

What a cheerful way to remember Christmases past! A Memory Shadow Box displays your holiday trinkets in a clever way. Use ornaments, photos, tags, cards...whatever you'd like! You'll find the instructions on page 434.

Is there someone you would especially like to remember at Christmas this year? Create a Memory Wreath! A loved one will be delighted to see his or her own photo tucked into the greenery along with holiday ornaments, mementos and ribbon. Learn how to make this very special decoration on page 434.

Among my treasures, I have a brooch that belonged to my Grandma. It is shaped like a Christmas tree and has multicolored rhinestones set in its branches. Grandma liked to wear that brooch every Christmas. She wore it to church, while she made the holiday dinner and even when playing with her rowdy great-grandchildren. And as much as that little tree sparkled, Grandma's smile was still brighter. My dear Grandma left us last year at Christmas. At the time, I couldn't imagine the holidays ever being happy again. But now I realize that she will spend every Christmas with the One whose birthdays she loved to celebrate. This year, I think I will wear Grandma's little Christmas tree brooch in her honor. It will be a sweet reminder of her beautiful smile.

—Susan Johnson
Little Rock, AR

I remember my annual CHRISTMAS SHOPPING TRIP with GRANDMA

All through the House

What's your favorite memory of Christmas? Is it a tree filled with heartfelt, handmade ornaments? Or a stack of gifts wrapped in vintage linens? Maybe it's greeting cards lined up to wish you holiday cheer? If you ask Mary Elizabeth, Holly, and Kate, you'll get three different answers, but the Gooseberry Patch friends all agree on one thing: There's nothing like filling your house with Christmas decorations to make you feel like a kid again!

Add a bit of whimsy this year…whip up a Latch-Hooked Rug and a Latch-Hooked Wreath with big, fluffy snowballs all over. Turn to pages 434 and 435 to learn how fleece fabric makes these holly-jolly decorations so much fun!

A Vintage Touch

Keeping Christmas is a tradition that comes from the heart. And since the Country Friends all have memories of their Grandmothers' pretty cotton handkerchiefs, they think this sweet holiday theme is extra-special. Now, no one wants to cut up Grandma's hankies, so it's probably best to use flea market or reproduction ones. You'll get the same lovely, vintage look, either way.

Holly's Hankie Garland

Here's a fast and easy decoration that will catch everyone's attention!

Make your garland as long as you like... make 2, make 3... it's easy as can be.
Simply cut 4 triangles from your hankie (figure one), or if your
hankie is smaller, cut 2 triangles (figure two).

FIG. ONE

FIG. TWO

Sew or glue the raw edges of your
triangles to a length of ribbon.
Attach buttons at the corners and
you're ready to decorate!

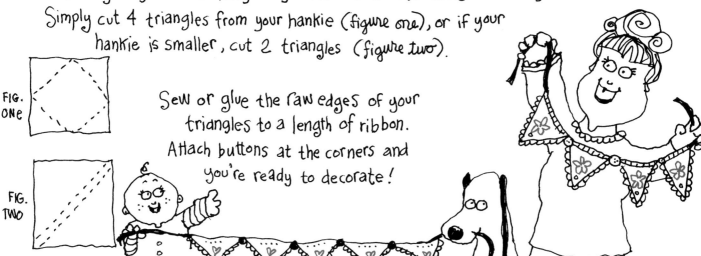

Sweet nostalgia makes these lovely ornaments even more beautiful. They're destined to become family heirlooms.

FRAMED HANKIE ORNAMENTS

Make your vintage handkerchiefs the focal point of your tree by framing them. Purchase wooden frames in various shapes and sizes and paint them cream. Remove the mats from the frames and cover with fabric. Cut a corner from a hanky and glue it to the mat or edge of the frame; you could even position a hankie to be a pocket! Adorn with decorative ribbons, rick-rack, tags, charms or buttons. On one of the frames, you may want to include a treasured photograph along with a decorated tag documenting the occasion. For hangers, glue the ends of a length of ribbon to the back of each frame.

VINTAGE PILLOW ORNAMENTS

Don't toss handkerchiefs that have a little wear! Cut a square from the usable portion (center the design if possible) and turn them into keepsakes for the tree! Start by cutting the hankie to the desired size. Cut a piece of backing fabric the same size. Sew rick-rack along edges of backing fabric. With right sides together and leaving an opening for turning, sew hankie piece and backing together. Turn right side out; stuff with polyester fiberfill and sew the opening closed. For hanger, cut a length of trim and tack ends to center top of ornament. Use fabric glue to embellish as desired with buttons, ribbons and trims.

This distinctive Nine Point Tree Skirt is a charming foundation for your tree. Turn to page 436 for instructions to fashion this timeless beauty.

HANKIE TUSSY MUSSIES

A tussy mussy is a dainty bouquet holder made from fabric or lace and filled with sweet-smelling flowers or herbs. These fragrant bouquets were carried by ladies of the Victorian era wherever they went. A lady would place the flowers a gentleman sent her in her tussy mussy to show she reciprocated his feelings.

To make your tussy mussy, fold a hankie in half twice. Fold opposite corners in and sew the two sides together to form a cone. Adorn the edges of the tussy mussy with rick-rack, ribbons and buttons. Add a ribbon hanger to proudly display your tussy mussy on the Christmas tree or door handle or even on the wall as a sconce. Fill with fresh greenery and berries or flowers from your special someone!

HANDKERCHIEF MANTEL SCARF

Add sentimental warmth to your mantel for the holidays by transforming vintage handkerchiefs into a mantel scarf. Measure the depth (including 3" for drop length) and length of your mantel; add 1" for seam allowances. Cut a piece of fabric this size for scarf. Press one long edge and ends of scarf 1/4" to wrong side. Press 1/4" to wrong side again, then topstitch to secure. Cut hankies in half diagonally. Cut triangles of white cotton fabric 1¼" larger than hankie triangles. Use fusible web tape to fuse short sides of each white triangle 1/4" to wrong side. Sew lengths of red rick-rack 1/2" from short edges of white triangles. Pin hankies 1/2" from edges of rick-rack and trim long edge of white triangle even with long edge of hankie triangle. Overlapping triangles to fit and matching right sides and raw edges, sew triangles to scarf; turn to right side and press.

The first time I went to a department store as a child and saw a Christmas tree, I wanted a tree as beautiful as the one I'd seen. Everything was perfect...matching bows and huge glass ball ornaments all perfectly arranged on the tree. Now, as a wife and mother, I have the perfect tree each year. It's decorated with cowboys, dolls and ornaments made in school...ones given to my children with their names on them. Even fishing bobbers adorn my tree. Each year, as my children decorate the tree with their beloved ornaments, I often think that we do have the most beautiful tree... a tree decorated with love, family and ornaments made from the heart.

—Angie Venable
Gooseberry Patch

Memories are not the key to the past, but to the future. ~ CORRIE ten Boom

FRAMED HANKIE CARD HOLDER

- cream wooden frame with a 23½"x12½" opening
- 24"x12" piece of foam core board
- ½ yard red & white striped fabric
- ½ yard green fabric
- red rick-rack and trim
- ¼"w mini red check ribbon
- dimensional foam dots
- assorted red buttons
- craft knife
- Christmas charms
- vintage hankies
- ¾" brass fasteners
- alphabet tags
- craft glue

1. For covered board, cut a piece of foam core board to fit frame. Cover foam core with striped fabric.

2. Cut a 36"x20" piece of green fabric. Fold fabric in half lengthwise.

3. With fold of fabric at top, overlap fabric 1" over sides and bottom of foam core. Glue sides in place. Making pockets 8" wide, create pockets with ½"w pleats (Fig. 1); glue overlap at bottom to back of foam core. Cut small holes through fabric and foam core ¼" from top and bottom of each pleat. Insert a brass fastener to secure pleat.

4. Cut hankies in half diagonally and fold over top of each pocket; tack to back of pocket top. Sew a charm to point of each hankie.

5. Insert covered board into frame. String alphabet tags onto a length of trim to spell "Merry Christmas!" Use foam dots to hold the trim ends to the frame.

6. Glue a button to each fastener and foam dot, then finish with rick-rack, ribbon and buttons.

Fig. 1

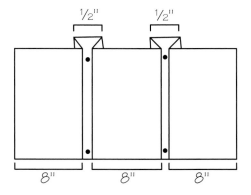

HANKIE WALL HANGING

- vintage handkerchiefs
- 1½ yards striped fabric
- 27½" square of background fabric
- red buttons
- 2½ yards red rick-rack
- assorted beads, bells and snaps
- fabric, ribbon and trim scraps
- embroidery floss
- batting
- hanging rod

Match right sides and use a ¼" seam allowance for all sewing unless otherwise indicated.

1. Leaving a 3¼" border on all sides and positioning one hankie for the pocket, arrange hankies on background fabric, overlapping as desired and pin in place. Sew hankies in place then sew a rick-rack border ½" from edges of hankies.

2. For fabric border, cut two 3¼"x27½" side strips and two 33½"x3¼" top/bottom strips from striped fabric. Sew side strips, then top and bottom strips to decorated background piece. Embellish as desired with folded hankies, trims, tags and buttons.

3. Cut one 33½" square of striped fabric for backing and a 3"x32" piece of striped fabric for hanging sleeve. Press ends, then edges of hanging sleeve ½" to wrong side. Center sleeve on backing 1" from top edge. Sew long edges in place, leaving ends open for the hanging rod.

4. Cut one 33½" square of batting. Place top piece and backing right sides together. Lay both pieces on top of batting and pin all three layers together. Leaving an opening for turning, sew along edges of wall hanging. Turn right side out and sew opening closed. Topstitch ¼" from edges of wall hanging. Sew layers together along seam of background fabric and borders and along edges of hankies.

There are few holidays when Mom doesn't include someone who would otherwise be alone. She always takes on the responsibility to make sure everyone has a happy day filled with love. Of course, growing up, we didn't realize all she did until we were grown with families of our own. Today, with four generations, she still manages to make each of us feel special and loved…our holidays are filled with joy and togetherness.

— Elena Tonkin
Powell, TN

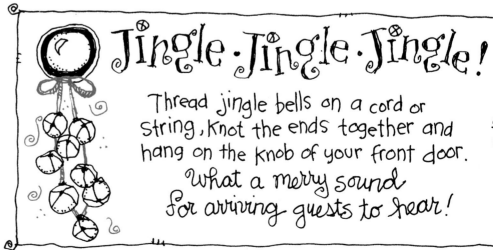

O Jingle · Jingle · Jingle!

Thread jingle bells on a cord or string, knot the ends together and hang on the knob of your front door. What a merry sound for arriving guests to hear!

Merrily monogrammed

Personalize a stocking for every member of your family with these quick & easy stockings that everyone is sure to love!

CROSS STITCHED MONOGRAM CHRISTMAS STOCKING

Using the stocking pattern on page 476, follow *Making Patterns*, page 427, to trace the stocking pattern onto tracing paper. Use the pattern to cut 2 stocking pieces from wool and 2 lining pieces from print fabric. Matching right sides, using a ½-inch seam allowance and leaving the top open, sew stocking pieces together; turn right side out. Repeat to sew lining pieces together; do not turn right side out.

For cuff, cut a 3½"x15" strip of 18 ct linen. Also cut a 1½"x15" strip and a 5½"x15" strip of print fabric. Matching long edges, sew 1½"w strip to top and 5½" strip to bottom of linen. Referring to *Cross Stitch*, page 430, and the alphabet, page 477, center and cross stitch monogram on linen. Matching sides and long edges, press. Matching right sides, sew ends of cuff together to form a ring. Matching wrong sides and raw edges, fold bottom of print fabric up into cuff.

Matching raw edges, place lining in stocking. Matching top edges and centering cuff seam at back, place cuff in lining. For the hanger, matching right sides and long edges, fold a 1½"x5" piece of print fabric in half; sew together along long edges. Turn right side out; press. Place the hanger between the cuff and stocking at heel-side seam. Sew pieces together along the top edges. Fold cuff to the outside.

Oh, what fun to decorate your window with Cross Stitched Monogram Ornaments!
You'll find the instructions for these letter-perfect pretties on page 437.

Those gifts are ever the most *acceptable* which the giver makes **precious.**

— OVID —

Beaded Monogram

Add some sparkle to your tree with beaded monogram ornaments. Simply print out a letter on your home computer and enlarge it to the desired size. Use the printed letter as a guide to bend a length of 20-gauge wire into the shape of the letter. Depending on the letter, you may have to use more than one piece of wire. Make a small eye loop at one end of the wire, thread beads onto the wire, then make a small eye loop at the remaining end to secure the beads in place. Repeat for additional beaded wire to complete the letter; twist beaded wires together at intersections to join them. Add a ribbon hanger to top of the beaded letter.

Make a sparkling gift in no time. It's as simple as threading beads onto wire, but oh-so dazzling! Beaded Monograms are wonderful ornaments for the tree, but Holly also likes to use them on gifts and wreaths.

Personalize a pillow. . .chenille yarn is stitched needlepoint-style on a purchased latch hook canvas pillow cover. *Turn to page 437 for the instructions.*

MONOGRAMMED HAND TOWEL

Turn a plain white cloth napkin into a vintage looking hand towel by adding a few simple details. Begin by sewing a length of crocheted lace along one edge of the napkin. Then cut a 2" wide strip of vintage fabric and press the raw edges ¼" to the wrong side. Topstitch the strip 1" from the edge of the napkin. Trace the desired monogram, page 477, onto tissue paper. Pin tissue paper in place above the fabric strip. Stitching through tissue paper, embroider letter using 3 strands of embroidery floss for *Satin Stitch* (page 423) and 2 strands for *Backstitch*, page 430. Carefully tear away tissue paper when embroidery is complete. Sew a rick-rack border around the monogram. Embellish with additional rick-rack and assorted vintage buttons.

A Monogrammed Tissue Box Cover brings holly-jolly cheer to the powder room. See page 437 to make this quick & easy tissue box cover.

Surprise an overnight holiday guest with her own pretty monogrammed hand towel in the bathroom!

Warm & Woolly

*If ever there's a fabric that looks as cozy as it feels,
it's good old-fashioned wool. These days, you can find hand-dyed wool
in a rainbow of colors. The rustic texture is reminiscent of country cabins and
a comfy evening by the fire. What a great way to make your Christmas décor…
and your Christmas gifts…as heartwarming as you could wish!*

I make the most
of all that comes
and the least of all that goes. - Sara Teasdale

The recipe for happy feet is a warm ottoman cover accented with wool appliqué! Once the Country Friends started creating these fancy footrest covers, they just couldn't stop until they finished three inviting designs (see pages 440-441). And can you guess the easy secret to shaping these wonderful wool trees? You can read all about it on pages 438-439.

Take your needle, my child, and work at your pattern; it will come out like a rose by and by. Life is like that; one stitch at a time taken *Patiently*, and the pattern will come out all right, like embroidery.
— Oliver Wendall Holmes

With its button berries, star appliqués and simple embroidery, the Stitched Wall Hanging reminds us that the best gifts come from the heart.

STITCHED WALL HANGING

- ½ yard of green felt
- ⅓ yard of oatmeal felt
- scraps of red and dark gold felt
- ½ yard red check homespun fabric
- ¼" and ¾" dia. red buttons
- ¼" dia. green shank buttons
- ½ yard of ¼"w variegated green silk ribbon
- gold, green and red embroidery floss
- ¾"w gold grosgrain ribbon
- 17" length of ½" dia. dowel rod
- two 1¼"dia. wooden balls
- tissue paper
- pinking shears

Refer to Embroidery Stitches, pages 422-423, before beginning project. Use 2 strands of floss for all stitching unless otherwise indicated.

For wall hanging front, cut a 14"x11" piece of oatmeal felt. Trace verse, page 481, onto tissue paper. Center and pin verse on oatmeal felt piece. Stitching through tissue paper and using green floss, work *Backstitches* (page 430) and *French Knots* over words. Carefully tear away tissue paper. For pine branches, cut silk ribbon in half; fold ribbon in half lengthwise and tack in place along each side of verse. Work gold floss *Straight Stitches* along silk ribbon to create pine needles. Cut assorted size "berries" from red felt. Work *Straight Stitches* to attach felt berries along pine branches, then sew ¼" red buttons for "berries" along branches.

Trace star patterns, page 481, onto tissue paper. Using patterns, cut 3 stars from gold felt. Work gold

Blanket Stitches along edges of stars to attach stars to front piece. For green backing, cut a 15½"x12½" piece of green felt. Work red *Blanket Stitches* to attach front piece to green backing. Cut scallops along edges of green backing. Work gold *Blanket Stitches* along edges of border scallops. Sew green buttons along scallops. Tear a 16½"x13" piece of homespun. Tack decorated felt piece to homespun. For hanging tabs, use pinking shears to cut three 1¼"x6" strips of green felt. Cut three 6" lengths of grosgrain ribbon. Work long red *Running Stitches* to attach ribbons to felt strips. Folding hangers in half, pin hangers evenly along top edge of wall hanging. Sew a red button through all layers. Insert dowel rod through hangers. Secure a wooden ball at each end of dowel rod.

EMBROIDERED TOTE BAG

Think of all the shopping you can do with this handy tote bag to help hold all your packages!

Match right sides and use a 1/2" seam allowance for all sewing unless otherwise indicated.

For front and back of bag, cut two 18½"x10½" pieces of burgundy wool. For bottom of bag, cut one 9¼"x11½" piece of burgundy wool. For borders, cut two 18½"x3¼" pieces of cream wool. Sew cream wool along bottoms of front and back pieces. With wrong sides together, sew short edges of front and back pieces together. With the side seams centered at each short edge of bottom piece and matching wrong sides, sew the bottom to the bag. Work green Blanket Stitches along top and bottom edges of borders and down side seams.

For the handles, cut two 2"x 34" strips of cream wool. Fold strips in half lengthwise; topstitch along raw edges. Sew ends of one strip 5" from each side of front of tote. Repeat for remaining strip on back of tote.

Trace patterns, page 480, onto tissue paper. Using patterns, cut appliqués from wool. Refer to photo and work *Blanket Stitches* to secure appliqués on front of bag.

For lining, cut one 9¼"x11½" and two 18½"x10½" pieces of cotton fabric. With right sides together, sew short edges of front and back pieces together. With the side seams centered at each short edge of bottom piece and matching right sides, sew the bottom to the lining. Turn top edge of lining under ¼" and press. Insert lining in tote bag and sew together along top edge.

Whether used as a handbag or to enclose a gift, this beautiful bag is meant to hold wonderful things! The Dyed Wool & Embroidery Drawstring Bag is as practical as it is pretty… its gathered closure keeps its contents secure, while the flat bottom helps it to stand upright. You'll find the instructions on page 440.

Print holiday sentiments on vellum using old-fashioned curly fonts for heartfelt wishes. Punch out the message using circular or square hand-held paper punches. Attach to packages with cotton string.

This Christmas, decorate with vintage accessories. You'll have a jolly time shopping at flea markets and resale shops for just the right pieces. Cheery red & white decorations deliver an extra measure of holiday joy.

FOUR-PATCH ORNAMENT

Cut squares from assorted tea towels and coordinating fabrics to make one of these ornaments. Sew four 3" squares together; baste crocheted lace along the edges. Cut a 10" length of twill tape for the hanger; matching ends and raw edges, baste ends to one edge of ornament front. Tack a crocheted doily and crocheted trim to center front of ornament. For backing, cut a 6" square from a tea towel or coordinating fabric. Matching right sides and leaving an opening at bottom for turning, sew ornament front to ornament back. Clip the seam allowance at the corners. Turn ornament right side out. Slipstitch opening closed.

Search out vintage fabrics in splashy vegetable prints, then make color photocopies. Cut out squares and attach to the front of a small brown paper bag using spray adhesive. Set a jar of relish inside, turn down bag edges and tie on a gift tag…so easy!

"What is Christmas? It is tenderness for the past, courage for the present, hope for the future. It is a fervent wish that every cup may overflow with blessings rich and eternal, and that every path may lead to peace."
— Agnes M. Pharo

Tag sale or flea market finds are perfect for giving your tree a vintage look. The four-patch ornament was made from a variety of tea towels found at a flea market.

Collectibles, such as this cute, crocheted dress, give a sweet, old-fashioned charm to your tree.

Shopping is a woman thing. It's a contact sport like football. Women enjoy the scrimmage, the noisy crowds, the danger of being trampled to death, and the ecstasy of the purchase.

FLEA

~ERMA BOMBECK~

TEA TOWEL TREE SKIRT

For a nostalgic holiday feel, create a clever tree skirt from vintage tea towels. If your towels aren't the same size, trim and hem them to match.

- six 18"x27" tea towels (cut and hemmed to size if necessary)
- four 10" squares of fabric for center
- six 4½" squares of fabric for points
- crocheted trim

Use a ½" seam allowance.

1. For center, press one corner of each 10" square 2" to wrong side. With wrong sides and pressed edges facing, refer to Fig. 1 to sew three sides of squares together; hem remaining two sides and pressed corners.

2. Overlapping towels and aligning inner edges according to Fig. 2, arrange tea towels over center; leaving one towel's edges open as indicated, pin towels in place.

3. Place 4½" fabric squares under towels to complete points; press outer edges to wrong side, then pin in place.

4. Leaving the designated opening unsewn, sew along the inner edges of the towels and triangles to join pieces together; hem edges of opening. Trim seam allowances as needed.

5. Pin, then sew crocheted trim along outside edges of tree skirt, adjusting trim as needed.

6. Hand sew decorative stitches along inner edges of towels (we chose a herringbone stitch, see Embroidery, pages 422-423).

Fig. 1

Fig. 2

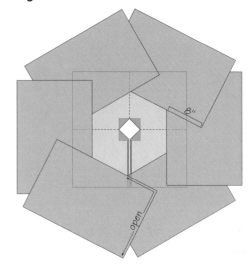

CROCHET CENTER PILLOW

A vintage tablecloth and crocheted potholders found at the flea market can be combined to make fantastic pillows for your home. Cut two 17" squares from the tablecloth. Baste crocheted lace to edges of pillow front. Tack crocheted potholder to center of pillow. Matching right sides and leaving an opening for turning, sew pillow front to pillow back. Clip the seam allowance at the corners. Turn pillow right side out; insert pillow form. Slipstitch opening closed.

A good conscience is a continual Christmas.
— BENJAMIN FRANKLIN —

QUILT

Yardage is based on 43"/44" wide fabric with a "usable" width of 40" after shrinkage and trimming selvages. Use a ¼" seam allowance.

- ½ yard each of six assorted fabrics
- 2¼ yards of backing fabric
- ½ yard of fabric for binding
- 60"x73" square of batting

Cut a total of eighty 7" squares from assorted fabrics. Sew 8 squares together to make a row. Sew 10 rows together to make quilt top.

To piece backing, cut backing fabric into two lengths. Place lengths with right sides facing and sew long edges together, forming a tube. Match seams and press along one fold. Cut along pressed fold to form single piece.

(continued on page 441)

A welcome spot of color on a winter day, this cozy quilt looks so inviting! You're sure to want to snuggle up and sit for a spell.

CRANBERRY-ALMOND BLONDIES

½ c. butter, softened
16-oz. pkg. brown sugar
3 eggs
1 T. vanilla extract
2 c. self-rising flour
1½ c. slivered almonds, toasted
   and divided
1 c. dried cranberries
Powdered sugar, for dusting

Preheat oven to 350 degrees. Beat butter and brown sugar together at medium speed with a mixer. Add eggs and vanilla until blended. Gradually add flour until blended. Fold ¾ cup almonds into batter. Spoon batter into a greased and floured 13"x9" baking pan. Sprinkle cranberries and remaining almonds over top of batter. Bake for 20 minutes; reduce temperature to 325 and bake 25 more minutes. Cool in pan on a wire rack. Dust with powdered sugar and cut into squares. Makes 16 servings.

TEA TOWEL GIFT BAGS

Transform vintage tea towels of your grandmother's into unique gift bags for the family. Simply fold a tea towel in half with right sides facing, then sew up the sides. Turn the bag right side out. Add some crocheted trim around the top edges and use a length of twill tape for the tie. Add your gift and you're done!

If you're looking for a sweet treat to make for the office Christmas party or church social, these Cranberry-Almond Blondies are just the thing! We used a vintage doily, picked up at the local flea market, to add a festive holiday look.

"Christmas in Bethlehem. The ancient dream: a cold, clear night made brilliant by a glorious star, the smell of incense, shepherds and wise men falling to their knees in adoration of the sweet baby, the incarnation of perfect love."
— Lucinda Franks

THE GREAT Disappearing Snack Mix!

THIS RED & WHITE MIX IS PERFECT TO TUCK INTO
TEA TOWEL GIFT BAGS WITH PLENTY LEFT OVER TO SNACK ON!

12-OZ. PKG. CHOCOLATE CHIPS
16-OZ. PKG. SALTED PEANUTS
11-OZ. PKG. SESAME STICKS
12-OZ. PKG. WHITE CHOCOLATE CHIPS
12-OZ. PKG. VANILLA YOGURT-COVERED RAISINS
2 6-OZ. PKGS. DRIED CRANBERRIES
10-OZ. CAN CASHEWS

MIX ALL INGREDIENTS TOGETHER IN A LARGE
MIXING BOWL. STORE IN PLASTIC ZIPPING BAGS.
MAKES 4 QUARTS.

A YUMMY RECIPE FROM
KRISTINE MERTES ★ LITTLE ROCK, AR

These reusable goodie bags will bring as many smiles as the treats packed inside! Fashioned from cheery red & white fabric, the gift sacks are sure to be used year round.

CHRISTMAS
with all the
trimmings

Make it homemade for the holidays! These terrific trims lend old-fashioned appeal to your Yuletide tree. Braided homespun garland winds around handcrafted stars, ribbon ornaments and greenery-filled flannel bags (see pages 109, 441 & 442). A fabric-trimmed basket is an ideal container for this charming tabletop accent.

FLANNEL BAG ORNAMENT

Trace the flannel bag pattern from page 482 onto tracing paper; cut out. Use the pattern to cut 2 bag pieces from flannel. Matching right sides, using a 1/2" seam allowance and leaving the top open, sew flannel pieces together; turn right side out. Press top edge of bag 1/4" to inside; topstitch in place. Cut one 18" length and two 6 1/2" lengths of 3/8" wide ribbon. Referring to Fig. 1 and taping ends down, lay 6 1/2" lengths of ribbon flat on a table; weave 18" ribbon through 6 1/2" lengths. Wrap woven ribbons around bag; stitch ribbon ends together at back. Sew top ribbon to top of bag. Cut an 8" length of ribbon for hanger; sew to each side of bag with a button. For flower, cut six 4" lengths of ribbon; tie a knot in center of each length. Form a loop with each ribbon length, stitching ends together at center to form flower. Work French Knots at center of flower; tack flower to gift bag.

Fig. 1

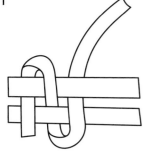

FLANNEL BAG

Enlarge the flannel bag pattern, page 482, by 200%. Follow instructions for Flannel Bag Ornament, above, changing ribbon lengths to three 11" ribbon lengths and a 39" length for woven band, and a 12" length of ribbon for handle.

SpRUCE UP a plain brown paper box with woven strips of homespun and ribbon ... hold them in place with double-stick tape. Add a festive ribbon bow and a gift tag made from a manila shipping tag, and you've got the **pRettiest gift** under the tree!

Give us Lord, a bit o' sun,
a bit o' work
and a bit o' fun;
Give us all, in the struggle and sputter
Our daily bread and a bit o' butter.
— from an old inn in Lancaster, England

HOLIDAY SWAG

Deck the halls, the windows, the china cabinet or anywhere else you want to spread holiday cheer! This striking swag will warm your home with the colors of Christmas. To make a more "scent-sational" version, use fresh greenery, berries and other jewels from Mother Nature. Decide how long you want your swag and cut two lengths of greenery that length. Wire the lengths together at the center and as necessary along the length. Wire berries along the center of the swag. Tear 1" wide strips of homespun…weave the strips and some ribbon through greenery. Tie a ribbon bow with streamers. Use wire to attach the bow to the center of the swag and it's ready to hang!

There's nothing quite as invigorating as a walk through the woods in the freshly fallen snow. Take along a basket and turn your walk into a treasure hunt. See what natural wonders you can gather to decorate your home… twigs of pine, cedar and holly, as well as colorful berries, pine cones and acorns are all fun finds. After you return home, take out a wooden bowl and line it with heavy-duty plastic wrap, then add water-soaked floral foam to create a base. Tuck the greenery and berry sprigs into the foam, making sure to let them overflow the bowl, then top with pine cones and acorns. For a burst of color, add apples or oranges. Be sure to water or mist as needed to keep your arrangement looking fresh.

So a-peeling…draw a design on an orange, lemon or lime using a felt tip marker. Carve along the marked design by removing the outside layer of the peel with a vegetable peeler or a lino tool from a hobby store. Stack several in a bowl or on a cake stand for a fragrant centerpiece.

Make your holiday gatherings even more warm and cozy by dressing your table with a fabulous flannel runner. Finished off with woven ribbons and buttons, this table topper can be used all winter long. Coordinating chairback covers lend country charm.

CHAIRBACK COVERS

Match right sides and use a ½" seam allowance for all sewing unless otherwise indicated.

Measure from the seat of your chair, over the top of the chairback, and back down to the seat for the length of your chairback cover, then measure the width of your chair. Add 1" to these measurements then cut a piece of flannel and a piece of fabric for lining this size. Cut a piece of fabric 6" narrower than flannel piece; press long edges of fabric ½" to wrong side, then center on flannel piece and sew in place. Lay flannel piece on a flat surface; lay lengths of ribbon down the length and pin in place. Weave additional lengths of ribbon across flannel piece and pin in place. Sew ribbons in place using decorative stitches. Sew buttons along ribbons. Cut four lengths of ribbon for ties. With right sides together and leaving an opening for turning, sew flannel and lining together catching ends of ties in seams at edges of cover. Clip corners, turn right side out and press. Topstitch along edges of cover.

TABLE RUNNER

Match right sides and use a ½" seam allowance for all sewing unless otherwise indicated.

Cut two pieces of flannel the desired size for your runner. Lay one flannel piece on a flat surface; lay lengths of ribbon down the length of flannel piece and pin in place. Weave additional lengths of ribbon across flannel piece and pin in place. Sew ribbons in place using decorative stitches. Sew buttons along ribbons. With right sides together and leaving an opening at one end for turning, sew flannel pieces together. Clip corners, turn right side out and press. Topstitch along edges of runner.

Write "Welcome One & All!" on a big, black chalkboard and hang on the front door for a festive greeting...a strip of flannel makes the ideal hanger.

Snowflake Follies

*Combine a sleigh full of sparkles and glitter and you're guaranteed
to have a white Christmas! This tree is sure to delight anyone who longs each year
for that first snowfall. It's flocked with a flurry of trims. . .from cozy mitten ornaments
that will remind you of playful snowball fights to a garland of shimmering icicles.
And the forecast calls for even more fun when you make the other frosty projects,
including gift bags, cards, candleholders, a wall hanging and soaps!*

You'll have "snow" much fun crafting these wintry tree trims for the most creative holiday ever! Instructions for the Round Box Ornaments are on page 119.

ICICLE GARLAND

Transform your home into a winter wonderland with glistening icicle garland. Trace pattern, page 483, onto freezer paper, repeating as needed for desired length. Iron freezer paper onto cotton batting; cut out. Peel off paper pattern. Spray garland with spray adhesive; sprinkle with mica snow glitter, shake off excess and allow to dry. Spray lightly with matte acrylic sealer and allow to dry.

SOFT MITTEN ORNAMENTS

Continue the snowflake theme on your tree with mitten ornaments. . . you can also tuck a small gift inside each mitten for extra fun! Enlarge mitten pattern, page 484, 115%; cut out. Iron interfacing onto one side of cotton batting. For each mitten, use pattern to draw two mitten shapes (one in reverse) onto interfaced side of batting. Cut out mittens; cut a 5"x7" piece from chenille for cuff. Trace small snowflake pattern, page 484, onto tracing paper and cut out; use pattern to cut a snowflake from blue felt. Using *French Knots* and *Straight Stitches*, pages 422-423, sew snowflake to front of one mitten shape. Sew a button to center of snowflake. With right sides matching and leaving wrist open, use a 1/2" seam allowance to sew mitten shapes together; clip curves. Sew short edges of cuff together. Matching wrong sides and long edges, fold cuff in half. Matching raw edges, slip cuff over mitten. Stitching through all layers, sew around top of mitten; turn mitten right side out then fold cuff to front. For hanger, tack ends of a length of ribbon inside mitten at sides.

SNOWFLAKE ORNAMENT

Polymer clay snowflakes sprinkled with mica snow glitter will add sparkle and shine to your tree. Read *Working with Polymer Clay*, page 431, then follow the polymer clay manufacturer's instructions to condition clay; run clay through a pasta machine (used for clay only) on the #1 setting. Using cookie cutters, cut out snowflakes. Following the instructions on the clay package, bake snowflakes in the oven. Once cooled, spray snowflakes with spray adhesive and sprinkle with mica snow glitter. Repeat on back of snowflake. Shake off excess glitter and allow to dry. Knot ends of a length of ribbon through snowflake and start decorating the tree!

CARDS WITH ENVELOPES AND TAGS

Think snow! Then gather up your snowflake stickers, ribbons, white and blue cardstock, and other papercrafting supplies to create your own wintery cards or tags for your gift bags. Mittens, sledding, icicles, a chance of flurries and thinking back to your childhood memories of the first snowfall of each year are sure to inspire your "cool" creations.

GIFT BAGS

Everyone will be saying "Let it Snow!" when you show up with this cascade of snow-studded gift bags. White textured bags topped with blue tissue paper and embellished with ribbons and snowflake stickers backed with blue felt are a quick and easy way to turn your gift into a winter wonderland!

Trim packages with a homemade pom-pom in place of a bow. Wind yarn tightly around a 4-inch cardboard square several times. Slide yarn off cardboard and tie in the center with an 8-inch length of yarn. Clip the looped ends and shake out to fluff.

A pair of woolly mittens makes a sweet gift long after the goodies have been enjoyed. Stitch white buttons in a simple snowflake pattern on a pair of blue mittens and tuck packages of snack mix inside.

Line a new paint can with gingham fabric and wax paper, then fill with freshly baked cookies. . .what a clever way to share sweet treats!

Weather forecast for tonight:
DARK.
~ GEORGE CARLIN ~

ETCHED SNOWFLAKE CANDLE HOLDERS

Brighten your holidays with snowflakes and candlelight. Scatter snowflakes over plain glass candle holders simply by applying the negative area from a sheet of snowflake stickers to the glass; following the manufacturer's directions, brush etching cream onto the open area and then wash. Nestle each candle in a bank of snow created by pouring Epsom salts into the base of each holder. Add embellishments of ribbons and charms around the neck of the candle holders, if desired.

Paper snowflakes cut from newspapers, brown paper bags or vintage maps turn a kid's room into a blizzard of holiday fun.

Let everyone know how you feel about snow! See page 442 to bring the frosty fun indoors with a trio of Snowflake Topiaries.

5. With wrong sides matching, use a ½" seam allowance to sew chenille squares together leaving raw edges out.

6. Stamp wintery sayings on handmade paper; tear around words. Tear fabric strips slightly larger than stamped pieces.

7. Centering each decorated felt square on a torn fabric strip and layering a stamped piece on a torn rectangle of fabric, arrange pieces on chenille squares then hand stitch in place using decorative stitches. To complete wall hanging front, add embellishments such as buttons, sequins, beads, and ribbons . . . we used sequins with bead centers and extra large snaps for the centers of snowflakes we stitched on with floss.

8. Lay wall hanging front over a piece of batting and cut to size. Cut a piece of chenille to the same size. Layer pieces and stitch together at outside edges leaving raw edges.

9. For hanger, cut a length of batting 4" wide; fold in half lengthwise. Sew hanger to top of wall hanging.

10. Trace Icicle Garland pattern, page 483, onto freezer paper repeating as needed for length of wall hanging. Iron freezer paper onto cotton batting; cut out. Peel off paper pattern. Sew batting to bottom of wall hanging; spray with spray adhesive and sprinkle with mica snow glitter.

This cheerful wall hanging will remind you of fun-filled days spent playing in the snow.

SNOWFLAKE AND MITTEN WALL HANGING

1. Cut four 12" squares of white chenille and four 7" squares of blue felt. Tear four 8" squares of fabric. Trace snowflake and mitten patterns, page 484, onto tissue paper; cut out. Using patterns, cut two large snowflakes, four small snowflakes, and two mittens from white felt. Cut four 3½"x3" pieces of chenille for mitten cuffs.

2. Using French Knots, page 422, and long Straight Stitches, page 423, sew a small snowflake to center of each mitten and each large snowflake; sew a button to center of each small snowflake.

3. Fold mitten cuffs in half lengthwise. Center mittens and cuffs on felt squares; glue in place with fabric glue.

4. Embellish large snowflakes with sequins and beads; center on remaining felt squares and glue in place.

Snowflakes are each unique, one-of-a-kind creations. Now you can give a gift that's just as original...snowflake soaps! The flurries are fashioned from cookie cutters.

SNOWFLAKE SOAPS

Homemade soap shaped like snowflakes is a thoughtful and unique way to say "Happy Holidays!" To make snowflake soaps, look in your local craft store for loaf soap. Melt the soap according to the manufacturer's directions on the package; pour ¼" into a plastic container sprayed with cooking oil. Before the soap totally hardens, turn the container over and carefully pop soap out onto wax paper. Use cookie cutters to cut snowflake shapes in soap. Allow soap to harden; clean edges as needed with a craft knife. Make a Round Box Ornament, page 119, without the hanger, to create a gift box. Nestle your snowflake soap in a bed of Epsom salts and your gift is complete.

ROUND BOX ORNAMENTS

- green scrapbook paper
- blue scrapbook paper
- lightweight cardboard
- spray adhesive
- craft knife
- mica snow glitter
- small snowflake stickers
- chenille rick-rack
- sequins
- seed beads
- craft glue
- tracing paper
- white felt

NOTE: *The following instructions make the Large Box Ornament. Use the measurements in parentheses for the Small Box Ornament. Use spray adhesive in a well-ventilated area.*

FOR BASE OF BOX:

1. For side of box, cut a 13½"x1¼" (11"x¾") strip from cardboard. For bottom of box, cut a 4" (3") dia. circle from cardboard.

2. Draw a line ¼" above bottom edge of cardboard strip; lightly score along line. Use craft knife to clip out wedges between raw edge and scored line.

Fig. 1

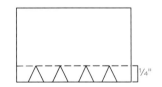

3. Wrapping a piece of green scrapbook paper around raw edge of cardboard strip from scored line on front to scored line on back, cut a piece of scrapbook paper to cover cardboard strip. Cut a circle of scrapbook paper to cover box bottom. Use spray adhesive to adhere green scrapbook paper to pieces.

Fig. 2

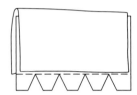

4. Fold strip along scored line and bend clipped edge to fit around box bottom. Glue clipped edge of strip around box bottom, overlapping clipped ends of strip.

5. Cut a 4" (3") dia. circle of scrapbook paper; glue to bottom of box to cover clipped edge.

FOR BOX TOP:

6. Repeat Steps 1-4, using blue scrapbook paper and the following measurements: 13¾"x1" (11¼"x½") strip for sides and 4¼" (3¼") dia. circle for bottom.

7. Cut a 4¼" (3¼") dia. circle of scrapbook paper; glue to box top to cover clipped edge.

8. Trace snowflake pattern, page 482, onto tracing paper; cut out. Use pattern to cut a snowflake from white felt. Adhere to top of box. Apply a snowflake sticker to center of felt snowflake.

9. Thin a small amount of craft glue with water; brush over top of box. Sprinkle mica snow glitter over glue; allow to dry, then tap off extra glitter.

10. Glue a length of rick-rack around sides of box top. For hanger, cut a 7" (6") length of rick-rack. Fold hanger in half; tack ends to rick-rack along sides of box. Tack a sequin and a seed bead to base of hanger.

Spray paint a papier-mâché box blue; let dry. Add a Star of David to the lid using silver paint and when dry, fill the box with a dreidel and an equal amount of pennies or chocolate coins…kids love playing this game! Replace the lid and secure this pretty packaging with silver ribbon.

In about the same degree as you are helpful, you will be happy. ～ KARL REILAND

It's A Kids' Christmas!

Get your kids in on the fun of holiday decorating by teaching them origami. . .the Japanese art of paper folding. They'll love making their own tabletop Christmas tree, as well as pleated ornaments for the family evergreen. See pages 443-444 to make the Origami Tree and Ornaments.

KRINGLES CAN

Change an ordinary 3" can of Pringles® into an attractive, delectable gift that is sure to please young and old alike! Begin by melting Dipping Chocolate in the microwave according to manufacturer's instructions. Line a baking sheet with wax paper. Dip chips in chocolate and set on wax paper; refrigerate until chocolate coating hardens.

Cover can with yellow cardstock; glue a circle of red cardstock to lid. For label, cut a piece of vellum, then tear a larger piece of scrapbook paper for background. Write "Kringles" on the vellum; layer, then glue label to can. Use a ¼" hole punch and a leaf punch to punch leaves and berries from scrapbook paper; glue to label. Place "chocolate chips" in can.

To make a snowman gift bag, fold down the top of a white lunch sack; round the edges of the folded-over flap with scissors. Add eyes and a mouth using a black pen and glue on an orange craft-foam nose. Top him off with an infant-size hat!

Kris Kringle will love to find these "chocolate chips" sitting out for him on Christmas Eve! The tasty treats also make great gifts for school friends and teachers. Dress up the original chip container to make your present even more festive.

I would be most content if my children grew up to be the kind of people who think decorating consists mostly of building enough *bookshelves.*

- Anna Quindlen -

Even little ones will love this clever craft. To create their own Wish List Album, they simply cut out pictures of the things they want and glue them on corrugated paper tags (instructions on page 444).

ACCORDION ALBUM

Cut two 4" squares from red mat board and a 24"x3⁷/₈" strip from green artist's paper. Accordion-fold paper into six 4" squares. Working in a well-ventilated area, use spray adhesive to adhere a mat board square to the outside ends of the folded paper to create a cover for your album. Cut photo corners from craft foam; trim photographs to fit pages and secure in place using photo corners. Embellish album with craft foam shapes.

PLAYING CARD ALBUM

Collect a "full house" of memories using a deck of playing cards. All decked out with stickers and journaling, this album is the picture-perfect place to display your favorite family snapshots. Simply cover one side of several cards with assorted scrapbook papers then punch a hole in the upper corner of each card. On the covered side, add a photo and stickers along with some journaling. Tie the cards together with a ribbon tied into a bow. Embellish the front of your album as desired...we cut out pieces of leftover playing cards and attached them using dimensional foam dots.

*W*hat fun! Colorful handprint tags add a personal touch to packages for everyone on your gift list. And they're so easy the whole family can make them! Draw around your hand onto colorful paper (like scrapbooking paper or craft paper) and cut out. Cut a rectangle from coordinating paper to make a cuff for a boy's hand. Glue on tinsel pom-poms for rings or a bracelet on a girl's hand. If you'd like, make a hole for the hanger near the cuff or bracelet and thread embroidery floss through it, tying the ends into a knot to hang from the present. Don't forget to write the "to" and "from" information on the tag before attaching it to your gift!

Take note of this fun project! The Notepad Booklet is great for jotting down phone numbers, important reminders, and more. You'll find the instructions on page 444.

CHRISTMAS is for Sharing

Handmade gifts can't help but get noticed! Because they show how much you care, they're sure to be appreciated. A warm & cozy fleece scarf is ready in a jiffy for someone special. Family & friends will love a whimsical mug cozy, fun wire bookmarks, or a sentimental paperweight. And don't forget your four-legged friends. Our dog quilt and cat bed will soon be your pets' favorite places to snuggle.

Something for everyone on your Christmas list! These gifts from the heart are oh-so thoughtful and will be treasured for years to come. Instructions begin on page 128.

The jolly old elf himself would like to see this Santa Doll under the tree. Any little girl will love a sweet, rosy sweater or one with a playful snowman. Instructions for these festive gifts are found on pages 444-445.

"So remember while December brings the only Christmas Day, in the year let there be Christmas in the things you do and say."
— Anonymous

"Christmas is doing a little something extra for someone."
— Charles Schultz

There is Glory in a great mistake.
— Nathalia Crane.

EMBELLISHED GLOVES

The design on these knitted gloves is done with a technique called duplicate stitch using embroidery floss. Duplicate stitch is a V-shaped stitch worked over the weave of the knitting (Fig. 1). For placement of stitches, follow the chart on page 490. Leave a 3" tail at the beginning and ending of your stitching. To secure the stitches, thread the needle with one of the tails, run it under several stitches, then go back under several stitches in the opposite direction; trim tail.

Repeat to secure the rest of the tails. To complete each stitch, come up at 1, go down at 2, come up at 3, and go back down at 1.

Fig. 1

FLEECE SCARF

Whip up this gift as quick as quick can be. Cut a 7"x63" piece of fleece for the body of your scarf. Layer pieces of assorted colors of fleece 3" from each end to create your design. Using invisible thread, machine sew zigzag stitches to secure edges of pieces in place. We used a diamond pattern, but you could pick something as simple as stripes. Cut ½" wide strips in ends for fringe.

hot COCOA MOCHA

...a yummy cocoa mix to give along with your mug cozy!

─♥─

3 c. hot cocoa mix
½ c. instant coffee
¾ t. cinnamon
½ c. mini marshmallows

Mix hot cocoa mix, instant coffee and spice together. Store in an airtight container. Give mix & marshmallows with serving instructions:

Add 3 tablespoons mix to ⅔ cup boiling water.

MUG COZY

Refer to Embroidery Stitches, pages 422-423, before beginning.

Wash an old sweater in hot water, then dry it on hot to create felted wool. Cut a piece of felted wool to fit around your mug. Using the pattern on page 490, follow *Making Patterns*, page 427, to trace the snowman pattern onto tracing paper. Use the pattern to cut snowman from white felt. Use two strands of grey embroidery floss to work *French Knots* for eyes and six strands of orange floss to work a *Straight Stitch* for nose. Using two strands of white floss, work *Blanket Stitches* along edges of snowman to secure it near one end of wool piece. Use two strands of grey floss to work *Back Stitches* for arms. For snow, use two strands of white floss to work scattered *Cross Stitches* around snowman. Using six strands of green floss, work a running stitch along top and bottom edges of cozy. Sew three buttons along one side edge of cozy; tacked on the other side edge, form loops with embroidery floss for closures. Wrap cozy around mug; loop closures around buttons. Pour yourself a cup of hot cocoa, sit back and relax!

Need a quick hostess gift? Use a dainty, flea-market find teacup and tuck in a little herb plant. Wrap it up in cellophane and add a jolly note...easy, sweet and long lasting!

dear santa,
I need a
silly hat for
christmas.

TRAVEL JEWELRY BOX

- 4½"x4½"x2½" papier-mâché box with lid
- travel rubber stamps
- brown ink
- light brown ink
- scrapbook paper with lettering
- travel stickers
- metal letters
- black felt
- lightweight cardboard
- shank buttons
- craft glue

Tear an approximately 4" square of scrapbook paper; glue to box lid. Use light brown ink to darken edges of box, lid, and paper square. Use both inks to stamp various travel sayings on box and lid. Adhere stickers and metal letters to lid of box. For inside of box, cut a 4" square of felt; glue to inside bottom of box. Cut a 2½"x16" strip of felt; glue around insides of box. For dividers, cut 3⅞" squares from cardboard and felt; glue squares of felt to both sides of each square. Sew a shank button to the center of each covered square. Insert dividers into box.

TRAVEL TRAY

This travel tray is a useful and unique way for travelers to keep their keys, pocket change, and jewelry together while away from home. The sides of the tray untie to lay flat in your suitcase. To create yours, cut one 8½"x11" piece each of cotton fabric and flannel, three 8½"x11" pieces of low-loft batting, and four 8" lengths of ⅜"w satin ribbon. Matching right sides and raw edges, place fabric pieces together; stack batting on top of the fabric pieces. Using a ½" seam allowance, leaving an opening for turning, and catching a ribbon end in the seam (approximately 1¼" from each corner) sew pieces together. Turn right side out and sew opening closed. Topstitch, through all layers, 1¼" from edges and your travel tray is ready to pack. When you reach your destination, tie the ribbons together at each corner to create the sides on your travel tray and you're ready to empty your pockets!

"It isn't the holly; it isn't the snow. It isn't the tree, nor the firelight's glow. It's the warmth that comes to the hearts of men when the Christmas spirit returns again."
— Anonymous

BOOKMARKS

Colorful beads make these bookmarks extra special. For each marker, thread four small beads onto a length of 18-gauge craft wire. Bend the wire on each side of the beads to hold beads in place. Form bends in the remainder of the wire, then curl the ends to finish. For dangles, add a small bead, a large bead, then a small bead to an eyepin; bend end in a loop around marker between small beads; if necessary, use wire cutters to trim wire.

"Books are the quietest and most constant of friends; they are the most accessible and wisest of counselors, and the most patient of teachers."
— Charles W. Eliot

PAPERWEIGHT

This paperweight is a gift that Dad can proudly display on his desk. Invert a clear glass ashtray onto craft foam; draw around the ashtray onto the foam and cut out. Repeat with a photograph. Use craft glue to glue photo to craft foam. Add names to photo, if desired, using alphabet tiles or stickers. If using alphabet tiles, make sure tiles will be in the bowl area of the ashtray and not along the edges. Invert ashtray on photo and use craft glue to adhere in place. Embellish paperweight with clear adhesive phrases, tags, and a ribbon.

Tie lengths of tulle around packages and position bows along the narrow or front side of the gift instead of top and center...great for stacking presents.

Everywhere, we learn only from those whom we love.
- JOHANN WOLFGANG VON GOETHE -

Animals are such agreeable friends — they ask no questions, they pass no criticisms.

— GEORGE ELIOT

DOGGY QUILT

- red corduroy for quilt blocks
- heavy-duty washable fabric for quilt blocks
- heavy-duty washable fabric for backing
- high-loft polyester batting
- embroidery floss

Use a ½" seam allowance for all sewing unless otherwise indicated.

For blocks, cut ten 9" squares each from red corduroy and heavy-duty fabric. Alternating fabrics, sew four squares together to make a row. Sew five rows together to make quilt top. Matching right sides and raw edges, place quilt top and backing together; stack batting on top of the fabric pieces. Leaving an opening for turning, sew pieces together. Clip edges and turn right side out; sew opening closed. Sew floss ties at intersections of each block, through all layers. Tie floss in a knot; leave strings long.

Take your animals to the pet store for some fun holiday shopping. Take along a notepad so you can make your pets a "wish list."

CAT BED

- ½ yard beige fleece
- ½ yard plaid fabric
- cream and red felt
- beige, green, red and black embroidery floss
- 8" dia. circle of 3"-thick foam rubber
- 6"x40" piece of 2"-thick foam rubber
- spray adhesive

Use a ½" seam allowance for all sewing unless otherwise indicated. Refer to Embroidery Stitches, pages 422-423, before beginning.

1. For sides of cat bed, cut a 13"x41" strip of fleece; sew ends together. Using spray adhesive in a well-ventilated area, adhere ends of 6"x40" piece of foam together. Wrap fleece around 6"x40" piece of foam; sew edges of fleece together with the seam along the inside bottom edge of cat bed.

2. For bottom of cat bed, cut two 14" dia. circles from plaid fabric. Matching right sides and raw edges, place circles together. Leaving an opening for turning, sew circles together. Clip edges and turn the cover right side out. Insert the circle of foam into the cover; sew opening closed. Insert bed bottom into center of cat bed.

3. Using the patterns on page 490, follow *Making Patterns,* page 427, to trace the patterns onto tracing paper, cut out. Use the patterns to cut cat from cream felt and letters to spell "KITTY" from red felt. Work *Satin Stitches,* with red floss for cat's nose; work black *French Knots* for cat's eyes. Attach cat to side of bed by working green *Straight Stitches* for cat's whiskers. Work beige *Running Stitches* along edges of letters to attach to bed.

Here Kitty*Kitty cookies

1 PKG. ACTIVE DRY YEAST
¼ C. WARM WATER
1 C. ALL·PURPOSE FLOUR
1 ENV. UNFLAVORED GELATIN MIX
1 C. POWDERED MILK
¼ C. CORN OIL
1 EGG
6·OZ. CAN TUNA
¼ C. WATER

DISSOLVE YEAST IN WARM WATER; SET ASIDE. COMBINE FLOUR, GELATIN MIX & MILK IN MIXING BOWL; STIR IN YEAST, OIL, EGG, TUNA & WATER. STIR 'TIL WELL BLENDED. DROP DOUGH BY HALF-TEASPOONFULS ONTO UNGREASED BAKING SHEETS. BAKE AT 300 DEGREES FOR 25 MINUTES. COOL COMPLETELY. STORE IN REFRIGERATOR. MAKES 8 TO 10 DOZEN.

Don't limit your creativity to the gift. Take it a step further and make a clever container, too! From whimsical to elegant, this charming assortment of gift wraps is simple and fun to make. Turn corrugated cardboard into a Pillow Gift Box and tie with a pretty bow. . .so easy! The Cone Gift Box and Gift Card Holder can be made to please anyone by choosing the perfect scrapbook paper design. And a Santa Pocket Envelope is just right for homemade "coupon" books.

CONE GIFT BOX

The Country Friends embellished their Cone Gift Box with buttons to match their scrapbook paper, but you could use other embellishments such as charms or stickers or leave it plain. Enlarge or reduce the pattern, page 491, to create gift boxes of different sizes. With all the types of scrapbook papers that are available, the possibilities are endless! Kate wants to let you know this cone isn't suited for ice cream!

Use spray adhesive (in a well-ventilated area) to adhere a sheet of scrapbook paper to a piece of Bristol board. Photocopy pattern, page 491; cut out. Tape pattern to back of covered board. Cut out pattern along solid lines and fold along dotted lines; remove pattern then glue sides together. Use a hole punch to punch a hole in each side of box. For handle, thread the ends of a length of wire-edged ribbon through holes then knot on inside to secure. Randomly, glue buttons to cone. For closure, glue one end of a length of ribbon to under side of lid; wrap remaining end around a button to secure.

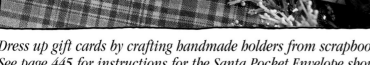

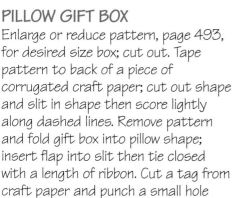

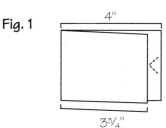

Collect old jars & covered bowls to fill with candy gifts.

There are some days when I think I'm going to die from an overdose of satisfaction. — SALVADOR DALI —

Dress up gift cards by crafting handmade holders from scrapbook paper. See page 445 for instructions for the Santa Pocket Envelope shown below.

PILLOW GIFT BOX

Enlarge or reduce pattern, page 493, for desired size box; cut out. Tape pattern to back of a piece of corrugated craft paper; cut out shape and slit in shape then score lightly along dashed lines. Remove pattern and fold gift box into pillow shape; insert flap into slit then tie closed with a length of ribbon. Cut a tag from craft paper and punch a small hole near top of tag then thread a length of string through hole to tie tag to ribbon. Apply "JOY" stickers to buttons then use dimensional foam dots to adhere buttons to tag.

GIFT CARD HOLDER

Use spray adhesive in a well-ventilated area.

Cut a 7³/₄"x2⁷/₈" rectangle from white cardstock and scrapbook paper; use spray adhesive to adhere papers together. Score holder 3³/₄" from one end; fold along score mark. For closure, use craft knife to cut a small "V" in paper (Fig. 1). Scuff up edges of scrapbook paper with sandpaper. Cut a square of white cardstock slightly larger than beaded snowflake sticker then trim with decorative-edge craft scissors. Cut a square of green cardstock larger than the white one. Layer and glue squares together; center and glue to front of holder. Use a dimensional foam dot to adhere sticker to center of white square. Cut a narrow strip of green cardstock; glue to end of holder. Use double-stick tape to secure gift card inside holder.

Fig. 1

4"

3³/₄"

EMBOSSING GIFT WRAP, CARDS AND SIMPLE-TO-MAKE PROJECTS

The Country Friends love to emboss! Holly loves the way embossing dresses up the cards she makes, Mary Elizabeth likes to emboss gift bags and tags for her baked goods, and Kate likes playing with the embossing heat tool.

Holly and Mary Elizabeth promise that embossing is as easy as these four simple steps. The most important thing to remember is that you have to apply the embossing powder while the ink is still wet.

1. Stamp your image. Mary Elizabeth likes to add accents with an embossing marker, like the green border on the poinsettia card. (Work with one color at a time.)

2. Sprinkle embossing powder over the image while the ink is still wet.

3. Lightly tap excess powder off image.

4. Heat image with an embossing heat tool until powder melts and turns shiny. It's magic!

*C*reate nostalgic ornaments that are miniature works of art. Pull out that box filled with Christmas cards you've received over the years, then give the cards a place of honor on your evergreen. Trim each scene as desired, then back the card cutout with a paper doily. Embellish with charms, ribbon roses, scraps of ribbon tied into bows or other pretty trims.

PHOTO WRAPPING PAPER

Bring back memories and make personalized wrapping paper at the same time! Simply photocopy several photos, side-by-side, all at once, then print on the largest paper possible. Use the paper to wrap your gifts, piecing paper as necessary to cover larger packages.

Recycle your shoe boxes into handy holiday storage containers. Spray paint the boxes with your favorite holiday colors. Cover the lid with Christmas cards and finish by adding a decorative trim around the edge.

"The best of all gifts around any Christmas tree: the presence of a happy family all wrapped up in each other."

— Burton Hillis

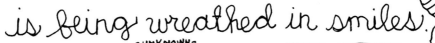

Perhaps the best yuletide decoration is being wreathed in smiles.
—UNKNOWN—

CRAFT FOAM CONTAINERS

Enlarge or reduce pattern, page 492, to make desired size container; cut out. Tape pattern to a piece of craft foam. Cut out shape. Use a small hole punch to punch a hole at end of each point. Place gift at center of craft foam. Bend points toward center; lace ribbon through holes and tie in a bow. To embellish your container, punch or cut circles or other designs from fun foam; glue to container. . .you can also buy pre-cut, self-adhesive shapes to decorate with.

Transform a window box into a Christmas garden with young potted evergreens, such as short-needle pines and blue spruce, which can be planted in the yard later. Be sure to select trees that are tall enough to be enjoyed from indoors as well as out, then fill in with real or faux plants and berries.

Cheery holiday potholders with pockets can be found at any kitchen store. When filled with Crispy-Crunchy Crouton Sticks (recipe is on page 148) and a few favorite dip recipes, they're handy keep-on-hand gifts.

"We make a living by what we get, we make a life by what we give."
— Sir Winston Churchill

Tasteful offerings

This year, give gifts that your family and friends will rave over! Holly, Mary Elizabeth and Kate have been busy in the kitchen cooking up some tasty treats. From savory pita snacks for munching to scrumptious granola for crunching, these recipes will have friends asking for more. And for an extra measure of homemade cheer, deliver your presents in containers you've either crafted or decorated yourself.

Joyful holidays begin with gifts for every taste. Trimming-the-Tree Pita Snacks, Cranberry-Chip Cookies, Homemade Maple Syrup and other taste-tempting treats make up this delectable collection. In addition to great recipes, you'll also find fun and easy ways to present your goodies.

BARLEY QUICK BREAD

In November of 2000, my sisters and I traveled to Finland to see the town where our ancestors had once lived. Prior to leaving, we collected letters from some of the children in our hometown to take to Santa Claus. It was there in Santa's kitchen at Santa Park that we enjoyed this delicious bread. We will always cherish the memory of Santa's kindness and the sweet aroma of freshly baked Finnish bread.

2 c. all-purpose flour
$\frac{1}{2}$ c. pearled barley, uncooked
1 t. salt
1 t. sugar
1 t. baking powder
$\frac{1}{2}$ t. baking soda
1 c. buttermilk
$\frac{1}{4}$ c. butter, melted

Mix together first 6 ingredients; stir in buttermilk. Turn dough onto a lightly floured surface; knead. Roll dough into an oval shape, $\frac{1}{2}$- to $\frac{3}{4}$-inch thick. Score dough with a knife and prick with a fork; place on a lightly greased and floured baking sheet. Bake at 375 degrees for 15 to 25 minutes. Cool on a wire rack and brush with melted butter. Serves 4 to 6.

Sherry Saarinen
Hancock, MI

OH GOODIE! IT'S

APPLE SYRUP

Re·warm in the microwave & serve over pancakes!

1 c. UNSWEETENED APPLE JUICE
1 c. SUGAR
$\frac{1}{4}$ c. APPLE LIQUER
1 CINNAMON STICK

...great over vanilla ice cream!

Combine all ingredients in a saucepan over medium heat. Bring to a boil, stirring constantly, and boil for about 15 minutes or until slightly thickened. Remove from heat and pour, including the cinnamon stick, into a sterilized 12-ounce bottle. Cap tightly and refrigerate up to one week. ⟿ Cindy Lawrence★ Topeka, KS

December will always be a most special month for me. In past years, we anticipated the arrival of family & friends by spending many hours baking cookies and candies and decorating our home both inside and out. But December 2000 will always be the most precious of all. After spending 22 days in a foreign country, my husband and I returned home just in time for Christmas with not one, but two babies! What a wonderful gift we were given! We were able to share with our family their two new grandsons, nephews and cousins. This arrival was truly a miracle and brought back the real reason we celebrate Christmas to the front of our family celebrations.
— Beth Hoffman
Santa Claus, IN

"Good bread is the most fundamentally satisfying of all foods; and good bread with fresh butter, the greatest of feasts."
— James Beard

"The smell of good bread baking, like the sound of lightly flowing water, is indescribable in its evocation of innocence and delight."
— M.F.K. Fisher,
The Art of Eating

"In cooking, as in all the arts, simplicity is the sign of perfection."
— Curnonsky

Even when freshly washed and relieved of all obvious confections, cHildren tend to be STicky.

—FRAN LEBOWITZ—

SYRUP BOTTLE

For each label (one for each side of container), use a 2¼" circle punch to punch a circle from corrugated olive craft paper and a 1½" circle punch to punch a circle from natural paper. To create your label, stamp "maple syrup" on natural circle and handwrite "homemade" above stamp; layer and glue circles together. Use a ½" hole punch to punch "berries" from red cardstock and a holly leaf punch to punch a leaf from green cardstock. Glue leaf and berries at top of label. To attach labels, punch a ⅛" hole on each side of both labels. Weave a length of ribbon through the holes; remove spout from syrup bottle and slip label over bottle then knot ribbon and trim ends behind a label. Add syrup and replace spout.

Get that special someone's day off to a great start with a real breakfast treat…Homemade Maple Syrup. The oh-so-sweet topping will make Christmas morning pancakes or waffles even more tasty.

HOMEMADE MAPLE SYRUP

I always keep a batch in my fridge…it's yummy!

4 c. sugar
2 T. corn syrup
½ c. brown sugar, packed
2 c. water
1 t. vanilla extract
1 t. maple flavoring

Stir together first 4 ingredients in a saucepan until sugar dissolves. Heat over medium heat until boiling; boil one to 2 minutes. Remove from heat and cool 5 to 10 minutes. Stir in vanilla and maple flavoring. Makes about 4 cups.

Jana Warnell
Kalispell, MT

Tuck pancake mix into a basket along with a bottle of Homemade Maple Syrup, a new extra-large spatula and some flavored tea bags. Any busy family will enjoy this breakfast treat.

BROWN SUGAR GRANOLA

Decorate a brown paper bag and fill with this yummy snack…so handy to nibble on while traveling to visit family.

2 T. butter
1/4 c. corn syrup
1/4 c. honey
2 3/4 c. quick-cooking oats, uncooked
1/2 c. sliced almonds
1/2 c. brown sugar, packed
1 1/2 t. cinnamon
1/2 c. flaked coconut, toasted

Melt butter with corn syrup and honey in a small saucepan; set aside. Combine remaining ingredients except coconut in a large bowl; blend in butter mixture. Spread in a well-greased 13"X9" baking pan; press firmly to pack. Bake at 350 degrees until dark and golden, about 20 to 30 minutes; turn onto aluminum foil to cool. Break into bite-size pieces; mix in coconut. Store in an airtight container. Makes 1 1/4 pounds.

Once upon a time, on a snowy day when I was very young, Mom was in the kitchen making her heavenly potato soup. Taking her eyes off the soup for just a minute, she asked my brother Bob and me if we knew where snowflakes came from…and then she told us angels in heaven were having a pillow fight. Now every time it snows I think of angels, Mom and her potato soup.
— Dianne Selep
Warren, OH

Make Brown Sugar Granola, and you'll have holiday snacking all wrapped up. Transform a plain brown bag into a jolly gift sack with scrapbook paper and a few other trims. Pack the crunchy munchies inside and it's ready to go.

EMBELLISHED BROWN BAG

Use spray adhesive for all gluing unless otherwise indicated. Use spray adhesive in a well-ventilated area.

Using decorative-edge craft scissors, cut a piece of black scrapbook paper 1/4" smaller on all sides than front of a lunch-size brown bag. Cut a piece of red scrapbook paper 1/2" smaller on all sides than front of bag. Using spray adhesive, adhere papers together, then to front of bag.

Fold top of bag down to form a 3" flap. Cut a 1 1/2"-wide strip of black scrapbook paper and tear a 1"-wide strip of newsprint scrapbook paper to fit across flap; glue papers together, then to flap. Use craft glue to glue a length of chenille rickrack to underside of flap so it peeks out from underneath; glue a length of ribbon across newsprint. Embellish with buttons, bells and thin jute. Make handmade black-rimmed tags from cardstock. Write greeting then punch holes for jute tie and glue to bag.

Wake Up Smiling!
Blueberry ★ Sour Cream
Breakfast Cake

BROWN SUGAR, CINNAMON & NUTS, SWIRLED WITH BLUEBERRIES — CAN YOU SAY YUM?

1 c. BUTTER
2 c. SUGAR
2 EGGS
1 c. SOUR CREAM
½ t. VANILLA EXTRACT
2 c. CAKE FLOUR
¼ t. SALT
1 t. BAKING POWDER
½ c. BLUEBERRIES,
    WELL DRAINED
GARNISH: POWDERED SUGAR

CREAM BUTTER & SUGAR; ADD EGGS. FOLD IN SOUR CREAM AND VANILLA. SIFT TOGETHER DRY INGREDIENTS ✓ ADD TO MIXTURE. FOLD IN BLUEBERRIES. POUR ⅓ BATTER INTO A GREASED & FLOURED BUNDT® PAN; SPRINKLE WITH HALF THE FILLING. POUR ⅓ BATTER OVER TOP; SPRINKLE WITH REMAINING FILLING. TOP WITH REMAINING BATTER. GENTLY SWIRL CAKE WITH A SPATULA. BAKE AT 350 DEGREES FOR ONE HOUR. COOL AND INVERT ONTO A SERVING PLATTER. DUST WITH POWDERED SUGAR. SERVES 12 TO 16.

FILLING:

½ c. BROWN SUGAR, PACKED
1 t. CINNAMON
½ c. CHOPPED NUTS
MIX UNTIL COMBINED.

A RECIPE FROM LAVERNE FANG ★ JOLIET, IL

PECAN MINI MUFFINS

Just the right size for little fingers to pick up and enjoy!

1 c. brown sugar, packed
⅓ c. all-purpose flour
⅛ t. salt
1 c. chopped pecans
2 eggs
½ t. vanilla extract

Mix all ingredients by hand just until moist. Divide dough into mini muffin tins coated with non-stick vegetable spray. Bake at 350 degrees for 20 minutes. Immediately remove muffins from pans and cool on wire racks. Makes 2 dozen.

Tisha Brown
Elizabethtown, PA

Granny used to make homemade biscuits for our family breakfast each Christmas morning. One year, we decided to save her the work and bought biscuits at a fast food restaurant the day before; however, not everyone in the family was in on this little secret. As we ate breakfast my cousin said, "Granny, these are the best biscuits you've ever made!" My how we all laughed! For the record, although she didn't use a recipe, Granny did make the best biscuits in the world.

— Robin Wilson
Altamonte Springs, FL

TRIMMING-THE-TREE PITA SNACKS

Add variety...sprinkle with bacon bits, diced pepperoni, dried tomatoes or any other favorite "trimmings."

8 pita rounds
olive oil
²/₃ c. grated Parmesan cheese
4 t. dried basil
1 t. garlic powder

Carefully split pitas into 2 rounds; slice each round into 6 wedges. Arrange wedges smooth-side up on aluminum foil-lined baking sheets; brush lightly with olive oil. Flip wedges over; brush with olive oil. Set aside. Combine cheese, basil and garlic powder; sprinkle evenly over wedges. Bake at 350 degrees for 12 to 14 minutes; remove to a wire rack to cool completely. Makes 16 servings.

Like a lot of mothers, I don't measure ingredients when I bake or cook...it's always been a pinch of this, a scoop of that. One day, my daughter asked me how she was ever going to learn to cook when I didn't write anything down. From that day on, I began to measure ingredients and wrote each recipe down. It took me most of the year but, by Christmas, I had completed her cookbook. I can still see the look of joy on her face as she leafed through it. What a wonderful way to preserve family recipes.

—Sally Davis
Payne, OH

Give a gift of Trimming-the-Tree Pita Snacks and you're likely to start a new holiday tradition. Decorating for Christmas can work up quite an appetite...these crunchy treats are just the answer!

Make a Trimming The Tree Snack Box

Unfold a cake box and apply spray adhesive to the right side... now smooth the box onto the wrong side of a piece of wrapping paper.

Use a craft knife to trim the paper along the sides of the box and cut through the slits. Cut a 3" square "window" in lid of box. Cover window from wrong side with clear cellophane.

Ok! Now refold the box. Add a length of ribbon, then a length of fringe trim to the flap. Embellish box lid with scrapbook paper pieces, photo corners, stickers, buttons, brads and a homemade tag. Place your pita snacks inside!

ZESTY MOZZARELLA CHEESE BITES

A tasty take-along nibbler.

16-oz. pkg. mozzarella cheese
¼ c. roasted garlic oil
2 t. balsamic vinegar
2 T. fresh basil, chopped
1 T. whole mixed peppercorns,
  coarsely ground

Cube cheese into ½-inch cubes; place in a medium mixing bowl. Set aside. Whisk remaining ingredients together; pour over cheese cubes. Toss to coat; cover and refrigerate up to 3 days. Makes 14 servings.

PAINTED GIFT TIN

Paint a cream stripe along the top of a small tin pail; allow to dry, then paint a smaller green stripe in center of cream stripe. Thread a length of red jute through two buttons; sliding buttons to sides of pail, glue a button to each side of pail and tie jute in a bow in the front. Cut a tag from orange cardstock; embellish with a "friends" charm and a small piece of ribbon, then personalize tag. Thread jute through a hole in tag, then attach to pail with dimensional foam dots.

A laugh is a smile that bursts.

—MARY WALDRIP—

Do something that makes you giggle:

* take silly pictures wearing Santa hats!
* sit on red and green balloons!
* paint your toe nails red and green!
* watch a funny holiday movie with the kids!

Give your favorite cheese lover a sumptuous surprise this Christmas. Lightly coated with fresh basil and ground peppercorns, the Zesty Mozzarella Cheese Bites have just the right zip.

CRISPY-CRUNCHY CROUTON STICKS

These big dunkers are just right for dips, spreads and even soups.

8-oz. loaf French baguette
½ c. butter
1 T. fresh basil, chopped
¼ t. garlic powder
⅛ t. onion salt

Slice baguette in half horizontally; cut widthwise into one-inch wide sticks. Set aside. Melt butter in a 12" skillet; stir in basil, garlic powder and onion salt. Add half the crouton sticks; sauté until coated. Arrange in a single layer in an ungreased jelly-roll pan; repeat with remaining crouton sticks. Bake at 300 degrees for 25 to 30 minutes; flip crouton sticks halfway through baking. Cool completely. Store in an airtight container up to 3 days or freeze up to 3 months. Makes 2 dozen.

Croutons aren't just for salads. The perfect size for dipping, these Crispy-Crunchy Crouton Sticks are a great alternative to chips and crackers. Put them in decorated cellophane bags and keep them on hand for drop-in guests.

Christmas in our family is the best time to bake all those wonderful recipes that have been passed down from generation to generation or even from friend to friend. Sometimes the aromas bring back the most wonderful memories and hopefully create more for those new little ones around us.

— Rosalie Colby
Hiram, ME

Polka Dot Bag

Punch assorted sizes of circles from red scrapbook paper. Use alphabet stamps to stamp the name of food item on some of the circles. Use double-sided tape or glue dots to adhere the circles to a cellophane bag. Add crouton sticks to the bag; tucking in a sprig of berries and adding a gift tag, tie bag closed with a length of pretty ribbon!

MUSTARD JAR

Cut a circle of scrapbook paper to fit top of lid. Use craft glue to glue circle to lid; glue a length of natural jute along edges of circle. For label, cut a strip of plain cardstock long enough to wrap around jar and overlap, then cut a wider strip of scrapbook paper. Use a paint pen to write "MUSTARD" on cardstock strip, then use a fine-point pen to write "sweet" on one side and "tangy" on the other side. Center and glue cardstock strip to paper strip; glue label to jar. Glue lengths of jute along top and bottom edges of label. Add short pieces of ribbon and buttons to resemble a cluster of holly berries and leaves.

Bundle up a bag of home-baked cookies in a holiday apron and tie with a length of rick-rack. Fill the apron pocket with the recipe and a cookie cutter or two. The happy baker will be oh-so pleased.

Sweet and Tangy Mustard

Give a bag of pretzels with this tasty dip!

14-oz. can sweetened condensed milk

8-oz. jar mustard

2 T. prepared horseradish

2 T. Worcestershire sauce

★

Stir all ingredients together; spoon into an airtight container. Refrigerate up to 3 months. Makes 3 cups.

~Hope Davenport
Portland, Tx

Sweet and Tangy Mustard is a treat for the taste buds! The unique blend of mustard, sweetened condensed milk, horseradish and Worcestershire sauce makes a zesty dip and will also add zip to sandwiches.

Condensed milk is wonderful. I don't see HOW they can get a cow to sit down on those little cans.
-FRED ALLEN-

CRANBERRY-CHIP COOKIE MIX

A new spin...substitute dried strawberries!

1⅛ c. all-purpose flour
½ c. quick-cooking oats,
    uncooked
½ t. baking soda
½ t. salt
⅓ c. brown sugar, packed
⅓ c. sugar
½ c. dried cranberries
½ c. white chocolate chips
½ c. chopped walnuts

Mix all ingredients; pour into a one-quart plastic zipping bag; close bag. Place bag and baking instructions in gift bag.

Instructions: Cream together ½ cup softened butter, one egg and one teaspoon vanilla extract in a medium bowl. Add bag contents; mix until well blended. Drop by rounded teaspoonfuls onto greased baking sheets. Bake at 350 degrees for 8 to 10 minutes or until the edges turn golden. Cool on wire racks. Makes about 3 dozen.

*Lynne Takayesu-Wulfestieg
Downely, CA*

Share the joy of holiday baking with our Cranberry-Chip Cookie Mix. Packed with cranberries, white chocolate chips and walnuts, these cookies are berry delicious! Tuck a batch of mix into a wintry fabric bag, and don't forget to include the directions.

FABRIC BAG

Match right sides and use a ½" seam allowance for all sewing.

Cut a 7"x27" piece of white canvas. Press short edges ½" to wrong side; sew in place. Matching right sides and raw edges and referring to Fig. 1, fold fabric to middle. Pin edges of body together; finger press fold of flap, then turn flap to right side. For snowflakes on flap, leaving 1" along sides unadorned and sewing through top of flap only, use two strands of white embroidery floss to work Straight Stitches (page 423) to make four snowflakes; work French Knots (page 422) to attach sequins to flap and to centers of Straight Stitches. Turn flap back, as in Fig. 1; pin edges of flap in place. Sew along long edges of bag. For flat bottom bag, match bottom side seams to bottom; sew across each corner 1" from point, Fig. 2. Turn right side out. Use fabric glue to glue a doubled length of white pom-pom fringe across underside of flap. Adorn a white tag with sequin snowflakes; attach to bag with a length of floss.

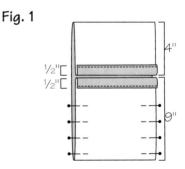

Fig. 1

½"
½"
4"
9"

Fig. 2

1"

HOLLY JOLLY COOKIES
Almost too pretty to eat!

1¾ c. all-purpose flour
1½ t. baking powder
½ t. salt
½ c. shortening
1 c. sugar
1 egg
¾ t. vanilla extract
¼ t. almond extract
¼ c. finely chopped
    blanched almonds
1 egg white, beaten
green decorating sugar
red cinnamon candies

Stir together flour, baking powder and salt; set aside. In a separate bowl, cream shortening; gradually add sugar, beating until fluffy. Blend in egg, vanilla and almond extract. Fold in almonds. Stir in dry ingredients; chill mixture for 3 hours. Divide dough in half and roll out each half between 2 sheets of wax paper to ⅛-inch thickness. Cut out cookies with a leaf-shape cutter. Arrange leaves in groups of 2 or 3 on an ungreased baking sheet; brush surfaces with egg white. Sprinkle green sugar over top of cookies and place 3 to 4 cinnamon candies at the base of the leaves. Bake at 375 degrees for 8 to 10 minutes. Cool on wire racks. Makes 3 dozen.

Kathy McLaren
Visalia, CA

"Christmas! The very word brings joy to our hearts."
— Joan Winmill Brown

Holly Plates

Holly loves to personalize gift plates for giving goodies to friends. She uses her favorite paint pens & glass paints to add designs that enhance the holly-themed cookies! Use your favorite holiday designs to decorate a plain glass plate ∼ just along the edges, though, for food safety — then let your friend know to handwash and dry the plate after every morsel is gone!

Bring out the holly…Holly Jolly Cookies that is! A sprinkling of green decorating sugar and cinnamon candy "berries" make these cookies as pretty as they are delicious. Give them on a hand-painted plate for added pizzazz.

GINGERBREAD MAN CARD AND BAG

Place a gingerbread man cookie in a cellophane bag and tie closed with lengths of ribbons. For card, use spray adhesive (in a well-ventilated area) to glue a 4³⁄₄"x9¹⁄₂" piece of scrapbook paper to a same size piece of cardstock. Fold card in half.

For front of card, tear a 4¹⁄₂" square of scrapbook paper, use decorative-edge craft scissors to cut a 3³⁄₄" square of scrapbook paper, and tear a 3" square of fabric. Layer fabric and paper squares; attach to card using small brads. Adhere a dimensional sticker to center of card.

Cookies are made of butter and love.

– NORWEGIAN PROVERB –

THE EASIEST GINGERBREAD MEN

A cake mix means this recipe is so simple, even the kids can make them!

18¹⁄₂-oz. pkg. spice cake mix
1 c. all-purpose flour
2 t. ground ginger
2 eggs
¹⁄₃ c. oil
¹⁄₂ c. molasses

Place cake mix, flour and ginger in a large mixing bowl; stir with a fork until blended. Mix in remaining ingredients. Beat with an electric mixer on medium speed for 2 minutes. Cover dough and refrigerate for 2 hours. Place dough on a floured surface; roll out to ¹⁄₄-inch thickness using a floured rolling pin. Cut out gingerbread people and place on greased baking sheets. Bake at 375 degrees for 8 to 10 minutes or until edges start to darken. Let cool on baking sheets for 5 minutes, then remove to wire racks to cool completely. Makes 1¹⁄₂ dozen.

Tanya Robinson
Ontario, Canada

A holiday tradition just got a little easier! By using cake mix, you can create these munchable men in a snap. Drop one in a cellophane bag tied with a bow, then add a handmade card for a quick-to-fix gift.

Graham Cracker Brownies

a recipe from Peggy Duzik ★ Sioux City, IA

2 c. graham cracker crumbs
1 c. semi-sweet chocolate chips ★
1 t. baking powder
⅛ t. salt
14-oz. can sweetened condensed milk

(★ substitute mint chocolate chips for a whole new taste!)

Combine all ingredients in a medium mixing bowl. Spread into a greased 8"x 8" baking pan. Bake at 350 degrees for 30 to 35 minutes or until a toothpick inserted near the center comes out clean. Cool on a wire rack and cut into squares. Makes 1½ dozen.

Fun Ideas!

This is an easy and yummy recipe to make with kids in the kitchen...

★ Let a little kid make the graham cracker crumbs ~ smash ★ smash ★ smash!

★ Kid-size aprons and potholders make chores pint-size.

★ Enjoy the finished product with a cold glass of milk!

GRANDMA'S MOLASSES POPCORN BALLS

My grandmother made these with my mom, and my mom made them every Christmas with me as a child. The best part was when the baking soda and butter were added...Mom said it was magic.

4 qts. popped popcorn
1 c. molasses
4 T. sugar
1 t. baking soda
1 t. butter

Place popcorn in a large bowl; set aside. Bring molasses and sugar to a boil in a large saucepan; boil for 20 minutes until mixture reaches the soft-ball stage, or 234 to 243 degrees on a candy thermometer. Remove from heat and quickly stir in baking soda and butter. Pour mixture over popcorn, stirring to coat. Grease hands with butter; shape popcorn into apple-size balls. Wrap individually in plastic wrap. Makes one to 2 dozen.

Cindy Hertz
Hummelstown, PA

OLD SOUTH POUND CAKE

If you thought the days were gone when pound cake really did take a pound of each ingredient...you were wrong!

1 lb. butter
1 lb. sugar
10 eggs, separated
1 lb. all-purpose flour
½ t. salt
1 t. lemon flavoring or
   vanilla extract

Cream butter; add sugar and beat well. In a separate bowl, beat egg yolks; add to creamed mixture. Combine flour and salt; stir into creamed mixture. Add lemon flavoring or vanilla. Beat egg whites until stiff peaks form; fold into cake batter. Pour into a greased Bundt® pan. Bake at 300 degrees for 1½ hours. Serves 10 to 12.

Delinda Blakney
Bridgeview, IL

"Sharing food with another human being is an intimate act that should not be indulged in lightly."
— M.F.K. Fisher

CINNAMON CAKE

Inside each slice, you'll find sweet swirls of cinnamon.

18¼-oz. pkg. yellow cake mix
3.4-oz. pkg. instant vanilla
    pudding mix
¾ c. oil
¾ c. water
1 t. vanilla extract
½ t. butter flavoring
4 eggs
¼ c. sugar
1¼ t. cinnamon

Combine first 6 ingredients in a large mixing bowl. Beat in eggs, one at a time, until mixture is smooth; set aside. In a separate bowl, combine sugar and cinnamon. Grease a Bundt® pan and sprinkle with half the cinnamon-sugar mixture. Pour half the cake batter in pan; sprinkle remaining cinnamon-sugar mix on top. Pour remaining batter on top. Bake at 350 degrees for one hour or until golden. Allow cake to cool for several minutes before removing from pan; pour icing over top while still warm. Serves 10 to 12.

Icing:
1 c. powdered sugar
3 T. milk
¼ t. butter flavoring

Mix all ingredients until smooth.

L. Santa Ana
Lomita, CA

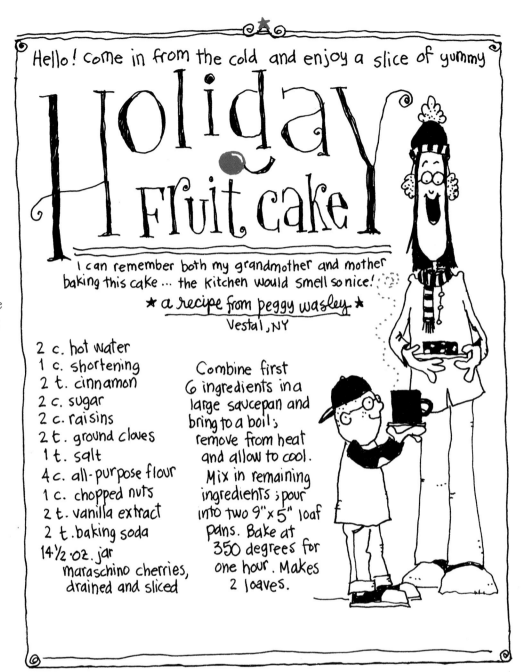

Hello! Come in from the cold and enjoy a slice of yummy

Holiday Fruit cake

I can remember both my grandmother and mother baking this cake ... the kitchen would smell so nice!

★ a recipe from peggy wasley ★
Vestal, NY

2 c. hot water
1 c. shortening
2 t. cinnamon
2 c. sugar
2 c. raisins
2 t. ground cloves
1 t. salt
4 c. all-purpose flour
1 c. chopped nuts
2 t. vanilla extract
2 t. baking soda
14½-oz. jar
    maraschino cherries,
    drained and sliced

Combine first 6 ingredients in a large saucepan and bring to a boil; remove from heat and allow to cool. Mix in remaining ingredients; pour into two 9" x 5" loaf pans. Bake at 350 degrees for one hour. Makes 2 loaves.

Need a gift in a flurry? Line a clean, new one-gallon paint can with a tea towel, glue homemade paper snowflakes on the outside and then fill to the rim with homemade cookies. Wrap it all up in cellophane and tie with a homespun bow.

Trim a tea party tree...tie dainty teacups to the ends of branches, gather lacy hankies and clip onto tree using vintage costume jewelry pins. Dangling teaspoons and tea caddies add even more charm and sparkle.

Stir up a batch of Sugar-Dusted Pecan Squares to satisfy the sweet tooth on your Christmas list. The nutty-sweet goodness will be a much appreciated treat.

SUGAR-DUSTED PECAN SQUARES

Be sure to include these at your Christmas cookie exchange!

2 c. brown sugar, packed
½ c. plus 2 T. all-purpose flour
¼ t. baking soda
2 c. chopped pecans
4 eggs
4 T. butter, melted
2 t. vanilla extract
Garnish: powdered sugar

Line a 9"X13" baking pan with aluminum foil, extending foil over ends of pan; grease foil. Mix together brown sugar, flour, baking soda and pecans in a small bowl; set aside. In a separate bowl, beat eggs; stir in melted butter. Stir in brown sugar mixture and vanilla. Pour mixture in pan; do not stir. Bake at 350 degrees for 20 minutes. Cool in pan on a wire rack. Use ends of foil to lift from pan. Cut into squares. Sprinkle lightly with powdered sugar. Makes 2 dozen.

Tamara Lucas
Guysville, OH

Star light, star bright. Place a well greased star-shaped open cookie cutter on a greased aluminum foil-lined baking sheet. Fill with coarsely chopped peppermint candies and bake at 325 degrees until candy melts. Gently push out of form...pretty swirled candy stars!

Kate's
Wooden Treat Basket!

Paint a wooden basket **RED**. tie a short length of silk ribbon through each end of a CHRISTMAS charm and glue to front of basket. For "TREATS" tags, CUT rectangles of green cardstock slightly larger than your alphabet charms, and rectangles of dark green cardstock larger than the green ones. layer and GLUE rectangles together. Center a charm on each rectangle; punch a hole in paper through hole in the charm. Attach a jump ring through holes in each charm and rectangle. Thread tags onto a length of jute; wrap and knot around basket, spacing tags evenly.

Now line the basket with a festive piece of homespun... and you're all done!

Flavors of the Season

Oh, the happiness of Christmas…
all our loved ones gathered together,
the aroma of roasted turkey, savory side
dishes and sweet pies. Perhaps the only
thing more wonderful than sharing holiday
foods is the laughter that follows the
dishes around the table. These recipes for
fabulous feasts and yummy treats will help
spread the joy throughout your holidays.

*Herb-Roasted Turkey tastes fabulous, and it looks so festive when
surrounded by lady apples, orange slices and fresh herbs!*

good friends good food

Christmas and friendship…each are good, but together they're better! Share these tempting dishes with the special people in your life or ask a friend to join you in the kitchen. The laughter will add its own special seasoning!

Herb-Roasted Turkey, Fresh Cranberry Relish, Feta & Walnut Salad

HERB-ROASTED TURKEY

A terrific turkey for dinner and for sandwiches the day after.

14-lb. turkey
1 T. salt
1 t. pepper
18 sprigs fresh thyme, divided
4 onions, peeled and sliced
1 lb. leek, chopped
2 carrots, chopped
4 stalks celery, chopped
3 bay leaves
1 T. peppercorns
1½ c. butter, melted
1 t. fresh sage, chopped
1 t. fresh thyme, chopped
1 t. fresh chives, chopped

Carefully rinse and dry turkey inside and out; set aside giblets. Rub all surfaces with salt and pepper, including cavity. Insert meat thermometer into thickest part of thigh without touching bone. Place 12 sprigs of thyme inside turkey. Place vegetables, bay leaves, remaining thyme sprigs, peppercorns and giblets in bottom of large, heavy roasting pan. Place turkey on top of vegetables. Cover opening of cavity with aluminum foil. Brush butter over all surfaces of turkey; sprinkle with sage, thyme and chives. Cover loosely with tent of aluminum foil. Roast at 350 degrees for 2½ hours, undisturbed; remove aluminum foil to let skin brown. Roast and baste every 20 minutes for an additional hour and 15 minutes or until an internal temperature of 180 degrees is reached. Remove from oven. Transfer to platter and cover with aluminum foil; pan juices may be reserved for making gravy. Let turkey rest 15 to 20 minutes before carving. Serves 12 to 14.

Jo Ann
Gooseberry Patch

Everybody knows a turkey and some mistletoe help to make the season bright. ❧ Mel Torme & Robert Wells

FRESH CRANBERRY RELISH

I make this simple recipe every Thanksgiving and Christmas at the request of my dad and husband. It nicely complements all the holiday favorites…turkey, ham, pork roast and stuffed winter squash. I like to garnish it with stars cut from the orange peel with a small cookie cutter.

12-oz. pkg. cranberries
2 apples, cored, peeled and
    quartered
2 pears, cored, peeled and
    quartered
2 oranges, peeled and sectioned
½ c. coarsely chopped pecans,
    optional
orange zest to taste
¾ c. honey or to taste

Coarsely chop the fruit with a food processor. Mix in nuts and orange zest; sweeten to taste with honey. Turn into a serving dish. Makes about 8 cups.

Karen Healey
Rutland, MA

FETA & WALNUT SALAD

If I think my guests won't care for the tart taste of cranberries, I just substitute cherry tomatoes.

5-oz. pkg. mixed salad greens
¾ c. dried cranberries
½ c. feta cheese, crumbled
½ c. chopped walnuts, toasted
2 T. balsamic vinegar
1 T. honey
1 t. Dijon mustard
¼ c. olive oil

Toss greens, cranberries, feta cheese and walnuts together in a large bowl. In a small bowl, whisk vinegar, honey and mustard until well blended; gradually add oil, whisking until combined. Pour over salad and toss to coat. Serves 4 to 6.

Denise Neal
Clayton, CA

AMBROSIA

Mom made this 5-cup salad in the 1950's and it's still popular today!

1 T. sugar
1 c. sour cream
1 c. miniature marshmallows
1 c. crushed pineapple, drained
1 c. flaked coconut
1 c. mandarin oranges, drained
Garnish: maraschino cherries
    (optional)

Stir sugar into sour cream; add next 4 ingredients. Stir well; chill. Garnish before serving, if desired. Makes 5 cups.

Mary Ann Nemecek
Springfield, IL

"Remember, no man is a failure who has friends."

— Clarence the Angel,
It's a Wonderful Life

Ambrosia

Need a Quick Centerpiece for your holiday table?

Wrap different-size boxes, stack them into a tower and glue on inexpensive ornaments where you can.

GREEN BEAN-CORN CASSEROLE

Try this quick & easy side dish. It's a terrific change from the more traditional green bean casseroles.

14½-oz. can French-style green
    beans, drained
15¼-oz. can corn, drained
1 c. shredded sharp Cheddar cheese
½ c. onion, chopped
1 c. sour cream
8-oz. can sliced water chestnuts,
    drained
10¾-oz. can cream of celery soup
½ c. butter, melted
1 sleeve round buttery crackers,
    crushed

Spread green beans on the bottom of an ungreased 13"x9" baking pan; layer corn on top. In a separate bowl, mix cheese, onion, sour cream, water chestnuts and celery soup together; spread over the vegetables. Combine butter and crackers; sprinkle on top. Bake at 400 degrees for 40 minutes or until golden. Serves 6.

Jennifer Thomas
Coffeyville, KS

Green Bean-Corn Casserole

CORNBREAD STUFFING

Mound stuffing on a large platter and top with a baked turkey breast…add teaspoonfuls of cranberry sauce evenly spaced around the rim for a meal that's pretty and filling.

16-oz. pkg. cornbread stuffing mix
3 c. water
½ c. butter, divided
1 c. onion, chopped
1 c. celery, chopped
1 c. ground Italian sausage,
    browned and crumbled
1 c. sweetened, dried cranberries
½ c. chopped pecans

Prepare stuffing according to package directions using 3 cups water and ¼ cup butter; set aside. Sauté the onion and celery in remaining butter until translucent. Stir onion, celery, sausage, cranberries and pecans into stuffing; toss well to coat. Spread in a lightly greased 13"x9" baking pan; bake at 350 degrees for 30 minutes. Makes about 12 cups.

Kathy Grashoff
Fort Wayne, IN

Play holiday music quietly during family dinners…try jazz, contemporary and country themes, and find your family's favorites.

A row of red apples tucked into pine boughs arranged down the middle of the table offers guests a simple country welcome.

SUNDAY DINNER POTATO ROLLS

Growing up, Sunday dinner was the most important meal in our home, and these rolls were always served fresh from the oven.

2 pkgs. active dry yeast
2 c. warm water
1/2 c. sugar
1 1/4 T. salt
1 c. warm mashed potatoes
1/2 c. butter, softened
2 eggs
7 1/2 c. all-purpose flour, divided
3 T. butter, melted

Dissolve yeast in water; add sugar, salt, potatoes, butter and eggs. Gradually beat in 3 1/2 cups flour; continue beating for 2 minutes. Mix in remaining flour; knead dough several strokes. Coat dough with melted butter; place in a bowl and refrigerate 2 hours. Punch down; refrigerate overnight. Punch down and knead. Divide dough in half; shape each half into 24 rolls. Place rolls on lightly greased baking sheets; let dough rise in a warm place. Bake at 325 degrees for 40 minutes. Makes 4 dozen rolls.

Mary Murray
Gooseberry Patch

"Peace on earth will come to stay, when we live Christmas every day."
— Helen Steiner Rice

"To get the full value of joy, you must have someone to divide it with."
— Mark Twain

CARAMEL PECAN PIE ...ooey. Gooey and unbearably GOOD!

36 CARAMELS, UNWRAPPED
1/4 c. BUTTER
1/4 c. MILK
3/4 c. SUGAR
3 EGGS
1/2 t. VANILLA EXTRACT
1/4 t. SALT
1 c. PECAN HALVES
9-INCH PIE CRUST

COMBINE CARAMELS, BUTTER & MILK IN HEAVY SAUCEPAN; HEAT UNTIL MELTED & CREAMY, STIRRING OFTEN. REMOVE FROM HEAT; SET ASIDE. BLEND SUGAR, EGGS & VANILLA & SALT TOGETHER; GRADUALLY MIX IN CARAMEL MIXTURE. FOLD IN PECANS; SPREAD IN PIE CRUST. BAKE AT 350 DEGREES FOR 45 TO 50 MINUTES; COOL 'TIL FIRM. SERVES 8.

JOAN BROCHU
HARDWICK, VT

Caramel Pecan Pie

They'll Never Know It's Not Homemade!

The recipe for "seasoned" greetings begins in the kitchen with this festive array of soon-to-be holiday favorites! Even Kate can whip up these yummy dishes, because they all feature ready-made foods from the grocery store. So, with just a pinch of work, you'll have a pound of wonderful treasures!

HERBED FAN DINNER ROLLS

When baked, the layers of the roll spread out to mimic a fan.

¼ c. butter or margarine, melted
½ t. dried Italian seasoning
11-oz. pkg. refrigerated loaf bread

Combine butter and Italian seasoning, stirring well. Roll dough into a 13" square. Cut into four equal strips. Stack strips on top of each other. Cut strips crosswise into 6 equal pieces. Place each piece, cut side up, into greased muffin pan; brush with butter mixture. Cover and let rise in a warm place (85 degrees), free from drafts, 25 minutes or until doubled in bulk. Bake at 375 degrees for 22 to 25 minutes or until golden. Brush with butter mixture again, if desired. Makes 6.

Make-Ahead: Place dough pieces in muffin pan; brush with butter mixture. Cover and freeze. Thaw, covered in a warm place 2 hours or until doubled in bulk. Bake as directed.

ITALIAN CHEESE TERRINE

Have provolone cheese and salami thinly sliced at a deli. Packaged, pre-sliced cheese and salami are too thick for this recipe.

1 lb. thinly sliced provolone cheese
2¾-oz. jar pesto sauce
¾ lb. thinly sliced salami
3 T. commercial Italian salad dressing
Garnish: fresh thyme sprigs
marinara or pasta sauce

Place one slice of cheese on a large piece of heavy-duty plastic wrap; spread one teaspoon of pesto over cheese. Top with 3 slices of salami. (Do not stack salami.) Brush salami lightly with salad dressing. Repeat layers, using all of cheese, pesto, salami, and salad dressing, and ending with cheese. Surround stack with a few sprigs of thyme, if desired. Fold plastic wrap over layers, sealing securely. Place a heavy object, such as a small cast-iron skillet, on top of cheese terrine. Cover and chill at least 24 hours or up to 3 days. Remove plastic wrap to serve terrine. Cut into wedges, using an electric knife or sharp knife. Serve with breadsticks, crackers, and desired sauce. Makes about 12 appetizer servings.

Herbed Fan Dinner Rolls

sweet treats

Quick 'n Easy Pie

WALNUT CRANBERRY SAUCE

A hint of cinnamon, splash of dark vinegar and handful of toasted nuts make this cranberry sauce worthy of gift giving. Deliver it in a jar tied with ribbon.

16-oz. can whole-berry cranberry
    sauce
1/3 c. strawberry preserves
1 1/2 T. sugar
1/4 t. cinnamon
1/2 c. coarsely chopped walnuts,
    toasted
1 T. balsamic vinegar or red wine
    such as Pinot Noir

Combine first 4 ingredients in a saucepan. Cook over medium heat, stirring often, just until thoroughly heated. Remove from heat; stir in walnuts and vinegar. Cover and chill until ready to serve. Serve with turkey or ham. Makes 2 1/4 cups.

QUICK 'N EASY PIE

This pie will vanish so fast...you'd better make two!

1 qt. vanilla ice cream, softened
6-oz. chocolate cookie crumb
    crust
14 1/2-oz. jar milk chocolate ice
    cream topping
3 1.4-oz. English toffee candy
    bars, chopped

Spread vanilla ice cream in crumb crust. Cover and freeze until ice cream is firm. Spread ice cream topping over ice cream; sprinkle with chopped candy, and freeze until firm. Serve immediately.

Sugar-n-spice makes everything nice.

— Old Saying

Snowball Sandwich Cookies

Little fingers will enjoy dipping these cookies in melted chocolate!

6·oz. pkg. white chocolate, chopped

2 12·oz. boxes Danish wedding cookies

Melt white chocolate in a heavy saucepan over low heat, stirring occasionally. Dip flat sides of half the cookies in white chocolate, and top with flat sides of remaining cookies. Let stand until white chocolate is firm. Makes 4 dozen.

HALF DIP TIPS

Make store-bought chocolate cookies more irresistible with even more chocolate! Here are some ideas worth dipping into.

Biscotti:
Melt 12 ounces chocolate candy coating or semi-sweet chocolate in top of a double boiler over hot water. Remove from heat. Fill a large mug with melted chocolate coating. Dip biscotti halfway into coating. Shake off excess coating and let dry on wax paper over a wire rack. Refill mug as needed.

Chocolate Snaps:
Follow procedure above, only using 10 ounces vanilla candy coating or white baking bars.

Dipped Cookies:
Place one cup milk chocolate morsels in a 2-cup glass measure. Microwave at HIGH one to 2 minutes or until melted, stirring every 30 seconds. Dip 20 cookies halfway into chocolate. Let dry on wax paper over wire racks. Repeat with another one cup morsels and remaining cookies. (It takes about 2 hours for milk chocolate coating to dry.)

Dipped and Drizzled Cookies:
Dip cookies as previously directed. Then seal $^1/_2$ cup chocolate or vanilla morsels in a heavy-duty, plastic zipping bag. Dip bag in very hot water 2 to 3 minutes or until chocolate melts. Remove bag from water; snip a tiny hole in one corner of bag. Drizzle chocolate over dipped cookies.

Dipped and Drizzled Fruit:
Dip various fruits such as fresh strawberries or dried apricots in melted semi-sweet chocolate. Let dry on wax paper-lined trays. Or drizzle fruit, if desired, as directed above.

Speedy Sorbet

SPEEDY SORBET
What a fun way to eat fruit!

2 21-oz. cans blueberry or cherry pie filling

Freeze unopened cans of pie filling until frozen solid, at least 18 hours or up to one month. Submerge unopened cans in hot water one to 2 minutes. Open both ends of cans, and slide frozen mixture into a bowl. Break into chunks. Position knife blade in food processor bowl; add chunks. Process until smooth, stopping as necessary to scrape down sides. Pour fruit mixture into an 8"x8" baking pan. Freeze until firm. Let stand 10 minutes before serving. Makes 6 servings.

Pineapple Sorbet: Substitute two 20-oz. cans chunk pineapple in heavy syrup for pie filling.

Strawberry Sorbet: Substitute three 10-oz. packages frozen strawberries in syrup for pie filling.

CHOCOLATE MINT TORTE

Serve this refrigerated or frozen...it's delectable either way.

17-oz. loaf marble pound cake
¼ c. plus 2 T. chocolate syrup, divided
4.67-oz. pkg. chocolate-covered mint wafer candies, divided
2 c. whipping cream, divided
½ c. sifted powdered sugar, divided

Slice pound cake in half horizontally; slice each half in half again horizontally. Brush top of each layer with 1½ tablespoons chocolate syrup; let stand 15 minutes for layers to absorb syrup. Reserve 8 whole candies for garnish. Finely chop remaining candies. Combine one cup whipping cream and ¼ cup powdered sugar in a large mixing bowl; beat at high speed with an electric mixer until stiff peaks form. Fold chopped candies into sweetened whipped cream. Place one cake layer on a serving plate; spread ½ cup whipped cream mixture on cake layer. Repeat procedure with next 2 cake layers, stacking layers. Top with remaining cake layer and freeze until firm. Beat remaining whipping cream and remaining powdered sugar together. Frost top and sides of torte with mixture. Cover and chill or freeze until ready to serve or up to 8 hours. Pull a vegetable peeler down sides of reserved 8 candies to make tiny shavings. Sprinkle candy shavings over torte before serving. Makes one 9" torte.

Chocolate Mint Torte

LEMON FONDUE

Whereas melted chocolate is typically blended with cream and liqueur, we've concocted a luscious lemon version of the popular dessert fondue. Pears and gingersnaps are a must for dipping.

11¼-oz. jar lemon curd
⅓ c. sweetened condensed milk
¼ c. half-and-half
Garnish: lemon zest

Combine first 3 ingredients in a small bowl, and stir well. Spoon into a footed serving dish. Serve with fresh fruit, gingersnaps, and pound cake cubes. Garnish dish, if desired. Makes 2 cups.

Give kazoos as party favors, then everyone can play along with the Christmas music.

Make A Joyful noise!

Cook Slow, Save Time!

There's just something magical about a meal from a slow cooker. All those wonderful flavors mingling gently together produce meats that are more tender, and broths & sauces that seem more robust. And while your favorite dishes slowly simmer, you're free to make good use of the time you would otherwise have spent in the kitchen!

Tried & True Meatloaf

TRIED & TRUE MEATLOAF
Save any leftovers for tasty meat loaf sandwiches.

1 ¹/₂ lbs. ground beef
³/₄ c. bread crumbs
2 eggs
³/₄ c. milk
1 onion, chopped
1 t. salt
¹/₄ t. pepper
¹/₄ c. catsup
2 T. brown sugar, packed
1 t. dry mustard
¹/₄ t. nutmeg

Combine beef, bread crumbs, eggs, milk, onion, salt and pepper; form mixture into a loaf. Place in a slow cooker; heat on high setting one hour. Reduce to low setting and cook 4 to 5 hours. Whisk remaining ingredients together; pour over beef. Heat on high setting an additional 15 minutes. Serves 4 to 6.

Take a child to the grocery store to help choose dinner ingredients with all the fixings to drop off at a local food pantry…a tradition well worth keeping.

SHREDDED BEEF BBQ

A family favorite.

2¾-lb. beef chuck roast
1 onion, sliced
½ c. water
½ c. plus 1 T. brown sugar, packed
    and divided
1 T. vinegar
2 t. lemon juice
7-oz. bottle catsup
¼ t. salt
1½ t. Worcestershire sauce
½ t. dried mustard
pepper to taste

Place roast in a 2-quart slow cooker; add enough water to cover. Top with onion; heat on high setting for one hour. Reduce to low setting and cook 7 hours. Shred roast with 2 forks; place in a 10" skillet. Add ½ cup water; bring to a boil. Stir in ½ cup brown sugar; heat until liquid evaporates. Combine remaining ingredients with remaining brown sugar in a mixing bowl; pour over beef mixture. Heat until warmed through. Serves 6.

LANDSLIDE FRENCH DIP

Put ingredients in the slow cooker before leaving in the morning and dinner's ready when you come home!

3-lb. rump roast
1 cube beef bouillon
3 to 4 peppercorns
½ c. soy sauce
1 bay leaf
1 t. garlic powder

Place roast in a slow cooker; add remaining ingredients. Pour in enough water to cover the roast; heat on high setting for one hour. Reduce to low setting and cook 9 hours. Remove and discard bay leaf before serving. Serves 6.

Shredded Beef BBQ

SLOW COOKER Smothered Steak

⅓ c. all-purpose flour
1 t. garlic salt
½ t. pepper
1½ lbs. round steak,
    cut into strips
1 onion, sliced
2 green peppers, sliced
4-oz. can sliced mushrooms,
    drained
10-oz. pkg. frozen
french-style green beans
¼ c. soy sauce
9 c. prepared white rice

Add first 3 ingredients to a one-gallon plastic zipping bag; shake to mix. Place steak strips in bag; shake to coat. Arrange steak in a slow cooker; layer onion, green peppers, mushrooms & green beans on top. Pour soy sauce over top; heat on high setting for one hour. Reduce heat to low and heat for 8 hours; serve on bed of warm rice. Serves 6.

...Worth the Wait.

Jalapeño-Chicken Chili

ARTICHOKE-CHICKEN PASTA

So easy to make and so yummy!

16-oz. frozen grilled chicken
    breast strips
1 T. chicken bouillon granules
¼ c. water
17-oz. jar alfredo sauce
6½-oz. jar marinated artichoke
    hearts, drained
6-oz. pkg. angel hair pasta, cooked

Place chicken strips in a 4-quart
slow cooker with bouillon and water.
Cook on low for 2 to 3 hours. One
half hour prior to serving, turn
cooker to high and place sauce and
artichokes over chicken. Serve over
pasta. Makes 4 servings.

Mary Luinstra
Great Falls, MT

CHOW-DOWN CORN CHOWDER

Hearty and delicious.

6 slices bacon, diced
½ c. onion, chopped
2 c. potatoes, peeled and diced
2 10-oz. pkgs. frozen
    whole-kernel corn
16-oz. can cream-style corn
1¼ T. sugar
1½ t. Worcestershire sauce
1¼ t. seasoned salt
½ t. pepper
1 c. water

In skillet, fry bacon until crisp.
Remove bacon; reserve drippings.
Add onion and potatoes to drippings
and sauté for about 5 minutes; drain
well. Combine all ingredients in a
3½-quart slow cooker; stir well.
Cover and cook on low for 4 to 7
hours. Makes 4 servings.

Marian Buckley
Fontana, CA

*Try serving chili and chowder in
bread bowls…yummy! Scoop out
bread rounds and brush the insides
with olive oil or corn oil. Bake in a
350-degree oven for 10 minutes,
then fill with soup.*

JALAPEÑO-CHICKEN CHILI

*Jalapeño peppers and salsa spice up
this chili.*

2 c. chicken, cooked and cubed
4 15-oz. cans Great Northern
    beans
1 onion, chopped
½ c. red pepper, diced
½ c. green pepper, diced
2 jalapeño peppers, finely diced
2 cloves garlic, minced
1½ t. cumin
½ t. dried oregano
¾ t. salt
¼ c. water
½ t. chicken bouillon granules
1 to 2 c. salsa

Stir all ingredients except salsa
together; spoon into a slow cooker.
Heat on high setting for 5 hours,
or cook on high setting one hour
and reduce to low setting and cook
7 to 9 hours; stir occasionally. Add
salsa during last hour of heating.
Serves 4 to 6.

Good things come to those who Wait.

Mom's Spaghetti Sauce

1 onion, diced
3 cloves garlic, chopped
1 T. butter
3 14-½-oz. cans tomatoes
3 6-oz. cans tomato paste
2 c. water
¼ t. salt
½ t. pepper
½ t. dried basil
½ t. dried oregano
½ t. garlic powder
½ t. dried thyme
1 t. Italian seasoning
2 bay leaves
1 T. dried parsley

⅛ t. sugar
3 T. olive oil

Sauté onion and garlic in butter; set aside. Blend tomatoes and tomato paste in a blender until smooth; stir in onion and garlic. Pour into slow cooker; mix in remaining ingredients. Heat on high setting for approximately 3 hours, stirring occasionally; remove bay leaves before serving. Makes about 5 cups.

Everybody's Favorite!

Slow-Cooker Potato Soup

SLOW-COOKER POTATO SOUP

This soup will warm you from the inside out.

4 to 5 potatoes, peeled and cubed
10¾-oz. can cream of celery soup
10¾-oz. can cream of chicken soup
1⅓ c. water
4⅔ c. milk
6.6-oz. pkg. instant mashed potato flakes
Garnish: bacon bits, green onions and shredded Cheddar cheese

Place potatoes, soups and water into a slow cooker; heat on high setting until potatoes are tender, about 2 to 3 hours. Add milk and instant mashed potatoes to reach desired consistency, stirring constantly. Heat 2 to 3 hours longer; spoon into bowls to serve. Top with garnishes. Serves 4 to 6.

GOOD HONEY-GARLIC CHICKEN WINGS

These delicious wings will be ready when the "big game" starts.

3 lbs. chicken wings,
    cleaned and halved
salt and pepper to taste
1 c. honey
1/2 c. soy sauce
2 T. oil
2 T. catsup
1 clove garlic, minced

Sprinkle chicken with salt and pepper. In a mixing bowl, combine remaining ingredients and mix well. Place chicken in a 4-quart slow cooker and pour sauce over. Cook on high for one hour. Reduce to low and cook 5 to 7 hours. Makes 8 to 12 servings.

Mary Murray
Gooseberry Patch

CHICKEN & GREEN BEAN BAKE

A full meal in one dish.

2 to 3 boneless, skinless chicken
    breasts
salt, pepper and garlic powder to
    taste
10 3/4-oz. can cream of mushroom
    soup
1/2 c. milk
14 1/2-oz. can green beans, drained
2.8-oz. can French fried onions

Place chicken breasts in a slow cooker; season with salt, pepper and garlic powder. Heat until juices run clear when chicken is pierced with a fork, approximately 2 to 3 hours on high setting; drain. Add mushroom soup, milk and green beans; sprinkle top with French fried onions. Cover and heat 30 minutes longer. Serves 4.

POT ROAST & VEGGIES

Come home to a perfect dinner!

2- to 4-lb. pot roast
salt and pepper to taste
4 T. all-purpose flour
1/4 c. cold water
1 t. browning sauce
1 clove garlic, minced
2 onions, coarsely chopped
5 potatoes, peeled and coarsely
    chopped
3 carrots, coarsely chopped

Cut pot roast in half; place in a 4-quart slow cooker. Sprinkle with salt and pepper. Make a paste of flour and cold water; stir in browning sauce and spread over roast. Add garlic, onions, potatoes and carrots. Cover and cook on high setting for one hour. Reduce to low setting and cook 7 to 9 hours. Serves 4 to 6.

Donna Dye
London, OH

No longer forward nor behind I look in hope or fear; But, grateful, take the good I find, The best of now and here.
—JOHN GREENLEAF WHITTIER—

Pot Roast & Veggies

CARAMEL PIE

They'll never believe you made it in a slow cooker!

2 14-ounce cans sweetened
    condensed milk
9-inch graham cracker pie crust
8-oz. container frozen whipped
    topping, thawed
1.4-oz. English toffee candy bar,
    coarsely chopped

Pour condensed milk into a 1-quart glass measuring cup; cover with foil. Place in a 3½-quart slow cooker, adding water around cup to milk level. Cook, covered, 8 to 9 hours or until mixture is the color of peanut butter; stir with a wire whisk. Pour into pie crust; chill one hour or until firm. Spread whipped topping over top of pie, and sprinkle evenly with chopped candy bar. Makes 6 to 8 servings.

Caramel Pie

MACARONI & CHEESE

An all-time favorite of kids everywhere.

12-oz. can evaporated milk
3 eggs, beaten
½ c. butter, melted
7-oz. pkg. macaroni, cooked
salt and pepper to taste
3 c. Cheddar cheese, grated
    and divided

Combine milk, eggs and butter, whisking until blended. Cook over medium heat, stirring constantly, until slightly thickened. Stir in macaroni, salt and pepper and 2 cups cheese; stir well. Pour into a 5-quart slow cooker and sprinkle with remaining cheese. Cover and cook on low for 3 hours. Do not take lid off until ready to serve. Makes 12 servings.

Stacie Seiders
Oakton, VA

"May peace and plenty be the first to lift the latch on your door, and happiness be guided to your home by the candle of Christmas!"
— Irish Blessing

Prayer is the simplest form of speech that infant lips can try;

Prayer the sublimest strains that reach The Majesty on high.

~ James Montgomery ~

A CUP of CHEER

A mug of Candy Cane Cocoa is just the thing to chase the chill after a day of building snowmen. Or maybe you need Apple-Cranberry Sparkler to help you cool down from a long evening of trimming the tree. Remember to make at least two servings for everyone, because these refreshments will disappear almost as fast as you can pour them.

Candy Cane Cocoa

CANDY CANE COCOA

This will warm you head to toe on those snowy nights.

4 c. milk
³/₄ c. sugar
1 t. peppermint extract
1 ¹/₂ c. baking cocoa
1 pt. mint chocolate chip ice cream
chocolate syrup
8 candy canes, crushed

Combine milk, sugar, peppermint extract and cocoa in a large saucepan. Heat over medium heat until hot; do not boil. Divide evenly into 8 large mugs. Float a scoop of ice cream in each mug; drizzle with chocolate syrup and sprinkle with candy cane pieces. Makes 8 servings.

Pat Ghann-Akers
Bayfield, CO

PINEAPPLE WASSAIL

Bring to a holiday open house while warm...mmmm.

4 c. unsweetened pineapple juice
12-oz. can apricot nectar
2 c. apple cider
1½ c. orange juice
2 3-inch cinnamon sticks
1 t. whole cloves
4 cardamom seeds, crushed

Combine ingredients in a 3-quart saucepan; heat to boiling. Reduce heat and simmer 15 to 20 minutes; strain into serving glasses or punch bowl. Serve warm. Makes about 2 quarts.

COMFY CIDER

Grab a mug of cider and snuggle down in front of the fireplace.

4 c. apple cider
2 c. cranberry juice
46-oz. can apricot nectar
1 c. orange juice
¾ c. sugar
2 3-inch cinnamon sticks
1 orange, peeled and sectioned

Place ingredients in a slow cooker; heat on low setting until warmed through, 4 to 6 hours. Strain before serving, discarding solids. Serves 10 to 12.

Add a bit of sparkle and spice to holiday drinks...tie a little ornament or bauble onto a cinnamon stick. The cinnamon stick is a great stirrer, while the ornament dangles over your mug of hot cocoa, mulled cider or creamy eggnog.

Pineapple Wassail

Snow Cocoa

Stir this cocoa all together in the slow cooker and plug in before heading out to go sledding!

2 c. WHIPPING CREAM
6 c. MILK
1 t. VANILLA EXTRACT
12-oz. PKG. WHITE CHOCOLATE CHIPS

Combine all ingredients in slow cooker. Heat on low for 2 to 2½ hours or until chocolate is melted and mixture is hot. Stir well to blend. Serves 10 chilly sledders! ❧ KENDALL HALE ★ LYNN, MA

Creamy Nog Punch

~ Better Than a Pile o' Presents! ~

1 gal. vanilla ice cream
½ gal. eggnog
1 t. nutmeg
½ t. cinnamon
16-oz. container frozen
    whipped topping, thawed

*

Scoop ice cream into a punch bowl. Pour eggnog over ice cream and sprinkle with nutmeg & cinnamon; gently stir in whipped topping. Serve immediately. Stir as needed. Makes 1-½ gallons.

Creamy Nog Punch

SPICED HOT COCOA MIX

The 1st Day of Winter is December 21st...chase those flurries away with this warm mix.

1 vanilla bean
1 1/3 c. sugar
1 1/3 c. powdered milk
1 c. baking cocoa
3 T. instant espresso
1/2 t. cinnamon
1/4 t. vanilla powder
1/8 t. ground cardamom

Split vanilla bean; scrape seeds and place in a medium mixing bowl, discarding shell. Add sugar; stir to blend. Add remaining ingredients; mix well. Spoon into an airtight container; attach instructions. Makes about 3 1/2 cups.

Instructions: Stir 1/4 cup mix into one cup boiling water; stir until dissolved. Makes one serving.

CHRISTMAS MORNING CAPPUCCINO MIX

Slip a jar into a stocking for an early-morning treat.

2/3 c. instant coffee granules
1 c. powdered sugar
1 c. powdered non-dairy creamer
1 c. chocolate drink mix
1/2 c. sugar
3/4 t. cinnamon
3/8 t. nutmeg
2 12-oz. jars and lids

Blend coffee granules until fine; place in a large bowl and add remaining ingredients. Stir until well mixed. Divide mixture between the 2 jars; secure lids and attach instructions. Makes 2 jars.

Instructions: Mix 3 tablespoons cappuccino mix with 3/4 cup hot water or milk. Makes one serving.

Jennifer Clingan
Dayton, OH

Apple-Cranberry Sparkler

MOM'S CRANBERRY TEA

Makes plenty for your holiday visitors.

3 6-inch cinnamon sticks
30 whole cloves
4 qts. water, divided
16-oz. can jellied cranberry sauce
2 6-oz. cans frozen orange juice
    concentrate, thawed
1 c. sugar
6 T. lemon juice

Combine cinnamon sticks, cloves and 2 cups water in a small saucepan; bring to a boil and boil for 10 minutes. In a large bowl, combine cranberry sauce, orange juice, sugar and lemon juice; add boiling liquid, straining cinnamon sticks and cloves. Pour mixture and remaining water into a slow cooker; heat on low setting to keep warm until serving. Makes about 5 quarts.

APPLE-CRANBERRY SPARKLER

Looks oh-so pretty when served in lovely holiday glasses.

4 teabags
2 c. boiling water
1 c. cranberry juice cocktail, chilled
1 c. apple juice, chilled
2 t. sugar

Place teabags in boiling water and brew for 5 minutes; remove teabags. Combine tea, juices and sugar in a pitcher and chill. Makes one quart.

Ranae Scheiderer
Beallsville, OH

*"Have a holly jolly Christmas,
It's the best time of the year.
I don't know if there'll be snow,
But have a cup of cheer."*
— Johnny Marks

I know well that happiness is in the little things.

— JOHN RUSKIN

sweet holiday treasures

A Christmas without sweets just wouldn't be Christmas! This assortment of cakes, pies, cookies and candy offers everything from traditional flavors to flavorful new recipes...and every morsel is just as scrumptious as the one before!

PEPPERMINT CANDY CHEESECAKE

Drizzle strawberry syrup on each slice right before serving for a merry little touch.

1 c. graham cracker crumbs
3/4 c. sugar, divided
6 T. butter, melted and divided
1½ c. sour cream
2 eggs
1 T. all-purpose flour
2 t. vanilla extract
2 8-oz. pkgs. cream cheese, softened
¼ c. peppermint candies, coarsely crushed
Garnish: frozen whipped topping, thawed; crushed peppermint candies

Blend crumbs, ¼ c. sugar and ¼ cup melted butter in bottom of ungreased 8" round springform pan; press evenly over bottom. Blend sour cream, remaining sugar, eggs, flour and vanilla in a blender or food processor until smooth, stopping to scrape sides. Add cream cheese and blend; stir in remaining 2 tablespoons melted butter until completely smooth. Fold in crushed candy and pour over crust. Bake at 325 degrees for 45 minutes. Remove from oven and run a knife around edge of pan. Cool, then refrigerate overnight. Loosen pan sides and remove springform; serve garnished with whipped topping and crushed candy. Makes 12 servings.

Bobbi Carney
Centennial, CO

Peppermint Candy Cheesecake

COOKIES & CREAM CAKE

For even more chocolatey taste, try using chocolate sandwich cookies with chocolate filling…yum!

18½-oz. pkg. white cake mix
1¼ c. water
⅓ c. oil
1 t. vanilla extract
3 eggs
1 c. chocolate sandwich cookies, crushed

Combine cake mix, water, oil, vanilla and eggs in a large mixing bowl; blend on low speed until just moistened. Blend on high for 2 minutes; gently fold in crushed cookies. Line two 8" round baking pans with wax paper; grease and flour pans. Pour mixture into pans; bake at 350 degrees for 25 minutes or until a toothpick inserted in the center removes clean. Cool for 10 minutes; remove from pans to a wire rack to cool completely. Frost. Serves 12.

Frosting:
½ c. butter or shortening
1 t. vanilla extract
4 c. powdered sugar
¼ c. milk

Beat together butter and vanilla until creamy. Add powdered sugar and milk alternately to creamed mixture, beating until desired consistency.

Shari Miller
Hobart, IN

Dip pretzel rods in melted chocolate, then coat with chopped nuts and crushed peppermint candies…arrange in a holiday glass filled with coarse sugar for a stand-up treat.

Cookies & Cream Cake

SOFT GINGERBREAD COOKIES

My mother always made these cookies at Christmastime when I was a little girl. I carried on the tradition for my children and now make them for my grandson. They are so soft and moist…a true favorite.

1 c. margarine
1½ c. brown sugar, packed
2 eggs, beaten
1 T. ground ginger
½ c. molasses
1½ c. boiling water
1½ t. baking soda
5 c. all-purpose flour
2 t. baking powder
1½ t. salt
1 T. cinnamon
1 c. chopped walnuts

Blend margarine and sugar in a large mixing bowl; blend in eggs. Mix in ginger and molasses; stir in boiling water. Set aside. Combine remaining ingredients except for the nuts; add to sugar mixture. Fold in walnuts; cover and refrigerate dough for at least 2 hours. Drop by teaspoonfuls onto ungreased baking sheets; bake at 425 degrees for 10 to 12 minutes. Makes about 6 dozen.

Bev Johnstone
Delaware, OH

Merry Munchers!

My daughter's favorite cookie! This recipe can easily be doubled... perfect for holiday cookie exchanges and parties.

½ c. butter
1 c. sugar
½ c. brown sugar, packed
3 eggs
1 c. creamy peanut butter
1 t. vanilla extract
1 T. baking soda

4½ c. quick-cooking oats, uncooked
½ c. semi-sweet chocolate chips
½ c. candy-coated chocolates
1 c. chopped nuts

Cream butter & sugars in a large bowl until fluffy. Add eggs, peanut butter, vanilla & baking soda, beating well. Stir in remaining ingredients and mix well. Spoon onto greased baking sheets; bake at 350 degrees for 12 to 15 minutes. Makes 25 cookies.

~ Janie Branstetter * Fairview, OK ~

Merry Munchers

PUMPKIN PRALINE LAYER CAKE

I think this is the type of dessert that's so delicious, it makes your toes curl up!

1 c. brown sugar, packed
½ c. butter
¼ c. whipping cream
¾ c. chopped pecans
2 c. all-purpose flour
1 t. baking powder
2 t. pumpkin pie spice
1 t. baking soda
1 t. salt
1⅔ c. sugar
1 c. oil
4 eggs
2 c. canned pumpkin
1¾ c. whipping cream
¼ c. powdered sugar
¼ t. vanilla extract
Garnish: toasted chopped pecans

Combine first 3 ingredients in a heavy saucepan over low heat until brown sugar dissolves; stir occasionally. Divide equally between 2 greased 9" round cake pans. Sprinkle evenly with pecans; let mixture cool slightly. Sift together flour, baking powder, spice, baking soda and salt in a bowl; set aside. Blend sugar, oil and eggs; alternately add pumpkin and reserved dry ingredients. Spoon batter evenly over pecan mixture in cake pans. Place pans on a baking sheet and bake at 350 degrees for 35 to 45 minutes or until centers test clean. Cool cakes in pans on a wire rack for 5 minutes; invert and cool completely on wire rack. Beat whipping cream until soft peaks form; stir in powdered sugar and vanilla. Continue beating until stiff peaks form. To assemble cake, place one layer on a serving plate, praline-side up; spread with whipped topping. Add second layer, praline-side up, and top with remaining whipped topping. Garnish with toasted pecans. Serves 8.

Judy Phelan
Macomb, IL

CHOCOLATE TRUFFLES

Wrap these sweets in colorful foil papers for a festive assortment.

³/₄ c. butter
³/₄ c. baking cocoa
14-oz. can sweetened
    condensed milk
1 T. vanilla extract
Garnish: baking cocoa, powdered
    sugar, chopped nuts, candy
    sprinkles, flaked coconut

Melt butter in heavy saucepan over low heat; add cocoa and stir until smooth. Add sweetened condensed milk; cook and stir constantly until mixture is thick, smooth and glossy, about 4 minutes. Remove from heat; stir in vanilla. Cover and refrigerate 3 to 4 hours or until firm. Shape into 1¹/₄-inch balls; roll in desired garnish. Refrigerate again until firm, one to 2 hours. Store, covered, in refrigerator. Makes 2¹/₂ dozen.

Vickie

Chocolate Truffles

GRANDMA'S PEANUT BUTTER PIE

My grandma is a wonderful cook and baker. When we would visit, she always had a fresh-baked pie waiting.

¹/₂ c. boiling water
4 T. cornstarch, divided
³/₄ c. powdered sugar
¹/₂ c. creamy peanut butter
³/₄ c. sugar, divided
1 T. all-purpose flour
¹/₈ t. salt
3 eggs
3 c. milk
2 t. butter
2 t. vanilla extract
9-inch deep-dish pie crust, baked
¹/₄ t. cream of tartar

In a small saucepan, mix together boiling water and one tablespoon cornstarch. Cook and stir constantly until clear and thick; set aside to cool. In a small bowl, combine powdered sugar and peanut butter to resemble coarse crumbs; set aside. In a 2-quart saucepan, stir together ¹/₂ cup sugar, remaining cornstarch, flour and salt. Separate eggs, placing whites in a separate bowl; set aside to warm to room temperature. Add egg yolks and milk to sugar mixture; whisk until combined. Bring mixture to a boil over medium heat; cook and stir for 2 minutes. Remove from heat and stir in butter and vanilla. Sprinkle ¹/₃ peanut butter mixture over pie crust bottom; layer half of batter over crumbs. Sprinkle another ¹/₃ peanut butter mix over batter and top with remaining batter; set aside. Add cornstarch

mixture and cream of tartar to egg whites; beat until soft peaks form. Gradually sprinkle remaining sugar over mix until stiff peaks form. Spread meringue over pie, being sure to touch edges of crust to seal. Sprinkle remaining ¹/₃ peanut butter crumbs around top edge of pie. Bake at 375 degrees for 8 to 10 minutes or until meringue is golden. Cool completely before serving. Serves 6 to 8.

Kristina Wyatt
Madera, CA

"Christmas is not a time nor a season, but a state of mind. To cherish peace and goodwill, to be plenteous in mercy, is to have the real spirit of Christmas."
— Calvin Coolidge

Peppermint Pinwheels

PEPPERMINT PINWHEELS
The prettiest cookies for the holidays!

1/2 c. shortening
1/2 c. butter, softened
1 1/4 c. sugar, divided
1 egg
1 1/2 t. almond extract
1 t. vanilla extract
2 1/2 c. all-purpose flour
1 t. salt
1/2 t. red food coloring
2 t. egg white powder
1/4 c. water
1/4 c. peppermint candy sticks,
    crushed, or coarse sanding sugar

Mix together shortening, butter, one cup sugar, egg and almond and vanilla extracts. Sift together flour and salt; blend into butter mixture. Divide dough in half and blend red food coloring into one half. Chill both halves until firm. Roll light dough on a lightly floured surface to form a 6"x6" square. Roll red half to same size and lay on top of light dough. Wrap in plastic wrap and chill until firm. Roll the double layer with a rolling pin to a 12"x12" square. Tightly roll up jelly-roll style; wrap in plastic wrap and chill for one hour. Slice chilled dough into 1/4-inch thick cookies. Place on ungreased baking sheets; bake at 375 degrees for 13 minutes or until lightly golden. Mix egg white powder with water; brush on warm cookies. Mix crushed candy with remaining sugar; sprinkle candy mixture or coarse sugar on top of cookies. Makes 2 to 3 dozen.

Kathy McLaren
Visalia, CA

RED VELVET CAKE
This colorful cake is a terrific choice for a holiday dessert buffet.

1/2 c. shortening
1 1/2 c. sugar
2 eggs
2-oz. bottle red food coloring
2 t. baking cocoa
1 t. salt
2 1/2 c. all-purpose flour
1 t. vanilla extract
1 c. buttermilk
1 t. baking soda
1 t. vinegar

Blend together shortening, sugar and eggs. In a separate bowl, mix together food coloring and cocoa; add to sugar mixture. Add salt, flour, vanilla and buttermilk. Alternately add baking soda and vinegar until just blended. Pour batter into 2 greased and floured 8" round baking pans. Bake at 350 degrees for 30 minutes. Cool. Spread frosting on layers and stack to form a 2-layer cake. Serves 6 to 8.

Frosting:
3 T. all-purpose flour
1 c. milk
1 c. sugar
1 c. shortening
1 t. vanilla extract

Combine flour and milk in a saucepan; cook over medium heat until thick. Cool. Mix together sugar, shortening and vanilla until fluffy; add to flour mixture. Beat until light and fluffy.

Stephani Hobert
Huber Heights, OH

Use a white paint pen to draw simple snowflakes or stars away from the rim on the side of a large blue mug. Let the paint dry, then fill the mug with candy. A perfect quick gift for a snacker!

ROCKY ROAD FUDGE BROWNIES

"DELICIOUS WARM... MY HUSBAND HAS TO EAT AT LEAST 2 AS SOON AS THEY COME OUT OF THE OVEN!"

1 c. BUTTER, SOFTENED
3/4 c. BAKING COCOA
1/4 c. OIL
4 EGGS
2 c. SUGAR
1⅓ c. ALL-PURPOSE FLOUR
1/2 t. SALT
1/2 c. HOT FUDGE

TOPPING:
1 c. CHOPPED PECANS
1 c. BUTTERSCOTCH CHIPS
2 c. MINI MARSHMALLOWS
combine & mix well.

Combine first 3 ingredients in small saucepan; heat 'til melted and smooth, stirring often. Remove from heat; set aside. Blend eggs in large mixing bowl 'til light and fluffy; mix in cocoa mixture and next 3 ingredients. Spread in a greased 13"x9" baking pan; bake at 350 degrees 'til brownies pull away from sides of pan ~ about 25 minutes. Sprinkle topping evenly on top and drizzle with hot fudge sauce. Continue baking 5 minutes; cool. Cut into bars to serve. Makes 15.

~ Rita Miller ✦ Wirtz, VA

Rocky Road Fudge Brownies

ORANGE POUND CAKE

I wanted to share this old Southern recipe that our family has been enjoying for over 35 years. We just love it!

1½ c. butter, softened
3 c. sugar
5 eggs
3½ c. all-purpose flour
1 t. cream of tartar
1½ t. baking powder
¼ t. salt
½ c. milk
½ c. plus 5 T. orange juice, divided
1 t. vanilla extract
1 t. almond extract
4 T. orange zest, divided
1½ c. powdered sugar

Cream butter; gradually add sugar, mixing until light and fluffy. Add eggs, one at a time, blending after each addition. Combine flour, cream of tartar, baking powder and salt; add to creamed mixture alternately with the milk and ½ cup plus 2 tablespoons orange juice, beginning and ending with flour mixture. Mix until just blended; stir in extracts and 2 tablespoons orange zest. Pour into a greased and floured 10" Bundt® pan; bake at 325 degrees for about one hour and 25 minutes. Cool. Combine powdered sugar, remaining orange zest and enough remaining orange juice to make a desired consistency to pour over cooled cake. Serves 12.

Juanita McLane
Wilmington, DE

ENGLISH TOFFEE

Sprinkle with coarsely chopped red & white peppermints or toffee chips for an extra-special delight.

1 c. butter
1 1/3 c. sugar
1 T. light corn syrup
3 T. water
2 1/2 c. finely chopped slivered almonds, toasted and divided
3   1.55-oz. milk chocolate candy bars, divided

Line a 13"x9" baking pan with aluminum foil. Butter foil; set aside. Combine first 4 ingredients in a 4-qt. heavy saucepan. Cook over medium-low heat until mixture comes to a boil. Wash down crystals from sides of pan with a small brush dipped in hot water. Cook until mixture reaches the hard-crack stage or 300 degrees on a candy thermometer, stirring occasionally to prevent scorching. Remove from heat and stir in 1 1/2 cups almonds. Spread candy in prepared pan; cool completely (about 30 minutes). Break 1 1/2 chocolate bars in pieces and place in a small glass bowl. Microwave at HIGH 50 seconds; stir until candy melts. Spread melted chocolate over toffee mixture; sprinkle with 1/2 cup almonds. Let cool until set (about one hour). Lift foil and candy from pan. Place a 15"x10" jellyroll pan over candy and invert candy onto jellyroll pan; remove foil. Melt remaining chocolate bars as above. Spread melted chocolate over toffee; sprinkle with remaining almonds. Chill, uncovered, 30 minutes or until firm; break into pieces. Makes about 2 pounds.

Rochelle Sundholm
Creswell, OR

AMISH SUGAR COOKIES

During my three daughters' elementary school years, these cookies were served at all class events. I would get a thrill out of watching the parents send their kids up to the cookie counter for yet another one...not for the kids, but for themselves!

2 c. sugar
1 c. shortening
3 eggs
1 c. sour cream
1 t. vanilla extract
5 t. baking powder
5 c. all-purpose flour
1 1/2 t. baking soda

Mix together sugar, shortening and eggs; add sour cream and vanilla. Gradually blend in remaining ingredients; mix well. Cover and refrigerate overnight. Drop by teaspoonfuls onto ungreased baking sheets; flatten slightly with the bottom of a sugar-coated glass. Bake at 350 degrees for 9 to 11 minutes; cool completely on wire racks. Frost. Makes about 4 dozen.

Frosting:
5 T. sugar
2 T. water
3 c. powdered sugar
2/3 c. shortening
1 t. vanilla extract

Add sugar and water to a small saucepan; bring to a boil. Stir and boil until sugar dissolves; remove from heat. Pour into a medium mixing bowl; set aside to cool to lukewarm. Blend in powdered sugar; mix well. Add shortening and vanilla, blending until smooth and creamy.

Patty Vance
Paulding, OH

Handy Candy Temperatures
(Temperatures are Fahrenheit)

230°-233° = thread stage
234°-243° = soft ball stage
244°-249° = firm ball stage
250°-269° = hard ball stage
270°-289° = soft crack stage
290°-310°= hard crack stage

English Toffee

Chocolate Pecan Pie

CHOCOLATE PECAN PIE

A winning combination…ooey, gooey pecan pie and chocolate!

8 sqs. semi-sweet baking
  chocolate, divided
2 T. butter
9-inch pie crust
3 eggs, beaten
$^1/_4$ c. brown sugar, packed
1 c. corn syrup
1 t. vanilla extract
1$^1/_2$ c. pecan halves

Coarsely chop 4 squares of chocolate and set aside. In a small bowl, microwave remaining chocolate and butter together at HIGH for one minute or until chocolate begins to melt. Whisk until chocolate mixture is smooth. Brush bottom of pie crust with a small amount of beaten egg; set aside. Stir sugar, corn syrup, remaining eggs and vanilla into a large bowl; whisk in chocolate mixture. Add nuts and chopped chocolate. Pour into pie crust and bake at 350 degrees for 40 minutes. Cool on wire rack. Serves 8.

Debi DeVore
Dover, OH

WALNUT CRUNCH PUMPKIN PIE

This brings back special memories of evenings spent shelling nuts with my mother. What a good time we would have…the jokes and laughter flew faster than the nutshells!

16-oz. can pumpkin
12-oz. can evaporated milk
2 eggs
$^3/_4$ c. brown sugar, packed
1$^1/_2$ t. cinnamon
$^1/_2$ t. salt
$^1/_2$ t. ground ginger
$^1/_2$ t. nutmeg
9-inch pie crust
Garnish: frozen whipped topping,
  thawed

*S*prinkle snowflake-shaped glitter onto a clear glass plate, then top with another clear glass plate to hold glitter in place…so sweet for serving cookies!

Blend first 8 ingredients in a large bowl with hand mixer at medium speed until well mixed. Place pie plate with crust on oven rack; pour in pumpkin mixture. Bake at 400 degrees for 40 minutes or until a knife inserted one inch from the edge comes out clean. Cool; sprinkle walnut topping evenly over pie. Change oven to broiler setting. Place pie 5 to 7 inches below broiler and broil about 3 minutes or until topping is golden and sugar dissolved. Cool on wire rack; garnish with whipped topping. Makes 10 servings.

Walnut Topping:
1 c. chopped walnuts
$^3/_4$ c. brown sugar, packed
4 T. butter, melted

Mix ingredients well in a small bowl.

Judy Voster
Neenah, WI

Memories of
the Season

years Gone by

What are your favorite recollections of Christmas? Do you remember wearing your grandmother's apron while helping her make holiday treats? Maybe it's the memory of bundling up and piling into the car to see the neighborhood lights? Or do you find yourself recalling that first Christmas away from home, when you discovered that friends could be almost as dear as family? Keep those memories bright and shining with these clever ideas. Your thoughtfulness will be appreciated by all your loved ones for many years to come!

Many years have gone by since these star-shaped decorations twinkled atop a Christmas tree, but they continue to sparkle surrounded by fresh-cut greenery. For a festive display, make your own holiday collectibles part of an evergreen arrangement.

open a box full of *sweet* memories

Start a new holiday tradition that everyone in the family can enjoy. Have each person write down his or her favorite memory of the season, then put their notes in a Christmas Memory Box. As each Yuletide arrives, bring out the box and read the old notes before adding new ones. Instructions to make your memory keeper are on page 446.

Cheery Gift Tag Ornaments are more than just another pretty way to label packages. Make one for each member of your family and they'll have a new ornament for next year's Christmas tree. You'll find the instructions on page 446.

Put a new spin on a ribbon memory board by arranging the ribbons into a snowflake design! What a great way to keep track of holiday party invitations, cards and photos.

"It's Christmas in the mansion,
Yule-log fires and silken frocks;
It's Christmas in the cottage,
Mother's filling little socks;
It's Christmas on the highway,
in the thronging, busy mart.
But the dearest truest Christmas,
is the Christmas in the heart."
— Unknown

Christmas~
tHat magic blanket
that wraps itself
around us....

AUGUSTA RUNDEL

When you look at your life, the greatest happinesses are family happinesses.

~Joyce Brothers

An Accordion-Fold Album holds lots of sweet reminiscences in a small space, making it perfect to tuck into a scrapbook or a large stocking. Turn to page 446 to begin this fun project.

My grandmother has a journal that she has had for as long as I can remember. This journal is brought out every year at Christmas and placed next to her chair in the living room. It contains memories from Christmases in our family for the past 20 years. Each year, we take turns reading through the pages, each of us remembering something different as we look through. After looking the book over, we each try to write a little something about this year's happenings so that we can reflect on them again in the coming years. This year, I get to write about my first baby's first Christmas. And someday I know she will be able to look back and read exactly how I was feeling that day. I think that's pretty special.

— Jennifer Smith
Manchester, CT

More than Santa, your sister knows when you've been BAD and GOOD. —LINDA SUNSHINE

The Best Present

From Santa

EMMA

adorable

puppy love

CHRiSTMAS

Does your family have a favorite dish that is a "must-have" at Christmastime? Frame that famous recipe along with a photo of the much-loved cook who first introduced it to your celebrations. Read all about this delicious idea on page 446.

Sometimes it's the smaller souvenirs that really bring back special memories. Try placing a single ornament, a greeting card or a holiday photograph inside a paperweight.

A small photo in a large frame? Give the photo a clever mat of vintage buttons...lovely!

Candied apples

8 COOKING APPLES (We LiKE ROME APPLES)
1¾ C. SUGAR
¾ C. WATER
9·oz. PKG. SMALL RED CINNAMON CANDIES

Peel, core and cut apples into eighths. In a Dutch oven, combine sugar, water and candies. Stirring constantly, cook over medium heat about 10 minutes or 'til candies dissolve. Add apples and bring to a boil. Cook about 7 minutes until apples are tender. Cool; cover and store in refrigerator. Serve chilled. Makes 6½ cups.

When I decided to use a bare-branched sweet gum tree covered in "snow" instead of a Christmas tree, I tried for weeks to remember how my talented mother, who passed away many years ago, made the snow out of common household ingredients. No one in our family could remember, either! The day before friends were coming to lunch, I sat down, slightly panicked, to eat my breakfast toast. I picked up a cookbook that happened to be on the kitchen table; it was a book I never used and had placed in a stack to donate to a charity. The book fell open to the very page that told how to mix 2 cups Ivory Snow with ½ cup water to make "snow." "Thank you, Mama," I said. "That was close!"

— Wanda Scott Wilson
Hamilton, GA

Every year during the last few days before Christmas, we make a new "Memory List." The list has questions that stay the same, but with four children, our answers differ each year. Some examples of questions are favorite food, favorite song, best friend, teacher, and what do you want to be when you grow up. We also add a new question every year. As we write our new list, we review the old year's answers. We laugh and laugh, and it's a highlight of mine that I wait for each year.

— Tammy Young
St. Peters, MO

NESTLE A BRIGHT GREEN APPLE IN A BOX OR BOWL FULL OF PEPPERMINTS!

12 Tags of Christmas

Celebrate the holidays by making "The 12 Tags of Christmas." The clever designs are simple to craft so children can get in on the fun! Kids will especially enjoy whipping up the oatmeal and glitter Magic Reindeer Mix to give to their classmates. To make these terrific tags, *turn to page 197.*

SleepyTime Tag:
Hang one on the door at naptime.

Dear Santa,
Here's a bit of help in case you get a tear.
From Lori

DogTag:
use dog treats and a collar to wrap up a tag for your best friend!

santa's Best Friend

You'll find dozens of uses for these jolly tags! Label presents, trim the Christmas tree, decorate a scrapbook page, serve up a dinner placecard...there's even a tag with everything Santa needs to mend his red suit.

THE 12 TAGS OF CHRISTMAS

Standard 2³/₈"x4³/₄" shipping tags were used as the base of each of these tags. Follow our easy suggestions and use your imagination and favorite scrapbook embellishments to make each tag.

MERRY

Pair this tag with the "Christmas" tag below for a unique Christmas greeting. The patterns on page 504 make it easy to recreate this tag. Simply zigzag a fabric "M" to cardstock and color the Santa with colored pencils before adhering them to your tag. Stencil stickers and a few metal embellishments complete your creation.

CHRISTMAS

This tag says it all in one word . . . "Christmas." Make a layered cardstock and fabric "C"; then finish spelling the word with newsprint stickers and letter tiles. (The "C" pattern is on page 504.) Attach metal stars and string red thread through the hole in the tag.

(continued on page 446)

Color copy nostalgic Christmas postcards...they make such pretty gift tags and jar labels.

Come Home for Christmas

Home is where
Christmas dreams come
true, so gather your loved ones
near for a wonderful visit among
these fun and festive decorations.
Friends & family will all agree…from
porch to living room and mantel to
tree, your home at holiday-time
is the best place to be!

*Trimming the snowy tree in style
is a merry mixture of handmade ornaments,
purchased snowflakes and large glass
ball ornaments. Instructions for this winter
wonderland begin on page 201.*

Let It Snow!

The weather outside might be frightful, but frosty decorations inside are delightful! These wintry ideas were inspired by a lucky find at the department store…the little snowman atop the mantel on page 199.

To make Decorative Packages (top) for your mantel, embellish a variety of boxes with scrapbook papers and ribbon. Your holiday fireplace isn't complete until you add Fleece & Chenille Stockings (bottom) in wintry blue and white.
See page 447 to make them cozy with chenille, felt and pom-poms.

DECORATIVE PACKAGES

Use spray adhesive in a well-ventilated area.

Trimming and folding the paper at the corners as necessary, use spray adhesive to cover the boxes and lids with kraft or scrapbook paper. For a snowy lid, spray the lid with adhesive and sprinkle it with mica flakes. Allow the adhesive to dry; then shake off the excess flakes. Tape or tie ribbon and trim around the packages.

I like nonsense.
It wakes up the brain cells.

– THEODOR GEISEL "DR. SEUSS"

CHENILLE STEM ORNAMENTS
CANDY CANES

Twist red and white chenille stems together and bend the ends into a candy cane shape. We found red and white chenille stems that were already twisted together and twisted them together for extra-thick candy canes.

SNOWFLAKES

For each snowflake, twist 3 pieces cut from white bumpy chenille stems together at the center; then do the same thing with 3 pieces cut from silver chenille stems. Hot glue the pieces together at the center. Hot glue red beads to the centers of the snowflakes.

CLOWN HAT ORNAMENTS
- tracing paper
- assorted scrapbook papers
- double-sided tape
- craft glue
- $1/16$"w white satin ribbon
- red and white pom-poms
- assorted embellishments (We used tissue paper, pom-pom trims, rickrack, snowflake and circle punches, cardstock and mica flakes.)

1. For each ornament, use the pattern on page 498 and make a cone hat from scrapbook paper.

2. For the hanger, glue the ends of a 9" ribbon length inside the top of the hat. Glue a pom-pom to the top of the hat.

3. Decorate the hat. (We added pleated tissue paper ruffles, trims, rickrack, cardstock circles and mica-flaked snowflake punch-outs.)

It's not what you look at that matters, it's what you see.

— Henry David Thoreau

This frosty friend is so adorable, he'll warm your heart! Turn to page 448 to make your own too-cute Snowman Chairback Cover. For a whimsical way to bring wintertime fun indoors, fill a large bowl with simple-to-form Yarn Snowballs. Add homemade charm to your gifts by turning to page 449 to make a Noel Gift Tag and a Monogram Gift Tag.

YARN SNOWBALLS

For each snowball, apply a spot of glue on a foam ball. Wrap yarn around the ball and tuck and glue the yarn end under. Arrange the snowballs in a large bowl.

SNOWFLAKE TREE SKIRT

- 1¼ yards of 60"w dark teal fleece
- string
- fabric marking pen
- thumbtack
- tracing paper
- light blue and white felt
- fabric glue
- 3½ yards red pom-pom trim

1. For the skirt, cut a 42" fleece square. Follow *Making a Fabric Circle* on page 427 and use a 19½" string measurement for the outer cutting line. Remove the tack and use a 1" string measurement for the inner cutting line.

2. Cut through all fleece layers along the drawn lines. Unfold the skirt and cut an opening from the outer edge to the center opening.

3. Using the pattern on page 503, cut snowflakes from felt and glue them to the tree skirt. (We used a photocopier to enlarge and reduce the pattern for different-sized snowflakes.)

4. Glue the fringe to the wrong side of the skirt along the outer edge.

Share your wish for peace on earth or joy to the world with handmade greeting cards. But why stop there? Stamped Gift Wrap and the Gift Box with Snowflake Embellishment are two fun ways to make your present just as unique as your cards! Instructions for these happy ideas begin on page 449.

CELEBRATE PACKAGE BANNER

Make a package sparkle with a glittery "CELEBRATE" banner. Die-cut white cardstock letters; then, working in a well-ventilated area, spray adhesive on the letters and sprinkle them with glitter. Once the adhesive has dried, shake off the excess glitter and glue the letters along a length of narrow ribbon. Tie the banner around a package for an extra-special gift.

I wish for 5 kittens!

Featuring Santa's red suit, this Ho Ho Ho Card is as jolly as the old elf himself. Send a Wish Card to let someone know that they're never too old to have Christmas wishes. What's a 6-letter word for this Crossword Puzzle Gift Bag? Clever! It's the ideal way to present a gift to your favorite crossword enthusiast. Instructions begin on page 450.

ACROSS

4. a 3 letter word for happiness
5. Christmas bread
6. Saint Nick
7. Hung by the chimney w/ door decoration
8. Custom or ritual
12. __ the red-nosed reindeer
15. holiday beverage
17. 4 letter word for christmas

DOWN

1. Dec.
2. Let __
3. __ joy
4. El __
9. rejoice, party, enjoy, make merry
10. __ upon a star
11. when you __
13. christmas flower
14. famous snowman
16. rhymes with Jolly
18. new born King
20. Kiss under this

Crossword grid answers:
4. JOY
2. PEACE
10. W
13. WISH
12. RUDOLPH
20. MISTLETOE

christmas sweet dreams ...come true.

Naturally Inviting

Transform your entryway into a scene of seasonal delights! Whether you prefer wintry accents or a display of fruit and greenery, one of our four inviting entryways is sure to inspire you to create a welcoming entry full of Yuletide fun! Instructions for this natural setting are on page 451.

Light the way to Christmas cheer with the warm glow of a Candle Centerpiece and snowy Luminaries! With a few simple embellishments, purchased pillows are transformed into Tufted Pillows and a Button Wreath Pillow. The frosty setting provides a welcome spot to reflect on the true reason for the season.

FROSTY

CANDLE CENTERPIECE

Never leave burning candles unattended.

Button-studded pillar candles, frosty greenery and shiny ornaments make up a winter wonderland in this shimmering centerpiece. The tray is a large picture frame backed with a thin piece of wood and dry brushed with thinned white acrylic paint. Insert glittered button picks into aqua candles of different sizes and shapes. Arrange button-studded candles and small votive cups holding red candles on the tray. Fill in around the candles with green, pearl and red ornaments. Tuck frosted greenery picks around the bottom of the centerpiece. Sprinkle mica snow over the tray and your centerpiece is complete!

RAILING SWAG

Use floral wire to join frosted greenery picks to form a swag. Loosely wrap the swag with red beaded garland and aqua ribbon. Insert glittered button picks along the swag; then, add aqua, pearl and red ornaments.

(continued on page 452)

F*or a reminder that Santa's on his way, wire a length of sleigh bells to a fresh greenery wreath…a jolly jingle every time the door opens!*

APPLES & SPICE

REVERSIBLE THROW

Even a beginner can sew this simple reversible throw. You will need a total of 3$\frac{1}{2}$ yards of fleece in various colors. (We used $\frac{7}{8}$ yard each of four colors.) Cut 120 total 6" fleece squares. Using a $\frac{1}{2}$" seam allowance, sew the squares into 10 rows of 12 squares each. Sew the rows together, with seams facing the same side of the throw. Fringe the seams and the outer edges of the throw by clipping every $\frac{1}{4}$".

PATCH PILLOW

To make the matching pillow, you will need $\frac{1}{2}$ yard of fleece in various colors. Cut 18 total 6" fleece squares. Using a $\frac{1}{2}$" seam allowance, sew the squares into 6 rows of 3 squares each. Sew 3 rows together for the pillow front and 3 together for the pillow back. Matching wrong sides, sew the front and back together, leaving one edge open. Insert a 14" square pillow form into the opening and sew it closed. Fringe the edges of the pillow by clipping every $\frac{1}{4}$".

Spiced Apple Cider

3 QTS. APPLE CIDER
12 WHOLE CLOVES
10 WHOLE ALLSPICE
1 T. CANDIED GINGER
10 CINNAMON STICKS
3/4 C. BROWN SUGAR, PACKED

★

COMBINE ALL INGREDIENTS EXCEPT SUGAR AND BOIL. LOWER HEAT, ADD SUGAR AND SIMMER 15 TO 20 MINUTES. STRAIN AND POUR INTO INSULATED CONTAINER TO SERVE STEAMING HOT.

For a fresh approach to an entryway, place trees in tubs on either side of the door and fill in the top of each tub with artificial apples.

TREE CENTERPIECE
- 6" dia. metal bucket
- spray primer
- paintbrushes
- cream and burnt umber acrylic paints
- matte clear acrylic sealer
- kitty litter
- hot glue gun
- boxwood picks
- 17"-tall Christmas tree
- holly picks
- small artificial apples

Allow primer, paint and sealer to dry after each application.

Working in a well-ventilated area, prime the bucket. *Dry brush (page 429)* the bucket with acrylic paints, apply sealer and fill with kitty litter. Hot glue boxwood picks into the tree until it looks full. Add a few holly picks and apples and place the tree in the bucket.

BOXWOOD MONOGRAM
Tired of wreaths that all look the same? This wreath is sure to be the envy of everyone who sees it! Start by using a computer to print a letter and use a photocopier to enlarge it to the desired size. Draw around the letter onto a 2" thick green floral foam sheet and use a serrated knife to cut it out. For stability, wrap the foam with hardware cloth and secure with floral wire. Insert boxwood picks into the foam, covering the sides and front of the letter. Add some holly picks and an artificial apple to one corner. Make a floral wire hanger on the back of the wreath.

SMALL WREATH
Form a wreath with grapevine wire. Hot glue boxwood picks into the wreath. Decorate the wreath with holly picks and an artificial apple.

SNOWBALLS 5¢

WELCOME

TRADITIONAL

Swag with Ornaments

This traditional decorating theme, featuring greenery and red ribbons, is sure to bring out the holiday spirit in everyone! Begin by cutting a length of garland long enough to swag across the doorway and drape down each side. Wire in pieces of holly. Wrap ribbon around the top of the garland and allow the ends to drape down each side. Tie 2 ribbon bows and wire one to each side of the swag. Wire over-sized ornaments to each side and small ornaments to the center.

Door Spray

Continue the traditional decorating theme with a matching door spray. Insert artificial greenery picks into the sides and top of a foam brick. Wire in pieces of holly. Wire a bow to the spray. Wire an over-sized ornament below the bow and small ornaments to the spray.

Snowballs for Sale

Add a touch of whimsy to your doorstep with a tub of snowballs. To make the snowballs, wrap various sizes of foam balls with batting. Add filler, such as crumpled newspapers, to the bottom of a galvanized tub; then, cover with a layer of batting. Arrange the snowballs on top of the batting.

For the sign, cut a piece of foam core. Write "SNOWBALLS 5¢" on the sign using a black permanent marker. Glue a strip of batting across the top of the sign. Wrap a yardstick with red & white striped fabric and glue the sign to one end. Insert the sign into the tub of snowballs.

Working in a well-ventilated area, spray adhesive on the snowballs, sign and batting in the tub and sprinkle with mica flakes. Spray the snowballs and batting with adhesive again to seal the mica flakes to the surfaces.

Doormat

- 18"x30" sisal doormat
- white spray paint
- black permanent marker
- tracing paper
- paintbrush
- red, white and black acrylic paints

Use spray paint in a well-ventilated area. Allow paint to dry after each application.

Coat the mat with white spray paint. Draw a 5"x22" rectangle in the center of the mat with the marker. Using the large diamond pattern on page 506, draw rows of harlequin diamonds across the mat with the marker. Paint alternating diamonds red and the remaining diamonds and rectangle white. Use black paint to spell "WELCOME" in the rectangle. After the paint dries thoroughly, outline everything with the marker.

(continued on page 452)

pray for kindness for all creatures great & small.

He's checking HIS LIST!

*Santa Claus is coming to town,
so you'd better be good for goodness sake!
In his gift sack, he has a Christmas tree that's
trimmed with spirited red & white ornaments.
Cheery knit stockings hang from the banister,
and a handrail garland adds a merry touch.
This whimsical scene is sure to fill
your foyer with Yuletide cheer.*

*Santa is checking his list and getting ready to make the season
bright for all good little boys and girls. The jolly gift-giver and his
basket of presents let visitors know that you believe in holiday
magic. Instructions for these festive ideas begin on page 214.*

NO
PEEKING ALLOWED!
★ NO ★
PACKAGE
SHAKING!
NO
EARLY
UNWRAPPING!
★ NO ★
RIBBON
BREAKING!

BE GOOD FOR GOODNESS SAKE.

SANTA'S BAG

(shown on page 213)
For a clever change from the traditional tree skirt, you can make this bag in the blink of an eye! Match the short ends of a 3⅛-yard piece of 60"-wide red felt. Sew the sides together, leaving the top open and using a ½" seam allowance. Press the ends of a 119" length of 1¼"-wide twill tape ½" to the wrong side and topstitch. For the casing, begin at a side seam and pin the twill tape to the wrong side of the bag, 8" from the top edge. Topstitch the tape to the bag along the long edges. Turn the bag right side out. Open the side seam between the tape ends. Thread a 4½-yard length of ½"-diameter cord through the casing. Knot the cord ends and you're ready to bag that tree!

GOODY BASKET

- rectangular basket (ours measures 12"x18"x9")
- red felt
- 1"-tall white self-adhesive felt letters
- fabric glue
- white eyelash trim

Use a ¼" seam allowance for all sewing unless otherwise indicated.

What fun it will be to fill this basket with goodies! For the liner, measure the inside bottom of the basket and add ½" to each measurement. Cut a felt rectangle the determined size. For each side panel, measure the width of the side and add ½". Measure the height of the side and add 4½" for the flap. Cut a piece of felt the determined size. Sew each side panel to the bottom felt piece and sew the sides together. Turn the top edge ½" to the wrong side

and topstitch. Place the liner in the basket and fold the flap over the rim. Adhere the felt-letter message to the flap. Glue the trim along the inside bottom edge of the flap.

HANDRAIL GARLAND

(shown on page 213)
To spruce up your staircase, weave white eyelash trim and olive green and red ribbons through a greenery garland that you've tied to the handrail. Add frosted holly and greenery picks and you're done!

"Here comes Santa Claus!
Here comes Santa Claus!
Right down Santa Claus Lane!
He's got a bag that is filled with toys
for the boys and girls again."
— Gene Autry and Oakley Haldeman

STRIPED KNIT STOCKING

Refer to Knit, page 424, before beginning the project.

Finished Size: 7 1/2"x31" (19x78.5 cm)

Materials
Bulky Weight
Novelty Eyelash Yarn
  [1 3/4 ounces, 47 yards
  (50 grams, 43 meters)
  per skein]:
  White - 3 skeins
Bulky Weight Brushed Acrylic
Yarn
  [3 1/2 ounces, 142 yards
  (100 grams, 129 meters)
  per skein]:
  White - 1 skein
Bulky Weight Yarn
  [5 ounces, 255 yards
  (140 grams, 232 meters)
  per skein]:
  Red - 1 skein
Straight knitting needles, size 13
  (9 mm) **or** size needed for gauge
Stitch holders - 3
Yarn needle

GAUGE: Holding one strand
of **each** White together, in
Stockinette Stitch, 9 sts
and 13 rows = 4" (10 cm)

CUFF
Holding 2 strands of Red together,
cast on 36 sts.

Work in K1, P1 ribbing for 7" (18
cm).

LEG
Note: Carry unused yarn **loosely**
along edge.

Row 1 (Right side): Holding one
strand of **each** White together,
knit across.

Row 2: Purl across.

Row 3: Knit across.

Row 4: Purl across.

Row 5: Holding 2 strands of
Red together, knit across.

Row 6: Purl across.

Row 7: Holding one strand of **each**
White together, knit across.

Row 8: Purl across.

Row 9: Knit across.

Row 10: Purl across.

Rows 11-64: Repeat Rows 5-10,
9 times.

Cut yarns.

(continued on page 454)

For a fun change, knit these cheery Striped and Dotted stockings and hang them from the staircase instead of the mantel. Instructions for the Dotted Knit Stocking are on page 455.

Wrap bulky weight yarn around foam balls to create Striped and Dotted Ball Ornaments, and remake an old red sweater into Already-Knit Ball Ornaments and Santa's Hat Ornaments. Then wrap up your tree trimming with Package Ornaments.

IT'S HARD TO BE GOOD.

STRIPED AND DOTTED BALL ORNAMENTS

Your kitty may want to join in when you make these fast and fuzzy ornaments! Dab a spot of glue on each foam ball and wrap with white or red bulky weight yarn. Tuck the end and use fabric glue to add yarn stripes or swirled dots. For a hanger, knot a yarn loop around a large-headed pin. Dab glue on the sharp end and insert the pin in the ornament.

SANTA'S HAT ORNAMENTS

For each of these playful ornaments, cut an 8¹/₂"x12" rectangle from a red knit item. Matching the right sides, sew the long edges together. Zigzag around both openings and turn right side out. For the cuff and pom-pom, follow Santa's Hat Tree Topper, using purchased trim or a 4-stitch-wide by 13¹/₂"-long knit band and a 2"-diameter foam ball.

ALREADY-KNIT BALL ORNAMENTS

For each ornament, cut a piece with one finished edge from a red sweater to fit around a foam ball. Wrap the piece around the ball with the finished edge at the bottom, and glue the sides together with fabric glue. Use embroidery floss to sew *Running Stitches* (page 423) around each end. Pull the stitches tight and knot. Glue white eyelash trim around the top of the ornament. For a hanger, knot a yarn loop around a large-headed pin. Dab glue on the sharp end and insert the pin in the ornament.

PACKAGE ORNAMENTS

- 3½"x3½" and 4½"x4½" papier-mâché boxes with lids
- craft glue stick
- white and red wool felt
- green hand-dyed wool
- scallop-edged craft scissors
- craft glue
- 1/16" dia. hole punch
- 1/8"w green variegated ribbon
- red chenille yarn

For each ornament, use a glue stick to adhere the box bottom to the center of a felt piece. Following Fig. 1, cut out the corners and adhere the side flaps to the box sides. Trim any excess felt. Repeat with felt or wool to cover the lid and scallop the edges if desired.

Fig. 1

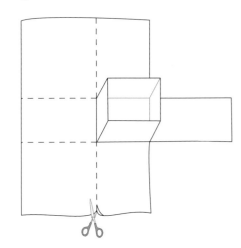

Glue wool or felt circles to the ornament with craft glue, or punch holes in 1/2"-wide scallop-edged felt strips and glue the strips and green ribbon lengths to the sides of the box. Tie chenille yarn around each box.

This oh-so sweet St. Nick (page 453) is sure to bring smiles to every child at heart! Make Santa's list more fun and personal by using names of friends and family members.

SANTA'S HAT TREE TOPPER

(shown on page 213)
- large red sweater
- white bulky weight novelty eyelash yarn
- white bulky weight brushed acrylic yarn
- size 17 (12.75 mm) knitting needles
- white embroidery floss
- 3" dia. foam ball
- fabric glue

Refer to *Knit*, page 424, before beginning the project, or use purchased trim for the cuff.

Cut the sleeve from the sweater at the shoulder. Zigzag around the raw edge. For the hat cuff, holding the 2 yarns together, knit a 7-stitch-wide by 24"-long band. Use white floss to *Whipstitch* (page 423) the cuff to the zigzagged opening.

For the pom-pom, dab glue on the foam ball and wrap it with eyelash yarn. Tuck the end and leave a tail. Use floss to sew *Running Stitches* around the sleeve hem. Pull the stitches tight and knot. Using the tail, tack the pom-pom to the sleeve hem.

MERRY MANTELS

A crackling fire on the hearth draws everyone near at Christmastime. To make your mantel oh-so merry, decorate it with one of these four festive themes. Turn to page 456 to broadcast the glad tidings with this Newsprint Noel Mantelscape.

Complete with a miniature gate bearing a word of good cheer, this Christmas Garden Mantelscape is naturally inviting. The peaceful scene includes tin doves, a pair of obelisks and papier-mâché apples. Instead of stockings, why not hang these embellished envelopes with gift cards tucked inside? The envelopes can also hold Christmas cards received from friends & family. Instructions are on page 457.

let it snow

let it snow let it snow

Does a rustic holiday retreat sound appealing? There's no need to pack your bags…this Lodge-Inspired Mantelscape is just the ticket! The woodsy scene includes miniature trees, candles wrapped with twigs, old-fashioned sock stockings and an easy-to-make log cabin picture. To create your own lodge look, *turn to page 457.*

…And I told Santa you are the bestest dog I know.

What's more cozy than gathering 'round the fireplace for hot cocoa and a chat? Stencil pine trees and stars on a large, galvanized tub. Fill the tub with wood and set by the fire to save trips out into the blustery evening.

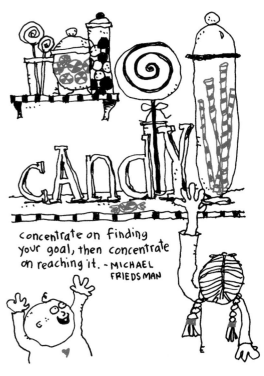

concentrate on finding
your goal, then concentrate
on reaching it. —MICHAEL
FRIEDSMAN

If your holiday mantel arrangement isn't as full-looking as you would like, tie some dinner napkins together, corner to corner, to create a mantel scarf.

May all your Christmas wishes come true! Shimmering stars make a heavenly backdrop for this Dreamy Mantelscape. Turn to page 458 to add sparkle with embellished candles, glittery letters and Tussie-Mussie "stockings."

Friends and Fun Ornament PARTY

What better way to kick off the holiday season than by hosting an ornament party? Invite your pals over for lunch and have each one bring as many handcrafted ornaments as there are guests. After lunch, have an ornament exchange. In this section, you'll find lots of great ideas to help you prepare for your party, including a recipe that's sure to make the day a sweet success…homemade chocolate-covered cherries!

It's an ORNAMENT PARTY!

YOU have been INVITED
to have LUNCH
(and some *chocolate covered cherries*- YUM!!)
with your FRIENDS

Where: LORI'S HOUSE
When: Saturday, December 9, 2006
Time: Noon

We will be swapping *handmade* ornaments.
Everyone needs to bring **6** of her ornament.

It's a place to raise your family
And a place to laugh with friends.
It's a place to put your feet up
And rest at the work day's end.

With space to store your treasures
And space to make your own
It's a place to play,
It's a place to love,
It's the place that you call

Home.

~ Andrea L. Mack ~

ORNAMENT PARTY INVITATIONS

• cream and red cardstock
• stylus
• craft glue
• assorted scrapbook papers
• $1/8$"w red ribbon with white stitching
• decorative-edged craft scissors
• alphabet rub-ons
• metal "O" and "P" charms
• $1/8$" dia. silver brads
• $1/2$"w silver foil tape
• $1/4$" dia. hole punch
• fabric scraps from Hostess Apron (page 224)
• ornament charms
• adhesive foam dots
• $5^{1}/4$"x$7^{1}/4$" cream envelopes

For each card, cut a 5"x12" cream cardstock piece. Use the stylus to score across the card 5" from one short edge; fold along the scored line. Use a computer to print party information on another cream cardstock piece. Trim the cardstock to 5"x7" and, aligning the top edge with the fold, glue it to the inside card back. Glue a $2^{1}/2$"x5" paper piece along the bottom edge of the inside back and glue ribbon along the top edge of the paper. Stack and glue paper and cardstock squares on the card front and embellish with cardstock strips, rub-ons, charms, brads and foil tape. Punch 2 holes, $1/2$" apart, in the center of the paper on the inside card back. Knot a 1"x$6^{1}/2$" fabric strip through the holes and use a brad to attach the ornament charm to the card through the knot. Secure the charm with a foam dot. Using craft scissors on one long edge, cut a 1"w red cardstock strip and glue it along the opening of each envelope.

Razzle, dazzle and recycle...paint burned-out light bulbs with glass paint and add swirls or polka dots with a paint pen. Twist florist's wire around the bases, leaving an end to shape into a loop for hanging.

Gather bowls and clear glass vases to pile full of ball-shaped ornaments for a pretty display.

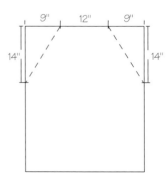

HOSTESS APRON

- 1 yard floral print cotton fabric
- 3 yards of 1¼"w twill tape
- ³/₈ yard coordinating fabric for pocket
- paper-backed fusible web
- green, red and white fabric scraps
- green, red and white thread
- ½" dia. black pom-pom

Yardages are based on fabric with a 40" usable width.

Cut a 30"x36" piece from floral fabric. For the top of the apron, follow Fig. 1 to mark a 12" section at the center of one short edge and mark each long edge 14" from the corner. Draw a line connecting the marks on each corner. Cut along the drawn lines.

Fig. 1

For the hem, press the top edge ³⁄₈", then ¹⁄₂" to the wrong side and topstitch. Repeat to hem the straight side edges and the bottom edge. Press the angled side edges ¹⁄₄", then 1" to the wrong side and topstitch along the pressed edge to make a casing. Press each end of the twill tape ¹⁄₂" to the wrong side. Fold the twill tape in half, matching the long edges, and topstitch the edges together. Starting at the top, thread the twill tape ends through the casings. Cut a 9"x12¹⁄₂" piece from the pocket fabric. Press the short edges and one long edge ¹⁄₂" to the wrong side. For the top of the pocket, press the remaining long edge ³⁄₈", then ¹⁄₂" to the wrong side; topstitch. Trace the patterns on page 501 onto the paper side of the fusible web and cut them out. Fuse the patterns to the wrong side of the appropriate fabric scraps. Remove the paper backing; then arrange and fuse the appliqués on the pocket. Machine satin stitch the appliqués to the pocket. Sew the pom-pom to the flower center. Sew the side and bottom edges of the pocket to the center of the apron front.

End your party on a sweet note with a Christmas classic...chocolate-covered cherries! Send each guest home with a few of the yummy morsels along with a Chocolate-Covered Cherries Recipe Tag. Follow the simple instructions on page 459 to make each tag.

Send your friends home with

CHOCOLATE ★ Covered CHERRIES

16·oz. PKG. POWDERED SUGAR
½ c. BUTTER, SOFTENED
1 T. EVAPORATED MILK
2 t. VANILLA EXTRACT
2 10·oz. JARS MARASCHINO CHERRIES,
        WITH OR WITHOUT STEMS, DRAINED
12 oz. CHOCOLATE-FLAVORED CANDY COATING
6·oz. PKG. SEMI-SWEET CHOCOLATE CHIPS

BLEND TOGETHER SUGAR, BUTTER, EVAPORATED MILK & VANILLA. WRAP EACH CHERRY IN ABOUT 1 TEASPOON SUGAR MIXTURE. ARRANGE ON WAX PAPER IN A BAKING PAN AND CHILL OVERNIGHT. MELT TOGETHER CANDY COATING & CHOCOLATE CHIPS IN A DOUBLE BOILER; STIR UNTIL MELTED AND BLENDED. USE A CANDY DIPPER TO DIP CHERRIES IN CHOCOLATE, TAPPING OFF EXCESS. PLACE ON WAX PAPER TO COOL. MAKES ABOUT 4½ DOZEN.

CHOCOLATE-COVERED CHERRIES

Cover a photo box with cheery fabric; then monogram and embellish the lid to create a Personalized Ornament Box! Turn to page 459 to get started.

FLOCKED ORNAMENT

- ³/₄" dia. foam brush
- red and green glass paints
- glass ball ornament
- black paint pen
- paintbrush
- Soft Flock® adhesive
- red and green
  Soft Flock® fibers
- red cardstock
- black fine-point
  permanent pen
- ¹/₈" dia. hole punch
- 12" length of ¹/₈"w black ribbon
  with white stitching

Allow the paint to dry after each application.

Use the foam brush to paint red dots on the ornament for cherries. Use the paint pen to draw stems. Freehand paint green leaves at the top of the stems. Follow the manufacturer's instructions to flock the cherries and leaves. Cut a 1"x1¹/₂" cardstock tag. Write a message on the tag and punch a hole at the top. Remove the wire hanger and cap from the ornament, thread the tag onto the hanger and replace. Knot the ribbon through the hanger.

SANTA ORNAMENT

- craft glue
- peach felt
- 5" dia. foam ball
- white and red fleece
- hot glue gun
- $^1/_2$" dia. pink shank button
- $^1/_4$" dia. black gemstones
- pink chalk
- white faux fur
- 1" dia. silver jingle bell
- 12$^1/_2$" length of $^1/_4$"w red grosgrain ribbon

Glue a 2$^1/_4$"x4" felt piece to the ball for the face. Cut a 2$^1/_2$"x15" white fleece strip for the long layer of the beard. Make 2"-long clips, $^1/_2$" apart, for fringe. Hot glue the strip around the ball. Fill in at the bottom with shorter, narrower strips, until the beard is full. For the mustache, fold a 4"x5" white fleece strip in half, matching the long edges. Make 1$^1/_4$"-long clips, $^3/_8$" apart, along the long raw edges. Hot glue the strip to the ball, overlapping the face and shaping into a mustache. Hot glue the button and stones to the face for the nose and eyes and add cheeks with chalk. Enlarge the pattern on page 506 to 125%. Using the enlarged pattern, cut a hat from red fleece. Matching the wrong sides, sew the side edges together with a $^1/_2$" seam allowance and turn right side out. Sew a 1$^1/_2$"w fur strip along the bottom edge and the bell to the tip of the hat. Hot glue the hat on Santa's head, covering any exposed edges of the face. Fold the ribbon length in half and glue it to the back of the hat to hang.

The Snowman Tag Ornament and Santa Card Ornament will give your tree whimsical charm. Grab your scrapbooking supplies and turn to pages 459-460 to make the jolly trims.

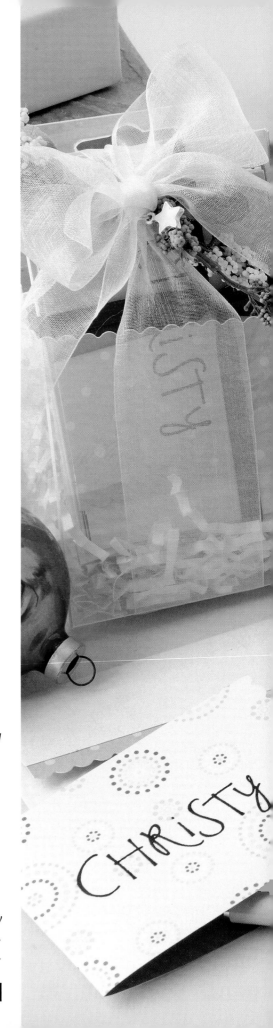

Simple Pleasures to Share

Handmade gifts are
so special...any present that includes
your gift of time and talent is one that's sure
to be cherished. Kate, Holly and Mary Elizabeth
have come up with some great gifts that you'll really
have fun making. A host of accessories will delight the
special women on your list, while a reindeer bath set and
snowman pillow/pajama bag are ideal for little
ones. And what man wouldn't appreciate a special
tray to hold all his valuable pocket items?

Pretty personalized cards and stationery sets will provide faraway
friends and family a means of keeping in touch throughout the year.
Instructions for these noteworthy projects and more begin on page 231.

Favorite Things

Send each of your friends a gift that's twice as nice because you made it with him or her in mind!

A Friendship ATC Gift Card not only shares holiday wishes, but also offers the recipient a collectible Artist Trading Card. To learn more about ATCs, see page 248.

Monograms always lend a personal touch, and these selections are beautiful examples of what you can create for everyone you know. Instructions for the Personalized Tags with Gift Box (above), Boxed Personalized Card Set (opposite, top) and Boxed Green & Brown Stationery Set (opposite, bottom) start on page 460.

FRIENDSHIP ATC GIFT CARD

- 2½"x3½" playing card
- craft glue
- ATC background paper or scrapbook paper
- friendship ephemera
- glue dots
- black fine-point permanent pen
- jewelry tag
- brown thread
- ⅛" dia. silver brads
- alphabet bottle caps and stamps
- square alphabet brads
- deckle-edged craft scissors
- brown and red cardstock
- variegated brown ink pad
- 6⅛" length of ³⁄₁₆"w ribbon
- 4"x5½" cream card with square-flap envelope
- black self-adhesive photo corners

See page 248 for more information about ATCs.

For the ATC, cover the playing card with background paper. Cut out and glue pieces of ephemera to the playing card, using glue dots to elevate areas as desired (we used one behind the girl's head). Write a message on the tag. Run thread through the hole in the tag and knot the ends together. Attach the tag and round brads to the ATC. Add bottle-cap and brad initials.

For the card, use the craft scissors to cut a 3⅝"x5⅛" brown cardstock piece; ink the edges. Wrapping the ends to the back, glue the ribbon along one long edge of the cardstock. Glue the cardstock to the center of the cream card front. Place photo corners over 2 opposite corners of the ATC and attach it to the cardstock ⅜" from the bottom. Stamp a message above the ATC.

Glue a ⅜"w strip of red cardstock, trimmed with the craft scissors, along the bottom edge of the envelope flap.

CARD WITH EARRINGS

- holly and 2½" square border stamps
- green ink pad
- 3½"x4⅞" cream card with square-flap envelope
- craft knife and cutting mat
- colored pencils
- sandpaper
- craft glue
- gold handmade paper
- ⅛" dia. hole punch
- 3½" length of ¼"w cream silk ribbon
- assorted cream beads
- silver beads
- 2½" Bali-style head pins
- crimp beads
- crimp and round-nose pliers
- wire cutters
- 16½" length of ⅛"w green variegated ribbon

Stamp a border in the center of the card front, ⅞" from the top edge. Use the craft knife to cut a 2" square opening in the center of the border. Randomly stamp holly on the outside of the card and color with colored pencils. Lightly sand the outside of the card. Ink the right edge of the card front and the bottom edge of the envelope flap. Glue a 3⅜"x4⅞" handmade paper piece to the inside card back. Punch 2 holes, ½" apart and 1½" from the top edge, in the center of the inside card back. Thread the cream ribbon ends through the holes from front to back. Cross the ends and thread them through the holes again from back to front; trim.

For each earring, thread cream beads and a silver bead onto a head pin as desired. Crimp a crimp bead onto the head pin above the other beads. Use the round-nose pliers to shape the head pin into an earwire. Cut off any excess wire. Attach the earrings through the holes in the inside card back. Wrap the variegated ribbon around the card front at the fold and tie the ends into a bow.

For a timely gift, make this stylish lapel pin that features a watch face.
Turn to page 462 to fashion the Brooch with Gift Box.

WOVEN SCARF

Refer to Crochet on page 426 before beginning the project.

FINISHED SIZE: 4¹/₂"w x 65"l
(11.5 cm x 165 cm)

 EASY

Materials

Bulky Weight Yarn
    [6 ounces, 185 yards (170
    grams, 169 meters) per ball]:
    Variegated - 3 balls

Bulky Weight Novelty Eyelash Yarn
    [1³/₄ ounces, 60 yards (50
    grams, 54 meters) per ball]:
    Blue - 1 ball

Crochet hook, size K (6.5 mm) **or**
    size needed for gauge

Yarn needle

GAUGE SWATCH: 4¹/₂" (11.5 cm)
square
Work same as Body for 5 rows.

Body

With Variegated, ch 13.

Row 1 (Right side): Dc in fourth ch
from hook **(3 skipped chs count as
first dc)**, ★ ch 1, skip next ch, dc in
next 2 chs; repeat from ★ 2 times
more: 8 dc and 3 ch-1 sps.

Note: Loop a short piece of yarn
around any stitch to mark Row 1 as
right side.

Row 2: Ch 3 **(counts as first dc)**,
turn; dc in next dc, (ch 1, dc in next 2
dc) across.

Repeat Row 2 for pattern until
Body measures approximately
65" (165 cm) from beginning ch;
finish off.

Weaving

Thread yarn needle with Blue.

Beginning at Row 1, weave Blue
through ch-1 sps to last row, being
careful not to pull too tightly.

Leaving an 8" (20.5 cm) tail on each
end, cut Blue. Tie tail around ch on
each end. Repeat, weaving 3 **more**
strands through same sps; then,
weave 4 strands of Blue through
remaining ch-1 sps on Body in same
manner.

Fringe

Cut a piece of cardboard 3" (7.5 cm)
wide by 9" (23 mm) long. Wind the
Blue **loosely** and **evenly** lengthwise
around the cardboard until the card
is filled; then cut across one end.
Repeat as needed.

Holding 3 strands of Blue together,
fold in half.

With **wrong** side facing and using a
crochet hook, draw the folded end up
through a stitch, or space and pull
the loose ends through the folded
end; draw the knot up **tightly**. Repeat
spacing evenly across short edges of
Scarf.

Lay flat on a hard surface and trim
the ends.

CD HOLDER

- 8½"x11" sheet of blue cardstock
- snowflake and snowflake border stamps
- white ink pad
- clear embossing powder
- embossing heat tool
- bleach pen
- white thread
- blue embroidery floss
- CD with recipient's favorite songs
- iridescent vellum
- vellum tape
- ¾" dia. blue button
- adhesive foam dots
- ⅛" dia. silver brads
- white handmade paper
- craft glue
- snowflake charms

1. For the holder, tear a 6⅛"x11" piece from cardstock. Stamp a snowflake border along one short edge on one side. While the ink is wet, sprinkle it with embossing powder. Shake off the excess powder. Follow the manufacturer's instructions to heat the powder with the embossing tool.

2. Stamp snowflakes and make dots with the bleach pen on the same side of the holder. Emboss some of the snowflakes if desired.

3. For the pocket, fold the end opposite the snowflake border 3¼" to the wrong side. Sew along the long edges of the holder, securing the pocket. Fold the bordered end 2¾" to the wrong side for the flap. Knotting one end

on the inside, stitch a 6" floss length through the center of the flap, ½" from the end.

4. Print the CD's song titles on vellum, tear it into a 2⅛"x4⅝" piece and tape it to the inside of the flap. Stitch the button with floss and use a foam dot to attach it to the center of the pocket, 1¼" from the top edge. Place the CD in the pocket and wrap the floss around the button to keep the holder closed.

5. Print a label on vellum and tear it into a 1¼"x1¾" piece. Use brads to attach the label to a torn handmade paper piece and glue it to the flap. Use pieces of foam dots to attach charms to the flap.

NECK WARMER

- tracing paper
- $1/2$ yard muslin
- funnel
- 3 lbs. uncooked rice
- white bath towel
- die-cutting tool and alphabet dies
- navy felt and thread
- 7" length of $5/8$"w hook-and-loop fastener
- blue cardstock
- snowman stamp
- white ink pad
- white pencil
- craft glue
- blue printed scrapbook paper
- $1/8$" dia. hole punch
- assorted fibers
- safety pin

Yardage is based on fabric with a 40" usable width.

For the rice bag, use a photocopier to enlarge the pattern on page 498 to 144%. Following *Making Patterns* on page 427 and excluding the tab, use the enlarged pattern and cut 2 bag pieces from muslin.

Matching the wrong sides, using a $1/2$" seam allowance and leaving a 1" opening, zigzag the pieces together. Use the funnel to fill the bag with rice and sew the opening closed. Trim the seam allowance to $1/4$".

For the cover, use the enlarged pattern and cut 2 cover pieces (with tabs) from the towel. For the back, cut away $3/4$" of the top tab edge of one piece. For the front, die-cut the recipient's initials from felt. *Whipstitch* (page 423) the pieces to the cover front as shown.

Matching the right sides, using a $1/4$" seam allowance and leaving the tab edges open, sew the cover pieces together. Turn right side out. Sew one half of the fastener to the outer top tab edge of the cover back and the other half to the inner top tab edge of the cover front. Insert the rice bag in the cover and secure the tabs with the fastener.

Cut a $2^1/8$"x$3^7/8$" cardstock tag. Stamp the snowman on the tag. Use the pencil to add names, snowflakes, the words "Microwave 2 to 4 Minutes" and a message on the tag. Glue the tag to scrapbook paper and cut the paper slightly larger than the tag. Punch a hole in the top of the tag. Knot fibers on the safety pin and use it to attach the tag to the cover.

A good book should leave you... slightly exhausted at the end. You live several lives while reading it. ~WILLIAM STYRON

READER'S SCARF

- 2¼" yards cream fleece
- 1 yard floral fabric

Yardage is based on fabrics with a 40" usable width.

1. For the scarf, cut a 24"x80" piece from fleece; round the corners.

2. For each pocket, cut a 9¾"x10½" fabric piece; round the corners on one end. Clipping the curves, press the bottom and side edges ½" to the wrong side. Press the top edge ½" to the wrong side twice; topstitch. Center and topstitch a pocket 2½" from each scarf end.

3. For the binding, cut a 23" fabric square. Follow *Continuous Bias Binding* on page 428 to cut a 2"x207" continuous bias strip from the fabric square.

4. Press one end and one long edge of the binding ½" to the wrong side. Beginning with the pressed end and matching the long raw edges, place the right side of the binding on the wrong side of the scarf. Using a ¼" seam allowance and overlapping the pressed end with the raw end, sew the unpressed edge of the binding to the wrong side of the scarf.

5. Wrap the pressed binding edge to the front; pin and topstitch.

For a doubly delightful present, tuck a new book inside the Reader's Scarf.

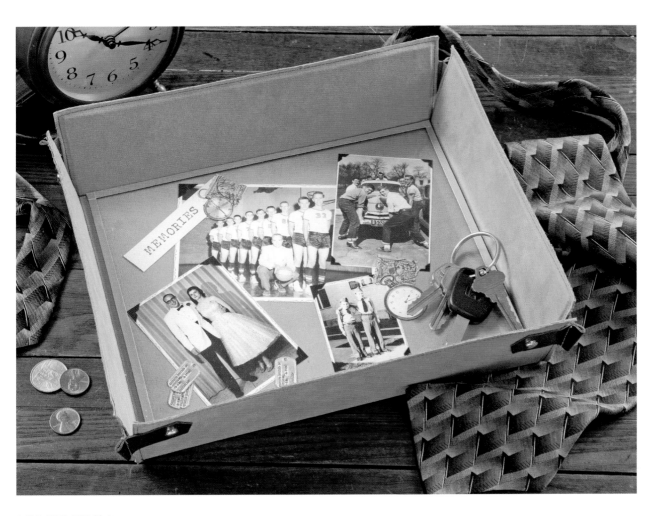

VALET TRAY

- mat board
- fusible stabilizer
- two 15¼"x17¼" pieces of camel faux suede
- spray adhesive
- dark brown faux leather
- ⁵⁄₁₆" dia. silver studs
- craft glue
- clothespins
- 8"x10" piece of glass from a photo frame
- ½"w silver foil tape
- photos and paper memorabilia

Use spray adhesive in a well-ventilated area. Allow adhesive to dry after each application.

1. Cut two 2½"x8", two 2½"x10" and one 8"x10" piece from mat board. Fuse stabilizer to the wrong side of each suede piece. Leaving ⅛" between pieces and securing with spray adhesive, arrange the mat board pieces on the wrong side of one suede piece as shown in Fig. 1.

Fig. 1

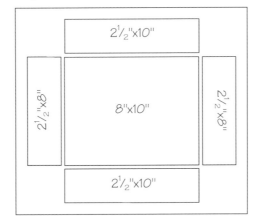

2. Adhere the remaining suede piece to the remaining side of the mat board, tucking the suede between the pieces. Machine sew along the creases between the mat board pieces and around the outer edges close to the mat board. Cut away the excess suede.

3. Cut four 1"x4" leather strips. Trim each end into a point; attach studs at the ends. Fold each strip in half. Starting ⅜" from the fold and working toward the fold, sew a diagonal line across the strip.

4. Fold the tray sides up and glue a strip to each corner as shown. Secure the strips with clothespins until the glue dries.

5. Cover the glass edges with foil tape. Place photos and memorabilia, then the glass in the tray.

"Laughter is the closest distance between two people."

—*Victor Borge*

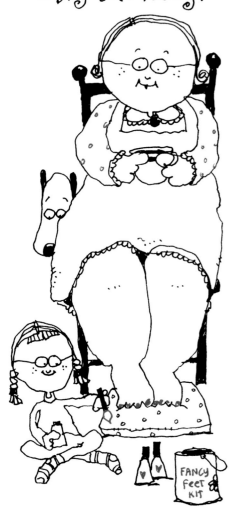

Take a load off,
hoist your feet
for a treat
that can't be beat:

No socks, no shoes
let's paint your
toesies

∽ pinkies green
& big toes rosey!

PEDICURE KIT

- deckle-edged craft scissors
- assorted cardstock and scrapbook papers
- brown alphabet rub-ons
- brown gel pen
- small and large flower punches
- ½" dia. circle punch
- brown ink pad
- double-sided tape
- new pint-size paint can with lid
- mini pedicure set and nail polish
- ⅝ yard of ⅝"w polka-dot grosgrain ribbon
- tracing paper
- ⅛" dia. hole punch
- blue cording

For the label, use the craft scissors to cut a 2¾"x4" piece of cardstock. Use rub-ons to spell "fancy feet kit" on the label. Draw a border on the label ¼" from the edges.

Punch flowers from scrapbook papers and circles from cardstock and scrapbook paper. Ink the edges of the flowers, circles and label. Tape the flowers and circles to the label and the label to the can. Tape a scrapbook paper circle to the lid.

Place the pedicure set and polish in the can. Tie ribbon around the can. Using the pattern on page 498, cut a scrapbook paper tag. Tape the tag to cardstock and cut the cardstock slightly larger than the tag. Punch a hole in the top of the tag and add "pamper!" with rub-ons. Tie the tag onto the ribbon with the cording.

When making Pedicure Kits, remember to make one for yourself. After a long day of shopping, your feet will deserve a little pampering!

GIRL'S FLEECE CAPELET

- 1¼ yards of 60"w pink fleece
- string
- fabric marking pen
- thumbtack
- ½ yard of 60"w dark pink fleece
- pencil with eraser
- tracing paper
- scrap of green fleece
- pink and green embroidery floss
- 4 yards pink and green pom-pom fringe with a ⅝"w flange

Our capelet measures 16¼" from the collar to the bottom edge. You may need to adjust the measurements of your capelet to fit your child. Use a ½" seam allowance for all sewing.

1. Cut a 41" pink fleece square. Follow *Making a Fabric Circle* on page 427 and use a 20" string measurement for the outer cutting line. Remove the tack and use a 2½" string measurement for the inner cutting line.

2. Cut through all layers along the drawn lines. For the front opening, cut through one layer along one folded edge from the outer to the inner edge; unfold. Pin the front opening edges ¾" to the wrong side and topstitch.

3. Enlarge the collar pattern on page 502 to 126%. Following *Making Patterns* on page 427, cut 2 collars from dark pink fleece. Matching the right sides and leaving the neck edge open, sew the collar pieces together. Clip the curves. Turn the collar right side out and topstitch ¼" from the seam.

4. Pin the raw edge of the collar to the wrong side of the capelet. Sew the collar to the capelet; clip the curves. Turn the capelet and collar right side out. Topstitch ¼" from the neck seam.

5. For each tie, cut a 2½"x17" strip from dark pink fleece. Matching the right sides and long edges, sew along the long edges. Trim the seam allowance to ¼". Use the eraser end of the pencil to help turn the tie right side out.

6. For each pom-pom, cut forty ½"x3" strips and one ½"x8" strip from dark pink fleece. Stack the short strips and tightly tie the long strip around the middle. Tack a pom-pom to the end of each tie. Tack the remaining tie ends to the capelet front under the collar.

7. Using the patterns on page 502, cut a dark pink fleece flower and a green fleece center. *Blanket Stitch* (page 422) the center to the flower with 3 strands of pink floss, then the flower to the capelet with 3 strands of green floss.

8. Folding the flange ends ½" to the wrong side and aligning the top of the flange with the bottom raw edge of the capelet, pin the fringe to the right side of the capelet. Zigzag along the bottom edge of the flange. Fold the bottom edge of the capelet ¾" to the wrong side and topstitch.

SNOWMAN PILLOW WITH JAMMIE BAG HAT

- ⁵⁄₈ yard of 60"w white plush fleece
- string
- fabric marking pen
- thumbtack
- orange and black felt scraps
- orange, black and blue embroidery floss
- 1" dia. black flower buttons
- pink chalk or blush and applicator
- polyester fiberfill
- ¹⁄₂ yard of ultra-soft 60"w blue dotted fleece
- ¹⁄₂" dia. white pom-poms
- fabric glue
- 28" length of red jumbo chenille rickrack

Use a ¹⁄₂" seam allowance for all sewing.

Cut two 17" squares from white fleece. Follow *Making a Fabric Circle* on page 427 and use a 7¹⁄₂" string measurement to cut a 15" circle from each square for the pillow front and back.

Cut a nose and mouth from felt. Using 6 strands of floss, sew the buttons to the pillow front for the eyes. *Blanket Stitch* (page 422) the nose and *Whipstitch* the mouth to the pillow front. Blush the cheeks.

Matching the right sides and leaving an opening for turning, sew the pillow front and back together.

Turn the pillow right side out, stuff it and sew the opening closed.

For the hat, cut a 15"x29" blue fleece piece. Matching the right sides, sew the short edges together and turn right side out. Sew a 1" hem along one end for the bottom. Leaving the back open for the jammie bag, tack the bottom edge of the hat to the pillow front only. *Sew Running Stitches* 2" from the top of the hat. Pull the thread tight, wrap it around the gathers 3 times and knot to secure. Make ¹⁄₄"w cuts in the top edge for fringe. Randomly sew pom-poms to the fringe. Glue rickrack along the bottom edge of the hat.

REINDEER TOWEL & BATH MITT

- two 16"x30" tan hand towels and a 30"x56" tan bath towel
- tan, brown, black and white thread
- tracing paper
- brown, black and white felt
- polyester fiberfill
- Sizzix® die-cutting tool and upper-and lowercase "O" dies
- fabric glue
- 1" and ³/₄" dia. red pom-poms

Match the right sides and use a ¹/₂" seam allowance unless otherwise indicated.

TOWEL

1. Using a photocopier, enlarge the hood pattern on page 503 to 150% and cut it out. Fold one hand towel in half, matching the short edges. Aligning the bottom edge of the pattern with the short edges of the towel, use the enlarged pattern to cut 2 hood pieces from the folded towel.

2. Leaving the bottom and front edges open, sew the hood pieces together. Fold the front edge ¹/₂" to the wrong side twice and topstitch. Turn the hood right side out.

3. Using the patterns on page 502, cut 4 ears from the hand towel scraps and 4 antlers (2 in reverse) from brown felt. Leaving the bottom edges open, sew the ears together in pairs; turn right side out. Pinching the bottom of the ears to pleat, *Whipstitch* (page 423) the ears to the hood as shown.

4. Matching the wrong sides and using a ¹/₄" seam allowance, sew the antlers together in pairs; do not turn. Trim the seam allowance to ¹/₈". Stuff the antlers. *Whipstitch* the antlers to the hood behind the ears.

5. For each eye, use the uppercase die to cut an "O" from black and white felt. Using the outlines from the white die-cuts and the centers from the black die-cuts, glue the eyes to the hood as shown. Tack the 1" pom-pom to the hood for the nose.

6. Center and sew the bottom edge of the hood on one long edge of the bath towel.

(continued on page 462)

Several years ago, I was watching my nieces and nephews open many, many gifts. Although elated to see the joy in their faces, it saddened me to think of others not even having one brightly wrapped package. The next year was to be different. Each child received a gift especially for him or her, but instead of gifts on end, there was also a check to be donated to a charity of the child's choice. For example, one nephew loves to eat so he was given gift certificates to some of his favorite food chains…he, in turn, used his other half of the gift to feed a dozen homeless men a turkey dinner at our local shelter. An animal-loving niece received a large stuffed animal because she chose to send her gift to Animal Friends. It has expanded to the adults. Our family gardener was given new gloves and a few tools while crops were planted in Guatemala in her name. It is fun and feels so good (twice!). It is always better to give than to receive.

—Karen Petrie

Love thE animals.

PET ALBUMS

- freezer paper
- wool felt for the background and in colors to match your pet
- coordinating embroidery floss
- pinking shears
- polyester fiberfill
- ⅛" dia. hole punch
- assorted ribbons and trims
- fabric glue
- spiral-bound album
- brads

For the Cat Album:
- jingle bell

For the Dog Album:
- two ⅝" dia. brown buttons
- leather watchband
- cardstock
- alphabet rub-ons
- clear dimensional glaze
- ¹⁄₁₆" dia. hole punch
- jump ring

CAT ALBUM

1. For the appliqués, trace the cat patterns on page 504 onto the dull side of the freezer paper; cut them out. Iron the shiny side of the patterns to the wrong side of the desired wool colors; cut them out. Cut wool "spots" as desired.

2. Leaving a tail, wrap floss around the ball for yarn. Layer the pieces on a pinked felt background cut to fit on the album cover. *Blanket Stitch* (page 422) the pieces in place with 3 strands of floss, lightly stuffing as you sew. Add *Straight Stitch* details as desired.

3. For the collar, punch a ⅛" hole in the background on each side of the cat's neck. Thread the bell onto the center of a 4" ribbon length. Thread the ribbon through the holes and knot at the back.

4. Glue the appliquéd background to the front album cover. Punch ⅛" holes through both layers at the background corners. Attach brads through the holes. Knot ribbon and trim around the binding.

DOG ALBUM

1. Using the dog pattern on page 504, follow Step 1 of the Cat Album.

2. Layer the pieces (except the nose and mouth) on the center of a pinked felt background cut to fit on the album cover. *Blanket Stitch* (page 422) the pieces in place with 3 strands of floss, lightly stuffing as you sew. Add *Straight Stitch* details as desired.

3. Glue the nose and mouth in place. Sew the buttons to the face for the eyes.

4. For the collar, cut the buckled watchband to fit across the dog's neck. Cut a bone from cardstock. Use rub-ons to spell "rruff" on the bone. Apply glaze to the bone and allow to dry. Punch a ¹⁄₁₆" hole in the bone and attach it to the collar with the jump ring. Glue the collar in place.

5. Follow Step 4 of the Cat Album.

SANTA DOORMAT

- red and green felt
- tracing paper
- dark brown wool
- fabric glue
- dark brown embroidery floss
- chenille doormat
- green jumbo rickrack

Use a computer to print "Santa's Been Here." Enlarge the letters to the desired size with a photocopier. Using the enlarged letters as a pattern, cut felt letters. Using the patterns on page 496, cut wool footprints. Glue the letters and use floss to sew the footprints to the mat as shown. Layer and glue rickrack and red felt strips along the short edges of the mat.

Gifts in the Nick of time

Dec. 23

*Christmas is the season
for sharing! As your gift list grows,
it's sometimes difficult to think of things
to give everyone. Rather than making a
different gift for each person, make several of
the same gift. Everyone could use a Christmas
Address Book to make sending cards a snap,
while a manicure set or handmade earrings are
just right for all your friends. So pick a
gift and get started crafting…Christmas
will be here soon!*

*Who wouldn't love a new manicure set for Christmas? Add a playful
touch to a purchased set by painting the pieces with whimsical dots
and stripes. A white candy box tied with polka-dot ribbon makes a
perfect presentation. See page 462 to make this gift in a flash!*

CHRISTMAS ADDRESS BOOK

You'll remember everyone on your Christmas card list with this Christmas Address Book. Glue a scrapbook paper cover to a journal. Apply a large "C" sticker to a wavy-edged green cardstock square; then sew the green square to a torn red cardstock square, leaving long thread ends. Glue the square to the front cover and use rub-ons to finish spelling "Christmas" on the cover. Tack red jute to the end of the page marker and tie jingle bells onto the ends. Use rub-ons to spell "address book" on a ribbon length. Tie the ribbon around the book to keep it closed.

Need a quick but festive way to wrap a two-part gift? See page 463 to make a Penny Sack and matching Gift Box (below).

In the early 1800s, it was a tradition to send holiday letters to friends and relatives who lived far away. But in 1843, an Englishman named Henry Cole was too busy to write his usual letters, so he hired John C. Horsley, an artist, to design an illustrated card. The card featured three panels…the middle was a scene of a celebrating family, while the two side panels represented acts of Christmas charity. Before long, the tradition of sending Christmas cards began!

above the 2" cardstock square. Punch another hole 1" above the first. Attach the rivet through the top hole. For the tag, write a message on a 1/2"x3/4" cardstock piece and sandwich it between the clear adhesive tags. Knot the snowflake ornament and tag onto the center of the brown ribbon. Thread one ribbon end through the bottom hole to the inside front, then through the rivet to the outside front. Tie a bow on the card front.

GIFT CARDS

- craft glue
- green striped and mauve and cream polka-dot scrapbook papers
- cream cardstock
- brown ink pad
- black fine-point permanent pen
- black alphabet rub-ons
- brown and cream thread
- 1/8" and 1/4" dia. hole punches
- double-sided tape
- candy cane
- 5/8 yard of 1/4"w cream silk ribbon
- hot glue gun
- cream buttons
- snap-on scrapbooking rivet
- two 5/8"x1" clear adhesive tags
- 2" snowflake ornament
- 3/8 yard of 1/8"w brown ribbon

CANDY CANE CARD

Glue a 4"x5 5/8" striped paper piece to a 4 1/4"x6" cardstock piece; then, gluing only at the center, glue two 2"x3" pieces of polka-dot paper to the striped paper as shown. Ink the card as desired and use the pen and rub-ons to add a message. Zigzag along all the paper edges with brown thread. Punch two 1/4" diameter holes, 1 1/2" apart, in the center of the card. Tape the candy cane to the card between the holes. Thread silk ribbon through the holes from back to front and knot the ends at the front around the candy cane. Knot a few extra ribbon lengths around the first and hot glue buttons, threaded with cream thread, over the knots.

SNOWFLAKE CARD

Matching the short edges, fold a 5"x10" cardstock piece in half. Gluing only at the centers, adhere a 4 5/8" polka-dot paper square to the center of the card front and a 2" cardstock square near the bottom of the polka-dot square. Ink the card as desired. Zigzag along the edges of the squares on the front with brown thread. Glue a 5" cardstock square to the inside card front. Punch a 1/8" diameter hole in the card front just

Treat your friends to a pair of handmade earrings! Instructions for crafting the earrings and jolly gift tag are on page 463.

card. Use a brad to attach a charm to the snowflake paper and glue the paper to the card front.

For the label, cut a 1³/₄"x2" green cardstock square with craft scissors and glue it to a 2"x2¹/₈" handwriting paper piece. Zigzag along the left edge with brown thread. Add a message on the label. Use a brad to attach a charm to the label and glue it to the card back. Wrap ribbon around the card as shown, knotting and trimming the ends at the front.

Punch 2 green cardstock circles. Attach a circle and charm to the envelope flap with a brad. Close the flap and attach a circle to the envelope, just below the flap, with a brad. Wrap jute around the brads to close the envelope.

CHRISTMAS ATC

Artist Trading Cards, or ATCs, are a popular way to exhibit scrapbooking skills on a smaller scale. The cards are made by decorating 2¹/₂"x3¹/₂" playing cards. You can display your completed cards or trade them with other scrapbook enthusiasts. Check on the Internet or at your local scrapbook store to join in the trading fun. Follow our easy suggestions and use your imagination and favorite scrapbook embellishments to make each card.

- craft glue
- 2¹/₂"x3¹/₂" playing card
- red and green cardstock
- snowman and Christmas greeting ephemera
- deckle-edged craft scissors
- snowflake and handwriting scrapbook papers
- silver brads
- silver snowflake charms
- brown thread
- alphabet and date stamps
- brown ink pad
- black fine-point permanent pen
- 12" length of ¹/₄"w red ribbon
- 3"x4" white vellum envelope
- ³/₄" dia. circle punch
- jute

Cover the card face with red cardstock. Trim the ephemera edges with craft scissors. Mat the snowman ephemera with red cardstock and glue it and the greeting to a snowflake paper piece slightly smaller than the

An original is hard to find but easy to recognize.

– JOHN MASON –

ATC ALBUM WITH CARD

- 22"x28" cream cardstock sheet
- stylus
- clear plastic sheets
- brown thread
- ⅛" dia. eyelets
- eyelet setter
- red and brown cardstock
- assorted hole and shape punches
- craft glue
- alphabet stamps
- brown ink pad
- light blue scrapbook paper
- 21" length of ½"w brown rickrack
- tracing paper
- red embroidery floss
- 2½"x3½" playing card
- Christmas ephemera

1. For the album, cut a 6"x28" cream cardstock piece. Mark seven 4" wide sections on the cardstock. Use the stylus to score the back or front of the album as indicated in Fig. 1. Referring to the photo, accordion-fold the album.

Fig. 1

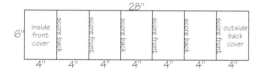

2. For the pockets, cut five 2½"x3" plastic pieces. Center a plastic piece, 1" from the bottom, on each inside album section. Sew the pockets to the album along the side and bottom edges. Attach eyelets at the top corners of each pocket.

3. Cut a 3½"x5¼" red cardstock rectangle. Punch shapes from the rectangle and glue it to the album front. Glue the punched shapes to the album as desired. Stamp "A.T.C." onto a ¾"x2¼" scrapbook paper piece. Trim a punched shape and glue it to the paper. Layer and glue a ⅞"x2½" brown cardstock piece and the scrapbook paper piece on the album front.

Looking for an ideal gift for your scrapbooking friends? Give them ATC Albums so they'll have a clever way to store and display their Artist Trading Cards.

4. Close the album. Center and glue the rickrack across the back cover; tie the ends into a bow at the front. Cut a tag from brown cardstock. Stamp "for you!" on a small scrapbook paper piece and glue it to the tag. Punch a hole in the top of the tag and tie it onto the rickrack with floss.

5. For the card inside the album, cover the playing card with brown cardstock. Layer and glue cream cardstock and red punched cardstock on the brown cardstock. Glue Christmas ephemera to the card.

First ponder, then DARE.
-HELMUTH VON MOLTKE

S'MORE BARS PACKAGE

- 12"x12" sheets of brown and cream cardstock
- brown chalk
- craft glue
- brown thread
- 1 yard of 1½"w green satin ribbon
- ⅜ yard each of 1"w cream and ⅜"w pink satin ribbons
- black alphabet rub-ons
- white vellum
- deckle-edged and scallop-edged craft scissors
- ⅛" square silver brads
- sandpaper
- pink striped and pink floral print scrapbook paper
- ⅜" dia. grommet and grommet kit
- 6¼" length of ¼"w brown velvet ribbon
- Kelly's S'more Bars
- cellophane bag
- twist tie
- ⅝ yard each of ¼"w green, pink and cream silk ribbons
- tracing paper
- alphabet stamps
- brown ink pad
- ⅛" dia. hole punch
- adhesive foam dot

1. Tear away ½" of each long edge of a 7"x12" brown cardstock piece. With the short edges at the top, fold the cardstock into three 4" sections for the package.

2. Chalk the edges of a 3¾"x5½" cream cardstock piece. Gluing at the center only, attach the cardstock to the package front and sew along the edges in a random pattern.

3. Machine sew decorative stitches along one long edge of a 13" green satin ribbon length. Layer and glue the green ribbon and a 13" length each of cream and pink satin ribbon down the front of the package, wrapping the ends to the wrong side. Use rub-ons to spell "s'more bars" on vellum; trim to 1¼"x2" with deckle-edged scissors. Use brads to attach the vellum to the package front.

4. For the top flap, sand a 5"x6¼" striped paper piece and fold it in half, matching the long edges. Cut a 1"x6¼" floral print paper strip and trim away ¼" of one long edge with scallop-edged scissors. Glue the strip to the back of the flap along one long edge for the front. Attach the grommet to the center front of the flap, 1" from the fold. Glue the velvet ribbon along the front edge of the flap. Overlapping ⅝" of the top back edge of the package, zigzag the back edge of the flap to the package.

5. Place S'more Bars in the bag and close with the twist tie. Tie a 22" green satin ribbon length into a bow around the top of the bag. Place the bag in the package. Loop a 22" length of each silk ribbon around the bow, thread the ends through the grommet and tie into a bow at the front to close the package.

6. Using the pattern on page 505, cut a floral print paper tag and stamp it with a message. Chalk the edges and punch a hole in the top. Tie one silk ribbon end to the tag and secure it on the package with the foam dot.

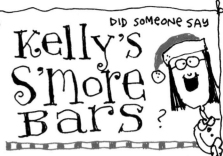

DID SOMEONE SAY

Kelly's S'more Bars?

6 graham crackers (2½"x5"), finely crushed
4 T. butter, melted
1⅓ c. semi-sweet chocolate chips
3/4 c. sweetened condensed milk
1 t. vanilla extract
2½ c. mini marshmallows
2 graham crackers (2½"x5"), coarsely crushed

★

Line an 8"x8" pan with foil; spray bottom with cooking spray. Mix finely crushed crackers with butter; press into bottom of pan. Melt chocolate chips and milk over low heat. Remove from heat and stir in vanilla; pour over crust. Press marshmallows into warm chocolate and sprinkle coarsely crushed crackers on top. Chill for 3 hours, remove foil and cut into bars.
—Makes 32 bars.

Glue a stamped round cardstock label to the tag. Punch a hole through the tag and tie it to the bag with jute. Fill the pot with excelsior and place the bag inside. Place the pot in the box and fill in with ornaments and berries. Wrap ribbons around the box and tie into a bow at the front.

Offering the promise of spring in the middle of winter, the paperwhite narcissus is one of the easiest bulbs to force into bloom in your home. Paperwhite Kits are an ideal gift for co-workers, your garden club, or your book club. Other bulbs that will work are amaryllis and hyacinth. What a nice way for anyone to add color or fragrance to their days!

PAPERWHITE KIT

- 4³⁄₄"x4³⁄₄"x6" papier-mâché box
- ceiling tin paintable wallpaper
- greenery
- scallop-edged craft scissors
- small brown paper bag
- paperwhite bulbs
- ¹⁄₃ yard each of ¹⁄₄"w green-checked and ¹⁄₈"w blue-green ribbons
- red jute
- craft glue
- alphabet and leaf stamps
- brown ink pad
- 1³⁄₄" dia. circle punch
- green cardstock

- 2" dia. metal-rimmed tag
- ¹⁄₈" dia. hole punch
- 4³⁄₈" dia.x3¹⁄₈" tall clay pot
- wood excelsior
- vintage ornaments
- tallow berries
- 1 yard each of ⁷⁄₈"w red and ³⁄₈"w blue-green ribbons

Cover the box with wallpaper and fill with greenery. Trim the top of the bag with craft scissors. Place the bulbs in the bag and tie ribbon and jute into a bow around the top.

Seasoned greetings

Christmas is a time of celebrating…and cooking! When loved ones gather for the holidays, the merriment usually takes place around the dinner table. Kate, Holly & Mary Elizabeth know that a good meal stimulates good conversation, so they've served up an array of flavorful fare that's sure to get the party started! Their recipes will help you create festive feasts…from breakfast to dinner…not to mention all the delightful desserts and savory snacks in between!

Featuring Fruited Pork Loin, Dressed-Up Holiday Stuffing and Parsley Biscuits, this mouthwatering meal is sure to satisfy! Each dish is a treat for the eyes as well as the taste buds.

A Special Invitation Dinner

Host a holiday gathering the fun & easy way! For a Special Invitation Dinner, you prepare the main dish while giving each guest a different menu item to cook. Put a recipe in each invitation, and include a note that a similar dish may be substituted.

"Must-Have-Recipe" Salad

"MUST-HAVE-RECIPE" SALAD

A light, fruity salad that looks so pretty on a festive plate.

2 5-oz. pkgs. romaine lettuce
1 c. shredded Swiss cheese
1 c. cashews
1 apple, coarsely chopped
1 pear, coarsely chopped
¼ c. sweetened, dried cranberries

Combine all ingredients in a large serving bowl; toss to mix. Pour salad dressing over salad and toss. Serves 8 to 10.

Salad Dressing:
½ c. sugar
⅓ c. lemon juice
2 t. red onion, finely chopped
1 t. salt
⅔ c. oil
1 T. poppy seed

Combine sugar, lemon juice, onion and salt in blender container; cover and blend well. While blender is running, add oil in a slow, steady stream; blend until thick and smooth. Add poppy seed and blend an additional 10 seconds to mix.

Holly Peters
Lino Lakes, MN

FRUITED PORK LOIN

Slices of this pork loin make a beautiful holiday presentation.

½ c. dried dates, coarsely chopped
¼ c. dried apricots, coarsely
    chopped
¼ c. pecans, finely chopped
1 clove garlic, minced
1½ t. dried thyme, crushed
2 T. molasses, divided
½ t. salt, divided
¼ t. pepper
2-lb. boneless pork loin roast
⅔ c. bourbon or chicken broth
⅔ c. chicken broth
¼ c. whipping cream

Blend together dates, apricots, pecans, garlic, thyme, one tablespoon molasses, ¼ teaspoon salt and pepper; set aside. Butterfly pork loin roast by making a lengthwise cut down center of one side, cutting within ½ inch of the bottom. (Do not cut through roast.) Open roast, forming a rectangle. Starting at the center of the open loin, make another lengthwise cut on the left portion, cutting to within ½ inch of the edge. Repeat with right portion of the open loin. Spread date mixture evenly over open roast and starting with the short end, roll up stuffed roast jelly-roll style. Tie roast securely every 2 to 3 inches with kitchen string and place roast, seam side down, in a shallow roasting pan; set aside. Blend together bourbon or chicken broth, ⅔ cup chicken broth and remaining one tablespoon molasses in a small saucepan. Bring mixture to a boil and pour over roast. Roast pork at 350 degrees for one hour or until meat thermometer inserted into thickest portion registers 150 degrees, basting occasionally. Remove roast from roasting pan; reserve drippings. Cover roast with foil and let stand 10 minutes or until thermometer registers 160 degrees before slicing. Stir together cream and remaining ¼ teaspoon salt in a small saucepan; blend in reserved drippings. Cook over medium heat, stirring constantly, until mixture slightly thickens. Serve sauce with roast. Serves 6.

Tina Wright
Atlanta, GA

DRESSED-UP HOLIDAY STUFFING

My mother gave me this basic recipe 25 years ago and, over the years, I've added my own touches...either way, it's simply delicious!

2 24-oz. loaves white bread
2 6.2-oz. pkgs. long-grain and
    wild rice, prepared
20 to 25 green onions, chopped
3 to 4 c. celery, chopped
2 c. slivered almonds
3 eggs, beaten
salt and pepper to taste
1 t. garlic, minced
dill weed to taste
1 1/2 c. butter, melted

Tear bread into bite-size pieces; place in a very large bowl. Add rice, green onions, celery, almonds and eggs; mix well. Stir in salt, pepper, garlic and dill weed. Pour butter over stuffing; mix well. Place in 2 lightly greased 13"x9" glass baking dishes; bake, uncovered, at 350 degrees for one hour. Serves 16 to 20.

John Boyd Brandon
Jemez Springs, NM

PARSLEY BISCUITS

Enjoy these warm from the oven.

2 c. all-purpose flour
1 T. baking powder
1/2 t. salt
3 T. fresh parsley, chopped
zest of one lemon
1/2 c. vegetable shortening
1/2 c. milk
1/4 c. whipping cream

In a large mixing bowl, combine flour, baking powder and salt; add parsley and lemon zest. Using a pastry cutter or 2 knives, cut in shortening until mixture resembles oatmeal. Add milk and cream; blend until mixture forms a ball. Place dough on a lightly floured surface and knead 5 times. Roll out dough to 1/2-inch thickness and cut out biscuits. Place on lightly greased baking sheets and bake at 425 degrees for 15 minutes or until golden. Makes eight 2 1/2-inch biscuits.

Jo Ann

Cream of Pumpkin Soup

Make your own crusty loaf o' bread and serve a big Caesar salad with this soup...tasty!

*

2 T. butter
1 onion, diced
3 14-oz. cans chicken broth
29-oz. can pumpkin
2 carrots, chopped
1 T. brown sugar, packed
1 bay leaf
1 c. whipping cream
1/2 t. nutmeg
Garnish: fried ham cubes,
    optional

*

In a large saucepan, melt butter and sauté onion. Add broth, pumpkin, carrots, brown sugar & bay leaf. Bring to a boil, reduce heat and simmer for 15 minutes. Remove bay leaf. Purée mixture in blender and return to pan; stir in cream & nutmeg. Garnish with ham, if desired. Makes 8 servings.

~Janice Gilmer ∗ Merrimack, NH~

Cream of Pumpkin Soup

SNOWFLAKE BREAD

Golden honey-glazed loaves with a snowflake design...so pretty for Christmas dinner.

1 pkg. active dry yeast
1/4 c. warm water
3/4 c. milk
1/2 c. butter, melted
1/4 c. honey
4 3/4 c. all-purpose flour, divided
2 eggs
2 t. vanilla extract
1 1/2 t. anise seed, crushed
1/2 t. salt

Combine yeast and warm water in a measuring cup; let stand 5 minutes. Combine milk, butter and honey in a large bowl. Stir in yeast mixture, 2 cups flour, eggs, vanilla, anise seed and salt. Beat with an electric mixer until smooth. Stir in another 2 cups flour until a soft dough forms. Turn dough onto a lightly floured surface; knead until smooth, gradually adding remaining 3/4 cup flour. Place in a greased bowl, turning dough to coat; cover and let rise 45 minutes or until doubled in bulk. Punch dough down and divide in half. Form each half into a 7 1/2-inch round loaf; place on greased baking sheets. Cover dough and let rise 15 minutes or until almost doubled in bulk. Use a knife to make a snowflake design in each loaf. Bake loaves at 350 degrees for 20 minutes. Brush glaze over loaves; return to oven for 5 to 10 minutes or until tops are golden. Serves 10 to 12.

Glaze:
1 egg, beaten
1 T. honey
1 T. water

Stir together all ingredients.

Vickie

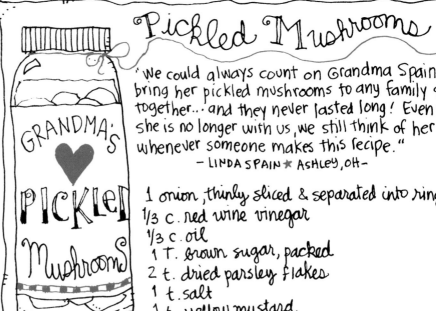

Pickled Mushrooms

"We could always count on Grandma Spain to bring her pickled mushrooms to any family get-together...and they never lasted long! Even though she is no longer with us, we still think of her whenever someone makes this recipe."
— LINDA SPAIN ★ ASHLEY, OH —

1 onion, thinly sliced & separated into rings
1/3 c. red wine vinegar
1/3 c. oil
1 T. brown sugar, packed
2 t. dried parsley flakes
1 t. salt
1 t. yellow mustard
3 7-oz. jars button mushrooms, drained

In a small saucepan, combine all ingredients except mushrooms. When mixture comes to a boil, add mushrooms and simmer for 5 minutes. Pour into a bowl, cover & chill for several hours or overnight, stirring occasionally. Drain before serving. Makes 3 cups.

Snowflake Bread

HOT PECAN DIP

Very simple, yet elegant appetizer when served with baguette slices.

8-oz. pkg. cream cheese, softened
1 onion, grated
3-oz. pkg. dried beef, chopped
½ c. sour cream
¼ c. green pepper, chopped
2 t. milk
¼ t. pepper

Combine all ingredients; mix well. Spread in a buttered 9" pie pan; sprinkle with toasted pecans. Bake at 350 degrees for 20 minutes. Serves 12.

Toasted Pecans:
½ c. chopped pecans
2 t. butter, melted
¼ t. salt

Toss all ingredients together; spread on an ungreased baking sheet. Broil until golden; stir often.

Jana Warnell
Kalispell, MT

CINNAMON & GINGER TREATS

You won't be able to stop nibbling on these.

3 c. assorted nuts
1 egg white
1 T. orange juice
⅔ c. sugar
1 t. cinnamon
½ t. ground ginger
½ t. allspice
¼ t. salt

Place nuts in a large mixing bowl; set aside. Blend egg white and orange juice together until frothy; mix in remaining ingredients. Pour over nuts; mix thoroughly. Spread coated nuts onto an aluminum foil-lined baking sheet; bake at 275 degrees for 45 minutes, stirring every 15 minutes. Cool; store in an airtight container. Makes 3 cups.

Debbie Isaacson
Irvine, CA

Yam Risotto

YAM RISOTTO

Not your ordinary side dish.

2 T. butter
1 shallot, minced
1 clove garlic, minced
¾ c. Arborio rice, uncooked
15.5-oz. can yams, mashed
3 c. chicken broth, divided
¼ t. cinnamon
¼ t. salt
⅛ t. pepper
3 T. pumpkin seeds, toasted
Garnish: toasted pumpkin seeds (optional)

Melt butter in a saucepan; add shallot and garlic. Sauté for one minute or until soft; stir in rice. Heat for one minute; mix in yams and ½ cup chicken broth. Heat until liquid is absorbed; stir in an additional ½ cup broth. Continue heating for 15 minutes, stirring constantly; add broth, ½ cup at a time, as previous additions have been absorbed. Remove from heat; stir in cinnamon, salt, pepper and 3 tablespoons pumpkin seeds. Sprinkle with additional pumpkin seeds, if desired. Serve warm. Serves 4.

Stephanie Moon
Nampa, ID

VEGETABLE BAKE

My Italian son-in-law first made this dish for our family on Thanksgiving...we love it!

13¼-oz. can mushroom pieces, drained
1 onion, diced
¼ c. butter
10¾-oz. can cream of mushroom soup
10¾-oz. can cream of chicken soup
11-oz. can cut green beans, drained
11-oz. can yellow wax beans, drained
11-oz. can sliced carrots, drained
8-oz. pkg. shredded Cheddar cheese
8-oz. pkg. shredded mozzarella cheese

Sauté mushrooms and onion in butter until tender; add soups, beans and carrots. Remove from heat; spread into a 13"x9" baking pan. Combine cheeses; sprinkle on top. Bake at 350 degrees about 30 minutes or until bubbly. Makes 12 to 15 servings.

Glory Bock
Lee's Summit, MO

Christmas Champagne Punch

SUGAR COOKIES

2 18-oz. pkgs. refrigerated sugar
    cookie dough
assorted cookie cutters
drinking straw (optional)
assorted candies and sprinkles

Roll out the dough to ¼-inch thickness. Cut out with cookie cutters (for cookie ornaments, before baking, use the straw to make a hole in each cookie for hanging). Place on ungreased baking sheets and bake at 350 degrees for 5 to 7 minutes or until golden. Decorate with frosting, candies and sprinkles, if desired. Makes 36 to 40.

Sugar Cookie Frosting:
5 c. powdered sugar
5½ to 6½ T. water
1½ t. almond extract
paste food coloring

Combine powdered sugar, water and almond extract in a medium bowl; beat until smooth. Transfer frosting into small bowls and tint with food coloring. Spread onto cooled cookies.

CHRISTMAS CHAMPAGNE PUNCH

A good punch to start any occasion!

1 qt. frozen, unsweetened
    strawberries, thawed
½ to 1 c. sugar, to taste
2 bottles white Rhine or Moselle
    wine, chilled
1 bottle dry champagne, chilled
Garnish: fresh strawberries on
    wooden skewers (optional)

Crush fruit in a large bowl and stir in sugar; allow sugar to dissolve. Add wine and chill for 4 hours. Just before serving, pour mixture into a punch bowl and add champagne. Garnish with fresh strawberries, if desired. Makes 24 punch cups.

May our house always be too small to hold all of our friends.
    —Traditional Holiday Toast

NEW ENGLAND PUMPKIN PIE

Make this special pie for your gathering.

6 T. brown sugar, packed
2 T. sugar
2 t. cinnamon
½ t. nutmeg
½ t. salt
¼ t. ground cloves
½ c. molasses
3 eggs, separated
15-oz. can pumpkin
1½ c. half-and-half
2 T. rum
2 9-inch pie crusts

Combine first 6 ingredients. Add molasses and egg yolks; mix well. Stir in pumpkin, half-and-half and rum. Beat egg whites until stiff; fold into pumpkin mixture. Pour into unbaked pie crusts. Bake at 425 degrees for 30 minutes or until knife inserted in center comes out clean. Serves 16.

Joan Merling
Bethel, CT

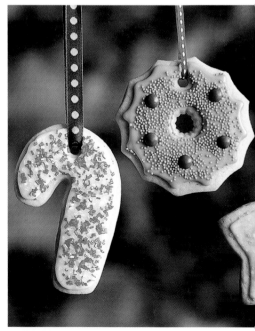

Sugar Cookies

SWEET ALMOND COFFEE

Enjoy this sweet cocoa-almond blend on a frosty night.

1/2 c. sugar
1/4 c. baking cocoa
1/4 c. instant coffee granules
1/4 c. finely ground almonds
2 t. powdered non-dairy creamer
1/4 t. salt
4 1/2 c. milk

In an electric blender, combine sugar, cocoa, instant coffee, almonds, creamer and salt. Cover and blend on high speed for 10 seconds. Heat milk in a 2-quart saucepan. Do not boil. Add cocoa mixture to hot milk; stir to combine. Pour into mugs. Makes 5 cups.

Vickie

Sweet Almond Coffee &
Luscious Layered Brownies

Luscious Layered Brownies

No need to frost 'em...
these are good just the way they are!

3/4 c. all-purpose flour
3/4 c. baking cocoa
1/4 t. salt
1/2 c. butter, sliced
1/2 c. sugar
1/2 c. brown sugar, packed
3 eggs, divided
2 t. vanilla extract
1 c. chopped pecans
3/4 c. white chocolate chips
1/2 c. caramel ice cream topping
3/4 c. semi-sweet chocolate chips

Mix together flour, cocoa & salt in a bowl; set aside. In another bowl, blend together butter & sugars until creamy. Add 2 eggs, one at a time, beating well after each addition. Mix in vanilla. Gradually beat in flour mixture. Reserve 3/4 cup batter; spread remaining batter into a greased 8"x8" baking pan. Sprinkle pecans & white chocolate chips over batter. Drizzle caramel topping over top. Beat remaining egg into reserved batter until light in color; stir in chocolate chips. Spread evenly over caramel topping. Bake at 350 degrees for 30 to 35 minutes. Cool & cut into squares. Makes 12 to 16.

All these recipes are so delicious, there may not be any food left over...but if there is, use take-out containers to send everyone home with a goodie box. You can also make a full set of recipe cards for each guest, so they can re-create the meal for themselves at a later time.

Sugar Cookies

Stack·It·Up Breakfast

Flapjacks, griddlecakes, hotcakes…no matter what name you prefer for the traditional breakfast skillet bread, you're sure to call these new variations "scrumptious!" Be sure to try each one of these pancake and topping recipes. We think you'll find several new ways to start your holiday morning.

HAM & APPLE FILLED PUFFED PANCAKE

A hearty way to start your day!

3 T. butter, divided
¾ c. milk
⅔ c. all-purpose flour
2 eggs
½ t. salt
1 c. cooked ham, cubed
21-oz. can apple pie filling
1 c. shredded Cheddar cheese

In a 9" glass pie plate, melt 2 tablespoons butter in oven. In a large bowl, combine milk, flour, eggs and salt. Using a wire whisk, beat until smooth; pour batter into pie plate. Bake, uncovered, at 400 degrees for 20 to 25 minutes or until golden brown. Meanwhile, in a 10" skillet, melt remaining one tablespoon butter until sizzling; add ham and apple pie filling. Cook over medium heat, stirring occasionally, until heated through. Spoon filling into center of hot pancake; sprinkle with cheese. Cut into wedges. Makes 4 servings.

Gail Prather
Bethel, MN

Ham & Apple Filled Puffed Pancake

COUNTRY CRUNCH PANCAKES

A favorite recipe that was shared with me by an Amish friend in our community. The crunchy topping makes these terrific!

2 c. all-purpose flour
1/3 c. whole-wheat flour
1/2 c. plus 1/3 c. quick-cooking oats, divided
2 T. sugar
2 t. baking powder
1 t. baking soda
1 t. salt
2 t. cinnamon, divided
2 1/4 c. buttermilk
2 eggs, beaten
2 T. oil
1 c. blueberries
1/4 c. chopped almonds
1/4 c. brown sugar, packed

For batter, combine flours, 1/3 cup oats, sugar, baking powder, baking soda, salt and one teaspoon cinnamon in a mixing bowl. In a separate bowl, combine buttermilk, eggs and oil. Stir into dry ingredients until blended. Fold in blueberries. For topping, mix together remaining 1/2 cup oats and one teaspoon cinnamon. Blend in almonds and brown sugar. Sprinkle about one teaspoon topping for each pancake onto a hot, lightly greased griddle. Pour 1/4 cup batter over topping. Immediately sprinkle with another teaspoonful of topping. Turn when bubbles form on top of pancakes. Cook until second side is golden brown. Makes 19.

Kathy Grashoff
Fort Wayne, IN

Country Crunch Pancakes with Cinnamon, Pecan & Honey Syrup

CINNAMON, PECAN & HONEY SYRUP

In our family, my husband always makes the pancakes and waffles!

2 c. maple syrup
3/4 c. chopped pecans
1/2 c. honey
1/2 t. cinnamon

Combine all ingredients; stir well. Pour mixture into an airtight container. Store at room temperature. Serve over waffles or pancakes. Makes 3 cups.

Flo Burtnett
Gage, OK

Lay pancakes on a baking sheet and place in oven at a low temperature to keep warm until all the batter is used.

BUTTERY MAPLE SYRUP

Leave out the butter for a more traditional maple syrup.

2 c. water
2 c. corn syrup
1 c. sugar
3 T. butter
1/2 t. salt
1 1/2 t. maple flavoring

Combine water, corn syrup, sugar, butter and salt in a heavy saucepan. Cook over medium heat until mixture reaches a full boil, stirring occasionally. Continue to boil syrup for 7 minutes; remove from heat and allow to cool for 15 minutes. Stir in maple flavoring; allow to cool to warm before serving. Makes one quart.

Regina Vining
Warwick, RI

Santa's favorite!

Jelly ♥ roll Pancakes

1 c. ALL-PURPOSE FLOUR
1½ t. BAKING POWDER
½ t. SALT
1 c. MILK
2 EGGS
3 T. OIL
⅓ c. JAM OR JELLY
Garnish: Powdered Sugar

♥

STIR TOGETHER FLOUR, BAKING POWDER & SALT IN MEDIUM BOWL; SET ASIDE. BLEND TOGETHER MILK, EGGS & OIL IN SMALL BOWL; STIR INTO FLOUR MIXTURE 'TIL JUST BLENDED. DROP BY ½ CUPFULS ONTO A HOT, GREASED GRIDDLE. COOK PANCAKES ON EACH SIDE 'TIL LIGHTLY GOLDEN. SPREAD ABOUT 2 TEASPOONS JAM OR JELLY ON ONE SIDE OF EACH PANCAKE; ROLL UP, PLACE SEAM-SIDE DOWN ON SERVING PLATE AND SPRINKLE WITH POWDERED SUGAR. MAKES ABOUT EIGHT 6-INCH PANCAKES.

♥ A RECIPE FROM RENAE SCHEIDERER
BEALLSVILLE, OH

♥ Idea!
TRY PUMPKIN BUTTER OR APPLE BUTTER INSTEAD OF JELLY! YUM!

Buttermilk Pancakes with Orange Butter

ORANGE BUTTER

Spread on bagels, toast, muffins or pancakes…yummy!

1 c. butter, softened
2 t. orange zest
⅛ t. mace or nutmeg

Blend ingredients together until creamy; pack in a crock. Chill until ready to serve. Makes one cup.

Liz Plotnick-Snay
Gooseberry Patch

A *glassful of fresh-squeezed orange juice is always a treat at breakfast. Set out a juicer along with a bowl of oranges cut in half so everyone can take a turn at squeezing their own!*

BUTTERMILK PANCAKES

These pancakes are good and so easy to make…have the kids help!

1 c. all-purpose flour
3 T. sugar
1 t. baking powder
½ t. baking soda
½ t. salt
1 c. buttermilk
1 egg
2 T. butter, melted

In a large mixing bowl, combine flour, sugar, baking powder, baking soda and salt. Stir in remaining ingredients. Drop by ¼ cupfuls onto a hot, lightly greased griddle. Cook until bubbling; flip and cook other side. Use your favorite cookie cutter to cut out pancakes. Makes 4.

Jackie Crough
Salina, KS

Santa Face Pancakes

In the late 1940s, my father made these for breakfast on Christmas morn'. Served with whipped cream, we always had great fun making Santa's beard!

a recipe from Susan Young ♥ Madison, AL

1¼ c. all-purpose flour
2 T. sugar
3 t. baking powder
½ t. salt
1 egg

2 T. oil
¾ to 1 c. milk
6 bacon slices, cut into fourths & cooked
Garnish: strawberry preserves & whipped cream

Sift dry ingredients into a large bowl. Make a well in the center and add egg, oil and ¾ cup milk. Quickly stir until just blended; batter should not be thin. Add more milk if needed. When griddle is hot, pour ¼ cup batter per pancake onto griddle. When edges bubble, turn pancake over. Continue cooking until golden brown. Place pieces of bacon to resemble eyes, nose and mouth. Serve with preserves for Santa's hat and whipped cream for his beard and pom-pom. Makes 6 to 9 pancakes.

That is the BEST ~ to laugh with someone because you both think the same things are funny. — GLORIA VANDERBILT

CHOCOLATE CHIP PANCAKES

These ooey-gooey pancakes don't need syrup, but you'll want to make sure there are plenty of napkins on hand!

1 c. milk
2 eggs, beaten
2 c. buttermilk biscuit baking mix
¼ t. cinnamon
½ c. mini semi-sweet chocolate chips
Optional: powdered sugar

Combine first 4 ingredients, stirring until moistened. Fold in chocolate chips, being sure not to overblend. Drop by ¼ cupfuls onto a hot, greased griddle; flip over when bubbles appear around edges. Cook on each side until lightly golden. Sprinkle with powdered sugar, if desired. Makes 12 to 16.

Carolyn Demel
Houston, TX

DUBLIN POTATO PANCAKE

Yummy with eggs and bacon…a hearty farmhouse breakfast!

2 potatoes, shredded
1 onion, finely chopped
½ c. shredded Cheddar cheese
1 egg, beaten
2 bacon slices, cooked and chopped
salt and pepper to taste

Mix all ingredients together in a bowl. Spray a skillet with non-stick vegetable spray and place over medium-high heat until warm. Pour potato mixture into skillet, pressing down to form a pancake. Cook over medium-high heat until golden brown on the bottom and middle is set. Check edges periodically by gently lifting. Turn pancake using 2 spatulas and cook second side until golden. Serves 4.

Virginia Konerman
Virginia Beach, VA

Festive Tree·Trimming Feast

Trimming the Christmas tree is a popular holiday custom. And a tree-trimming party is just the thing to bring the family together for food and fun! The following pages are packed with delicious recipes…from a hearty Whole Baked Ham to Mom's Special Occasion Cherry Cake. Keep the festivities going with a tasty assortment of appetizers, drinks and desserts.

Whole Baked Ham & Sweet Hot Mustard

WHOLE BAKED HAM

A yummy ham that can be served hot or refrigerated and sliced for sandwiches.

12- to 14-lb. fully cooked boneless
    or bone-in ham
12 whole cloves
1 1/2 c. pineapple juice
1/2 c. maple-flavored syrup
6 slices canned pineapple
1 c. water
3/4 c. brown sugar, packed
3 T. mustard

Place ham, fat side up, in a shallow roasting pan. Press cloves into top of ham. Stir together pineapple juice and syrup; pour over ham. Arrange pineapple slices on ham. Bake at 325 degrees for 1 1/2 hours. Add water and bake for 1 1/2 additional hours. Remove from oven; remove pineapple slices. Mix together brown sugar and mustard; spread over ham. Bake an additional 30 minutes. Makes 18 to 20 servings.

Jacqueline Kurtz
Reading, PA

SWEET HOT MUSTARD

This mustard really spices up ham sandwiches.

2 2-oz. containers dry mustard
2 1/4 c. white vinegar
1 1/2 c. sugar
1/4 c. all-purpose flour
1 t. salt
3/4 t. red pepper
1 1/2 T. butter
3 eggs, lightly beaten

Combine mustard and vinegar in a large bowl; cover and let stand 8 hours. Combine sugar and next 3 ingredients; whisk into mustard mixture. Melt butter over medium heat. Add mustard mixture; cook 8 minutes or until slightly thickened. Gradually whisk about 1/4 of hot mixture into beaten eggs; add to remaining hot mustard mixture, stirring constantly. Cook 3 minutes or until a thermometer registers 160 degrees and mixture is slightly thickened. Remove from heat. Cool completely. Store in an airtight container for up to 2 weeks. Makes 3 cups.

Brie Kisses

Brie Kisses

a recipe from KATHY GRASHOFF FORT WAYNE, IN

... LITTLE CHEESY BITES YOU'LL LOVE FOR HOLIDAY PARTIES!

2/3 LB. BRIE CHEESE
17.3-OZ. PKG. FROZEN PUFF PASTRY
RED & GREEN HOT PEPPER JELLY

CUT BRIE INTO 32 HALF-INCH CUBES; ARRANGE ON A PLATE AND PLACE IN THE FREEZER. LET PASTRY THAW AT ROOM TEMPERATURE FOR 30 MINUTES; UNFOLD EACH PASTRY AND ROLL WITH A ROLLING PIN TO REMOVE CREASES. SLICE EACH SHEET INTO QUARTERS; SLICE EACH QUARTER IN HALF. CUT EACH PIECE IN HALF ONE MORE TIME FOR A TOTAL OF 32 SQUARES. PLACE SQUARES INTO GREASED MINI MUFFIN CUPS; ARRANGE SO CORNERS OF DOUGH POINT UPWARDS. BAKE AT 400 DEGREES FOR 5 MINUTES. PLACE ONE BRIE CUBE IN CENTER OF EACH PASTRY. BAKE 10 MINUTES OR 'TIL EDGES ARE GOLDEN. REMOVE FROM PAN IMMEDIATELY TOP WITH PEPPER JELLY.

Makes 32

BURGUNDY MEATBALLS

This recipe has become a New Year's favorite in our house!

1½ lbs. ground beef
⅓ c. milk
¼ c. bread crumbs
1 egg, beaten
1½ t. salt
⅛ t. pepper
2 T. dried, minced onion, divided
1 T. butter
1½ T. all-purpose flour
¼ t. garlic powder
1 c. beef broth
2 T. tomato paste
½ c. raisins
Optional: ¼ c. burgundy wine or
   cranberry juice

Mix first 6 ingredients together; add one tablespoon onion. Shape into 18 balls; brown in butter in a skillet. Remove meatballs; whisk flour and garlic powder into drippings in skillet. Stir in remaining onion, beef broth, tomato paste and raisins; add meatballs. Cover and simmer for 10 minutes. Remove meatballs to a hot serving dish; stir wine or juice into remaining sauce in skillet, if desired. Heat and pour sauce over meatballs before serving. Serves 4 to 6.

Suzanne Flinn
Bedford, IN

WRAPPED WATER CHESTNUTS

Crunchy with just the right amount of sweetness.

1 lb. bacon, slices halved
16-oz. can whole water chestnuts
½ c. mayonnaise
½ c. brown sugar, packed
¼ c. chili sauce

Cook bacon until almost crisp; drain. Wrap one slice around each water chestnut; secure with a toothpick. Arrange in an ungreased 9"x9" baking pan; set aside. Mix remaining ingredients together; pour over water chestnuts. Bake at 350 degrees for 45 minutes. Makes about 2 dozen.

Jan Fishback
Carmi, IL

PINEAPPLE BALL

Serve with an assortment of crackers and bread sticks and watch it disappear!

2 8-oz pkgs. cream cheese,
   softened
2 T. green pepper, chopped
2 T. onion, finely chopped
2 t. seasoned salt
¼ c. crushed pineapple, drained
2 T. sugar
2 c. chopped pecans, divided

Mix first 6 ingredients with one cup pecans; shape into a ball. Cover and chill one hour. Roll in remaining one cup pecans; cover with plastic wrap and refrigerate until firm. Makes about 2½ cups.

Janice Patterson
Black Forest, CO

Pineapple Ball

Citrus Mimosa

HOMEMADE EGGNOG

There's nothing like the taste of homemade eggnog...sprinkle with cinnamon or nutmeg before serving.

2/3 c. sugar
4 egg yolks
1/2 t. salt
4 c. milk
8 c. half-and-half
nutmeg to taste
1 pt. whipping cream, chilled
3 T. sugar
2 t. vanilla extract
Garnish: frozen whipped topping, thawed, and cinnamon or nutmeg

Beat sugar into egg yolks in a saucepan; add salt and stir in milk. Cook mixture over medium heat, stirring constantly, until mixture coats the back of a metal spoon. Remove from heat and set pan in ice water to cool quickly. Pour through a sieve to remove lumps. Add half-and-half to cooled mixture; sprinkle with nutmeg. In a separate bowl, whip cream with sugar and vanilla; fold into egg mixture. Stir well before serving. Serve with a dollop of whipped topping and a sprinkle of cinnamon or nutmeg. Makes 12 servings.

Rebecca Ferguson
Carlisle, AR

Citrus Mimosa

makes the champagne go a little further!

∘∘ ☆ ∘∘

1 c. PREPARED STRAWBERRY DAIQUIRI MIX

6 OZ. COLD WATER

6-OZ. CAN FROZEN ORANGE JUICE CONCENTRATE, THAWED

3/4 c. FRESH GRAPEFRUIT JUICE

1/3 c. FROZEN LEMONADE CONCENTRATE, THAWED

3 T. FROZEN LIMEADE CONCENTRATE, THAWED

1 BOTTLE CHAMPAGNE *, CHILLED

garnish : orange rind curls

∘∘∘ ☆ ∘∘∘

COMBINE PREPARED DAIQUIRI MIX, WATER, ORANGE JUICE CONCENTRATE, GRAPEFRUIT JUICE, LEMONADE & LIMEADE CONCENTRATES IN A PITCHER OR BOWL. STIR 'TIL WELL COMBINED. COVER & CHILL. TO SERVE, POUR AN EQUAL AMOUNT OF THE CHILLED JUICE MIXTURE & CHAMPAGNE INTO 8 GLASSES. GARNISH WITH ORANGE RIND CURLS. MAKES 8 SIX-OUNCE SERVINGS.

* Note: For a non-alcoholic drink, substitute carbonated water for the champagne!

BLACK & WHITE SALSA

This salsa looks as great as it tastes.

15½-oz. can black beans, rinsed
    and drained
10-oz. pkg. frozen shoepeg corn,
    partially thawed
1 bunch green onions, diced
1 red tomato, diced
1 yellow tomato, diced
juice of 2 limes
1 jalapeño pepper, diced
1 T. olive oil
½ t. salt
⅛ t. pepper
fresh cilantro, chopped, to taste

Combine beans, corn, onions
and tomatoes; set aside. Mix
remaining ingredients together;
combine mixtures before serving.
Makes 3 to 4 cups.

Kristen Halverson
Folsom, CA

SWEET RED PEPPER DIP

*Serve this with fresh vegetables and
bagel chips.*

2 sweet red peppers
1 c. sour cream
2 3-oz. pkgs. cream cheese
¼ t. salt
¼ t. paprika
⅛ t. cayenne pepper

Cut sweet red peppers in half
lengthwise; remove stems and
seeds. Place peppers, cut side
down, in an 8"x8" baking dish.
Cover and microwave at HIGH for
8 to 10 minutes or until peppers
are tender. Put peppers in cold
water and remove skins. Combine
peppers and remaining ingredients
in a food processor or blender and
process until smooth. Refrigerate
12 hours before serving. Makes
about 1¾ cups.

Liz Plotnick-Snay
Gooseberry Patch

CRAB-STUFFED MUSHROOMS

*A delicious appetizer...plan to
make extras!*

6-oz. can crabmeat
¾ c. grated Parmesan cheese
½ c. butter, melted
⅓ c. bread crumbs
2 to 3 cloves garlic, chopped
¼ to ½ c. onion, chopped
salt and pepper to taste
12-oz. pkg. fresh mushrooms, caps
    washed and stems removed

Mix all ingredients together, except
mushrooms. Stuff mushroom caps
with crab mixture and place on
a lightly oiled baking sheet. Bake
at 375 degrees for 20 minutes.
Makes about 15.

Nicole Shira
New Baltimore, MI

A RECIPE FROM
BRENDA HARRELL ★ BEULAVILLE, NC

CARAMEL APPLE DIP

QUICK & EASY - PERFECT TO BRING TO
A WINTER GATHERING!

★

8-OZ. PKG. CREAM CHEESE, SOFTENED
½ C. CARAMEL ICE CREAM TOPPING
¼ C. HONEY
¼ t. CINNAMON
3 TO 4 GREEN & RED APPLES,
    CORED & SLICED

GARNISH: Cinnamon

★

IN A MEDIUM SERVING BOWL,
COMBINE CREAM CHEESE, CARAMEL
TOPPING, HONEY & ¼ TEASPOON
CINNAMON; BEAT UNTIL SMOOTH.
STORE IN REFRIGERATOR 'TIL
CHILLED. SPRINKLE WITH CINNAMON
AND SERVE WITH APPLE SLICES.

~ makes 2 cups ~

Caramel Apple Dip

Raspberry Bars & Coffee Hermits

RASPBERRY BARS

Whip up these fruity treats for a potluck and watch them disappear!

1 c. butter, softened
3/4 c. sugar
1 egg
1/2 t. vanilla extract
2 1/2 c. all-purpose flour
10-oz. jar seedless raspberry jam
1/2 c. chopped pecans, toasted

Beat butter and sugar until creamy. Add egg and vanilla, beating until blended. Add flour, beating until blended. Reserving one cup dough, press remaining dough firmly into a lightly greased 9"x9" baking pan. Spread jam evenly over crust. Stir pecans into reserved one cup dough. Sprinkle evenly over jam layer. Bake at 350 degrees for 25 to 28 minutes or until golden. Cool completely on a wire rack. Makes about 1 1/2 dozen.

*S*et the mood for your tree-trimming party by playing Christmas music. Whether you select traditional holiday hymns or whimsical songs, be sure to have the family sing along!

COFFEE HERMITS

A delicious coffee-flavored cookie.

1/2 c. shortening
1 c. brown sugar, packed
1 egg
2 T. water
1 1/2 c. all-purpose flour
2 t. instant coffee granules
1/2 t. baking soda
1/2 t. cinnamon
1/4 t. salt
1/4 t. nutmeg
1/2 c. raisins
1/2 c. chopped pecans
1/2 c. chocolate chips

Combine shortening and brown sugar; blend in egg. Add water and set aside. Combine next 6 ingredients; mix into sugar mixture. Fold in remaining ingredients; drop rounded teaspoonfuls of dough about 2 inches apart onto lightly greased baking sheets. Bake at 350 degrees for 10 minutes. Makes about 5 dozen.

Pamela Raybon
Edna, TX

MOM'S SPECIAL OCCASION CHERRY CAKE

A special occasion cake.

2 1/4 c. cake flour
2 1/2 t. baking powder
1/4 t. salt
1/2 c. shortening
1 1/3 c. sugar
3 egg whites
2/3 c. milk
10-oz. jar maraschino cherries, drained with juice reserved
1/2 c. chopped walnuts
4-oz. jar maraschino cherries with stems

Combine flour, baking powder and salt in a small bowl; set aside. Beat shortening in a large bowl for 30 seconds; beat in sugar. Gradually add egg whites, beating well after each addition; set aside. Whisk milk and 1/4 cup reserved cherry juice together; add alternately with flour mixture to sugar mixture, mixing well. Fold in nuts and drained cherries; divide batter evenly into 2 lightly greased and floured 8" round baking pans. Bake at 350 degrees for 25 to 30 minutes; cool on a wire rack for 10 minutes. Remove from pans to cool completely; spread frosting between layers and on the top and sides of cake. Decorate top with a ring of stemmed cherries. Makes 8 to 10 servings.

Butter Frosting:
3/4 c. butter, softened
6 c. powdered sugar, divided
1/3 c. milk
1/4 t. salt
1 1/2 t. vanilla extract
4 to 6 drops red food coloring

Beat butter until fluffy; mix in 3 cups powdered sugar. Gradually blend in milk, salt and vanilla; add remaining 3 cups powdered sugar, mixing well. Stir in food coloring to desired tint.

Roger Baker
La Rue, OH

It All Starts With A Cake Mix

Whipping up a batch of delicious baked goods for your holiday entertaining and gift giving is a piece of cake! Just start with a package of cake mix and you can easily bake muffins, cookies, bars, brownies and of course, cakes.

···in all things, the supreme excellence is simplicity.
— LONGFELLOW —

SANTA'S HELPER

Sugar-Topped Muffins

SUGAR-TOPPED MUFFINS

Enjoy these muffins warm for a real treat!

18¼-oz. pkg. white cake mix
1 c. milk
2 eggs
½ t. nutmeg
⅓ c. sugar
½ t. cinnamon
¼ c. butter, melted

Blend cake mix, milk, eggs and nutmeg on low speed with an electric mixer until just moistened; beat on high speed for 2 minutes. Fill paper-lined muffin cups ⅔ full. Bake at 350 degrees until golden, about 15 to 18 minutes. Cool for 5 minutes. Combine sugar and cinnamon on a small plate. Brush muffin tops with butter; roll in sugar and cinnamon mixture. Serve warm. Makes 2 dozen.

As a little girl, I can remember going to my grandparents' house to help bake Christmas cookies. Mother would tell my brother and me to come to Grandmother's house right after school that day. All day long while in school, I would be daydreaming about baking cookies. We would eat supper and then start baking the delicious butter cookies. Grandmother always gave my mother more than half of the fresh-baked cookies to take home, but when we would visit, she always had plenty of cookies for us there, too! I looked forward to this time every year.

— Henrietta Loveland
Baltimore, MD

Devil's Food Sandwich Cookies

Devil's Food Sandwich Cookies

... great for dunking!

a recipe from
SHEILA GWALTNEY
★ JOHNSON CITY, TN

18¼·OZ. PKG. DEVIL'S FOOD CAKE MIX
¾ C. SHORTENING
2 EGGS
8·OZ. PKG. CREAM CHEESE, SOFTENED
½ C. MARGARINE, SOFTENED
½ t. ALMOND EXTRACT
16·OZ. PKG. POWDERED SUGAR

COMBINE CAKE MIX, SHORTENING & EGGS. FORM INTO SMALL BALLS AND FLATTEN SLIGHTLY ON UNGREASED BAKING SHEET. BAKE AT 350 DEGREES FOR 8 TO 10 MINUTES. IN MEDIUM BOWL, BLEND CREAM CHEESE, MARGARINE & ALMOND EXTRACT. GRADUALLY BLEND IN POWDERED SUGAR UNTIL DESIRED CONSISTENCY. BEAT WITH A SPOON 'TIL SMOOTH; REFRIGERATE. WHEN COOKIES ARE COOL, SPREAD FILLING BETWEEN 2 COOKIES; REPEAT. KEEP REFRIGERATED. MAKES 2 DOZEN.

PISTACHIO CAKE

A popular cake in the 1970's…it's still very good, easy to make and looks so festive!

18¼-oz. pkg. white cake mix
3.4-oz. pkg. instant pistachio
    pudding mix
1 c. oil
1 c. club soda
3 eggs
½ c. pistachios, chopped
Garnish: chopped pistachios

Combine first 6 ingredients; blend for 4 minutes. Pour batter into a greased and floured 10" tube pan; bake at 350 degrees for 45 to 50 minutes or until toothpick inserted in center of cake comes out clean. Cool in pan for 10 to 15 minutes; remove and cool completely on a wire rack. Frost and garnish with nuts; refrigerate until ready to serve. Makes 12 servings.

Frosting:
2 envelopes whipped topping mix
1½ c. cold milk
3.4-oz. pkg. instant pistachio
    pudding mix

Combine whipped topping mix and milk; beat until soft peaks form. Add pudding mix; beat until fluffy.

Ethel Bolton
Vienna, VA

KATE'S HOLIDAY DREAM: PEPPERMINT SWIRL ICE CREAM and A GIGANTIC CHOCOLATE CUPCAKE WITH SPRINKLES ON TOP!

Pistachio Cake

GRANDMA GRACIE'S LEMON CAKE

This recipe has become a New Year's favorite at our house!

18¼-oz. pkg. yellow cake mix
3.4-oz. pkg. instant lemon pudding mix
¾ c. oil
¾ c. water
4 eggs

Mix together all ingredients. Pour into a greased 13"x9" baking pan. Bake at 350 degrees for 35 to 40 minutes or until toothpick inserted in center comes out clean. Remove cake from oven and immediately poke holes through the cake with a fork; pour glaze over top. Serves 10 to 12.

Glaze:
2 c. powdered sugar
⅓ c. lemon juice
2 T. butter, melted
2 T. water

Combine all ingredients.

Denise Grace Musgrave
Shelbyville, IN

RASPBERRY UPSIDE-DOWN CAKE

Great served warm or cold, and it couldn't be easier to prepare!

18¼-oz. pkg. yellow cake mix and
    ingredients to prepare cake
1 c. raspberries
¾ c. sugar
½ c. whipping cream

Prepare cake mix according to package directions. Pour into greased and floured 10" cake pan. Place raspberries over top of cake mix. Sprinkle sugar over raspberries. Gently pour whipping cream over top. Bake for 25 to 35 minutes in a 350 degree oven. Let stand for 10 minutes. Turn upside down on plate to serve. Makes 10 to 12 servings.

Becky Rogers
Saline, MI

Keep plenty of cake mix on hand so you can be ready to bring a sweet treat to any holiday get-together.

PUMPKIN CRISP

Everyone comes together at dinnertime when they know there's pumpkin crisp for dessert!

16-oz. can pumpkin
12-oz. can evaporated milk
3 eggs
1 c. sugar
2 t. cinnamon
18¼-oz. pkg. yellow cake mix
1½ c. chopped pecans
1 c. margarine, melted
8-oz. pkg. cream cheese, softened
½ c. powdered sugar
¾ c. thawed whipped topping

Mix pumpkin, milk, eggs, sugar and cinnamon together with mixer until well blended. Pour into greased 13"x9" baking pan. Sprinkle dry cake mix over the top. Sprinkle pecans over cake mix. Drizzle margarine over all; don't stir. Bake at 350 degrees for one hour. Cool and invert on a large platter. Blend together cream cheese, powdered sugar and whipped topping and spread over cooled crisp. Refrigerate until ready to serve. Makes 10 to 12 servings.

Judy Wilson
Hutchinson, MN

NUT ROLL BARS

Kids gobble up these rich and tasty treats.

18¼-oz. pkg. yellow cake mix
¼ c. butter, melted
1 egg
3 c. mini marshmallows
2 c. peanuts, chopped
2 c. crispy rice cereal
10-oz. pkg. peanut butter chips
½ c. corn syrup
½ c. butter
1 t. vanilla extract

Combine cake mix, butter and egg; press into a 13"x9" baking pan. Bake at 350 degrees for 10 to 12 minutes. Arrange marshmallows on top and return to oven for about 3 minutes or until marshmallows puff up. Combine peanuts and cereal. Melt peanut butter chips, corn syrup and butter in a saucepan over low heat; stir in vanilla. Pour mixture over peanuts and cereal mixture, stirring to coat; spread evenly over marshmallow layer. Refrigerate overnight and cut into bars. Makes 2 dozen.

Shelly Schenkel
Sioux Falls, SD

DROP THAT BACKPACK and DIG IN! MOM'S GOT

CARAMEL Brownies

...a great after-school treat with a glass of icy-cold cider!

14-oz. pkg. CARAMELS, unwrapped
⅔ c. EVAPORATED MILK, divided
18¼-oz. pkg. GERMAN CHOCOLATE CAKE MIX
⅔ c. BUTTER, MELTED
1 c. CHOPPED PECANS
12-oz. pkg. CHOCOLATE CHIPS

COMBINE CARAMELS & ⅓ CUP EVAPORATED MILK IN A MICROWAVE-SAFE BOWL. HEAT, STIRRING OCCASIONALLY, UNTIL CARAMELS HAVE MELTED; SET ASIDE. COMBINE CAKE MIX, BUTTER, REMAINING ⅓ CUP EVAPORATED MILK & PECANS. PRESS HALF OF CAKE MIXTURE INTO BOTTOM OF GREASED & FLOURED 13"x9" BAKING PAN. BAKE AT 350 DEGREES FOR 8 MINUTES; REMOVE FROM OVEN. SPRINKLE WITH CHOCOLATE CHIPS; SPREAD CARAMEL MIXTURE OVER THE TOP. DROP REMAINING CAKE MIXTURE BY SPOONFULS ON TOP OF CARAMEL MIXTURE; BAKE AN ADDITIONAL 15 TO 18 MINUTES. COOL SLIGHTLY; REFRIGERATE 30 MINUTES TO FIRM CARAMEL LAYER. CUT INTO BARS. MAKES 2 DOZEN.

~JODY KOMARNITZKI ★ VENICE, FL~

Nut Roll Bars

transforming traditions

What can you do when you're far from family and can't go home for the holidays? Transform your traditions! Some of your friends probably can't have Christmas with their families either, so invite them over to enjoy a combination of customs. Have guests bring dishes that reflect their family's regional or ethnic heritage. We've included recipes for some universal favorites to help you get the party started.

Herb-Roasted Holiday Turkey

HERB-ROASTED HOLIDAY TURKEY

So easy…just pop the turkey in a roasting bag!

1 T. all-purpose flour
1 onion, sliced
2 stalks celery, chopped
1 carrot, chopped
12- to 16-lb. turkey
2 T. oil
1 T. dried sage
1 t. dried thyme
1 t. dried rosemary
1 t. seasoned salt
1 t. pepper

Shake flour in a turkey-size oven bag; arrange in a 2-inch deep roasting pan. Add vegetables to bag; set aside. Remove neck and giblets from turkey and reserve for another use; rinse turkey, pat dry and brush with oil. Combine herbs, salt and pepper; sprinkle over turkey. Place turkey in bag on top of vegetables; close bag with nylon tie provided and tuck ends into pan. Cut six 1/2-inch slits in top of bag; insert meat thermometer into thickest part of inner thigh. Bake at 350 degrees for 2 to 2 1/2 hours or until meat thermometer reads 180 degrees. Let stand in bag for 15 minutes before opening; pour off drippings and reserve for gravy. Serves 10 to 12.

Turkey Gravy:
drippings from roasted turkey
1/4 c. all-purpose flour
1/4 t. salt
1/4 t. poultry seasoning

Pour drippings into a large, deep bowl. Spoon off fat, reserving 3 to 4 tablespoons; discard remaining fat. Measure drippings; add water, if necessary, to equal 2 1/2 cups. Place reserved fat in a skillet; stir in flour, salt and poultry seasoning. Heat over medium-high heat, stirring constantly until smooth and bubbly, about one minute. Gradually stir drippings into flour mixture; heat to boiling, stirring frequently. Boil for 5 to 7 minutes until thickened. Makes about 2 cups.

Vickie

GREAT-GRANDMA'S DRESSING

My Italian great-grandmother would make this dish for holidays and special occasions. It's almost a meal in itself!

2 T. olive oil
1 lb. mushrooms, sliced
5 stalks celery, chopped
1 onion, chopped
3 cloves garlic, minced
8-oz. stick pepperoni, chopped
4-oz. can sliced black olives
3/4 c. fresh parsley, chopped
1 t. poultry seasoning
pepper to taste
15 to 18 slices bread, torn
1 1/2 t. chicken bouillon granules

Heat oil in a large skillet; add mushrooms, celery, onion and garlic. Sauté for 5 minutes over medium heat. Add pepperoni, olives, parsley, poultry seasoning and pepper; sauté 5 additional minutes. Place bread in a lightly greased 13"x9" baking pan; mix in sautéed mixture until moistened. Gradually stir in chicken bouillon. Bake at 325 degrees for 40 to 45 minutes. Serves 4 to 6.

Lori Van Aken
Arvada, CO

Get the kids in on the fun by having them make traditional Christmas crafts from various countries around the world.

ALOHA CHICKEN WINGS

A staple at any gathering.

¼ c. butter
½ c. catsup
1 clove garlic, minced
3 lbs. chicken wings
1 c. bread crumbs
14-oz. can pineapple chunks,
    drained and juice reserved
2 T. brown sugar, packed
1 T. whole ginger, minced
1 T. Worcestershire sauce
hot pepper sauce to taste

Place butter in a jelly-roll pan; heat in a 400-degree oven until melted. Stir catsup and garlic together; brush over wings. Coat with bread crumbs; arrange in jelly-roll pan, turning to coat both sides with melted butter. Bake at 400 degrees for 30 minutes. While baking, add enough water to reserved pineapple juice to equal ¾ cup liquid; pour into a small mixing bowl. Whisk in remaining ingredients; pour over wings. Continue baking until juices run clear when chicken is pierced with a fork, about 20 to 30 additional minutes. Place pineapple around wings, baking until heated through. Serves 4.

Dianne Gregory
Sheridan, AR

DEBBIE'S LONG-DISTANCE MICHIGAN CORN CHIP DIP

This will serve a large group.

16 oz. cream cheese, softened
32 oz. sour cream
1 t. seasoned salt
1 tomato, chopped
6 green onions, sliced
6-oz. can large pitted olives,
    drained and sliced
8 oz. Colby or mild Cheddar
    cheese, shredded
Garnish: parsley, paprika and
    green onions

Beat cream cheese until fluffy. Add sour cream and mix thoroughly. Add seasoned salt. Add tomato, onion and olives. Mix sour cream mixture with tomato mixture. Pour into a 13"x9" dish. Sprinkle cheese on top of dip mixture. Garnish with parsley, paprika and green onions. Serve with corn chips, vegetables, dip-size chips or round butter-flavored crackers. Makes about 6 cups.

Dawn Marshall

POLENTA WITH TOMATO

Polenta is an Italian version of cornmeal mush…it's good; try it!

2 c. water
½ c. cornmeal
½ t. salt
1 c. onion, chopped
1 clove garlic, minced
1 T. oil
2 t. dried marjoram, divided
1 tomato, cut into 6 slices
¼ c. crumbled Gorgonzola cheese

Bring water to a boil; stir in cornmeal and salt. Cook, stirring constantly, until mixture thickens and comes to a boil; boil one minute. Cover and cook over low heat 7 minutes. Remove from heat; cool to room temperature. Sauté onion and garlic in oil; add one teaspoon marjoram. Stir onion mixture into polenta; spread into a greased 11"x7" baking dish. Cover and refrigerate at least 6 hours. Cut into 6 squares and arrange on a lightly greased baking sheet. Bake at 425 degrees for 25 minutes; top each square with one tomato slice. Sprinkle with cheese and remaining one teaspoon marjoram; bake for 5 minutes or until cheese begins to melt. Serve warm. Makes 6 servings.

Gail Prather
Bethel, MN

"Friendship! mysterious cement of the soul!
Sweetener of life! and solder of society!"

— Robert Blair

Polenta with Tomato

CREOLE GREEN BEANS

A wonderful green bean side dish . . . a twist on the usual recipe!

6 bacon slices, crisply cooked,
    crumbled and drippings reserved
$1/2$ c. green pepper, chopped
$1/4$ c. onion, chopped
2 T. all-purpose flour
2 T. brown sugar, packed
1 T. Worcestershire sauce
$1/2$ t. salt
$1/4$ t. pepper
$1/8$ t. dry mustard
16-oz. can peeled whole tomatoes,
    cut into fourths
16-oz. can green beans, drained

In skillet with bacon drippings, sauté green pepper and onion until tender. Blend together next 6 ingredients; stir into skillet. Add tomatoes and continue to stir until mixture thickens. Add green beans and heat through; sprinkle with crumbled bacon. Serves 6.

Cheryl Chapman
Union, MO

Creole Green Beans

TAKE-ALONG POTATOES

My family's favorite potato dish!

10 to 12 potatoes, peeled
    and thinly sliced
1 to 2 onions, sliced
$2/3$ c. shredded Cheddar cheese
$1/2$ c. butter, melted
15-oz. can chicken broth
1 T. dried parsley
2 T. Worcestershire sauce
salt and pepper to taste

In a greased 13"x9" pan, layer potatoes, onion and cheese. Pour butter over mixture. Mix remaining ingredients and pour over mixture. Bake, covered, at 425 degrees for 45 to 50 minutes or until potatoes are tender. Uncover, turn off oven and leave dish in oven for 10 minutes. Makes 10 to 12 servings.

Linda Murdock
Selah, WA

Baked Butternut Squash and Apples

This is an old-fashioned recipe from the Midwest; the apples and maple syrup are wonderful together!

2 butternut squash, peeled & seeded
$2 1/4$ lbs. Granny Smith apples, peeled & cored
3/4 c. dried currants
freshly grated nutmeg
salt & pepper to taste
3/4 c. maple syrup
1/4 c. butter, cut into pieces
$1 1/2$ T. fresh lemon juice

Cut squash & apples crosswise into 1/4-inch slices. Cook squash in large pot of boiling, salted water for 3 minutes or until almost tender. Drain well. Combine squash, apples & currants in 13" x 9" glass baking dish. Season with desired amounts of nutmeg, salt & pepper. Combine maple syrup, butter & lemon juice in small saucepan. Whisk over low heat 'til butter melts. Pour syrup over squash mixture and toss to coat evenly. Bake at 350 degrees until squash and apples are very tender, about one hour, stirring occasionally. Cool 5 minutes. Makes 8 servings.

OH BOY! Olliebollen (DOUGHNUTS)

A FAVORITE CHRISTMAS MORNING TRADITION FROM OUR DUTCH ANCESTORS, BUT GOOD ANY TIME, ANY DAY!

1 PKG. ACTIVE DRY YEAST
1 t. SUGAR
1/4 C. WARM WATER
2 1/4 C. CAKE FLOUR
1 1/2 C. RAISINS
1 C. WARM MILK (100 TO 110 DEGREES)
1/4 C. SUGAR
1 EGG, BEATEN
3/4 t. CINNAMON
1/2 t. SALT
1/4 t. NUTMEG
OIL
1 C. POWDERED SUGAR

DISSOLVE YEAST WITH ONE TEASPOON SUGAR & WATER — LET SIT FOR ABOUT 10 MINUTES. IN LARGE BOWL, COMBINE THE NEXT 8 INGREDIENTS 'TIL WELL BLENDED; ADD YEAST MIXTURE. COVER & LET RISE FOR ONE HOUR. DROP 2 TABLESPOONFULS OF DOUGH INTO HOT OIL IN DEEP FRYER; FRY 'TIL GOLDEN BROWN. DRAIN ON PAPER TOWELS. ROLL IN POWDERED SUGAR. SERVE IMMEDIATELY. MICROWAVE TO REHEAT. MAKES 2 DOZEN.

~ SALLY BORLAND ✶ PORT GIBSON, NY ~

Dakota Bread

DAKOTA BREAD

Mom always has this hearty bread waiting in the cupboard when we visit. It's named for all the good grains in it, which are grown in the Dakotas.

1 pkg. active dry yeast
1/2 c. warm water
1/2 c. cottage cheese
1/4 c. honey
1 egg
2 T. oil
1 t. salt
2 1/4 c. bread flour, divided
1/2 c. whole-wheat flour
1/4 c. wheat germ, toasted
1/4 c. rye flour
1/4 c. long-cooking oats, uncooked
2 T. cornmeal
1 egg white, beaten
2 T. sunflower kernels

Combine yeast and water in a small bowl; let stand 5 minutes. In a large bowl, combine cottage cheese, honey, egg, oil and salt.

Beat at medium speed with an electric mixer until blended. Add yeast mixture and 2 cups bread flour, beating until smooth. Gradually stir in whole-wheat flour, wheat germ, rye flour and oats. Add enough remaining bread flour to make a soft dough. Knead dough on a lightly floured surface until smooth and elastic. Place in a greased bowl; cover and let rise one hour or until doubled in bulk. Punch dough down. Shape into one round loaf and place in a pie pan coated with non-stick vegetable spray and sprinkled with cornmeal. Cover with greased plastic wrap and let dough rise again until doubled in bulk. Brush with egg white and sprinkle with sunflower kernels. Bake at 350 degrees for 35 to 40 minutes. Cool on a wire rack. Makes 6 to 8 servings.

Margaret Scoresby
Mosinee, WI

Olliebollen (Doughnuts)

DANISH SPICE COOKIES

You will start a new tradition with these cookies.

2 c. sifted all-purpose flour
1 t. cinnamon
¹/₂ t. salt
¹/₄ t. baking soda
¹/₄ t. ground cloves
¹/₂ c. butter or margarine
1 c. brown sugar, packed
¹/₂ c. sour cream
1 egg
1 t. vanilla extract
1 c. chopped dates
¹/₂ c. chopped walnuts

Sift flour, cinnamon, salt, baking soda and cloves in a bowl. Melt butter in a medium-sized saucepan; remove from heat. Add sugar and beat with a wooden spoon until combined. Beat in sour cream, egg and vanilla until smooth. Stir in flour mixture until thoroughly combined. Stir in dates and nuts. Spread evenly into a greased 15"x10"x1" pan. Bake at 350 degrees for 30 minutes or until top springs up. Makes 4 dozen.

Jennifer Muller

Little bars of fragrant goodness, Danish Spice Cookies get a flavor boost from an unexpected ingredient...sour cream! And when it comes to getting lots of zing for a minimum of fuss, you can't beat Bar Harbor Cranberry Pie.

START A NEW TRADITION: SHARE THE SEASON'S BOUNTY OF SWEETS WITH AN ELDERLY NEIGHBOR! DELIVER A BASKET OF COOKIES & A DINNER INVITATION.

BAR HARBOR CRANBERRY PIE

Frozen berries can also be used...no need to thaw before preparing this pretty pie.

2 c. cranberries
1¹/₂ c. sugar, divided
¹/₂ c. chopped pecans
2 eggs, beaten
1 c. all-purpose flour
¹/₂ c. butter, melted
¹/₄ c. shortening, melted
Garnish: whipped cream and
    cinnamon (optional)

Lightly butter a 9" glass pie plate; spread cranberries over bottom. Sprinkle evenly with ¹/₂ cup sugar and pecans; set aside. In a separate bowl, mix together eggs and remaining one cup sugar. Blend in flour, butter and shortening; beat well after each addition. Pour over cranberries; bake at 325 degrees for 55 to 60 minutes. Garnish each serving with a dollop of whipped cream and a sprinkle of cinnamon, if desired. Serves 8.

Jean Hayes
La Porte, TX

Bar Harbor Cranberry Pie

Taste Tempting TReATS

*Visions of sugarplums will dance in your head when you
start whipping up these sensational sweets. A perfect ending to
holiday meals or a special anytime snack, this collection of cookies, cakes,
pies and more will satisfy any sweet tooth. The taste-tempting treats
are also ideal to make for office parties or church potlucks.*

Mini Christmas Cheesecakes

MINI CHRISTMAS CHEESECAKES

These look so pretty on your dessert table.

3 8-oz. pkgs. cream cheese, softened
1½ c. sugar, divided
5 eggs
1½ t. vanilla extract
1 c. sour cream
2 cans cherry pie filling

Beat together cream cheese and one cup sugar. Add eggs, one at a time, beating well after each addition. Add vanilla and mix again. Pour into mini foil cups, filling ¾ full. Bake 20 minutes at 350 degrees. Remove from oven; let stand 5 minutes. Combine sour cream and remaining ½ cup sugar. Top each mini-cake with ½ teaspoon of the mixture and return to the oven for 5 minutes. When cooled, top each cheesecake with one cherry and a little of the filling. Keep refrigerated. Makes 8 dozen.

Mom's Gingerbread Cookies

MOM'S GINGERBREAD COOKIES

When I was little, Mom and I used to bake gingerbread men together at Christmas time. I remember peeking through the oven door, waiting for one of them to get up off the pan, just like the story!

½ c. shortening
2½ c. all-purpose flour, divided
½ c. sugar
½ c. molasses
1 egg
1 t. baking soda
1 t. ground ginger
½ t. cinnamon
½ t. ground cloves
candy-coated chocolate pieces

Beat shortening until softened. Add about 1¼ cups flour and next 7 ingredients. Beat until thoroughly combined. Stir in remaining 1¼ cups flour. Divide dough in half. Cover dough and chill for 3 hours or until easily handled. Roll each half of the dough to a ⅛" to ¼" thickness. Cut out 4½"-high cookies with gingerbread man cookie cutter. Place on ungreased baking sheets and bake at 375 degrees for 7 to 8 minutes or until edges are firm. Decorate with powdered sugar frosting and candies. Makes 2 dozen.

Powdered Sugar Frosting:
1 c. powdered sugar
¼ t. vanilla extract
1 T. milk

Combine all ingredients, stirring until smooth. Transfer frosting to a pastry bag fitted with a small round tip. Pipe frosting onto cookies. Makes ⅓ cup.

Michele Urdahl
Litchfield, MN

Amazing DOUBLE Chocolate Truffles

⭐ ..TRY MAKING FLAVORED TRUFFLES BY STIRRING IN DIFFERENT EXTRACTS... A TEASPOON OF ORANGE, PEPPERMINT OR RASPBERRY EXTRACT WILL DO THE TRICK.

6 1-OZ. SQS. SEMI-SWEET BAKING CHOCOLATE, CHOPPED
2 T. BUTTER
1/4 C. WHIPPING CREAM
12-OZ. PKG. WHITE CHOCOLATE CHIPS
2 T. SHORTENING
OPTIONAL: CHOPPED NUTS OR COLORFUL SPRINKLES

MELT BAKING CHOCOLATE IN A HEAVY SAUCEPAN OVER LOW HEAT, STIRRING CONSTANTLY; REMOVE FROM HEAT. ADD BUTTER AND WHIPPING CREAM; STIR 'TIL SMOOTH. REFRIGERATE FOR ONE HOUR. ROLL MIXTURE INTO ONE-INCH BALLS; PLACE ON AN ALUMINUM FOIL-LINED BAKING SHEET. FREEZE FOR 4 HOURS. MELT WHITE CHOCOLATE CHIPS AND SHORTENING OVER LOW HEAT, STIRRING 'TIL SMOOTH. DIP FROZEN TRUFFLES INTO WHITE CHOCOLATE ~ RETURN TO BAKING SHEET. ROLL IN NUTS OR SPRINKLES, IF DESIRED. REFRIGERATE TRUFFLES FOR 10 TO 15 MINUTES 'TIL COATING IS SET. STORE IN AIRTIGHT CONTAINER. MAKES ONE DOZEN.

PRALINE SHORTBREAD COOKIES

It just isn't Christmas at our house without these cookies!

1 1/2 c. butter, softened and divided
3 c. powdered sugar, divided
2 c. all-purpose flour
1 c. pecans, finely chopped
1 T. plus 1/2 t. vanilla extract, divided
1 c. brown sugar, packed
1/8 t. salt
1/2 c. evaporated milk

Beat together one cup butter and one cup powdered sugar. Add flour, stirring until well blended. Stir in pecans and one tablespoon vanilla. Shape into one-inch balls and place 2 inches apart on ungreased baking sheets. Make an indentation in center of each cookie. Bake at 375 degrees for 15 minutes; do not brown. Cool on wire racks. In saucepan, melt remaining 1/2 cup butter. Add brown sugar and salt; bring to a boil for 2 minutes, stirring constantly. Remove from heat, stir in evaporated milk and return to heat. Once again, bring to a boil for 2 minutes. Remove from heat and allow mixture to cool to lukewarm. Stir in remaining 2 cups powdered sugar and remaining 1/2 teaspoon vanilla with a wooden spoon, stirring until smooth. Fill indentations in cookies with praline filling. Makes about 3 dozen.

Carol Hickman
Kingsport, TN

MEXICAN WEDDING COOKIES

A crunchy, classic cookie.

1 c. butter or margarine, softened
1/4 c. powdered sugar
1 t. almond extract
2 c. all-purpose flour
1/4 c. walnuts, finely chopped
powdered sugar

Beat first 3 ingredients until creamy. Stir in flour and nuts. Chill for a couple of hours. Make small balls and bake at 375 degrees for about 17 minutes. Cool a little and toss in powdered sugar. Makes about 2 1/2 dozen.

Amazing Double Chocolate Truffles

Chocolate-Coconut Sweeties

CHOCOLATE ♥ COCONUT
SWEETIES
... they won't last long in the cookie jar!

1 c. BUTTER OR MARGARINE, SOFTENED
1 c. POWDERED SUGAR
½ t. SALT
1 t. VANILLA EXTRACT
2 c. ALL-PURPOSE FLOUR

BEAT BUTTER OR MARGARINE 'TIL FLUFFY; BEAT IN POWDERED SUGAR, SALT & VANILLA. GRADUALLY ADD FLOUR, BEATING WELL. COVER AND CHILL 8 HOURS. SHAPE INTO ONE-INCH BALLS. USING YOUR THUMB, GENTLY MAKE DEPRESSION IN CENTER OF EACH BALL; PLACE ON UNGREASED BAKING SHEETS. BAKE AT 350 DEGREES FOR 12 TO 15 MINUTES. SPOON A TEASPOON OF FILLING INTO EACH DEPRESSION WHILE WARM; DRIZZLE WITH FROSTING WHEN COOL. MAKES 4 DOZEN.

...a recipe from
BRENDA DONLEY
♥ LAKE ISABELLA, MI

FILLING:
6 oz. CREAM CHEESE, SOFTENED
2 c. POWDERED SUGAR
¼ c. ALL-PURPOSE FLOUR
2 t. VANILLA EXTRACT
1 c. CHOPPED WALNUTS
1 c. SWEETENED FLAKED COCONUT

Combine all ingredients.

FROSTING:
1 c. SEMI-SWEET CHOCOLATE CHIPS
¼ c. BUTTER OR MARGARINE
¼ c. WATER
1 c. POWDERED SUGAR

Microwave chips, butter and water in a one-quart glass bowl on HIGH for one minute or 'til it melts. Gradually whisk in sugar 'til smooth & creamy.

WHITE SUGAR COOKIES
My mother used this recipe for holidays and special treats when I was growing up.

5 c. all-purpose flour
5 t. baking powder
1 t. baking soda
1 t. salt
1 c. shortening
2 c. sugar
2 eggs
2 t. vanilla extract
¼ t. nutmeg
¾ c. milk

Combine flour, baking powder, baking soda and salt; set aside. In a large mixing bowl, beat shortening and sugar together. Beat in eggs, vanilla and nutmeg. Add milk alternately with dry ingredients, mixing well after each addition. Chill dough for at least 2 hours. Using approximately ¼ of the dough at a time, roll out on floured surface to ¼" thickness; cut out with cookie cutters. Bake at 350 degrees for 7 to 9 minutes on an ungreased baking sheet. When cooled, frost with Vanilla Frosting. Makes about 6½ dozen.

Vanilla Frosting:
3 c. powdered sugar
⅓ c. shortening
3 T. whipping cream or milk
1 T. margarine, softened
1½ t. vanilla extract
food coloring

Beat together all ingredients except food coloring. Frosting can be divided to make several different colors with food coloring. Spread frosting on cookies.

Sharon Lafountain

Cream-Filled Pumpkin Roll

CREAM-FILLED PUMPKIN ROLL

You can make this beautiful dessert...it's easier than you think!

1 c. sugar
¾ c. all-purpose flour
1 t. baking powder
1 t. cinnamon
⅛ t. salt
3 eggs, beaten
⅔ c. unsweetened canned
　　pumpkin
3 T. powdered sugar, divided

Butter a 15"x10" jelly-roll pan; line with wax paper. Butter the wax paper; set aside. Mix together first 5 ingredients; blend in eggs and pumpkin. Spread batter in prepared pan. Bake at 375 degrees for 12 to 15 minutes or until center tests done. Lay a kitchen towel down on a flat surface and sprinkle 2 tablespoons powdered sugar over top. Cut around sides of pan to loosen cake; invert onto sugared towel, wax paper-side up. Fold one side of towel over one long side of cake and roll up jelly-roll style. Cool cake completely. Unroll cake and leave on towel; peel off wax paper. Spread filling evenly over cake. Use towel to help roll up cake and place seam side-down on a serving platter. Trim ends of cake; cover and refrigerate until ready to serve. Dust cake with remaining one tablespoon powdered sugar. Serves 8 to 10.

Cream Cheese Filling:
8-oz. pkg. cream cheese,
　　softened
1 c. powdered sugar
2 T. unsalted butter, softened
1 t. vanilla extract
Optional: ½ c. chopped walnuts,
　　toasted

Combine cream cheese, powdered sugar, butter and vanilla; blend well. Stir in walnuts, if desired.

Susan Greeves
Frederick, MD

WARM TURTLE CAKE

A cake that reminds me of the boxes of chocolate-covered turtles that my dad used to bring home for us when we were little!

18¼-oz. pkg. Swiss chocolate
　　cake mix
½ c. plus ⅓ c. evaporated milk,
　　divided
¾ c. butter, melted
14-oz. pkg. caramels, unwrapped
1 c. chopped pecans
¾ c. chocolate chips

Beat cake mix, ⅓ cup evaporated milk and melted butter on medium speed with an electric mixer for 2 minutes. Pour half of mixture into a greased 11"x7" baking pan. Bake at 350 degrees for 6 minutes. In a double boiler or microwave, melt caramels in the remaining ½ cup evaporated milk. Drizzle over cake. Sprinkle pecans and chocolate chips over caramel mixture. Use a wet knife to spread the remaining cake mixture over the pecan pieces and chocolate chips. Bake at 350 degrees for 18 minutes. Serves 12.

Laurie Benham
Playas, NM

MINT CHOCOLATE CHIP CHEESE BALL

You'll love the flavor of this sweet cheese ball.

12-oz. pkg. mini semi-sweet
　　chocolate chips
12-oz. pkg. peppermint candies,
　　crushed
8-oz. pkg. cream cheese, softened
1 c. chopped pecans
chocolate sugar wafers

Blend chocolate chips, peppermint candies and cream cheese together; roll in pecans. Serve with chocolate sugar wafers. Makes 2½ cups.

CHRISTMAS PIE

If you take this festive pie to a holiday party, be sure to take copies of the recipe…everyone will want one!

8-oz. pkg. cream cheese, softened
1/2 c. powdered sugar
1 1/2 c. frozen whipped topping, thawed
9-inch graham cracker crust
1 c. fresh raspberries
1 c. water, divided
1 c. sugar
3 T. cornstarch
1/2 3-oz. pkg. raspberry gelatin

Beat cream cheese and powdered sugar until smooth; fold in whipped topping. Spread in crust; set aside. Place raspberries and 2/3 cup water in a saucepan; simmer for 3 minutes. Whisk sugar, cornstarch and remaining 1/3 cup water in a small bowl until smooth; add to raspberry mixture. Boil one minute, whisking constantly. Remove from heat. Add gelatin, whisking until smooth. Cool 5 to 7 minutes; pour over cream cheese mixture. Refrigerate 8 hours or until firm. Serves 8.

Caroline Wildhaber
Dayton, OR

CHOCOLATE CHESS PIE

This recipe was passed down from my grandma; it's truly wonderful.

5-oz. can evaporated milk
1 1/2 c. sugar
2 eggs, beaten
1/4 c. butter, melted
3 T. baking cocoa
1 t. vanilla extract
1/8 t. salt
9-inch pie crust

Combine first 7 ingredients; pour into an unbaked pie crust. Bake at 350 degrees for 40 to 45 minutes or until set. Makes 8 servings.

Michele Jones
Houston, TX

PRALINE-CREAM CHEESE POUND CAKE

My favorite because it has a rich caramel flavor that satisfies my most urgent sweet tooth!

1 c. butter, softened
8-oz. pkg. cream cheese, softened
1 lb. brown sugar
1 c. sugar
5 eggs
3 1/2 c. cake flour
1/2 t. baking powder
1 c. milk
1 1/2 t. vanilla extract
1 c. chopped pecans

Beat butter and cream cheese until well blended. Beat in brown sugar and sugar, one cup at a time, beating until light and fluffy. Add eggs, one at a time, beating well after each addition. Sift flour and baking powder together and add to creamed mixture alternately with milk, beginning and ending with flour. Add vanilla and nuts; mix well. Pour into a greased and floured tube pan.

Bake at 300 degrees for 2 hours or until cake tests done. Cool in pan for 10 minutes; remove from pan and cool on wire rack. Spread with Frosting. Serves 14.

Frosting:
3 c. sugar, divided
1/2 c. water
1 egg, beaten
1 c. milk
1/2 c. butter
1 t. vinegar
1/8 t. salt

Place 1/2 cup of sugar in a heavy skillet. Cook over low heat, stirring constantly until melted and brown. Add water and stir until dissolved. Add remaining 2 1/2 cups sugar. Mix egg with milk and stir into sugar mixture. Add butter, vinegar and salt. Cook to soft ball stage, 234 to 243 degrees on candy thermometer; cool. Beat until mixture reaches spreading consistency.

Vicki Jones
Rutherfordton, NC

Christmas Pie

Christmas
Cookbook

Country Breakfast
Sandwich (page 292)

Gooseberry Patch Family

holiday favorites

Vickie likes to serve savory Black-Eyed Pea Dip to her
family & friends during the holidays while Jo Ann bakes a casserole of
Country Breakfast Sandwiches to kick off her big holiday. Take a peek at
these and other time-honored recipes and memories that your friends
at Gooseberry Patch like to share throughout the season.

Black-Eyed Pea Dip

BLACK-EYED PEA DIP

16-oz. can black-eyed peas, rinsed,
    drained and divided
3 green onions, chopped
½ c. sour cream
1 t. garlic salt

½ c. salsa
4 slices bacon, crisply cooked and
    crumbled
Tortilla, corn or bagel chips
Garnish: sliced green onions

Set aside ⅓ cup peas. Place remaining peas in an electric blender and process until smooth. Add onions, sour cream and garlic salt to blender; process until smooth. Transfer to a bowl and stir in salsa, bacon and reserved peas. Garnish, if desired. Serve with chips. Serves 8.

"This dip is yummy with warm and crispy tortilla chips."
VICKIE
CO-FOUNDER

AUNT RUTHIE'S BREAKFAST CASSEROLE

Softened butter or margarine
16 slices bread, crusts removed
1 lb. shaved deli ham
4 c. (1 lb.) shredded Cheddar cheese
4 oz. grated Parmesan cheese
2 (4.5-oz.) cans sliced mushrooms,
    drained

4 eggs, lightly beaten
½ t. dry mustard
3 c. milk
½ t. salt
¼ t. pepper
¼ t. onion salt
½ c. corn flake crumbs

Butter one side of each bread slice. Layer one-third of bread, butter side up, in a greased 13"x9" baking dish. Layer a third each of ham, cheeses and mushrooms; repeat layers twice. Stir together eggs, mustard, milk, salt, pepper and onion salt; pour over mixture in dish. Cover and chill overnight in the refrigerator.
Let stand at room temperature 30 minutes before baking. Sprinkle casserole with corn flake crumbs. Bake, uncovered, at 350 degrees for 45 minutes. Let cool 10 minutes before serving. Serves 8 to 10.

"After everyone has gone to bed Christmas Eve, I put on some holiday music and prepare this dish. Always a family favorite, this tried & true recipe has been handed down to me by my Aunt Ruthie, who's now in her 70s."
TINA KNOTTS
SENIOR BUYER

AS A KID, IT JUST WOULDN'T HAVE BEEN CHRISTMAS WITHOUT CHOCOLATE FUDGE!
My mom had only one cookbook and one particular fudge recipe we always made together. We laughed and we agonized over that fudge! We didn't have a candy thermometer, so it was my responsibility to make sure it reached the "soft ball" stage. I prepared several cups of icy cold water (anticipating several "tests"). Once the fudge started boiling, I spooned a small amount of the creamy confection into the first cup...and I repeated the process as many times as necessary (sometimes a half dozen or more!) until a soft ball of fudge could be formed. There were times when the anticipation was so great I cut the "soft ball" process short and, as a result, we poured the "fudge" over ice cream or pulled it like taffy or caramel. It was never wasted, though. The best part...I always got the pan and spoon to "clean up" at the end. Thanks for all the sweet memories, Mom!

VICKIE
CO-FOUNDER

COUNTRY BREAKFAST SANDWICHES
(pictured on page 288)

(pictured on page 288)

"For a change, why not try pancakes or toasted bagels in place of the toast in these breakfast sandwiches? Whichever you choose, it'll be so scrumptious!"

Jo Ann
Co-Founder

3 T. butter or margarine, divided
1 Granny Smith apple, peeled, cored
   and thinly sliced
2 slices whole-wheat bread, toasted

3 links pork sausage, halved
   lengthwise and browned
¼ c. maple syrup, warmed

Heat 2 tablespoons butter in a skillet over low heat. Add apple; sauté until tender and golden, turning often.
Spread toasted bread with remaining butter; top each slice with sausages, apple slices and syrup. Serves 2.

MY FAVORITE ONE-POT MEAL

"Curry powder, raisins and chopped apple make this chicken dish just a little different."

Liz Plotnick-Snay
Chief Operating Officer

2 onions, diced
¼ c. oil, divided
2½ to 3 lbs. boneless, skinless
   chicken breasts
14½-oz. can diced tomatoes
½ c. white wine or chicken broth
1 T. curry powder
¼ t. garlic powder

¼ t. dried thyme
¼ t. ground nutmeg
1 apple, peeled, cored and cubed
¼ c. raisins
3 T. whipping cream
½ t. lemon juice
2 c. cooked rice

Sauté onions in 2 tablespoons oil in a large skillet over medium heat; remove onions and set aside.
Add remaining oil and chicken to skillet; cook chicken until golden. Return onions to skillet; add tomatoes, wine and next 4 ingredients, stirring well. Reduce heat, cover and simmer for 20 minutes.
Add apple, raisins and cream to skillet; simmer over low heat 6 to 8 more minutes. Stir in lemon juice. Serve over cooked rice. Serves 3 to 4.

ONE CHRISTMAS, MY MOM HAD A SPECIAL SURPRISE FOR ME. I was excited because it was rare that we did anything without at least one of my five brothers & sisters tagging along. To a 7-year-old, the drive from rural New Jersey to New York City was very long but it was well worth it. We were setting out alone to see...the Rockettes! What I remember about that day are the twinkling lights at Radio City Music Hall, the hustle & bustle on the street and my small hand held warm and tight in Mom's. Everything seemed to be touched with magic. We waited in line, then in our scratchy seats and finally, they took the stage. I was in heaven! The costumes were fantastic and music filled the entire hall. Best of all, my mom's face mirrored my own delight.

Jo Ann
Co-Founder

HEARTY WINTER PORK STEW

2 lbs. boneless pork loin, cubed
1 t. salt, divided
1 t. pepper, divided
1 T. olive oil
2 c. sliced parsnips
1¹/₂ c. sliced carrots

1 small butternut squash, peeled and
   cubed
¹/₂ c. chopped onion
4 c. chicken broth
¹/₄ c. all-purpose flour
3 T. butter or margarine, softened

Sprinkle pork with ¹/₂ teaspoon each of salt and pepper. Brown pork in hot oil in a
large skillet over medium-high heat.
Layer pork and vegetables in a 5-quart slow cooker. Pour broth over vegetables.
Sprinkle with remaining ¹/₂ teaspoon each of salt and pepper. Cover and cook on
low setting 6 hours.
Stir together flour and butter in a small bowl; gently stir into stew one
tablespoon at a time. Increase heat to high setting; cover and cook 30 minutes
until thickened, stirring occasionally. Serves 4 to 6.

"This stew's nutritious…and filling! Try other varieties of winter squash instead of butternut…they're all delicious!"

JENNIE GIST
BOOK EDITOR

MEXICALI CHICKEN

4 cooked chicken breasts, shredded
12-oz. jar salsa
2 c. shredded colby-Jack cheese

8-oz. pkg. noodles
1 T. butter or margarine
1 t. Italian seasoning

Place shredded chicken and salsa in a large skillet over medium heat; simmer for 10 minutes or until thoroughly heated. Sprinkle with cheese; cover and continue simmering until cheese is melted.
Meanwhile, cook noodles according to package directions; drain. Stir in butter and seasoning. Spoon chicken mixture evenly over individual servings of noodles. Serves 6 to 8.

"This is the first recipe my son actually created on his own. It was so easy, it became a standard and now is requested for reunions and other gatherings."
JANIE REED
PRINT PRODUCTION MANAGER

CANDIED FRUITCAKE

3 (7½-oz.) pkgs. pitted dates, chopped
16-oz. pkg. candied pineapple, chopped
16-oz. pkg. whole red candied cherries

2 c. all-purpose flour
2 t. baking powder
½ t. salt
4 eggs, beaten
1 c. sugar
2 (16-oz.) pkgs. pecan halves

Combine dates, pineapple and cherries in a large bowl. Stir together flour, baking powder and salt in a second bowl; add fruit mixture. Mix well with hands; separate pieces so that all are well coated.
In another bowl, blend eggs with a hand mixer until frothy; gradually blend in sugar. Add to fruit mixture; mix well with a large spoon. Add pecans; mix with hands until evenly distributed and coated with batter.
Grease 2 (9") springform pans or 2 (9"x5") loaf pans; line with parchment paper cut to fit, then grease paper. Spread mixture in pans; press mixture down with hands; rearrange pieces of fruit and nuts as necessary to fill up any empty spaces. Bake at 275 degrees for 1¼ to 1½ hours; tops will look dry when done. Remove from oven; cool 5 minutes on wire racks. Turn out onto wire racks, carefully peel off paper and cool thoroughly. Store loosely wrapped.
Makes 2 cakes.

BACK IN THE 1960S, my mom used to make lots of these fruitcakes every Christmas to send as gifts to relatives. I can still remember going to the Kresge's dime store with her to buy the candied fruit at the candy counter. We all love this fruitcake...it's all candied fruit, pecans and just enough batter to hold it together.
JENNIE GIST
BOOK EDITOR

Espresso Biscotti

ESPRESSO BISCOTTI

¼ c. ground espresso
2 T. coffee-flavored liqueur or
    double-strength brewed coffee
½ c. butter or margarine, softened
¾ c. sugar

2 eggs
2 c. plus 2 T. all-purpose flour
1½ t. baking powder
¼ t. salt
⅔ c. slivered almonds, toasted

Place espresso in a small microwave-safe bowl. Add liqueur and microwave on HIGH (100%) for 10 to 15 seconds to steep; set aside.
Beat butter and sugar at medium speed with an electric mixer until light and fluffy. Add eggs, one at a time, beating until blended; stir in coffee mixture. Combine flour, baking powder and salt; add to butter mixture, stirring until blended. Fold in nuts. Divide dough in half.
On a greased baking sheet, shape dough into two 13"x1½"x½" rectangles, spacing them about 2 inches apart. Bake at 325 degrees for 20 to 25 minutes or until golden. Remove to a wire rack; let cool 5 minutes.
Place biscotti on a cutting board; using a serrated knife, cut biscotti diagonally into ½-inch-thick slices. Place slices upright on baking sheet ½ inch apart and bake 10 more minutes. Let cool on rack. Store in a tightly covered container. Makes 2 dozen.

"Crunchy coffee dippers! Make them even better by stirring some white chocolate chips into the dough, then drizzle finished cookies with melted dark chocolate."

STACIE MICKLEY
BOOK ASSISTANT

FROSTED TURTLE COOKIES

1 1/2 c. all-purpose flour
1/4 t. baking soda
1/4 t. salt
1/2 c. butter, softened
1/2 c. brown sugar, packed

1 egg
1 egg, separated
1/4 t. vanilla extract
1/2 lb. pecan halves (80 halves)

Stir together flour, soda and salt. Beat butter at medium speed with an electric mixer until creamy; gradually add sugar, beating well. Add egg and egg yolk, beating well. Gradually add flour mixture, mixing well. Stir in vanilla. (Dough will be soft.) Cover and chill 30 minutes. Arrange pecan halves in groups of 5 on greased baking sheets to resemble head and legs of a turtle.
Shape dough into 1 1/2-inch balls, using a rounded teaspoonful of dough for each so tips of nuts will show when cookies are baked. Dip bottom of dough into unbeaten egg white and press lightly onto nuts; flatten tops slightly.
Bake at 350 degrees for 12 to 14 minutes. (Do not overbake.) Cool completely on wire racks. Generously spread frosting on top of cookies. Makes 16.

Chocolate Frosting
3 T. butter, softened
1 1/2 c. powdered sugar, sifted

6 T. baking cocoa
1/4 c. whipping cream

Beat butter in a small mixing bowl at medium speed with an electric mixer until creamy. Gradually add sugar, cocoa and whipping cream, beating until smooth. Makes 1 1/8 cups.

SNOW ICE CREAM

1 c. heavy cream
Sugar to taste

Vanilla extract to taste
4 c. clean snow

Beat cream at high speed with an electric mixer until stiff peaks form; add sugar and vanilla to taste. Fold in snow, blending well. Eat immediately or freeze until ice cream has hardened. Serves 4 to 6.

Frosted Turtle
Cookies

Holiday Beef Tenderloin (page 303),
Asparagus with Mushrooms & Bacon
(page 304) and Blue Cheese & Cheddar
Potato Gratin (page 303)

Merry Christmas
menu

Gather your family around the table for a memorable feast filled with heart-warming tradition, good food and lasting memories...it's easy with such savory selections as beef tenderloin and cheesy potatoes and such grand finales as Quick Italian Cream Cake and Chocolate-Macadamia Pie!

Menu for 8

Cheery Cheese Ring

Sweet Potato-Peanut Soup

Spinach & Cranberry Salad

Holiday Beef Tenderloin

Blue Cheese & Cheddar Potato Gratin

Asparagus with Mushrooms and Bacon

Quick Italian Cream Cake

Chocolate-Macadamia Pie

For an extra-special treat, look for vintage cake molds in festive shapes at flea markets and antiques shops in which to shape this cheese spread. Serve strawberry preserves on the side, if you'd like.

CHEERY CHEESE RING

16 oz. sharp Cheddar cheese, finely grated
4 oz. cream cheese, softened
1/4 c. mayonnaise
1 onion, minced

1 c. chopped walnuts
1/4 t. garlic powder
1/8 t. chili powder
1/8 t. hot pepper sauce
1 c. strawberry preserves

Combine all ingredients except strawberry preserves in a large bowl; mix well. Scoop mixture onto a serving platter; wet your hands and shape into a ring. Pour strawberry preserves into the center. Serve with assorted crackers. Serves 12.

SWEET POTATO-PEANUT SOUP

1 T. butter
1/2 large sweet onion, chopped
1 small celery rib, diced
2 carrots, sliced
1/4 t. ground red pepper
1 1/2 lbs. sweet potatoes, peeled and cubed

3 1/4 c. chicken broth
1 c. half-and-half
1/2 c. creamy peanut butter
Nutmeg-Molasses Cream
Chopped toasted peanuts

Melt butter in a large Dutch oven; add onion and next 3 ingredients and sauté over medium heat 3 minutes. Add sweet potato cubes and chicken broth; cook over medium heat 30 minutes, stirring occasionally.
Process mixture, in batches, in an electric blender or food processor until smooth. Return mixture to Dutch oven; whisk in half-and-half and peanut butter. Reduce heat to low and simmer 15 minutes, stirring often. Serve with Nutmeg-Molasses Cream and chopped toasted peanuts. Serves 8.

Nutmeg-Molasses Cream
1 c. whipping cream
3 T. molasses

1/4 t. ground nutmeg

Beat whipping cream at medium speed with an electric mixer until soft peaks form; gradually beat in molasses and nutmeg. Chill until ready to serve. Makes about 2 cups.

Ask a few questions to stir Christmas dinner conversation.
What's a favorite holiday memory? Does anyone have a Christmas wish this year? What about a New Year's wish? Asking questions is a nice way to share sweet memories and catch up with friends & family during this special time of year.

Sweet Potato-
Peanut Soup

Spinach &
Cranberry Salad

SPINACH & CRANBERRY SALAD

2 T. butter or margarine
1 1/2 c. coarsely chopped pecans
1 t. salt
1 t. freshly ground pepper
2 (6-oz.) pkgs. fresh baby spinach

6 slices bacon, crisply cooked and crumbled
1 c. dried cranberries
2 eggs, hard-cooked and chopped
Warm Chutney Dressing

Melt butter in a nonstick skillet over medium-high heat; add pecans and cook, stirring constantly, 2 minutes or until toasted. Remove from heat; add salt and pepper, tossing to coat. Drain pecans on paper towels.
Toss together pecans, spinach, bacon, cranberries and eggs. Drizzle with Warm Chutney Dressing, gently tossing to coat. Serve immediately. Serves 8.

Warm Chutney Dressing

6 T. balsamic vinegar
1/3 c. bottled mango chutney
2 T. Dijon mustard

2 T. honey
2 cloves garlic, minced
1/4 c. olive oil

Cook first 5 ingredients in a saucepan over medium heat, stirring constantly, 3 minutes. Stir in olive oil, blending well; cook one minute. Makes one cup.

HOLIDAY BEEF TENDERLOIN

(pictured on page 298)

1 T. salt
1 1/2 t. onion powder
1 1/2 t. garlic powder
1 1/2 t. black pepper
1 t. ground red pepper
1/2 t. ground cumin

1/2 t. ground nutmeg
5-lb. beef tenderloin, trimmed
1/4 c. olive oil
Garnishes: fresh rosemary sprigs,
    fresh sage sprigs (optional)

Combine first 7 ingredients in a small bowl.
Rub tenderloin with oil; coat with spice mixture. Place in a large roasting pan; cover and chill 8 hours.
Bake at 500 degrees for 15 minutes or until browned. Lower temperature to 375 degrees; bake 20 more minutes or to desired degree of doneness. Let stand 10 minutes; then slice and serve with horseradish mayonnaise. Garnish, if desired. Serves 8.

Nutmeg delivers a hint of sweetness that balances the spiciness from the black and red peppers in this tenderloin. Look for horseradish mayonnaise on the condiment aisle of your local supermarket.

BLUE CHEESE & CHEDDAR POTATO GRATIN

(pictured on page 298)

1/4 c. butter or margarine
1/4 c. all-purpose flour
1 c. whipping cream
1 c. milk
1/2 t. salt
1/2 t. ground white pepper
1/4 t. ground nutmeg
1/2 c. crumbled blue cheese
2 t. minced garlic

1 c. thinly sliced onion, separated
    into rings
2 lbs. red potatoes, peeled and thinly
    sliced
9-oz. pkg. frozen artichoke hearts,
    thawed and drained
1 c. (4 oz.) shredded white Cheddar
    cheese

Melt butter in a heavy saucepan over low heat; add flour, stirring until smooth. Cook, stirring constantly, one minute. Gradually add cream and milk and cook over medium heat, stirring constantly, until mixture is thickened and bubbly. Stir in salt, pepper and nutmeg.
Sprinkle blue cheese and garlic in a lightly greased 13"x9" baking dish. Arrange half of onion rings over blue cheese and garlic; top with half of potato slices. Arrange artichoke hearts over potato slices. Pour half of sauce mixture over artichoke hearts. Repeat layers with remaining onion, potato slices and sauce mixture. Bake, covered, at 350 degrees for one hour. Sprinkle evenly with Cheddar cheese. Bake, uncovered, 15 more minutes or until potatoes are tender. Let stand 10 minutes before serving. Serves 10.

ASPARAGUS WITH MUSHROOMS & BACON

(pictured on page 298)

(pictured on page 298)

A dash of dried crushed red pepper makes the flavor of this side dish lively...not hot.

2 lbs. fresh asparagus
8 slices bacon
3 c. sliced shiitake mushrooms
　(about 7 oz.)
$\frac{1}{4}$ c. chopped shallots
$\frac{1}{8}$ to $\frac{1}{4}$ t. dried crushed red pepper
$\frac{1}{2}$ t. freshly ground black pepper
$\frac{1}{4}$ t. salt

Snap off and discard tough ends of asparagus. Cut asparagus into pieces. Cook in boiling salted water to cover in a Dutch oven over medium-high heat for 4 minutes; drain. Plunge into ice water to stop the cooking process; drain and set aside.

Cook bacon in a large skillet over medium-low heat until crisp; remove bacon and drain on paper towels, reserving 1 $\frac{1}{2}$ tablespoons drippings in skillet. Discard remaining drippings. Crumble bacon.

Sauté mushrooms and shallots in hot drippings over medium-high heat 5 minutes or until shallots are tender. Add asparagus and crushed red pepper; sauté one to 2 minutes or until thoroughly heated. Stir in crumbled bacon, pepper and salt. Serves 8.

QUICK ITALIAN CREAM CAKE

Using a cake mix simplifies this holiday cake. The bonus: all the taste of the traditional method but less time in the kitchen. That's icing on the cake!

18$\frac{1}{4}$-oz. pkg. white cake mix with
　pudding
3 eggs
1 $\frac{1}{4}$ c. buttermilk
$\frac{1}{4}$ c. vegetable oil
3 $\frac{1}{2}$-oz. can flaked coconut
$\frac{2}{3}$ c. chopped pecans, toasted
3 T. rum (optional)
Cream Cheese Frosting
Garnish: pecan halves

Beat first 4 ingredients at medium speed with an electric mixer 2 minutes. Stir in coconut and pecans. Pour batter into 3 greased and floured 9" round cake pans.

Bake at 350 degrees for 15 to 17 minutes or until a wooden toothpick inserted in center comes out clean. Cool in pans on wire racks 10 minutes. Remove from pans and cool completely on wire racks. Sprinkle cake layers evenly with rum, if desired; let stand 10 minutes.

Spread Cream Cheese Frosting between layers and on top and sides of cake. Garnish, if desired. Chill 2 hours before slicing. Serves 12.

Cream Cheese Frosting

1 $\frac{1}{2}$ pkgs. (12 oz.) cream cheese,
　softened
$\frac{3}{4}$ c. butter or margarine, softened
6 c. powdered sugar
1 c. chopped pecans, toasted
2 t. vanilla extract

Beat cream cheese and butter at medium speed with an electric mixer until smooth. Gradually add powdered sugar, beating until light and fluffy. Stir in pecans and vanilla. Makes 4 cups.

Chocolate-
Macadamia Pie

CHOCOLATE-MACADAMIA PIE

4 eggs, lightly beaten
¾ c. light corn syrup
½ c. brown sugar, packed
¼ c. butter or margarine, melted
2 t. Kahlúa or other coffee-flavored liqueur

2 t. vanilla extract
1 c. semi-sweet chocolate chips
7-oz. jar macadamia nuts
1 unbaked 9" pastry shell
Coffee Cream
¼ c. shaved semi-sweet chocolate

This luscious mocha-flavored pie is just as good with pecans as with macadamia nuts, if you'd like to substitute.

Combine first 6 ingredients in a medium bowl; stir well. Stir in chocolate chips and nuts.

Pour into pastry shell; bake at 425 degrees for 10 minutes. Reduce oven temperature to 350 degrees and bake 30 more minutes or until set. (Cover edges of pastry with strips of aluminum foil to prevent excessive browning, if necessary.) Cool completely on a wire rack; cover and chill thoroughly.

To serve, dollop each serving with Coffee Cream and sprinkle with shaved chocolate. Serves 8.

Coffee Cream

1 c. whipping cream
2 T. powdered sugar

2 T. Kahlúa or other coffee-flavored liqueur

Combine all ingredients in a large bowl; beat at high speed with an electric mixer until stiff peaks form. Makes 2 cups.

WE SPENT EVERY CHRISTMAS AT GRANDMA'S. Her table was filled with great Italian dishes, good conversation and close relatives. One year, as we sat down to dinner, Grandma handed me a pen and told me to write my name on her linen tablecloth! She insisted I sign and pass the pen along to the others. The following Christmas Eve, I noticed she had embroidered all our names on that cloth with brightly colored thread. Even though several family members were not there that year, their names reminded us of many good times. Each of us will forever have a special place at our family dinner table. Years have gone by, yet we use that same tablecloth. This year, the tablecloth is well over 20 years old and we still each have our "special" place at the table!

DENISE GIDARO
BADEN, PA

Turkey with Maple Glaze (page 311), Holiday Yams (page 317), Homestyle Green Beans (page 314) and Cornbread Dressing (page 313)

Christmas classics

Memories of foods like your grandmother's dressing or your aunt's

light-as-a-feather yeast rolls always top the list of holiday

gatherings of yesteryear. Here you'll find a treasure of equally

enticing entrées, veggies, dressings...and of course desserts...that

will reward you with rave reviews for years to come.

Best-Ever Baked Ham

BEST-EVER BAKED HAM

8- to 10-lb. smoked fully cooked ham
   half (shank end)
8-oz. jar Dijon mustard

1-lb. pkg. brown sugar
12-oz. can cola-flavored beverage

Remove and discard skin from ham. Score fat on ham in a diamond design; place ham, fat side up, in a 13"x9" baking dish. Coat ham with mustard; pat with brown sugar. Pour cola into dish. Bake, uncovered, at 325 degrees for 2½ to 3 hours or until a meat thermometer inserted into center of ham and not touching fat or bone, registers 140 degrees. (Do not baste.) Remove ham from dish, reserving drippings. Let ham stand.
Meanwhile, bring drippings to a boil in a 1½-quart saucepan over medium-high heat. Reduce heat to medium and simmer, uncovered, 20 minutes or until sauce thickens. Serve sauce with ham. Serves 16 to 18.

Three ingredients are all it takes to make this ham the best ever!

TURKEY WITH MAPLE GLAZE

(pictured on page 308)

12-lb. fresh turkey
1 c. butter, melted
1½ T. salt

2 t. pepper
⅔ c. pure maple syrup

Remove giblets and neck from turkey; reserve for other uses. Rinse turkey with cold water; pat dry. Place in a large roaster, breast-side down, in 2 inches of water. Bake, uncovered, at 350 degrees for one hour.
Turn turkey breast-side up; pour butter over turkey and sprinkle with salt and pepper. Bake, uncovered, 30 minutes; pour maple syrup over turkey and bake 30 more minutes or until a meat thermometer inserted into meaty part of thigh registers 167 degrees or to desired degree of doneness. Transfer turkey to a platter and let stand 30 to 45 minutes before slicing. Serves 10 to 12.

"Leftovers make wonderful sandwiches!"
JO ANN CAIN
PALMYRA, IL

JUICY PRIME RIB

¼ c. black pepper
2 T. ground white pepper
2 T. salt
1½ t. dried thyme

1½ t. garlic powder
1 t. onion powder
8- to 10-lb. boneless beef rib-eye
   roast

Combine first 6 ingredients; rub evenly over surface of roast. Place roast in a shallow roasting pan; insert a meat thermometer into thickest part of roast, making sure it does not touch fat or bone. Bake, uncovered, at 350 degrees for 13 minutes per pound or until thermometer registers 145 degrees (for medium-rare) or 160 degrees (medium). Cover with foil and let stand 15 minutes before carving. Serves 16 to 20.

CUMIN PORK ROAST WITH WILD MUSHROOM SAUCE

Natural juices and browned bits left in the roasting pan form the base of the triple mushroom sauce that accompanies this cumin-scented roast.

3½-lb. boneless center-cut pork loin roast
1 T. ground cumin
1½ t. salt, divided
1¼ t. pepper, divided
2 T. butter or margarine
8-oz. pkg. sliced fresh mushrooms
¼ lb. sliced fresh oyster mushrooms
¼ lb. sliced fresh shiitake mushrooms

½ c. chopped shallots
1 clove garlic, minced
1 T. seeded and minced jalapeño pepper, divided
2 T. chopped fresh cilantro
2 T. chopped fresh oregano
1 t. ground cumin
2 T. all-purpose flour
¼ c. dry sherry
14½-oz. can chicken broth
1 T. butter or margarine

Place roast, fat side up, on a rack in a shallow roasting pan. Cut small slits in roast at ½-inch intervals. Combine one tablespoon cumin, one teaspoon salt and one teaspoon pepper; gently rub seasoning mixture over entire surface of roast.

Bake, uncovered, at 375 degrees for 50 minutes or until a meat thermometer inserted into thickest part registers 160 degrees. Let stand 10 to 15 minutes before slicing. Reserve drippings.

Meanwhile, melt 2 tablespoons butter in a large skillet over medium heat. Add mushrooms, shallots, garlic and one teaspoon jalapeño pepper; sauté 15 minutes or until mushrooms are very tender and beginning to brown. Remove from heat. Stir chopped cilantro, oregano, one teaspoon ground cumin, remaining ½ teaspoon salt and remaining ¼ teaspoon pepper into mushroom mixture; set aside.

Combine flour and sherry in a small bowl, whisking until smooth. Pour reserved drippings into a large skillet. Add chicken broth; bring to a boil and reduce heat to medium. Gradually whisk flour mixture into broth mixture; cook over medium heat until thickened, stirring constantly. Add one tablespoon butter and remaining 2 teaspoons jalapeño pepper; cook, stirring constantly, one minute. Stir in reserved mushroom mixture and cook 5 more minutes, stirring occasionally. Serve roast with sauce. Serves 6.

GRILLED BEEF TENDERLOIN DIABLO

1 1/2 c. dry sherry
2/3 c. dark sesame oil
1/2 c. orange juice
1 small onion, minced
3 cloves garlic, pressed
2 bay leaves
2 T. chopped green onions
1 T. chopped fresh basil
1 T. chopped fresh chives

1 T. chopped fresh oregano
1 T. Worcestershire sauce
1 T. soy sauce
1 t. salt
1 t. pepper
1 1/2 t. hot sauce
4- to 5-lb. beef tenderloin, trimmed
1 c. kosher salt

Combine first 15 ingredients in a large plastic freezer zipping bag. Add tenderloin; seal and chill 8 hours, turning occasionally. Remove tenderloin from marinade, discarding marinade. Roll tenderloin in kosher salt until meat is coated. Grill, covered with grill lid, over medium-high heat (350 degrees to 400 degrees) about 30 to 40 minutes or until a meat thermometer inserted into thickest part of tenderloin registers 145 degrees (medium-rare) or 160 degrees (medium). Serves 8 to 10.

This tenderloin grills up extra juicy with a marinade of sherry and fresh herbs and a coating of kosher salt that seals in the juices.

CORNBREAD DRESSING

(pictured on page 308)

2 c. cornmeal
1/2 c. all-purpose flour
2 t. baking powder
1 t. baking soda
1 t. salt
1 t. sugar (optional)
6 eggs, divided
2 c. buttermilk

2 T. bacon drippings or melted butter
1/2 c. butter or margarine
3 bunches green onions, chopped
4 celery ribs, chopped
16-oz. pkg. herb-seasoned stuffing mix
5 (14 1/2-oz.) cans chicken broth

Combine first 5 ingredients and sugar, if desired, in a large bowl. Stir together 2 eggs and buttermilk; add egg mixture to dry ingredients, stirring just until moistened.
Heat bacon drippings in a 10" cast-iron skillet or 9" round cake pan in a 425 degree oven 5 minutes. Stir hot drippings into batter. Pour batter into hot skillet. Bake, uncovered, at 425 degrees for 25 minutes or until golden; cool and crumble.
Melt butter in a large skillet over medium heat; add green onions and celery and sauté until tender. Stir together remaining 4 eggs in a large bowl; stir in cornbread, onion mixture, stuffing mix and broth until blended. Spoon dressing into one lightly greased 13"x9" baking dish and one lightly greased 9" square baking dish.
Bake 13"x9" dish, uncovered, at 350 degrees for one hour or until lightly browned. Bake 9" square dish, uncovered, 50 minutes or until lightly browned. Serves 12.

Cover and freeze the unbaked dressing up to 3 months, if desired; thaw in the refrigerator for 8 hours and bake as directed.

MAKE-AHEAD MASHED POTATOES

5 lbs. potatoes, peeled, quartered
   and boiled
3-oz. pkg. cream cheese, softened

2 c. sour cream
1 T. butter or margarine, softened
Salt, pepper and paprika to taste

Mash potatoes in a large bowl; blend in cream cheese, sour cream and butter. Add salt, pepper and paprika to taste. Spread in a greased 13"x9" baking dish; cover and chill overnight. Bake, covered, at 350 degrees for 30 minutes. Serves 8 to 10.

BROCCOLI WITH ORANGE SAUCE

1 lb. broccoli, cut into spears
2 T. butter or margarine
1 T. cornstarch
1 c. orange juice, divided
1 T. minced fresh parsley
1 T. lemon juice

1 T. orange zest
1/2 t. dried thyme
1/2 t. dry mustard
1/4 t. pepper
Garnish: orange slices or orange
   zest

Steam broccoli just until tender. In a separate saucepan, melt butter. Add cornstarch and 1/2 cup orange juice, stirring until blended. Stir in remaining orange juice, parsley and next 5 ingredients. Cook over medium heat until mixture thickens; pour over broccoli. Garnish, if desired. Serves 4.

Broccoli gets dressed up for the holidays with a zesty fresh orange sauce.

HOMESTYLE GREEN BEANS

(pictured on page 308)

1 1/2 lbs. fresh green beans, trimmed
1/2 c. balsamic vinegar
1/2 c. dried tomatoes
2 T. minced shallot

2 T. butter or olive oil
2 T. brown sugar
1/4 t. salt
1/8 t. pepper

Cook beans in boiling water to cover 10 minutes or until crisp-tender. Drain and set aside.
Bring vinegar to a boil in a saucepan; remove from heat. Add tomatoes; let stand 10 minutes. Drain tomatoes, reserving vinegar. Coarsely chop tomatoes. Cook shallot in butter in a large skillet over medium heat, stirring constantly, until tender. Add reserved vinegar, tomato, brown sugar, salt and pepper. Cook over low heat until sugar melts, stirring occasionally.
Add beans to skillet and toss gently. Cook just until thoroughly heated. Spoon mixture into a serving bowl. Serves 6.

Apple &
Sausage Stuffing

APPLE & SAUSAGE STUFFING

1 lb. sweet Italian sausage
1 T. vegetable oil
1 large onion, diced
2 celery ribs, chopped
1 apple, peeled, cored and diced

2½ c. water
½ cup butter or margarine, melted
1 lb. herb-seasoned stuffing mix
1 t. fennel seeds

"This is a favorite of ours that your family will love."
CAROL TOMASETTI-RECORDS
WINDHAM, CT

Remove and discard casings from sausage. Brown sausage in a large skillet over medium heat, stirring until sausage crumbles and is no longer pink; drain. Remove sausage to a large bowl. Heat one tablespoon oil in skillet. Sauté onion, celery and apple until tender; remove from heat. Combine water and melted butter in a large bowl. Combine stuffing mix with water and butter; toss lightly until moistened. (You can add more water if you prefer moister stuffing.) Add fennel seeds to stuffing mix and blend. Add stuffing and onion mixture to sausage; mix thoroughly. Place stuffing in a lightly greased 13"x9" pan and bake, uncovered, at 350 degrees for 30 minutes. Serves 8 to 10.

Macaroni au Gratin

MACARONI AU GRATIN

8-oz. pkg. elbow macaroni
   (about 1³/₄ c.)
¹/₄ c. butter or margarine
¹/₄ c. all-purpose flour
2 c. milk
¹/₂ (16-oz.) pkg. process American
   cheese, cubed

1 T. minced onion
¹/₂ t. salt
¹/₂ t. Worcestershire sauce
¹/₄ t. pepper
¹/₄ t. dry mustard
2 T. Italian-seasoned bread crumbs
Butter or margarine

Cook macaroni according to package directions; drain and set aside.
Meanwhile, melt ¹/₄ cup butter in a large heavy saucepan over low heat; whisk
in flour until smooth. Cook one minute, whisking constantly. Gradually whisk in
milk. Cook over medium heat, whisking constantly, until mixture is thickened and
bubbly. Reduce heat and add cheese, onion, salt, Worcestershire sauce, pepper
and mustard; stir until cheese melts. Add macaroni, and mix well.
Divide mixture evenly into 6 (8-ounce) greased ramekins or a greased 2-quart
baking dish. Sprinkle with bread crumbs and dot lightly with additional butter.
Bake, uncovered, at 375 degrees for 20 to 30 minutes. Serves 4 to 6.

HOLIDAY YAMS

(pictured on page 308)

29-oz. can sliced peaches
2 T. cornstarch
²/₃ c. brown sugar, packed
16-oz. can cranberry sauce

1 t. ground cinnamon
¹/₄ c. butter or margarine
2 (40-oz.) cans yams, drained

*"One of my favorite
recipes for holiday
cooking…I can't
get away without
making it!"*

LEAH-ANNE SCHNAPP
EFFORT, PA

Drain peaches, reserving juice. Stir together cornstarch and ¹/₄ cup reserved
juice. Pour remaining juice in a saucepan; stir in brown sugar, cranberry sauce,
cinnamon and butter. Cook over medium heat until butter is melted, stirring
constantly. Add cornstarch mixture; cook until thickened. Add yams and cook
10 minutes. Stir in peaches; cook 5 more minutes. Serves 10 to 12.

REFRESH YOUR COLLECTION OF HOLIDAY SERVING
CONTAINERS…swap them with friends! Invite everyone
to bring two serving dishes, glasses or bowls to a
mix-and-match party to trade. Everyone goes home with
something new.

LANE CAKE

1 c. butter or margarine, softened
2 c. sugar
3 c. sifted cake flour
1 T. plus 1 t. baking powder
³/₄ c. milk

¹/₂ t. vanilla extract
¹/₄ t. almond extract
8 egg whites
Lane Cake Filling
Seven-Minute Frosting

Beat butter at medium speed with an electric mixer until creamy; gradually add sugar, beating well.

Combine flour and baking powder; add to butter mixture alternately with milk, beginning and ending with flour mixture. Beat at low speed after each addition until blended. Stir in extracts.

Beat egg whites at high speed until stiff peaks form; fold into batter. Pour into 3 greased and floured 9" round cake pans.

Bake at 325 degrees for 18 minutes or until a wooden toothpick inserted in center comes out clean. Cool in pans on wire racks 10 minutes; remove from pans and cool completely on wire racks.

Spread Lane Cake Filling between layers and on top of cake. Spread Seven-Minute Frosting on sides of cake. Serves 12.

Lane Cake Filling

¹/₂ c. butter or margarine
8 egg yolks
1¹/₂ c. sugar
1 c. chopped pecans

1 c. chopped raisins
1 c. flaked coconut
¹/₂ c. chopped maraschino cherries
¹/₃ c. bourbon or sherry

Melt butter in a heavy saucepan over low heat. Add egg yolks and sugar; cook, stirring vigorously, until sugar dissolves and mixture thickens (18 to 20 minutes). Remove from heat; stir in pecans and remaining ingredients. Cool completely. Makes 3¹/₂ cups.

Seven-Minute Frosting

1¹/₂ c. sugar
¹/₃ c. warm water
2 egg whites

1 T. light corn syrup
1 t. vanilla extract

Combine first 4 ingredients in top of a large double boiler; beat at low speed with an electric mixer 30 seconds or until blended.

Place over boiling water; beat constantly at high speed 7 to 9 minutes or until stiff peaks form and temperature reaches 160 degrees. Remove from heat. Add vanilla; beat 2 minutes or until frosting is spreading consistency. Makes 4¹/₂ cups.

CHOCOLATE PECAN PIE

½ (15-oz.) pkg. refrigerated
   pie crusts
4 eggs
1 c. light corn syrup
6 T. butter or margarine, melted
½ c. granulated sugar
¼ c. light brown sugar, packed

1 T. vanilla extract
1 c. coarsely chopped pecans
1 c. (6 oz.) semi-sweet chocolate
   chips
Hot fudge topping, warmed
Frozen whipped topping
Chopped chocolate

Pecan pie is elevated to decadent status with the addition of chocolate inside and outside this classic holiday pie.

Fit pie crust into a 9" deep-dish pie plate according to package directions; fold edges under and crimp. Whisk together eggs and next 5 ingredients until mixture is smooth; stir in chopped pecans and chocolate chips. Pour into pie crust. Bake on lowest oven rack at 350 degrees for one hour or until set. Drizzle each serving with hot fudge topping, dollop with whipped topping and sprinkle with chopped chocolate. Serves 8.

Filet Mignon with
Mushrooms
(page 322)
and Roasted
Asparagus
(page 326)

In a wink
of an eye

As the big day draws nigh, you'll savor the

simplicity...and the flavor...of these speedy recipes.

Just take a look at 5-ingredient Mandarin Pork Chops, 20-minute

Stroganoff Skillet and microwave-easy Chocolate-Peanut Butter Fudge.

FILET MIGNON WITH MUSHROOMS

(pictured on page 320)

4 (6-oz.) beef tenderloin filets
½ t. salt
½ t. pepper
½ t. garlic powder

12-oz. pkg. sliced mushrooms
4 cloves garlic, chopped
6 T. Marsala wine

Sprinkle each filet with salt, pepper and garlic powder; set aside.
Coat a large skillet with non-stick vegetable spray and heat to medium-high.
Add mushrooms and garlic; cook for 5 minutes or until mushrooms are golden,
stirring frequently. Remove from heat and set aside.
Arrange filets on a broiler pan about 4 inches from heat. Broil about 4
minutes on each side or to desired doneness.
Meanwhile, reheat mushroom mixture in skillet over medium-high heat. Add
wine to mixture and bring to a boil; cook about 2 minutes or until wine is
reduced. Place each steak on a serving plate and top with mushroom mixture.
Serves 4.

MANDARIN PORK CHOPS

"A terrific dinner party recipe...it's simple and quick but tastes like you spent hours on it."

SUSAN YOUNG
MADISON, AL

1 T. vegetable oil
4 to 6 (1"-thick) pork chops
11-oz. can mandarin oranges, drained

½ t. ground cloves
⅛ t. pepper

Heat oil in a large skillet over medium-high heat; add pork chops. Cook pork
chops 3 to 5 minutes on each side. Top with oranges; sprinkle with cloves and
pepper. Cover and cook over medium heat 15 minutes or until chops are done.
Serves 4 to 6.

PARMESAN BAKED CHICKEN

With a prep time of about 5 minutes, you can have this dish on the table in 25 minutes! While the chicken is baking, cook spaghetti noodles to go alongside.

½ c. mayonnaise-type salad
   dressing
⅓ c. grated Parmesan cheese

¾ t. garlic powder
4 boneless, skinless chicken breasts
¾ c. Italian bread crumbs

Combine salad dressing, cheese and garlic powder in a medium bowl. Coat
chicken with dressing mixture and top with bread crumbs. Arrange chicken on
an ungreased baking sheet. Bake, uncovered, at 425 degrees for 15 to 20
minutes or until lightly golden and chicken is done. Serves 4.

Quick
Salisbury Steak

QUICK SALISBURY STEAK

1 lb. ground beef
1½-oz. pkg. dry onion soup mix
2 eggs, beaten

2 (10¾-oz.) cans golden mushroom
  soup

Combine ground beef, soup mix and eggs in a large bowl; form into 4 patties. Place patties in an ungreased 13"x9" baking dish; cover with soup. Bake, uncovered, at 350 degrees for 35 minutes. Serves 4.

Serve this family favorite over creamy mashed potatoes to soak in the savory mushroom sauce.

Jambalaya

JAMBALAYA

"Feel free to add a
little more hot
pepper sauce if you
like it spicy!"

Patricia Perkins
Shenandoah, IA

2 T. butter or margarine
7-oz. pkg. chicken-flavored
   rice vermicelli mix
2¾ c. water
¼ t. pepper
¼ t. hot pepper sauce

1 T. dried, minced onion
¼ c. diced celery
¼ c. diced green bell pepper
2 c. diced cooked ham
1 lb. cooked, peeled medium-size
   fresh shrimp

Melt butter in a large saucepan over medium heat. Add rice vermicelli mix and
sauté just until golden. Stir in water and next 6 ingredients; reduce heat,
cover and simmer 10 minutes. Add shrimp and cook for 5 minutes or until
thoroughly heated. Serves 4 to 6.

STROGANOFF SKILLET

1 lb. ground round
1 onion, chopped
10¾-oz. can cream of mushroom
    soup

8-oz. container sour cream
1 c. beef broth
½ c. water
3 c. wide egg noodles, uncooked

Brown ground round and onion in a large skillet over medium heat; drain. Gradually add soup and remaining ingredients; bring to a boil. Cover, reduce heat and simmer 10 minutes or until noodles are tender. Serves 4 to 6.

BBQ CHICKEN PIZZA

2 c. cooked and shredded boneless,
    skinless chicken breasts
½ to 1 c. barbecue sauce
1 prebaked pizza crust

1 red onion, sliced
1 green bell pepper, sliced
1 c. shredded mozzarella cheese

Combine chicken and barbecue sauce in a large bowl; spread over pizza crust. Arrange sliced onion and bell pepper over chicken; sprinkle with cheese. Bake at 450 degrees for 10 to 12 minutes or until cheese is melted. Serves 6 to 8.

LINGUINE WITH TOMATO-CLAM SAUCE

2 T. butter or margarine
1 T. minced garlic
1 c. thinly sliced mushrooms
14½-oz. can chicken broth
2 (6½-oz.) cans chopped clams,
    drained and ¾ c. liquid reserved

14½-oz. can diced tomatoes,
    drained
1 t. dried parsley
Salt and pepper to taste
¼ c. white wine or chicken broth
8-oz. pkg. linguine, cooked

Melt butter in a saucepan over medium-high heat. Add garlic and sauté 30 seconds; add mushrooms and sauté one minute. Add broth, clams and reserved liquid and next 4 ingredients; bring to a boil and simmer 5 minutes. Serve sauce over cooked linguine. Serves 4 to 6.

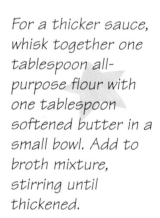

For a thicker sauce, whisk together one tablespoon all-purpose flour with one tablespoon softened butter in a small bowl. Add to broth mixture, stirring until thickened.

ROASTED ASPARAGUS

(pictured on page 320)

(pictured on page 320)

It's best to use fresh asparagus for this recipe because neither frozen nor canned roasts well.

1 lb. fresh asparagus
½ c. vertically sliced onion
½ c. sliced red bell pepper
1 T. olive oil

½ t. dried rosemary
⅛ t. garlic powder
½ T. balsamic vinegar

Place asparagus, onion and red bell pepper in a heavy roasting pan. Toss with oil, rosemary and garlic. Cook, uncovered, at 500 degrees for 10 minutes; drizzle with balsamic vinegar before serving. Serves 4.

SAVORY LIMAS

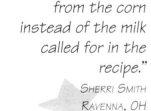

2 (9-oz.) pkgs. frozen baby lima
    beans
6 cloves garlic, chopped

2 T. butter or margarine
½ c. whipping cream
¼ t. salt

Place lima beans and garlic in boiling water to cover. Cook 10 to 12 minutes or until softened; drain. Stir in butter; mash with a potato masher. Add whipping cream and salt and mash until creamy. Serves 4.

CREAMED CORN

"If you have a little extra time, use fresh corn on the cob. Just use the liquid from the corn instead of the milk called for in the recipe."

Sherri Smith
Ravenna, OH

1 c. canned corn
½ t. milk
2 T. sugar
2 slices bacon, crisply cooked,
    crumbled and drippings reserved

3 T. all-purpose flour
½ c. water
Salt and pepper to taste

Combine corn and milk in a medium bowl; add sugar. Place corn mixture, bacon and bacon drippings in a large skillet.
Stir together flour and water in a measuring cup until smooth. Add enough additional water to the measuring cup to equal one cup. Add flour mixture to corn and cook over medium heat 10 to 15 minutes or until mixture is thickened; stir in salt and pepper to taste. Serves 4 to 6.

CHUNKY APPLESAUCE

2 small cooking apples, cored,
    peeled and cubed
½ c. sugar

½ t. ground cinnamon
¼ c. water

Combine first 3 ingredients in a medium-size microwave-safe bowl; add water, stirring gently. Cover and microwave on HIGH (100%) for 7 minutes; stir well. Makes 2 cups.

Roasted Walnut & Pear Salad

ROASTED WALNUT & PEAR SALAD

1 c. walnuts
2 T. butter or margarine, melted
¼ c. brown sugar, packed
1 head romaine lettuce, torn
2 c. thinly sliced pears

2 c. halved grape tomatoes
4-oz. pkg. crumbled blue cheese
8-oz. bottle raspberry white wine
   vinegar salad dressing

Toast walnuts in a medium skillet in butter until golden; add brown sugar and stir over low heat until walnuts are hardened with glaze.
Place lettuce in a large serving bowl; layer with pears and tomatoes. Add walnuts to salad; sprinkle with blue cheese and toss with vinegar dressing. Serves 6 to 8.

"This is a wonderful choice for a formal dinner or a casual, warm family gathering. Use fresh pears for the best flavor."

LAURIE JOHNSON
ROSENBERG, TX

YUMMY GARDEN BREAD

2 (12-oz.) tubes refrigerated
   biscuits
5 slices bacon, crisply cooked and
   crumbled
¼ c. chopped green bell pepper

¼ c. chopped onion
½ c. shredded sharp Cheddar
   cheese
¼ c. butter or margarine, melted

Quarter biscuits and place in a large bowl. Add bacon and remaining ingredients; toss with biscuits to coat. Spoon into a lightly greased 12-cup Bundt pan; bake at 350 degrees for 35 minutes or until lightly browned. Immediately invert onto a platter and serve hot. Serves 8.

"This is a savory version of the popular Monkey Bread."

CARA KILLINGSWORTH
SHAMROCK, TX

Chocolate Chip
Pudding Cake

Merry Treats

• **Invite family & friends to share tried & true favorites** and create a holiday recipe scrapbook...a great gift for a new cook in the family.

• **Surprise a neighbor with sweet treats at the doorstep!** Make a paper cone from vintage gift wrap and hang it from his or her doorknob...fill with candy canes and sweet treats.

• **As a special thanks for delivering Christmas wishes**...leave a tin of homemade goodies in your mailbox for the mail carrier.

• **Package holiday treats in an airtight container,** then slip them into gift bags tied with raffia. Set several in a basket by the door so there will always be a treat waiting for guests to take home.

• **Gather friends & family for a dessert party.** Everyone loves sweets...it's one of the best parts of the holidays!

CHOCOLATE CHIP PUDDING CAKE

3.4-oz. pkg. non-instant chocolate
  pudding mix
2 c. milk
18¼-oz. pkg. chocolate cake mix

12-oz. pkg. semi-sweet chocolate
  chips
Vanilla ice cream

Bring pudding and milk to a boil in a 2-quart saucepan over medium heat, stirring constantly. Remove from heat and stir in cake mix just until blended. Spread mixture into a greased and floured 13"x9" baking dish. Sprinkle evenly with chocolate chips. Bake at 325 degrees for 35 minutes. Serve warm with ice cream. Serves 15.

MOM'S NO-BAKE COOKIES

1 c. sugar
2 T. baking cocoa
¼ c. butter or margarine
¼ c. milk

¼ t. vanilla extract
¼ c. creamy peanut butter
1½ c. quick-cooking oats, uncooked
¼ c. toasted wheat germ

Combine sugar, cocoa, butter and milk in a large saucepan; cook, stirring constantly, over medium heat until sugar is melted. Remove from heat and add vanilla and peanut butter; stir until peanut butter is melted. Add oats and wheat germ to pan; stir until oats are well coated. Drop by tablespoonfuls onto wax paper-lined baking sheets and cool in refrigerator. Makes 2 dozen cookies.

EASIEST PECAN PRALINES

1 lb. box brown sugar
1 c. whipping cream

2 c. pecan halves
2 T. butter

Stir together brown sugar and whipping cream in a 4-quart microwave-safe bowl. Microwave on HIGH (100%) for 5 minutes; stir well. Microwave 4 more minutes; stir well. Microwave one more minute. Remove mixture from microwave; stir in pecan halves and butter. Stir one minute or just until candy starts to lose its luster. Working rapidly, drop by rounded teaspoonfuls onto wax paper; let stand until firm. Makes about 3 dozen.

What could be easier than microwave pralines? Drop the candy onto wax paper quickly before it hardens…a second pair of hands is helpful.

CHOCOLATE-PEANUT NUGGETS

1 T. oil
3 T. baking cocoa
24 oz. white almond bark
12-oz. pkg. semi-sweet chocolate chips

16 oz. unsalted, dry roasted peanuts
16 oz. salted, dry roasted peanuts

Place oil, cocoa, white almond bark and chocolate chips in a 3-quart slow cooker. Cover and cook on low setting 2 hours or until chocolate is melted and smooth. Add peanuts; stir well. Drop by tablespoonfuls onto wax paper; cool. Makes about 8 dozen candies.

CHOCOLATE-PEANUT BUTTER FUDGE

1 c. creamy peanut butter
1 c. butter
1-lb. pkg. powdered sugar

⅛ t. salt
¼ c. baking cocoa
1 t. vanilla extract

Combine peanut butter and butter in a large microwave-safe bowl. Microwave on HIGH (100%) for 2 minutes; stir. Microwave on HIGH 2 more minutes. Add powdered sugar and remaining ingredients; stir until smooth.
Line a 13"x9" pan with plastic wrap; press fudge into pan, smooth top and refrigerate until firm. Cut into bite-size pieces. Makes about 2½ pounds.

No candy thermometer is needed here, making this quick fudge extra easy!

CHOCOLATE ICE BOX PIE

5-oz. bar chocolate candy
12-oz. container frozen whipped topping, thawed

6-oz. chocolate pie crust

Place candy in a small microwave-safe bowl. Microwave on HIGH (100%) for 2 minutes or until melted, stirring once. Fold in whipped topping. Spoon chocolate mixture into pie crust; chill 3 hours or until firm enough to slice. Serves 6 to 8.

Turkey-Cheddar-
Broccoli Strata
(page 333)

Second Time
around

You can reinvent holiday leftovers into scrumptious meals for the rest of the
year with these clever recipes. Slice the leftover bird to roll Cranberry-Turkey
Wraps, chop the rest of the ham for Ham-Stuffed Baked Potatoes or use
extras from both entrées to stir up creamy Use-Your-Noodle Casserole.

Turkey-Walnut
Salad

ITALIAN BREAD SALAD

4 c. cubed Italian bread, toasted
3 tomatoes, diced and juice
    reserved
1 red onion, diced

1¾ c. chopped fresh basil leaves
1 c. olive oil
Salt and pepper to taste

Combine bread cubes, tomatoes and reserved juice, onion and basil in a large serving bowl. Add olive oil and toss to coat. Add salt and pepper to taste. Serves 10.

TURKEY-WALNUT SALAD

2 c. chopped cooked turkey
½ c. dried cranberries
½ c. light mayonnaise
¼ c. chopped walnuts, toasted
3 T. chopped fresh parsley
2 T. Dijon mustard

2 stalks celery, sliced
1 small red onion, chopped
    (about ½ c.)
¼ t. salt
¼ t. freshly ground pepper
Mixed salad greens

Stir together first 10 ingredients in a large bowl. Cover and chill at least 30 minutes. Serve over salad greens. Serves 10.

TURKEY-CHEDDAR-BROCCOLI STRATA

(pictured on page 330)

1 T. butter or margarine, softened
½ (12-oz.) pkg. French bread loaves,
    cubed
2 c. chopped cooked turkey
10-oz. pkg. frozen broccoli flowerets,
    thawed and chopped
½ c. diced celery
2 c. (8 oz.) shredded sharp Cheddar
    cheese

6 eggs, lightly beaten
2 c. milk
3 T. all-purpose flour
1 t. salt
1 t. curry powder
1 t. dry mustard
1 t. Worcestershire sauce
½ t. pepper

Grease bottom and sides of 7 (10-ounce) custard cups with butter. Layer half each of bread cubes, turkey, broccoli, celery and Cheddar cheese in custard cups; repeat layers, ending with Cheddar cheese.
Whisk together eggs and next 7 ingredients in a large bowl; pour evenly over cheese, pressing down lightly to absorb liquid. Cover and chill 8 hours.
Bake, uncovered, at 350 degrees for 30 minutes or until golden. Let stand 10 minutes before serving. Serves 7.

You can also make this in a 13"x9" baking dish…just adjust the baking time to 45 minutes.

CRANBERRY-TURKEY WRAPS

"Try dipping these wraps in extra cranberry sauce, too!"

LYNN WILLIAMS
MUNCIE, IN

1/2 c. water
1/2 c. brown sugar, packed
1/3 c. granulated sugar
1/4 c. cider vinegar
2 c. cranberries
1/2 c. raisins
1/2 c. chopped sweet onion
1 T. fresh ginger, peeled and finely chopped
1/2 t. red pepper flakes

2 (3-oz.) pkgs. cream cheese, softened
1 1/2 c. shredded sharp white Cheddar cheese
1 t. curry powder
6 (10") flour tortillas
1 1/2 lbs. cooked turkey slices
1/2 c. fresh cilantro, chopped and divided
6 T. chopped walnuts, divided

Add water, sugars and vinegar to a heavy saucepan; cook over medium heat until sugars dissolve, stirring often. Stir in cranberries, raisins, onion, ginger and red pepper; bring to a boil and cook 5 to 10 minutes until mixture thickens, stirring occasionally. Cool; cover and chill.

Combine cream cheese, Cheddar cheese and curry powder in a small bowl; stir well. Spread about 3 tablespoons cheese mixture over 2/3 of each tortilla, leaving a one-inch border; top with several turkey slices. Spread 2 to 3 tablespoons cranberry mixture on top; sprinkle with one heaping tablespoon cilantro and one tablespoon walnuts. Roll up tortillas starting with filled side, folding sides in; wrap tightly in parchment paper or aluminum foil. Arrange wraps on a baking sheet; bake at 350 degrees for 5 to 10 minutes or just until warm. Slice wraps in half diagonally and arrange on a serving plate; serve warm. Serves 6.

HOLIDAY LEFTOVERS CASSEROLE

You can use chicken instead of turkey in this recipe and enjoy it all year long. Substitute one jar of diced red bell peppers for the jar of pimentos, if desired.

7-oz. pkg. spaghetti, broken into 2" pieces
2 c. chopped cooked turkey
3/4 c. diced ham
2-oz. jar diced pimento, drained
1/4 c. minced green bell pepper
1/4 small onion, grated

10 3/4-oz. can cream of mushroom soup
1/2 c. chicken or turkey broth
1/8 t. celery salt
1/8 t. pepper
1 1/2 c. (6 oz.) shredded Cheddar cheese, divided

Cook spaghetti according to package directions in a large Dutch oven; drain well and return spaghetti to pot.

Stir in turkey and next 8 ingredients; cook 7 minutes or until thoroughly heated. Remove from heat and stir in one cup cheese. Pour into a lightly greased 8" square baking dish. Sprinkle evenly with remaining 1/2 cup cheese. Bake, uncovered, at 350 degrees for 15 minutes or until cheese melts. Serves 4 to 6.

Cranberry-Turkey
Wraps

EASY TURKEY POT PIE

"An irresistible way to turn leftover turkey into a meal."

KATHY MILLER
EASTON, PA

1 ½ c. frozen mixed corn, peas and carrots
1 ½ c. chopped cooked turkey
2 (10¾-oz.) cans cream of chicken soup

1 c. biscuit baking mix
¾ c. milk
1 egg

Stir together vegetables, turkey and soup; pour into an ungreased 9" pie pan. Combine baking mix, milk and egg in a medium bowl; pour over vegetable mixture and stir. Bake, uncovered, at 400 degrees for 35 minutes. Serves 8.

FIESTA TURKEY SOUP

1 medium onion, diced
1 t. vegetable oil
1 clove garlic, minced
3 c. chopped cooked turkey or chicken
15-oz. can chili beans
3 ½ c. chicken or turkey broth
11-oz. can whole kernel corn with red and green bell peppers, drained

10-oz. can diced tomatoes and green chiles
½ t. chili powder
½ t. ground cumin
⅛ t. salt
⅛ t. pepper
Toppings: sour cream, shredded Mexican 4-cheese blend

Sauté onion in hot oil in a large Dutch oven over medium heat 7 minutes or until tender. Add garlic and sauté one minute. Stir in turkey and next 8 ingredients. Bring to a boil, stirring occasionally; reduce heat and simmer 15 minutes. Serve with desired toppings. Serves 8.

USE-YOUR-NOODLE CASSEROLE

"Feeling creative in the kitchen, I pulled out all my tasty leftovers, tossed them together and invented this super casserole!"

JASON KELLER
CARROLLTON, GA

2 T. butter or margarine
2 T. all-purpose flour
1 c. milk
½ c. cubed cooked ham
½ c. cubed cooked chicken
1 c. cooked wide egg noodles

¼ c. chopped celery
¼ t. salt
¼ t. pepper
¼ c. shredded Cheddar cheese
Paprika to taste (optional)

Melt butter in a large saucepan over low heat; stir in flour and heat until bubbly. Slowly add milk, stirring constantly, until mixture is thick and smooth. Remove from heat; stir in ham, chicken, noodles, celery, salt and pepper. Transfer to an ungreased 1 ½-quart casserole dish. Bake at 400 degrees for 15 minutes. Sprinkle with cheese and, if desired, paprika. Bake 5 to 10 more minutes or until cheese is bubbly. Serves 4.

Ham-Stuffed
Baked Potatoes

HAM-STUFFED BAKED POTATOES

4 large potatoes (about 3 lbs.)
1 T. butter or margarine
3 c. chopped cooked ham
1 small onion, diced
2 cloves garlic, minced

½ c. sour cream
¼ t. salt
¼ t. pepper
¾ c. shredded Parmesan cheese
Garnish: chopped fresh chives

Bake potatoes at 450 degrees for one hour or until tender. Allow to cool to touch.

Cut potatoes in half lengthwise; scoop out pulp and place in a bowl, leaving shells intact. Set aside pulp and shells.

Melt butter in a small skillet over medium-high heat; add chopped ham, diced onion and minced garlic and sauté until onion is tender.

Mash potato pulp; stir in ham mixture, sour cream, salt and pepper. Stuff shells evenly with potato mixture; sprinkle evenly with Parmesan cheese. Place in a 13"x9" baking dish or pan. Bake, uncovered, at 350 degrees for 25 to 30 minutes. Garnish, if desired. Serves 8.

Baking Basics

• Let butter and eggs stand at room temperature before use but for no longer than 20 minutes for food safety reasons.

• Standard mixers on a stand are commonly used to test cakes. If you use a handheld mixer to mix your pound cake batter, beat the batter a few extra minutes. And if you're using a heavy-duty mixer, be sure not to overbeat it...use a shorter mixing time to accommodate this powerful mixer.

Foolproof Fudge

• Make fudge on a dry day for best results. The candy may have a more sugary texture on a humid day.

• Use a heavy saucepan; the thick sides and bottom will help conduct heat evenly.

• Use a clip-on candy thermometer and read it at eye level.

• Don't scrape sides of pan clean when pouring out fudge... this could lead to grainy fudge.

LEFTOVER POTATO PANCAKES

16-oz. pkg. frozen whole kernel corn, thawed
1 small onion, finely chopped
½ c. chopped green onions
2 t. vegetable oil
2 c. mashed potatoes

½ c. all-purpose flour
2 eggs, lightly beaten
¾ t. salt
½ t. freshly ground pepper
Salsa

Cook first 3 ingredients in hot oil in a large non-stick skillet over medium-high heat, stirring constantly, until crisp-tender. Remove from heat.
Combine mashed potatoes, flour and eggs, stirring well; stir in corn mixture, salt and pepper.
Lightly grease a large skillet. Place skillet over medium heat until hot. Drop mixture by rounded tablespoonfuls into skillet; cook 3 minutes on each side or until golden, wiping skillet with a paper towel as necessary. Drain; serve with salsa. Makes 14 pancakes.

SPICED EGGNOG POUND CAKE

1 c. butter, softened
3 c. granulated sugar
6 eggs
3 c. sifted cake flour
¾ t. baking powder
½ t. salt
1 c. refrigerated or canned eggnog
2 t. vanilla extract

2 T. brandy (optional)
1 t. ground cinnamon
¾ t. freshly grated nutmeg
½ t. ground allspice
¼ t. ground cloves
Powdered sugar
1 c. sifted powdered sugar
2 T. plus 1 t. whipping cream

Generously grease and flour a 12-cup Bundt® pan; set aside.
Beat butter at medium speed with an electric mixer about 2 minutes or until creamy. Gradually add granulated sugar, beating 5 to 7 minutes. Add eggs, one at a time, beating just until yellow disappears.
Combine flour, baking powder and salt. Add to butter mixture alternately with one cup eggnog, beginning and ending with flour mixture. Beat at low speed just until blended after each addition. Stir in vanilla and, if desired, brandy.
Pour half of batter into prepared pan. Stir cinnamon and next 3 ingredients into remaining batter. Spoon spice batter over plain batter. Swirl batters together, using a knife.
Bake at 350 degrees for 50 to 55 minutes or until a long toothpick inserted in center comes out clean. Cool in pan on a wire rack 15 minutes. Remove cake from pan; cool on wire rack. Place cake on a cake plate; dust with powdered sugar.
Combine one cup powdered sugar and whipping cream, stirring until smooth. Drizzle glaze over cake. Serves 16.

Eggnog Fudge

EGGNOG FUDGE

2 c. sugar
1 c. refrigerated eggnog
2 T. butter
2 T. light corn syrup
¼ c. chopped pecans, toasted

¼ c. slivered almonds, toasted and chopped
½ c. chopped red candied cherries
1 t. vanilla extract

Line an 8"x4" loaf pan with aluminum foil; butter foil and set aside. Combine first 4 ingredients in a 4-quart heavy saucepan. Cook over medium heat, stirring constantly, until mixture comes to a boil. Wash down crystals from sides of pan, using a pastry brush dipped in hot water. Insert a candy thermometer into eggnog mixture. Cook, stirring occasionally, until thermometer registers 238 degrees. Remove pan from heat and cool sugar mixture, undisturbed, until temperature drops to 190 degrees (15 to 18 minutes).
Stir in pecans and remaining 3 ingredients; beat with a wooden spoon until fudge thickens and just begins to lose its gloss (5 to 8 minutes). Pour candy into prepared pan. Cool completely; cut into squares. Makes about 1½ pounds.

Candied cherries and toasted nuts flavor this creamy fudge that's made with leftover eggnog.

Weekend Beef Burgundy
(page 347)

Potluck
pleasers

Hosting a potluck where everyone brings a favorite dish makes holiday get-togethers oh-so memorable! Whether you're the host or you're simply attending, mouthwatering casseroles like Hot Chicken Salad, Cajun Seafood Fettuccine and Ziti with Spinach & Cheese will have everyone wanting the recipes!

Mom's Broccoli
Casserole

MOM'S BROCCOLI CASSEROLE

2 (12-oz.) pkgs. fresh broccoli
   flowerets
2 c. fresh cauliflower flowerets
1 c. sliced carrots
½ c. butter or margarine, melted
10¾-oz. can cream of mushroom
   soup

1 c. mayonnaise
1 c. shredded sharp Cheddar cheese
½ c. chopped onion
1 c. crushed round buttery crackers
   (about 18 crackers)

Bring a large pot of water to a boil; add broccoli, cauliflower and carrots. Boil 3 to 4 minutes or until vegetables are crisp-tender. Drain and set aside. Pour melted butter into a 13"x9" baking dish; add cooked vegetables and set aside. Mix together soup, mayonnaise, cheese and onion in a medium bowl. Spread mixture over vegetables; top with crushed crackers. Bake, uncovered, at 350 degrees for 30 minutes. Serves 8.

"Mom was such a good cook, she could take nothing and turn it into something delicious! She was a truly wonderful lady."
JOAN MELO
DOYLESTOWN, PA

OLD-FASHIONED POTATO CASSEROLE

28-oz. pkg. frozen hashbrowns with
   onions and peppers
2 (10¾-oz.) cans cream of chicken
   soup

16-oz. container sour cream
2 c. shredded Cheddar cheese
2 c. crushed corn flake cereal
½ c. butter or margarine, melted

Spread hashbrowns in a lightly greased 13"x9" baking dish. Stir together soup and sour cream; spread on top of hashbrowns. Sprinkle with cheese; top with crushed corn flakes and drizzle with butter. Bake, uncovered, at 350 degrees for 30 to 35 minutes. Serves 6 to 8.

If you're packing a hot dish for a potluck, keep it hot for travel by wrapping the dish first in foil, then in several layers of newspaper.

HOT CHICKEN SALAD

¼ c. butter or margarine
½ c. chopped onion
4-oz. jar pimentos
6-oz. pkg. slivered almonds
⅓ green bell pepper, diced
4-oz. can mushroom pieces, drained

1 c. chopped celery
4 c. diced cooked chicken
1 c. mayonnaise
10¾-oz. can cream of celery soup
1 t. salt
1 c. crushed corn flake cereal

Melt butter in a large skillet over medium-high heat. Add onion and next 5 ingredients; sauté until vegetables are tender. Place in an ungreased 13"x9" baking dish. Add chicken, mayonnaise, soup and salt; stir well. Sprinkle with crushed corn flakes; bake, uncovered, at 350 degrees for 30 minutes. Serves 8.

"A tried & true favorite recipe that's been shared with 3 generations."
LYNNE DAVISSON
CABLE, OH

SHOEPEG & GREEN BEAN CASSEROLE

2 (7-oz.) cans shoepeg corn, drained
14½-oz. can green beans, drained
10¾-oz. can cream of celery soup
1 c. sour cream

1 c. shredded Cheddar cheese
1 c. crushed round buttery crackers
   (about 18 crackers)
¼ c. butter or margarine, melted

Stir together corn, beans, soup, sour cream and cheese; spread in a greased
2-quart baking dish. Top with cracker crumbs; drizzle with melted butter. Bake,
uncovered, at 350 degrees for one hour or until golden. Serves 6 to 8.

CAJUN SEAFOOD FETTUCCINE

"Sometimes this casserole serves only 4 in my family!"

SHELIA COLLIER
KINGWOOD, TN

¾ c. butter or margarine
2 (10-oz) pkgs. frozen seasoned
   vegetable blend
1 T. Cajun seasoning
½ t. garlic powder
¼ c. all-purpose flour
¼ c. water
16-oz. pkg. processed cheese, cubed

2 c. half-and-half
1½ lbs. medium-size fresh shrimp,
   peeled and deveined
1½ lbs. lump crabmeat, shell pieces
   removed
12-oz. pkg. fettuccine, cooked
1 c. shredded colby-Jack cheese

Melt butter in a large Dutch oven; add vegetables and sauté 5 minutes or
until tender. Sprinkle with Cajun seasoning and garlic powder; set aside.
Combine flour and water; stir well. Add flour mixture to Dutch oven; stir well.
Stir in cubed cheese and half-and-half; continue stirring until cheese is
melted. Add shrimp and crabmeat to vegetable mixture; let simmer on
medium-low heat for 5 minutes. Stir in fettuccine; pour into an ungreased
13"x9" baking dish. Sprinkle with colby-Jack cheese. Bake, uncovered, at 350
degrees for 20 minutes. Let stand 15 minutes before serving. Serves 8.

Create a family cookbook! At your next family potluck, have everyone
share their favorite recipes and any memories or even photos that go with the
recipes. The copy shop can easily make copies and bind them...everyone will want one!

Shoepeg & Green Bean
Casserole

Ziti with
Spinach & Cheese

ZITI WITH SPINACH & CHEESE

*"Three types of
cheese are added to
this ziti casserole!"*

KAREN PILCHER
BURLESON, TX

2 (10-oz.) pkgs. frozen chopped
   spinach, cooked and drained
15-oz. container ricotta cheese
3 eggs, beaten
2/3 c. grated Parmesan cheese
1/4 t. salt

1/4 t. pepper
16-oz. pkg. ziti pasta, cooked
26-oz. jar spaghetti sauce
2 t. dried oregano
16-oz. pkg. shredded mozzarella
   cheese

Combine spinach, ricotta cheese, eggs, Parmesan cheese, salt and pepper; set
aside.
Combine pasta, spaghetti sauce and oregano; place half the pasta mixture in
an ungreased 13"x9" baking dish. Layer with spinach mixture and mozzarella.
Add remaining pasta mixture. Cover with aluminum foil and bake at 375
degrees for 25 minutes. Uncover and bake 10 more minutes or until bubbly.
Remove from the oven and let stand for about 10 minutes before serving.
Serves 8.

TURKEY, ALMOND & WILD RICE CASSEROLE

1 onion, chopped
2 T. butter or margarine
½ c. all-purpose flour
2 (4½-oz.) cans sliced mushrooms,
　　drained and liquid reserved
3 c. half-and-half
½ c. chicken broth
2 c. prepared long-grain and wild rice

6 c. cubed cooked turkey
1 c. slivered almonds, toasted
½ c. diced pimentos
Salt and pepper to taste
¼ c. butter or margarine, melted
1 c. dry bread crumbs
¼ c. chopped fresh parsley

Sauté onion in butter in a saucepan over medium heat; remove from heat and
stir in flour. Set aside.
Combine reserved mushroom liquid with half-and-half and enough broth to
make 4 cups. Gradually stir into flour mixture; cook, stirring until thickened.
Add rice, mushrooms, turkey, toasted almonds, pimentos, salt and pepper.
Place in a lightly greased 13"x9" baking dish; set aside. Combine butter, bread
crumbs and parsley; sprinkle over top of casserole. Bake, uncovered, at 350
degrees for 40 minutes. Serves 6 to 8.

WEEKEND BEEF BURGUNDY

(pictured on page 340)

2 lbs. cubed stew beef
2 (10¾-oz.) cans cream of
　　mushroom soup
2.4-oz. pkg. herb and garlic soup mix
1 small onion, chopped

1 t. beef bouillon granules
2 (4½-oz.) cans sliced mushrooms,
　　drained
1 c. Burgundy wine or beef broth
6 c. cooked egg noodles

Combine first 5 ingredients in a large bowl; mix well. Spread mixture in a lightly
greased 13"x9" baking dish; bake, covered, at 325 degrees for 2 hours. Add
mushrooms and wine; bake 10 more minutes. Serve over noodles. Serves 8 to 10.

*"Try this easy dish
on a Saturday or
Sunday...it takes
some time to bake,
but it's well worth
the wait!"*

VIRGINIA WATSON
SCRANTON, PA

EARLY IN DECEMBER I get together with a group of 10 to
15 good friends for an ornament exchange and holiday
potluck. Everyone brings a homemade ornament and a
tasty dish to share, along with the recipe. It's a wonderful
afternoon as we sit around a toasty fire to exchange
ornaments, enjoy delicious food and chat about our holiday
plans. When the day's over, everyone goes home with several
handmade ornaments, new recipes to try and the spirit of
Christmas in their hearts.

KATHY FOX
EASTON, MD

ANYTIME ENCHURRITOS

2 c. shredded cooked turkey
1 1/2 c. salsa, divided
8-oz. container sour cream
2 to 3 T. diced green chiles
6 (8") flour tortillas

10 3/4-oz. can cream of chicken soup
2 c. shredded Mexican-blend cheese
Toppings: shredded lettuce, chopped tomatoes (optional)

Combine turkey, 1/2 cup salsa, sour cream and chiles. Spoon turkey mixture into tortillas; roll up and place seam-side down in an ungreased 13"x9" baking dish. Blend together soup and remaining salsa; pour over tortillas. Bake, uncovered, at 350 degrees for 30 minutes. Sprinkle with cheese and bake 5 more minutes or until cheese is melted. Top with shredded lettuce and chopped tomatoes, if desired. Serves 6 to 8.

NUTTY PUDDING CAKE

18 1/4-oz. pkg. yellow cake mix
4 (3.5-oz.) cups butterscotch
     pudding
2 eggs

1/3 c. sugar
1 c. butterscotch chips
1 c. sliced almonds

Combine first 3 ingredients in a bowl; spread in a greased and floured 13"x9" pan. Sprinkle top with sugar, butterscotch chips and almonds; bake at 375 degrees for 28 minutes or until a wooden toothpick inserted in center comes out clean. Serves 10 to 12.

CHRISTMAS IS A VERY SPECIAL TIME OF YEAR FOR MY FAMILY.
For two complete days, we get to spend almost every waking moment together. Over the years my grandmother kept a journal of our Christmas celebrations. She wrote down what we ate, what went on, what time Santa Claus arrived and even that special toy all the children loved. This past Christmas we received the best Christmas present ever. She gave each family a personal copy of our memories… so many things happened that we had almost forgotten. We were so thrilled by this sweet book of memories and will continue to add to it each year.

NICOLE ANDERSON
WARREN, OH

Anytime
Enchurritos

Buttermilk
Pound Cake

BUTTERMILK POUND CAKE

1/2 c. butter or margarine, softened	3 c. all-purpose flour
1/2 c. shortening	1/8 t. salt
2 c. sugar	2 t. lemon extract
4 eggs	1 t. almond extract
1/2 t. baking soda	Fresh strawberries
1 c. buttermilk	

Beat butter and shortening at medium speed with an electric mixer 2 minutes or until creamy. Gradually add sugar, beating 5 to 7 minutes. Add eggs, one at a time, beating just until yellow disappears.

Dissolve soda in buttermilk. Combine flour and salt; add to butter mixture alternately with buttermilk mixture, beginning and ending with flour mixture. Beat at low speed after each addition just until blended; stir in extracts.

Pour batter into a greased and floured 10" tube pan. Bake at 350 degrees for one hour or until a wooden toothpick inserted in center comes out clean. Cool in pan on a wire rack 10 to 15 minutes; remove from pan and cool completely on a wire rack. Garnish with fresh strawberries. Serves 14.

THE DAY AFTER THANKSGIVING, I welcomed the holiday season with a unique celebration. Instead of my usual weekly "girls-night-out," I opted for a "girls-night-in" and hosted a Potpourri-Making Party. I asked each person to bring two ingredients...one purchased and one found around the house or yard. Each was also asked to bring a special treat in the form of food or drink to share with the group. We had a fire, drank champagne, nibbled on shrimp, laughed, told stories and had a great time while we mixed up two huge bowls of Christmas and kitchen potpourris. Everyone left the party with generous samples of each potpourri to use themselves or to give as gifts. I think they also left feeling a little pampered before the holiday season began.

JOANNE MARTIN-ROBINSON

Store-bought items to choose:
- cinnamon sticks
- cinnamon oil
- bay leaves
- rosemary
- ground orris root
- whole allspice
- whole nutmeg
- star anise
- lemon balm
- balsam or fir oil

Things found around the house:
- orange, lemon and lime peels
- homegrown herbs & spices
- dried apple & orange slices
- large pinecone chunks
- tiny pinecones
- pine needles
- holly berries
- cranberries
- bayberry
- juniper
- cedar
- boxwood

Grapefruit Margaritas (page 355),
Sassy Shrimp (page 363) and
Roasted Red Pepper Bruschetta
(page 359)

Christmas
open house

Open your home to family & friends during the holidays
for good cheer, merry treats and festive fun. Sweet-tart sips
of Grapefruit Margaritas and savory bites of appetizers, such as
Crab Rangoon and Roasted Red Pepper Bruschetta, will encourage your
guests to linger as you celebrate this merry season together.

CINNAMON HOT CHOCOLATE

¼ c. baking cocoa	3 c. milk
¼ c. sugar	1 cinnamon stick
1 c. boiling water	1 t. vanilla extract

Combine cocoa and sugar in a heavy saucepan. Slowly add boiling water; bring to a boil and boil for 2 minutes. Add milk and cinnamon stick. Reduce heat and simmer for 10 minutes. Remove cinnamon stick and add vanilla; stir quickly to froth milk. Makes 4 cups.

CRANBERRY HOT TODDIES

16-oz. can jellied cranberry sauce	⅛ t. ground cloves
⅓ c. light brown sugar, packed	⅛ t. salt
¼ t. ground cinnamon	2 c. water
¼ t. ground allspice	2 c. pineapple juice
⅛ t. ground nutmeg	2 T. butter or margarine, sliced

Empty cranberry sauce into a large saucepan. Whisk in sugar and seasonings; add water and pineapple juice. Cover and simmer for about 2 hours. Pour into mugs and top each mug with a pat of butter. Makes 6 cups.

SPICED HOT BUTTERED RUM PUNCH

½ c. butter or margarine, softened	½ t. vanilla extract
½ c. brown sugar, packed	3½ c. boiling water
½ t. ground cloves	1¼ c. spiced rum
½ t. ground cinnamon	Garnish: 3" cinnamon sticks

Combine first 5 ingredients in a small bowl, stirring until smooth. Cover and chill until ready to serve.
To serve, combine butter mixture, boiling water, and rum in a small punch bowl, stirring until butter mixture melts. Serve warm with cinnamon-stick stirrers, if desired. Makes 5½ cups.

SPICED COFFEE-EGGNOG PUNCH

2 c. strong brewed coffee
1½ (3") cinnamon sticks
6 whole allspice
6 whole cloves
2 (32-oz.) cans eggnog, chilled

1 T. vanilla extract
1 c. whipping cream, whipped
1 qt. vanilla ice cream, softened
Ground nutmeg

Combine first 4 ingredients in a saucepan. Bring to a boil; reduce heat and simmer, uncovered, for 15 minutes. Pour coffee mixture through a wire-mesh strainer into a bowl, discarding spices; chill.
Combine coffee mixture, eggnog and vanilla in a large bowl; fold in whipped cream. Spoon softened ice cream into a punch bowl. Pour eggnog mixture over ice cream and stir gently. Sprinkle punch with ground nutmeg. Makes 11 cups.

APPLE-CINNAMON PUNCH

1 c. water
½ c. sugar
½ c. red cinnamon candies

2 (2-ltr.) bottles raspberry ginger
   ale, chilled
46-oz. can apple juice, chilled

Combine water, sugar and candies in a small saucepan; bring to a boil. Reduce heat and simmer, uncovered, for 5 minutes or until candies melt; stir occasionally. When mixture has cooled, combine with ginger ale and apple juice; stir well. Makes 25 cups.

Everyone will enjoy this punch...it has a great spicy taste!

GRAPEFRUIT MARGARITAS

(pictured on page 352)

6-oz. can frozen limeade
   concentrate
⅔ c. ruby red grapefruit juice

⅔ c. white tequila
¼ c. orange liqueur
Sparkling sugar

Combine first 4 ingredients in an electric blender, adding crushed ice to 5-cup level; process just until slushy. Pour into a pitcher and serve immediately, or cover and freeze. To serve, wet the rims of stemmed glasses and dip in sparkling sugar. Makes 3½ cups.

If you want slushy margaritas for a crowd, make several batches in advance and freeze until ready to serve. There's no need to thaw them; just stir and serve.

CHEDDAR FONDUE

"Dip bread cubes of all varieties and apple & pear slices into this dreamy fondue!"

LORI STEEN
ALOHA, OR

¼ c. butter
¼ c. all-purpose flour
½ t. salt
¼ t. pepper
¼ t. dry mustard

¼ t. Worcestershire sauce
1½ c. milk
2 c. (8 oz.) shredded Cheddar cheese

Melt butter in a saucepan. Whisk in flour, salt, pepper, mustard and Worcestershire sauce until smooth; gradually add milk. Bring to a boil; cook 2 minutes or until thickened, stirring often. Reduce heat; add cheese, stirring until melted. Transfer to fondue pot or slow cooker to keep warm. Makes 2½ cups.

CHRISTMAS BRIE

"This looks so festive and takes a short time to prepare...serve with lots of crunchy baguette rounds."

CLAYNETTE HEMKE
PORTLAND, OR

8-oz. pkg. Brie cheese
½ c. sun-dried tomatoes, minced
½ c. minced fresh parsley

5 cloves garlic, minced
2 T. olive oil

Carefully remove and discard the rind from top of cheese; set cheese aside. Combine tomatoes and remaining 3 ingredients in a microwave-safe bowl; microwave on HIGH (100%) for 2 to 3 minutes or until garlic has softened. Spread over top of cheese; microwave on HIGH for 45 seconds or until cheese melts. Serves 6 to 8.

CHUNKY GORGONZOLA DIP

Make this dip a day ahead and chill. Then let stand at room temperature 15 minutes before serving.

8-oz. carton mascarpone cheese
⅓ c. sour cream
⅓ c. chopped fresh chives
½ t. salt

¼ t. ground white pepper
4 oz. Gorgonzola cheese, crumbled
Garnish: chopped fresh chives

Combine mascarpone cheese and sour cream in a small bowl; stir with a wooden spoon until smooth. Stir in chives, salt and pepper. Gently stir in Gorgonzola cheese, leaving dip chunky. Garnish, if desired. Serve dip with sliced apples and pears, crackers and toasted walnuts. Makes 2 cups.

Cheddar Fondue

Florentine
Artichoke Dip

FLORENTINE ARTICHOKE DIP

To get 1¹/₂ cups
French bread
crumbs for this
recipe, tear off a
piece of a baguette.
Pulse in a food
processor until
coarse crumbs
form. Measure
crumbs, tear off
another chunk and
repeat procedure
until you get
1¹/₂ cups.

10-oz. pkg. frozen chopped spinach,
  thawed
12-oz. jar marinated artichoke
  hearts, drained and chopped
1¹/₂ (8-oz.) pkgs. cream cheese,
  softened
1 c. freshly shredded Parmesan
  cheese

¹/₂ c. mayonnaise
3 large cloves garlic, pressed
2 T. lemon juice
1¹/₂ c. French bread crumbs
  (homemade)
2 T. butter or margarine, melted

Drain spinach; press between layers of paper towels to remove excess moisture.
Combine spinach, artichoke hearts and next 5 ingredients in a bowl, stirring well.
Spoon into a lightly greased 11"x7" baking dish. Combine bread crumbs and
butter; sprinkle over spinach mixture.
Bake, uncovered, at 375 degrees for 25 minutes. Serve with assorted crackers,
bagel chips or bread sticks. Makes 4 cups.

SMOKY NUTS

1/4 c. honey
2 T. sugar
2 T. chipotle peppers with 1 t. pepper
    liquid, puréed

1 1/2 c. pecan halves
1 1/2 c. whole almonds
Salt

Instead of using both pecans and almonds, you can also use 3 cups of any one type of nut for this recipe.

Combine first 3 ingredients in a medium saucepan. Cook over medium heat until sugar dissolves, stirring often. Stir in nuts.

Spread coated nuts in a single layer in a lightly greased 15"x10" jelly roll pan. Bake at 300 degrees for 20 minutes; stir and bake 10 to 15 more minutes. Spread warm nuts onto aluminum foil or parchment paper; separate nuts with a fork. Lightly sprinkle with salt; cool. Store nuts between layers of parchment paper or wax paper in an airtight container up to 3 days. Makes 3 1/2 cups.

ROASTED RED PEPPER BRUSCHETTA

(pictured on page 352)

12-oz. jar roasted red bell peppers,
    drained well and finely chopped
1/2 c. finely chopped plum tomato
1/4 c. finely chopped red onion
2 T. balsamic vinegar
2 T. olive oil
1/2 t. salt
1/2 t. freshly ground pepper

Dash of sugar
1 baguette, cut diagonally into
    24 slices
1/4 c. olive oil
Salt and pepper
1/2 c. crumbled garlic-and-herb-
    flavored feta cheese

Combine first 3 ingredients in a bowl. Combine vinegar, 2 tablespoons olive oil, 1/2 teaspoon salt, 1/2 teaspoon pepper and sugar; pour over pepper mixture and toss well. Cover and chill until ready to serve.

Arrange baguette slices on a large ungreased baking sheet. Brush or drizzle slices with 1/4 cup oil; sprinkle with salt and pepper. Bake at 400 degrees for 4 minutes or until barely toasted.

Spoon about one tablespoon roasted pepper mixture onto each toast; top each with crumbled feta. Broil 5 1/2 inches from heat 3 minutes or until bubbly and barely browned. Serve warm. Makes 2 dozen.

CRANBERRY MEATBALLS

2 lbs. ground beef
1 t. parsley flakes
2 T. soy sauce
½ t. garlic salt
2 T. chopped onion

1 c. uncooked quick-cooking oats
2 eggs, beaten
¼ t. pepper
⅓ c. catsup

Combine all ingredients in a large bowl. Roll into 2-inch balls; arrange in a shallow baking pan. Bake at 350 degrees for 25 minutes; drain. Spoon sauce over meatballs and bake 15 more minutes. Makes 42 meatballs.

Sauce
16-oz. can jellied cranberry sauce
12-oz. bottle chili sauce

½ c. brown sugar, packed
1 T. lemon juice

Whisk together all ingredients in a medium bowl. Makes 3 cups.

HOT ANTIPASTO SQUARES

2 (8-oz.) cans crescent rolls, divided
¼ lb. thinly sliced cooked ham
¼ lb. thinly sliced Swiss cheese
¼ lb. thinly sliced salami
¼ lb. thinly sliced provolone cheese

¼ lb. thinly sliced pepperoni
2 eggs, beaten
7-oz. jar roasted red bell peppers,
    drained and chopped
3 T. grated Parmesan cheese

Unroll one can of crescent rolls; press into an ungreased 13"x9" pan, sealing edges. Layer the meats and cheeses in the order given; lightly press down. Combine eggs, peppers and Parmesan cheese in a small mixing bowl; pour over pepperoni layer. Unroll remaining crescent rolls; shape into a 13"x9" rectangle, pressing seams together gently. Carefully place on top of the egg mixture. Bake at 375 degrees for 30 minutes. Cool; cut into one-inch squares to serve. Makes about 5 dozen.

CLEVER PARTY FAVORS Purchase mini candy canes in the long, clear cellophane wrappers (the kind that are usually hanging on display racks). Tie on red and green bows between the candy canes. Hang them on the wall by your front door, along with a small pair of scissors. As guests leave, cut off a candy cane for them to take with them. You can also do this with small homemade gingerbread men. Simply wrap them in a long strip of plastic wrap.   LISA GLENN

Cranberry Meatballs

CHICKEN FINGERS WITH APPLE BUTTER-PEANUT SAUCE

1 lb. skinned and boned chicken
   breasts
¼ c. all-purpose flour
1 t. salt
½ t. pepper
1 egg, beaten

⅓ c. milk
½ c. Italian-seasoned bread crumbs
¼ c. sesame seeds
¼ t. salt
3 T. butter or margarine, melted
Apple Butter-Peanut Sauce

Cut chicken into ¼-inch lengthwise strips. Combine flour, one teaspoon salt and pepper in a large zip-top plastic bag. Add chicken strips, seal bag and shake to coat.
Combine egg and milk in a shallow dish, stirring well. Combine bread crumbs, sesame seeds and ¼ teaspoon salt in a shallow dish. Dip chicken strips in egg mixture and dredge in bread crumb mixture. Place in a lightly greased 13"x9" baking dish; drizzle with butter.
Cover and bake at 425 degrees for 20 minutes; uncover and bake 18 to 20 more minutes or until done. Serve with Apple Butter-Peanut Sauce, using short wooden skewers. Makes 10 appetizer servings.

Apple Butter-Peanut Sauce

½ c. creamy peanut butter
⅓ c. apple butter
1¼ c. chicken broth

1 T. freshly grated ginger
¼ t. salt

Combine all ingredients in a small saucepan over medium-high heat. Bring just to a boil; reduce heat and simmer, uncovered, 2 minutes or until thickened, stirring constantly. Remove from heat; cool. Serve at room temperature. Makes 1¾ cups.

MY FAMILY ARE CHRISTMAS CRAZIES! We start celebrating the Saturday after Thanksgiving by writing out our Christmas cards. We then have a party every weekend until Christmas. All the parties have a theme and we even give away door prizes! Last year we had a snowflake card party and decorated old mailboxes to store our cards in. In the past we have each decorated a door in my grandparents' house! The season doesn't end until New Year's Eve with a movie, game playing and pizza party. We are a family of 25 and every Christmas Eve is spent at my grandparents' house. All of this started when my husband and I first married and had our first child. Money was tight and we couldn't afford a lot of decorations. The relatives showed up and we created homemade decorations... paper chains and popcorn strings!

VIRGINIA HAGERMAN
JOLO, WV

Add a bit of elegance to your holiday open house...
type up the menu and place in a gold frame. Place at the beginning of the buffet table
with a bit of holly tucked into the frame.

CRAB RANGOON

8 oz. pasteurized crabmeat
12 oz. cream cheese, softened
¼ t. garlic powder
¼ t. seasoned salt

16-oz. pkg. won ton wrappers
  (3½" squares)
Oil for deep-frying

Combine first 4 ingredients in a medium bowl; mix well. Spoon about 2 teaspoons crab mixture into the center of each won ton; brush edges with water. Fold and pinch corners, completely enclosing filling.
Pour oil into a Dutch oven, filling at least half full; heat to 350 degrees over medium-high heat. Fry won tons, in batches, in hot oil 2 to 3 minutes or until golden. Drain on paper towels; serve immediately. Makes about 4 dozen.

"Serve these yummy appetizers by themselves or with your favorite dipping sauce, such as duck or plum sauce. They're also great with your favorite chicken dish!"
SUSIE BACKUS
GOOSEBERRY PATCH

SASSY SHRIMP

(pictured on page 352)

6 c. water
2 lbs. unpeeled, medium-size fresh
  shrimp
½ c. lemon juice
¼ c. vegetable oil
2 cloves garlic, crushed
1 bay leaf, crumbled
1 T. dry mustard
1 T. red wine vinegar
2 t. salt

½ t. paprika
Dash of ground red pepper
3¼-oz. can whole pitted ripe olives,
  drained
1 medium-size red onion, thinly
  sliced
1 lemon, thinly sliced
2-oz. jar diced pimentos, drained
2 T. chopped fresh parsley

Bring water to a boil; add shrimp and cook 3 to 5 minutes or until shrimp turn pink. Drain well; rinse with cold water. Peel shrimp and devein, if desired. Set aside.
Combine lemon juice and next 8 ingredients in a large bowl; stir with a wire whisk until blended. Add olives, onion, lemon, pimentos and parsley; stir well. Add shrimp; toss to coat. Cover and marinate in refrigerator one to 4 hours. Makes 8 appetizer servings.

Cream Cheese
Scrambled Eggs
(page 373),
Pears with Cranberry
Relish (page 367),
Crispy Brown Sugar
Bacon (page 370)
and Sunshine in a
Glass (page 366)

Breakfasts &
brunches

Rise and shine to the cinnamon aroma of Hot Percolator Punch.
If that doesn't get you going, then try a slice of hearty Savory Ham & Swiss
Breakfast Pie or nibble on a slice of Simple Citrus Coffee Cake. Whether
you're hosting a brunch or serving breakfast on Christmas morning, these
eye-opening selections are guaranteed to jump-start your day.

HOT PERCOLATOR PUNCH

This classic punch sends an inviting cinnamon aroma throughout your house as it perks. It's easily doubled if you're serving a large crowd and you have a party-size percolator.

3 c. unsweetened pineapple juice
3 c. cranberry-apple juice drink
1 c. water
⅓ c. light brown sugar, packed
2 lemon slices

2 (4") cinnamon sticks, broken
1½ t. whole cloves
Additional cinnamon sticks
   (optional)

Pour juices and water into a 12-cup percolator. Place brown sugar and next 3 ingredients in percolator basket. Perk through complete cycle of electric percolator. Serve with cinnamon sticks as stirrers, if desired. Makes 7 cups.

SUNSHINE IN A GLASS

(pictured on page 364)

1 c. frozen orange juice concentrate,
   partially thawed
½ c. milk

10 to 12 ice cubes
1 t. vanilla extract

Place ingredients in an electric blender; blend until smooth. Makes 2½ cups.

HOT VANILLA

"This is a warm and creamy change from hot cocoa!"

VICKIE

1 c. milk
1 t. honey

⅛ t. vanilla extract
⅛ t. ground cinnamon

Heat milk until very hot but not boiling in a saucepan. Pour milk into a mug. Add honey, vanilla and cinnamon. Mix well and serve immediately. Makes one cup.

WARM SPICED FRUIT

20-oz. plus 8-oz. cans pineapple
   chunks, juice reserved
29-oz. can sliced peaches, drained
29-oz. can pear halves, quartered
   and drained

¾ c. brown sugar, packed
¼ c. butter or margarine
2 (3") cinnamon sticks
½ t. ground ginger

Combine pineapple, peaches and pears; spoon into a 3½-quart baking dish. Stir together brown sugar, butter, cinnamon, ginger and reserved pineapple juice in a saucepan; bring to a boil. Reduce heat and simmer 5 minutes; discard cinnamon sticks. Pour juice over fruit and bake, uncovered, at 350 degrees for 30 minutes or until heated through. Serves 10 to 12.

PEARS WITH CRANBERRY RELISH

(pictured on page 364)

2 large Braeburn apples, cored and
    quartered
12-oz. pkg. fresh cranberries
1 lemon, quartered and seeded

1½ c. sugar
8 Bartlett pears, halved lengthwise
    and cored

Process apples in a food processor until well chopped; remove and place in a medium bowl. Add cranberries and lemon to food processor and process until well chopped; stir into apples. Add sugar, stirring well. Cover and chill 2 to 3 hours. Spoon relish into the pears and serve immediately. Serves 16.

A melon baller or grapefruit spoon is a great tool to use when removing the core from halved pears.

CAN'T-FAIL BISCUITS

2 c. self-rising flour

1 c. whipping cream

Mix together flour and whipping cream (dough will be stiff). Turn dough out onto a lightly floured surface and knead 10 to 12 times.
Roll dough to ½-inch thickness; cut with a 2-inch biscuit cutter. Place on a lightly greased baking sheet; bake at 450 degrees for 10 to 12 minutes or until lightly browned. Makes about one dozen.

"A really easy biscuit recipe. Tasty when spread with jams or honey."
ARLENE GRIMM
DECATUR, AL

CHOCOLATE GRAVY FOR BISCUITS

2½ c. sugar
¼ c. all-purpose flour
¼ c. baking cocoa

3 c. milk
1 t. vanilla extract
1 T. butter

Bring sugar, flour, cocoa and milk to a boil in a large saucepan. Reduce heat and simmer for 13 minutes or until thick and bubbly, stirring every 2 to 3 minutes. Stir in vanilla and butter. Serve over warm biscuits. Makes 4½ cups.

WE VISIT MY HUSBAND'S AUNT IN GEORGIA EVERY CHRISTMAS SEASON. Biscuits with Chocolate Gravy is one of my favorite memories. This recipe has been a tradition in my husband's family for at least 4 generations now! The men like it so much that they put the chocolate gravy over everything…eggs, bacon, sausage and pancakes.

KELLY SUMMERS
JEFFERSON, OH

CHEESE BISCUITS

2 c. self-rising flour
1 t. dry mustard
6 T. shortening

1 c. (4 oz.) shredded sharp Cheddar
   cheese
¾ c. buttermilk

Stir together flour and mustard; cut in shortening with a pastry blender until mixture is crumbly. Stir in cheese. Add buttermilk, stirring until dry ingredients are moistened. Turn dough out onto a lightly floured surface and knead 3 or 4 times. Roll dough to ¾-inch thickness; cut with a 2-inch biscuit cutter. Place biscuits on a lightly greased baking sheet. Bake at 450 degrees for 10 to 12 minutes or until lightly browned. Makes one dozen.

A little mustard boosts the cheese flavor in these quick biscuits. To get a head start, grate the cheese the night before.

SOUR CREAM TWISTS

¼-oz. pkg. active dry yeast
¼ c. warm water (100 degrees to
   110 degrees)
1 c. shortening, melted
8-oz. container sour cream
1 t. salt
1 t. vanilla extract
2 eggs

3½ c. all-purpose flour
1 c. granulated sugar
1 t. ground cinnamon
2 c. powdered sugar
2 t. vanilla extract
½ c. butter, melted
2 T. heavy whipping cream

Combine yeast and water in a small bowl; let stand 5 minutes.
Combine shortening, sour cream, salt and vanilla in a medium bowl; stir in yeast mixture and eggs. Stir in flour and mix well. Cover and chill 2 hours.
Combine granulated sugar and cinnamon in a small bowl. Roll out dough on a lightly floured surface into a 15"x10" rectangle. Sprinkle dough with ⅓ cup cinnamon-sugar mixture. Fold rectangle in thirds, like a letter. Roll dough into another 15"x10" rectangle; sprinkle with ⅓ cup cinnamon-sugar mixture. Fold rectangle into thirds again. Repeat entire procedure one more time, finishing with a 15"x10" rectangle. Cut final rectangle into 4"x1" strips; twist 2 times. Place twists one inch apart on greased baking sheets; bake at 400 degrees for 10 minutes.
Combine powdered sugar and remaining 3 ingredients, stirring well; drizzle glaze over warm twists. Makes about 4 dozen.

"My mom used to greet me at the door with these when I came home from school, but they're perfect anytime!"

EMILY FLAKE
COLORADO SPRINGS, CO

Blueberry-Croissant
French Toast

BLUEBERRY-CROISSANT FRENCH TOAST

1 c. half-and-half
2 eggs
⅓ c. granulated sugar
¼ c. milk
1 t. ground cinnamon
¼ t. salt

8 T. blueberry preserves, divided
4 croissants, sliced horizontally
½ c. butter or margarine, divided
2 c. blueberries
Toppings: maple syrup, powdered
    sugar

Combine first 6 ingredients in a bowl. Pour mixture into a 13"x9" baking dish;
set aside.

Spread 2 tablespoons preserves on each of 4 croissant halves; top with
remaining halves. Arrange croissants on top of egg mixture; turn to coat. Set
aside until liquid is absorbed, about 45 minutes; turn often.

Melt ¼ cup butter in a 12" skillet over medium heat; add 2 croissants and cook
until golden on both sides. Transfer croissants to serving plates and keep warm.
Wipe skillet clean; repeat with remaining ¼ cup butter and 2 croissants. Add
blueberries to skillet; cook for 3½ minutes or until heated thoroughly. Spoon
berries over croissants; serve with desired toppings. Serves 4.

*"Enjoy this simple
twist on a favorite
breakfast classic."*
Jo Ann

SIMPLE CITRUS COFFEE CAKE

¼-oz. pkg. active dry yeast	18¼-oz. pkg. white cake mix
½ c. warm water (100 degrees to 110 degrees)	3 eggs
	¼ c. orange juice
½ c. all-purpose flour	2 T. butter, melted
1 c. light brown sugar, packed	1 c. powdered sugar
1 T. ground cinnamon	½ t. grated orange zest
¼ c. butter, softened	2 T. orange juice

Combine yeast and warm water in a one-cup glass measuring cup; let stand 5 minutes.

Meanwhile combine flour, brown sugar and cinnamon. Cut in ¼ cup butter with a pastry blender or 2 forks until mixture resembles cornmeal; set aside.

Combine yeast mixture, cake mix and next 3 ingredients in a large mixing bowl; beat at low speed with an electric mixer just until moistened. Beat at medium speed 2 more minutes.

Pour half the batter into a greased and floured 12-cup Bundt® pan. Sprinkle brown sugar mixture over batter. Top with remaining batter.

Bake at 350 degrees for 35 minutes or until a wooden toothpick inserted in center comes out almost clean. Cool in pan on a wire rack 15 minutes; remove from pan and cool 15 minutes or until cake is just warm.

Combine powdered sugar, orange zest and 2 tablespoons orange juice, stirring until smooth; drizzle over cake. Serve warm. Serves 12 to 15.

CRISPY BROWN SUGAR BACON

(pictured on page 364)

1 lb. thick sliced hickory-smoked bacon slices	1 c. light brown sugar, packed
	1 T. cracked black pepper

Cut bacon slices in half. Combine sugar and pepper in a shallow dish. Dredge bacon in sugar mixture, shaking off excess. Twist each bacon slice, if desired. Place bacon in a single layer on a lightly greased baking rack in an aluminum foil-lined baking pan. Bake at 425 degrees for 20 to 25 minutes or until crisp. Allow bacon to cool before serving. Serves 6.

Family coming for a holiday brunch?

Copy one of Grandma's tried & true recipes onto a festive card, then punch a hole in the corner and tie the card to a napkin with a length of ribbon...a sweet keepsake.

Simple Citrus
Coffee Cake

SAVORY HAM & SWISS BREAKFAST PIE

1 2/3 c. water
1 c. whipping cream
2 cloves garlic, pressed
2 T. butter or margarine
1 t. salt
1/4 t. pepper
2/3 c. uncooked quick-cooking grits

1 1/4 c. (5 oz.) shredded Swiss
   cheese, divided
8 eggs, divided
1 T. vegetable oil
1/2 lb. cooked ham, diced
4 green onions, chopped
1/2 c. milk
Garnish: fresh chives

Bring first 6 ingredients to a boil in a saucepan; gradually whisk in grits. Cover,
reduce heat and simmer 5 to 7 minutes, whisking occasionally. Add 1/2 cup
cheese, stirring until cheese melts. Remove from heat; let stand 10 minutes.
Lightly beat 2 eggs and stir into grits mixture; pour into a greased 10" deep-dish
pie plate.
Bake at 350 degrees for 20 minutes; remove from oven. Increase temperature
to 400 degrees.
Sauté ham and onions in vegetable oil in a nonstick skillet over medium-high heat
5 minutes or until onion is tender. Layer ham mixture evenly over grits crust.
Whisk together milk and remaining 6 eggs; pour over ham mixture. Sprinkle
remaining 3/4 cup cheese evenly over egg mixture.
Bake at 400 degrees for 35 minutes. Let stand 10 minutes and cut into
wedges. Garnish, if desired. Serves 8.

CREAM CHEESE SCRAMBLED EGGS

(pictured on page 364)

12 eggs
1 c. half-and-half or milk
2 (3-oz.) pkgs. cream cheese, cubed
¾ t. salt

¼ t. pepper
¼ c. butter or margarine
Chopped fresh chives

Process first 5 ingredients in a blender until frothy, stopping to scrape down sides. Melt butter in a large heavy skillet over medium heat; reduce heat to medium-low. Add egg mixture and cook, without stirring, until mixture begins to set on bottom. Draw a spatula across bottom of skillet to form large curds. Continue cooking until eggs are thickened but still moist; do not stir constantly. Sprinkle with chives. Serves 6 to 8.

Stir the eggs only a few times during cooking. Stirring constantly makes them dry and crumbly.

SAUSAGE-FILLED CRÊPES

1 lb. ground sausage, browned
¼ c. diced onion
1½ c. shredded American cheese
3-oz. pkg. cream cheese, softened
3 eggs, beaten
1 c. milk

1 T. vegetable oil
1 T. water
1 c. all-purpose flour
½ t. salt
½ c. sour cream
¼ c. butter or margarine, softened

Combine first 4 ingredients until blended; set aside. Whisk together eggs, milk, oil and water. Stir in flour and salt. Lightly grease a 7" skillet and place over medium-high heat. Add 3 tablespoons of batter to pan; quickly tilt to coat bottom. Cook 3 minutes or until edges are golden and lift easily. Turn and cook 3 minutes. Repeat procedure with remaining batter. Place 3 tablespoons sausage mixture down the center of each crêpe; roll up and place in a greased 13"x9" baking dish. Bake, uncovered, at 375 degrees for 20 minutes. Combine sour cream and butter; spoon over crêpes. Bake, uncovered, 5 minutes. Serves 9.

"Enjoy a glass of freshly squeezed orange juice with these savory crêpes!"
RENAE REU
LUVERNE, MN

CREAMY CRAB BAKE

1 lb. lump crabmeat, shell pieces
    removed
8-oz. pkg. shredded sharp Cheddar
    cheese
2 c. seasoned croutons
2 c. milk

2 eggs, lightly beaten
1 T. dried, minced onion
1 T. dried parsley
½ t. salt
¼ t. pepper
¼ c. grated fresh Parmesan cheese

Combine first 9 ingredients in a bowl. Spoon into a lightly greased 11"x7" baking dish; sprinkle with Parmesan cheese. Bake, uncovered, at 325 degrees for 50 minutes or until a knife inserted into the center comes out clean. Serves 8.

White Chicken Chili
(page 382)

Heartwarming Soups & stews

Soup's on and it's never been tastier! For a crowd, ladle up bowls full of White Chicken Chili…it makes over 20 cups! Or snuggle in on a cold evening with Cream of Tomato Soup and grilled cheese sandwiches. Whether you're serving a big group or just your family, these soups & stews deliver comfort for the appetite and the soul.

LOBSTER & CHIVE BISQUE

This fancy bisque is laced with chunks of savory lobster, flavored with sherry and thickened with cream for a velvety taste and texture.

3 T. butter
1 T. minced onion
3 T. all-purpose flour
3 c. milk
1 c. heavy whipping cream

1/2 c. dry sherry
1 t. salt
1/8 t. paprika
1 c. cooked lobster (about 5 oz.)
2 T. chopped fresh chives

Melt butter in a Dutch oven over medium heat; add onion and sauté one minute or until tender. Add flour, stirring until blended. Cook one minute, stirring constantly. Gradually add milk and next 4 ingredients. Bring just to a simmer; cook, uncovered, 5 minutes or until slightly thickened (do not boil). Stir in lobster and chives. Makes 5 cups.

BISTRO ONION SOUP

4 large onions (about 2 lbs.), sliced
1/4 c. butter or margarine, melted
2 T. all-purpose flour
5 1/4 c. water
1/2 c. dry white wine
1/2 c. dry red wine
4 chicken bouillon cubes

4 beef bouillon cubes
2 bay leaves
1/2 t. salt
1/2 t. dried sage
1/4 t. pepper
8 (1/2") diagonally sliced French
   bread slices, toasted
8 slices Gruyère cheese

Sauté onion in butter in a Dutch oven over medium heat 15 minutes or until golden, stirring often. Stir in flour; cook one minute. Add water and next 8 ingredients. Bring to a boil; reduce heat and simmer, partially covered, 30 minutes. Discard bay leaves.
Ladle soup into 4 individual oven-proof soup bowls. Place on a baking sheet. Add 2 bread slices to each bowl and cover with 2 slices cheese. Broil 5 1/2 inches from heat 2 minutes or until cheese is bubbly. Serve immediately. Makes 6 cups.

Note: Equal amounts of chicken broth and beef broth can be substituted for the white and red wine, but omit the 1/2 teaspoon of salt.

There's nothing more cozy than a bowl of warm soup.
For extra comfort, warm up oven-safe bowls in a 200-degree oven before filling… the soup (and the guests) will stay warmer longer!

Bistro
Onion Soup

BAKED POTATO SOUP

4 large baking potatoes
⅔ c. butter or margarine
⅔ c. all-purpose flour
7 c. milk
4 green onions, sliced
12-oz. pkg. bacon, cooked and crumbled
1¼ c. (5 oz.) shredded Cheddar cheese

8-oz. container sour cream
¾ t. salt
½ t. pepper
Garnish: additional shredded Cheddar cheese, cooked and crumbled bacon, sliced green onions

Bake potatoes at 400 degrees for one hour or until done; cool. Cut potatoes in half lengthwise; scoop out pulp and reserve. Discard shells.
Melt butter in a Dutch oven over low heat. Whisk in flour until smooth. Cook one minute, stirring constantly. Gradually whisk in milk; cook over medium heat 10 minutes, whisking constantly, until mixture is thickened and bubbly.
Stir in potato pulp and green onions; bring to a boil. Cover, reduce heat and simmer 10 minutes. Add bacon and next 4 ingredients; stir until cheese melts. Garnish, if desired. Serve immediately. Makes 14 cups.

Soup Pointers

• **Make your soups ahead.** Many soups take on a richer flavor if made a day ahead...it gives the flavors time to blend.

• **To remove fat from soups,** either use a bulb baster or wrap an ice cube in damp cheesecloth and skim it over the soup's surface. The fat will firm up on contact and is easily removed. Or cover and chill the soup overnight. The fat will solidify on top and can be lifted off.

• **Soup too salty?** Drop a peeled, raw potato into the pot and let it cook for a few minutes. Remove the potato just before serving the soup.

• **To prevent mushy vegetables,** add the quicker-cooking foods, such as carrots or canned vegetables, after the meat is tender. Cook them until fork-tender, about 15 minutes.

• **To freeze,** package soups & stews in pint or quart plastic freezer containers or heavy-duty plastic freezer bags; label, date and freeze up to 3 months.

CHRISTMAS EVE OYSTER-CORN CHOWDER

1 large onion, chopped
2 celery ribs, chopped
¼ c. butter, melted
2 new potatoes, cut into ¼" cubes
2 medium carrots, cut into ¼"
   slices
¼ c. chopped fresh flat-leaf parsley

3 c. half-and-half, divided
7-oz. can cream-style corn
1 t. salt
½ t. sugar
¼ t. freshly ground pepper
1 to 2 (12-oz.) containers fresh
   oysters, undrained

Sauté onion and celery in butter in a Dutch oven over medium heat until tender. Add potatoes, carrots and parsley; cook one minute. Add 2 cups half-and-half and bring to a boil. Reduce heat and simmer, uncovered, 15 minutes or until potatoes are tender. Stir in remaining one cup half-and-half, corn and remaining ingredients. Bring to a boil; reduce heat and simmer, uncovered, 5 minutes or until edges of oysters curl. Serve immediately. Makes 8 cups.

CREAM OF TOMATO SOUP

3 lbs. plum tomatoes
2 T. butter or margarine
1 onion, coarsely chopped
1 clove garlic, minced
2 T. chopped fresh tarragon leaves
½ t. allspice
½ t. sugar

¼ t. salt
6 c. chicken broth
1 T. tomato paste
1 t. orange zest
1 c. whipping cream
Garnish: fresh chives, snipped

"Grilled cheese sandwiches are a must with this creamy soup."
CONNIE BRYANT
TOPEKA, KS

Bring 4 quarts water to a boil in a 6-quart Dutch oven. Cut an "X" in bottom of tomatoes with a small paring knife. Scald tomatoes, about one pound at a time, in hot water one minute or until skins begin to split; plunge into cold water. Drain, peel and coarsely chop.
Melt butter in Dutch oven over medium-low heat. Add onion and cook about 10 minutes or until softened. Add garlic, tarragon, allspice, sugar and salt; cook, stirring for one minute. Add tomatoes, chicken broth and tomato paste to the pot; bring to a boil. Reduce heat to medium, partially cover and simmer for 30 minutes. Stir in orange zest and cool for 20 minutes. Purée the soup, in batches, in a blender or food processor. Return to Dutch oven, stir in cream and heat thoroughly over low heat. Do not boil. Garnish with chives and serve. Makes 11 cups.

HEARTY HAM & BEAN SOUP

"I keep a mix of dried beans on hand to use for soup and to give as gifts. Just put the beans in a jar and tie on the recipe!"

KATHLEEN WESTBY
LANSING, MI

1/4 c. dried black beans
1/4 c. dried red beans
1/4 c. dried pinto beans
1/4 c. dried navy beans
1/4 c. dried black-eyed peas
1/4 c. dried Great Northern beans
1/4 c. dried lentils
1/4 c. dried split peas
2 qts. water

2 (8-oz.) pkg. diced cooked ham
1 large onion, chopped
1 clove garlic, minced
1 t. salt
14 1/2-oz. can diced tomatoes
10-oz. can tomatoes and green
   chiles, undrained
1/4 c. barley

Sort and wash beans; place in a Dutch oven. Cover with water 2 inches above beans; let soak overnight.

Drain beans. Add 2 quarts water, ham, onion, garlic and salt. Cover and bring to a boil. Reduce heat and simmer 1 1/2 hours or until beans are tender. Add tomatoes and remaining ingredients; simmer 30 minutes, stirring occasionally. Makes 12 1/2 cups.

CHICKEN SOUP WITH WILD RICE & MUSHROOMS

2 T. butter or margarine
2 small onions, diced
3 carrots, diced
3 celery ribs, diced
2 cloves garlic, minced
1 c. wild rice, uncooked
8 c. chicken broth

2 bay leaves
1 t. dried thyme
2 1/2 c. chopped cooked chicken
8 oz. pkg. sliced mushrooms
1/2 c. white wine
1/2 t. salt
1/2 t. pepper

Melt butter in a large stockpot; add onions, carrots, celery and garlic. Sauté until vegetables are tender. Add rice, broth and herbs. Simmer, covered, for one hour. Add chicken and remaining ingredients. Discard bay leaves. Makes 12 cups.

Delight family & friends with a "snowman" soup supper.

Using three plates, place the smallest at the top and largest at the bottom of each place setting. Decorate your snowman "face" with cheese cubes, oyster crackers or croutons; use a roll for his tummy and a bowl of soup for his base.

3-Bean Ravioli
Minestrone

3-BEAN RAVIOLI MINESTRONE

1 T. olive oil
1 onion, chopped
2 carrots, chopped
2 celery ribs, sliced
2 cloves garlic, minced
3 (14-oz.) cans chicken broth
9-oz. pkg. frozen baby lima beans,
   thawed
16-oz. can light red kidney beans,
   rinsed and drained

16-oz. can garbanzo beans, rinsed
   and drained
2 (14½-oz.) cans diced tomatoes
2 t. Italian seasoning
1 t. pepper
½ t. salt
7-oz. pkg. mini cheese ravioli
Shredded Parmesan cheese

Combine first 13 ingredients in a large stockpot. Cover and simmer 30
minutes. Add ravioli and cook 10 minutes or until tender. Serve with shredded
fresh Parmesan cheese. Makes 14 cups.

TORTILLA SOUP

For a heartier soup, add chopped, cooked chicken breasts.

6 (14½-oz.) cans chicken broth
2 (4.5-oz.) cans diced mild green
   chiles, drained
2 cloves garlic, minced
⅓ c. chopped fresh mint
1 t. chili powder
1 t. ground cumin
Red pepper flakes to taste

1 c. chopped tomatoes
2 avocados, pitted, peeled and
   chopped
4 slices bacon, cooked and crumbled
½ c. plus 2 t. chopped fresh cilantro,
   divided
Tortilla chips, slightly crushed
Sour cream

Combine first 7 ingredients in a large Dutch oven; bring to a boil. Cover, reduce heat to low and simmer for about one hour.
Meanwhile, combine tomatoes, avocados, bacon and ½ cup cilantro in a small bowl. To serve, ladle broth into individual soup bowls; place a scoopful of tomato mixture onto each and top with tortilla chips, sour cream and remaining cilantro. Serve immediately. Makes 12 cups.

TACO SOUP

"Try lime-flavored tortilla chips with this soup… yummy!"
SUSAN NAFZIGER
CANTON, KS

1½ lbs. ground chuck
1 medium onion, chopped
1.25-oz. pkg. taco seasoning
1-oz. pkg. Ranch dressing mix
1 c. water
16-oz. pkg. frozen corn

16-oz. can kidney beans, undrained
15-oz. can tomato sauce
14.5-oz. can diced tomatoes with
   green chiles, undrained
Toppings: corn chips, shredded
   Cheddar cheese, sour cream

Cook ground chuck and onion in a stockpot, stirring until beef crumbles and is no longer pink; drain. Add taco seasoning and next 6 ingredients to beef mixture. Bring to a boil; cover, reduce heat and simmer 30 minutes. Serve with desired toppings. Makes 11 cups.

WHITE CHICKEN CHILI
(pictured on page 374)

This soup makes a lot, so be sure to have plastic containers on hand to send everyone home with leftover soup…if there is any!

6 (15½-oz.) cans Great Northern
   beans, drained and rinsed
3 (5-oz.) cans chicken, drained
32-oz. container chicken broth
3 c. (12 oz.) shredded Monterey
   Jack cheese
2 (4½-oz.) cans diced green chiles

2 small onions, chopped
1½ c. sour cream
1 T. olive oil
2 t. ground cumin
1½ t. dried oregano
1 t. garlic powder
¼ t. ground white pepper

Combine all ingredients in a large stockpot. Simmer 30 minutes or until thoroughly heated. Makes 20½ cups.

KATHLEEN'S FABULOUS CHILI

1 lb. ground chuck
1 lb. bacon, uncooked and chopped
1 onion, chopped
1 c. chopped green bell pepper
16-oz. can dark red kidney beans, drained
16-oz. can pinto beans, drained
15.5-oz. can Sloppy Joe mix
15-oz. can pork and beans, undrained
14.5-oz. can diced tomatoes, undrained
1 c. water
1/4 c. brown sugar, packed
1 T. chili powder
1/2 t. salt
1/2 t. ground black pepper

Cook first 4 ingredients in a large skillet, stirring until beef crumbles and is no longer pink; drain.
Combine meat mixture, beans and remaining ingredients in a 6-quart slow cooker; cover and cook on high setting 4 hours. Makes 12 1/2 cups.

"This recipe is my own creation. It won 1st place for 'Overall Best Chili' at a church chili cook-off!"
KATHY STRUNK
MESA, AZ

FARMSTYLE BEEF STEW

1 T. vegetable shortening
3 lbs. cubed stew meat
3 3/4 c. water, divided
2 (14 1/2-oz.) cans diced tomatoes
2 medium onions, vertically sliced
2 celery ribs, chopped
2 cloves garlic, minced
1/4 c. chopped fresh parsley
1/2 t. dried thyme
1 T. salt
1/2 t. pepper
10 carrots, sliced (about 2 lbs.)
5 baking potatoes, cubed (about 2 lbs.)
1/4 c. all-purpose flour
12 green onions, sliced (about 2 bunches)
1 c. frozen petite green peas

Melt shortening over medium-high heat in a 6-quart Dutch oven. Cook meat, in batches, 6 minutes or until well browned, reserving drippings in pan. Add 2 1/2 cups water, tomatoes and next 7 ingredients. Bring to a boil; reduce heat, cover and simmer for 1 1/2 hours or until meat is tender, stirring occasionally.
Stir in carrots and potatoes. Bring to a boil; reduce heat, cover and simmer one hour. Gradually whisk remaining 1 1/4 cups water into flour. Stir flour mixture into stew; stir in green onions and peas. Bring to a boil; reduce heat and simmer, uncovered, 5 minutes or until slightly thickened, stirring often. Makes 19 cups.

"I found this recipe while looking through a cupboard at my dad's house…it was even written in my late grandmother's handwriting!"
CAROL BRASHEAR
MYERSTOWN, PA

It's the unexpected touches that make the biggest impressions. When serving soup or chili, offer guests a variety of fun toppings… fill bowls with shredded cheese, oyster crackers, chopped onions, sour cream and crunchy croutons; then invite everyone to dig in!

Giant Chocolate Malt
Cookies (page 391)

For kids Only

Let your children lend a hand in the kitchen with enticing recipes like Cheese Fries, Taco Pizza or Giant Chocolate Malt Cookies. You'll enjoy the ease of these kid-friendly recipes while the kids enjoy the taste!

KID'S "CHAMPAGNE"

1 ltr. white grape juice   2 ltrs. ginger ale

Combine ingredients and serve well chilled. Makes 12 cups.

WAKE-UP SHAKE

1 c. milk   Sugar to taste
1 T. frozen orange juice concentrate   4 to 6 ice cubes
1 t. vanilla extract

Pour all ingredients into an electric blender; process until smooth. Serves one.

MONKEY PAW BISCUITS

³/₄ c. granulated sugar   ¹/₄ c. evaporated milk
¹/₂ t. ground cinnamon   ¹/₂ c. brown sugar, packed
3 (12-oz.) cans refrigerated biscuits   ³/₄ c. butter or margarine

Combine granulated sugar and cinnamon; set aside. Separate biscuits; cut each one into fourths. Coat biscuits with sugar and cinnamon mixture; stack in bottom and around sides of a lightly buttered 12-cup Bundt® pan.
Bring evaporated milk, brown sugar and butter to a boil in a small saucepan and cook until thickened; pour over biscuits. Bake at 350 degrees for 35 minutes; cool slightly before removing from pan. Serve warm. Serves 12.

CHEESY CHICKEN & MAC

3 c. diced cooked chicken   1 c. onion, diced
2 c. macaroni or ziti, uncooked   8-oz. pkg. pasteurized process
1³/₄ c. milk   cheese spread, diced
2 (10³/₄-oz.) cans cream of chicken 8-oz. pkg. sliced mushrooms
   soup   ¹/₄ c. dry white wine
                                     ¹/₄ t. pepper

Mix all ingredients together in a large bowl; spoon into an ungreased 13"x9" baking dish. Refrigerate overnight. Let stand 30 minutes before baking. Bake, uncovered, at 350 degrees for 45 minutes; then cover and bake 15 more minutes. Serves 6 to 8.

CHEESE FRIES

32-oz. pkg. frozen French fries
1 T. chili powder
½ c. sliced green onions
½ c. crisply cooked and crumbled
   bacon (7 slices)

1 c. shredded Cheddar cheese
Ranch dressing

Leave the crumbling of the bacon to the kids, though you might want extra slices for nibbling on.

Bake fries according to package directions for crispier fries. Place baked fries in a broiler pan; sprinkle with chili powder, green onions, bacon and cheese. Broil for about 2 minutes or until cheese is melted. Serve with Ranch dressing. Serves 8.

Nachos Magnifico

NACHOS MAGNIFICO

1 lb. ground beef
1 c. chopped onion
3/4 t. salt
1/4 t. pepper
Tortilla chips
2 (16-oz.) cans refried beans
4.5-oz. can diced green chiles
1 c. salsa

1 c. shredded Cheddar cheese
1 c. shredded mozzarella cheese
1 c. shredded Monterey Jack cheese
12-oz. container guacamole
1 1/2 c. sour cream
2 1/4-oz. can sliced black olives, drained
1/2 c. chopped green onions

Cook ground beef and one cup onion in a skillet, stirring until beef crumbles and is no longer pink; drain well. Add salt and pepper.
Layer tortilla chips in a lightly greased 13"x9" baking dish; top with beans, beef mixture, green chiles and salsa. Sprinkle with cheeses. Cover and bake at 400 degrees for 8 to 10 minutes or until cheese melts. Top with guacamole, sour cream, olives and green onions. Serve with additional tortilla chips. Serves 6 to 8.

For added pizzazz, use blue and yellow tortilla chips and arrange them around the edges of the dish. Let the kids sprinkle on the toppings.

RAVIOLI LASAGNA

2 c. pasta sauce, divided
16-oz. container ricotta cheese
10-oz. pkg. frozen chopped spinach, thawed and drained
2 eggs, beaten

Salt and pepper to taste
1/2 c. grated Romano or Parmesan cheese
18-oz. bag frozen cheese ravioli
1/2 c. shredded mozzarella cheese

Spread 1/2 cup pasta sauce in a 5-inch-deep, 8"x8" baking dish. Stir together ricotta, spinach, eggs, salt, pepper and Romano cheese in a bowl. Layer one-third of the ravioli in the baking dish; top with half the ricotta mixture. Repeat layers, ending with remaining third of ravioli. Spoon remaining pasta sauce over top; sprinkle with mozzarella.
Cover with aluminum foil and bake at 375 degrees for 40 minutes. Remove foil and continue baking 10 more minutes. Serves 4.

"A friend shared this recipe with me and it's fabulous! Prep time is short enough to make it a tasty weeknight meal."

KAREN LEE PUCHNICK
LYNDORA, PA

SPAGHETTI BAKE

8- to 12-oz. pkg. spaghetti, cooked
2 lbs. ground beef, browned and drained
28-oz. jar spaghetti sauce

4-oz. can sliced mushrooms, drained
3 to 4 c. shredded mozzarella cheese
Grated Parmesan cheese to taste

Mix spaghetti, ground beef, sauce and mushrooms together. Spread in a greased 13"x9" baking dish; sprinkle with cheeses.
Bake, uncovered, at 350 degrees for 20 minutes or until cheese is melted. Serves 6.

"My family loves this much better than plain spaghetti...it's cheesy and delicious!"

JILL MEHRINGER
JASPER, IN

SALSA-CHIPPY CHICKEN

"If you like fresh cilantro, try sprinkling a handful on the chicken before pouring the salsa over the top. Yum!"

LESLIE STIMEL
POWELL, OH

2 T. oil
2 T. lime juice
1 t. honey
1 lb. boneless, skinless chicken
   breasts, sliced into 1" strips

12 taco shells, crushed
16-oz. jar salsa
2 c. shredded sharp Cheddar cheese

Combine oil, lime juice and honey in a medium bowl. Dip chicken strips into oil mixture; dredge in crushed taco shells. Arrange in an ungreased 13"x9" pan and bake, uncovered, for 25 minutes or until chicken is done.
Remove chicken from oven; pour salsa over chicken and sprinkle with cheese. Bake, uncovered, 5 to 7 more minutes or until cheese is melted. Serves 4.

CHEESEBURGER & FRIES CASSEROLE

"The kids love this recipe...it's so much fun!"

TRACY HOUSE
NICHOLS, NY

2 lbs. ground beef
10³/₄-oz. can golden mushroom
   soup

10³/₄-oz. can Cheddar cheese soup
20-oz. pkg. frozen French fries

Cook ground beef in a large skillet, stirring until it crumbles and is no longer pink; drain well. Stir in soups and pour into an ungreased 13"x9" baking dish; arrange French fries on top. Bake, uncovered, at 350 degrees for 50 to 55 minutes. Serves 6 to 8.

TACO PIZZA

"The kids' favorite... truly a can't-miss dinner idea! Set up a topping bar when making Taco Pizza. Everyone can just help themselves by adding their favorite toppings to individual servings."

RACHEL FIELDS
BEDFORD, IN

8-oz. pkg. corn muffin mix
1¼-oz. pkg. taco seasoning mix,
   divided
1 lb. ground beef, browned
½ c. taco sauce

1 c. shredded Cheddar cheese
Toppings: sour cream, chopped
   tomatoes, chopped green
   onions, hot peppers, salsa,
   shredded lettuce

Prepare corn muffin mix according to package directions; spread in a greased 8"x8" baking dish. Bake at 400 degrees for 6 to 8 minutes.
Stir ½ package of taco seasoning mix into beef, reserving remaining mix for another recipe. Add any additional ingredients according to taco seasoning mix directions, reducing each by half.
Remove cornbread from oven and spread with taco sauce. Top with beef mixture and cheese. Return to oven; continue baking 15 more minutes or until cheese is melted. Let stand 2 to 3 minutes; cut into squares. Serve with desired toppings. Serves 2 to 4.

CINNAMON PUFFS

8-oz. pkg. cream cheese
1 egg yolk
½ c. plus 2 T. sugar, divided
1 t. vanilla extract

1 loaf sliced white bread, crusts removed
1 T. ground cinnamon
1 c. butter, melted and cooled

Beat cream cheese, egg yolk, 2 tablespoons sugar and vanilla in a medium bowl at medium speed with an electric mixer. Roll bread slices flat; spread cream cheese filling on bread. Roll up jelly roll-style. Combine remaining ½ cup sugar and cinnamon in a small bowl. Dip bread in butter and then in cinnamon-sugar mixture. Place on baking sheets and freeze. Cut each roll into 3 pieces. Bake at 350 degrees for 15 minutes. Makes 45 bite-size pieces.

"A quick treat for the kids."
MARGARET SCHAEFER
FAIRVIEW PARK, OH

GIANT CHOCOLATE MALT COOKIES
(pictured on page 384)

1 c. butter-flavored shortening
1¼ c. brown sugar, packed
½ c. malted milk powder
2 T. chocolate syrup
1 T. vanilla extract
1 egg

2 c. all-purpose flour
1 t. baking soda
½ t. salt
1½ c. semi-sweet chocolate chunks
1 c. milk chocolate chips

Combine first 5 ingredients in a large mixing bowl; mix at medium speed with an electric mixer for 2 minutes. Add egg; mix well and set aside.
Stir together flour, soda and salt; add shortening mixture, mixing well. Fold in chocolate. Shape dough into ½-cup balls; press down to form 3½-inch round discs. Arrange 3 inches apart on ungreased baking sheets. Bake at 375 degrees for 15 minutes. Cool for 5 minutes; remove to a wire rack to cool completely. Makes 8 cookies.

"The next best thing to a good old-fashioned malted shake!"
PAT HABIGER
SPEARVILLE, KS

ALMOND GRAHAMS

12 whole graham crackers
1 c. butter or margarine
1 c. brown sugar, packed

½ t. vanilla extract
1 c. sliced almonds
1 c. flaked coconut

Place crackers in a greased 15"x10" jelly-roll pan; set aside. Bring butter and brown sugar to a boil in a saucepan, stirring constantly, for 2 to 3 minutes until sugar melts; add vanilla. Pour over crackers, spreading evenly. Sprinkle with sliced almonds and coconut. Bake at 400 degrees for 5 minutes; break or cut into pieces. Makes 8 cups.

"If you want larger servings (and you will!), simply serve them cut into squares."
PATRICIA MACLEAN
ONTARIO, CANADA

Holly-Jolly
Almond Brittle
(page 402)

Cookie & Candy exchange

The holidays and sweet treats go hand in hand. For old-fashioned cookie cutouts to decadent chocolaty treats, look no further. Check out the festive gift cards on page 403 that can be copied, cut and colored to "tag" along with these holiday confection gifts.

Waffle Cookies

WHITE CHOCOLATE-CRANBERRY COOKIES

18-oz. tube refrigerated white
    chocolate chunk cookie dough,
    softened
1 c. chopped pecans

3/4 c. sweetened, dried cranberries
1 t. orange extract
1 t. vanilla extract

Combine all ingredients in a large bowl; mix well. Drop by heaping teaspoonfuls, 2 to 3 inches apart, onto ungreased baking sheets. Bake at 350 degrees for 8 to 10 minutes. Makes 2 to 3 dozen.

"Cranberries add a chewy tartness to these cookies...a tasty treat."
SANDY BERNARDS
VALENCIA, CA

WAFFLE COOKIES

4 (1-oz.) squares unsweetened
    baking chocolate
1 c. butter or margarine
1 1/2 c. sugar

4 eggs
2 t. vanilla extract
2 c. all-purpose flour
Chocolate Frosting

Melt together chocolate and butter in a heavy saucepan over low heat; stir in sugar until dissolved. Remove from heat and whisk in eggs, vanilla and flour until blended. Drop by teaspoonfuls onto a heated waffle iron; bake according to manufacturer's instructions. Top with Chocolate Frosting. Makes 4 dozen.

Chocolate Frosting
2 (1-oz.) squares unsweetened
    baking chocolate
1/4 c. butter or margarine

1/4 c. milk
2 t. vanilla extract
3 c. powdered sugar, sifted

Melt chocolate and butter in a heavy saucepan over low heat; remove from heat and add milk and vanilla. Mix in powdered sugar to desired consistency. Makes 1 1/2 cups.

THERE'S NO EASIER GIFT BAG THAN A CLASSIC BROWN PAPER LUNCH SACK. Fill with treats, fold the top over, punch 2 holes and slide a peppermint stick or candy cane through. You could even thread a licorice whip through the holes and tie into a bow!

MORAVIAN SPICE CRISPS

¾ c. all-purpose flour
½ t. baking powder
¼ t. baking soda
¼ t. salt
½ t. ground cinnamon
½ t. ground ginger
½ t. ground white pepper
¼ c. ground cloves
⅓ c. light brown sugar, packed
3 T. butter, softened
¼ c. light molasses

Combine flour, baking powder, soda, salt and spices; set aside. Beat brown sugar and butter in a mixing bowl at high speed with an electric mixer until creamy. Beat in molasses at medium speed until blended. Stir in flour mixture. Drop batter by rounded teaspoonfuls about 4 inches apart on greased baking sheets; press each into a 2-inch circle. Bake at 350 degrees for 8 to 10 minutes. Let cool several minutes; remove to wire racks to cool completely. Store in a tightly covered container. Makes about 3 dozen.

STAINED GLASS COOKIES

½ c. butter or margarine, softened
½ c. shortening
1 c. sugar
1 egg
1 t. vanilla extract
2½ c. all-purpose flour
½ t. baking soda
½ t. salt
Colored hard candies, crushed

Beat butter and shortening in a large bowl at medium speed with an electric mixer until creamy. Add sugar, egg and vanilla; beat well. Stir together flour, baking soda and salt; add to butter mixture and beat well. Form dough into a ball; wrap in wax paper and chill one to 2 hours or until firm enough to shape. Shape dough by tablespoonfuls into 9-inch-long thin ropes; form ropes into closed shapes such as triangles, circles, hearts, bells or stars. Place shapes on parchment-lined baking sheets. Fill insides of shapes with crushed candies. Bake at 350 degrees for 10 to 12 minutes or until candy melts. Makes about 3 dozen.

OVERLAP COOKIES IN A WREATH SHAPE and dust with powdered sugar for a snowy look. Perfect for nibbling on before the cookie exchange begins.

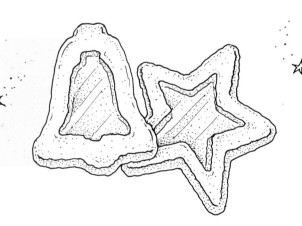

CHOCOLATE CUTOUTS

1 egg, beaten
2/3 c. butter, softened
3/4 c. granulated sugar
1½ c. all-purpose flour
¼ c. baking cocoa

1 t. baking powder
½ t. salt
1 t. vanilla extract
Optional: frosting, colored sugar

Beat egg, butter and 3/4 cup granulated sugar in a mixing bowl at medium speed with an electric mixer until creamy. Stir together flour and next 4 ingredients. Add to egg mixture, beating until combined. Form dough into 2 flattened rounds; cover and chill.
Roll dough out on a floured surface to ⅛-inch thickness. Cut with cookie cutters as desired; place on ungreased baking sheets. Bake at 350 degrees for 8 to 10 minutes. Let cool; frost and sprinkle with colored sugar, if desired. Makes 2 to 3 dozen.

"You'll have a hard time eating just one!"
NANCY CAVAGNARO
MOUNTAIN VIEW, CA

ORANGE-YOU-GLAD COOKIES

1 c. butter, softened
1 c. sugar
1 egg, beaten
2½ c. all-purpose flour

1 t. baking powder
2 T. orange juice
1 T. vanilla extract

Combine butter, sugar and egg in a large mixing bowl; beat at medium speed with an electric mixer until creamy, about one to 2 minutes. Add flour, baking powder, orange juice and vanilla; mix one to 2 more minutes. Cover and chill for 2 to 3 hours until dough is firm.
Roll dough to ¼-inch thickness and cut into shapes with cookie cutters. Place one inch apart on lightly greased baking sheets. Bake at 350 degrees for 6 to 10 minutes until edges are lightly golden. Cool and frost. Makes 2 dozen.

"I get requests for this cookie recipe all the time!"
JACKIE BALLA
WALBRIDGE, OH

Frosting
3 c. powdered sugar
1/3 c. butter, softened
1 t. vanilla extract

1 to 2 T. orange juice
Red and yellow food coloring

Combine all ingredients in a mixing bowl; beat at medium speed with an electric mixer until fluffy. Makes 1½ cups.

HOLIDAY GUMDROP COOKIES

1 c. butter, softened
1 c. sugar
2 eggs
1 t. vanilla extract
2 c. all-purpose flour
1 t. baking powder

½ t. baking soda
¼ t. salt
1 c. quick-cooking oats, uncooked
1 c. flaked coconut
1 c. pecans, coarsely chopped
1 c. gumdrops, sliced

Beat butter and sugar at medium speed with an electric mixer until creamy. Stir in eggs, one at a time, and vanilla until well mixed; set aside. Stir together flour, baking powder, soda and salt; add to butter mixture and mix well. Stir in oats and remaining ingredients just until mixed; refrigerate dough 30 minutes. With floured hands, roll dough into 1½-inch balls and flatten slightly; place on parchment paper-lined baking sheets. Bake at 375 degrees for 13 minutes. Makes about 2 dozen.

CHOCOLATE SNOWBALLS

2 c. granulated sugar
½ c. milk
¾ c. butter or margarine
6 T. baking cocoa

3 c. quick-cooking oats, uncooked
1 c. chopped pecans
1 t. vanilla extract
Garnish: powdered sugar

Combine granulated sugar, milk, butter and cocoa in a saucepan. Bring to a boil over medium heat, stirring constantly. When mixture comes to a boil, remove from heat; stir in oats, pecans and vanilla. Allow to cool to room temperature.
Shape into one-inch balls; roll in powdered sugar. Keep refrigerated in an airtight container. Makes about 3 dozen.

CAN'T-LEAVE-ALONE BARS

18¼-oz. pkg. white cake mix
2 eggs
⅓ c. oil
14-oz. can sweetened condensed milk

6-oz. pkg. semi-sweet chocolate chips
¼ c. butter, sliced

Combine cake mix, eggs and oil in a bowl; mix well. With floured hands, press two-thirds of mixture into a greased 13"x9" pan. Set aside.
Combine condensed milk, chocolate chips and butter in a microwave-safe bowl. Microwave, uncovered, on HIGH (100%) for 45 seconds. Stir and microwave 45 to 60 more seconds or until chips and butter are melted. Stir until smooth; pour over cake mixture in pan. Drop remaining cake mixture by teaspoonfuls over top. Bake at 350 degrees for 20 to 25 minutes or until light golden. Let cool before cutting into squares. Makes 3 dozen.

PEANUTTY CARAMEL BARS

14-oz. pkg. caramels, unwrapped
¼ c. water
¾ c. creamy peanut butter, divided
4 c. doughnut-shaped oat cereal

1 c. peanuts
1 c. milk chocolate chips
½ c. butter, melted

Heat caramels, water and ½ cup peanut butter in a large saucepan until melted. Add cereal and peanuts; stir until coated. Spread into a greased 13"x9" pan; set aside.
Heat chocolate chips, butter and remaining ¼ cup peanut butter in another pan over low heat until melted; spread over cereal mixture. Refrigerate before cutting into bars. Makes about 3 dozen.

"Nothing says holidays more than trays filled with cookies that have been made with love in your own kitchen!"
SHEILA PLACKE
CARROLLTON, MO

MINT BROWNIES

19½-oz. pkg. fudge brownie mix
3-oz. pkg. cream cheese, softened
½ c. butter, softened
1 T. milk

½ t. peppermint extract
3 or 4 drops green food coloring
2 c. powdered sugar
Garnish: chocolate frosting

Prepare brownies according to package directions, using the amount of eggs for cakelike brownies. Bake in a greased 13"x9" pan according to package directions. Let cool.
Mix cream cheese and butter in a bowl until creamy. Add milk, peppermint extract, food coloring and powdered sugar. Spread on cooled brownies; let mint layer harden. Spread with chocolate frosting; cut into squares. Makes 2½ to 3 dozen.

"When I make these for my husband, I usually end up getting only a small square...they go fast!"
BETH POWELL
POTOSI, WI

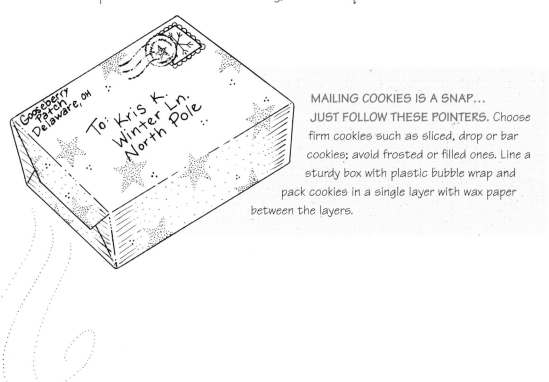

Gooseberry Patch
Delaware, OH

To: Kris K.
Winter Ln.
North Pole

MAILING COOKIES IS A SNAP...
JUST FOLLOW THESE POINTERS. Choose firm cookies such as sliced, drop or bar cookies; avoid frosted or filled ones. Line a sturdy box with plastic bubble wrap and pack cookies in a single layer with wax paper between the layers.

PEANUT BUTTER-COCOA TRUFFLES

3/4 c. butter
1 c. peanut butter chips
1/2 c. baking cocoa
14-oz. can sweetened condensed
    milk

1 T. vanilla extract
Garnish: baking cocoa, finely
    chopped nuts, graham cracker
    crumbs

Combine first 4 ingredients in a large saucepan over low heat. Stir constantly until mixture is thick and glossy, about 9 minutes. Remove from heat; stir in vanilla. Chill for 4 hours or until firm enough to handle.
Shape into one-inch balls; roll in cocoa, nuts or crumbs. Chill until firm, about one hour. Store, covered, in the refrigerator. Makes about 3 dozen.

CHOCOLATE-COCONUT BONBONS

2 (1-oz.) squares unsweetened
    baking chocolate
14-oz. can sweetened condensed
    milk

2 c. flaked coconut, packed
1/2 c. chopped walnuts

Melt chocolate over low heat in a heavy saucepan. Remove from heat and stir in condensed milk and remaining ingredients. Drop by teaspoonfuls onto greased baking sheets, shaping with hands into balls.
Preheat oven to 350 degrees; turn off heat. Place baking sheets in oven for 20 minutes. Remove from oven and let cookies cool completely on baking sheets. Makes about 6 dozen.

ONE OF MY FAVORITE MEMORIES involves creating a holiday treat with my then 4-year-old daughter, Raisa. I decided that my daughter and I should attempt to create a gingerbread house. Knowing my creative limitations, I opted for a "pre-fab" kit. After several attempts, we managed to get the house (which looked more like a shanty) to stand. My daughter then began to decorate it with pounds of gumdrops, peppermints, licorice sticks, wafers and candies. By the time we finished, it looked like a joke...frosting everywhere, candies scattered and the house looked like it would collapse if you stared at it too long. I was about ready to toss the whole mess out when my daughter whispered, "Isn't it the prettiest house you've ever seen? And we made it!" Nobody would ever suggest that our gingerbread house would win any blue ribbons, but to my daughter it was a glorious achievement. And what she taught me that year was that it was the effort and time we spent together that was important...not whether or not the gumdrops were lined up in a perfect row.

VALERIE ORLEANS
ANAHEIM HILLS, CA

Peanut Butter-
Cocoa Truffles

HOLLY-JOLLY ALMOND BRITTLE

(pictured on page 392)

2 c. sugar
½ c. water

6 T. butter, melted
2 c. whole almonds

Butter a large baking sheet; set aside.

Combine sugar and water in a 3-quart heavy saucepan. Bring to a boil, stirring gently to dissolve sugar. Wash down crystals on sides of pan with a small brush dipped in hot water. Insert a candy thermometer. Bring mixture to a boil over medium-high heat; cook until thermometer reaches 280 degrees, washing down crystals occasionally.

Reduce heat to medium; stir in butter and almonds. Mixture will crystallize, but continue to cook until mixture melts and thermometer registers 306 degrees, stirring often to blend melting sugar with crystallized sugar. Quickly pour mixture onto prepared baking sheet. Let cool. When hardened, break into pieces. Store at room temperature in an airtight container. Makes about 1½ pounds.

MERINGUE KISSES

3 egg whites
¼ t. cream of tartar
⅔ c. sugar

½ t. peppermint extract
¼ t. green liquid food coloring
½ c. semi-sweet chocolate mini chips

Beat egg whites at high speed with an electric mixer until foamy; beat in cream of tartar. Slowly beat in sugar, one tablespoon at a time, until sugar dissolves and stiff peaks form. Beat in peppermint extract and food coloring; fold in chocolate chips. Drop mixture by teaspoonfuls onto parchment paper-lined baking sheets.

Bake at 250 degrees for 45 minutes; turn off oven and leave overnight. Store in an airtight container at room temperature. Makes 4 dozen.

For Snowman-shaped Meringues:

Spoon meringue into a gallon-size heavy-duty zip-top plastic bag. Snip off one corner to get a ¾-inch opening. Pipe 2 circles (one bigger than the other); flatten with a spatula, if necessary. Decorate with additional candies as desired. Bake as directed. Makes 3 dozen.

To:

Let us eat Cookies!

From:

Baked with LOVE

From the Kitchen of:

Include these festive tags with your merry treats. Just copy, cut and color!

CANDY BAR FUDGE

½ c. butter
⅓ c. baking cocoa
¼ c. brown sugar, packed
¼ c. milk
3¾ c. powdered sugar
1 t. vanilla extract

30 caramels, unwrapped
2 T. water
2 c. salted peanuts
¾ c. milk chocolate chips
¾ c. butterscotch chips

"I hope you enjoy this recipe that I hold dear to my heart."
LORI BRANDES
WELLSVILLE, NY

Combine butter, cocoa, brown sugar and milk in a large microwave-safe bowl. Microwave on HIGH (100%) one minute; stir well. Continue to microwave on HIGH 2 more minutes or until mixture comes to a boil. Gradually stir in powdered sugar and vanilla. Press into a lightly greased 8"x8" pan; set aside. Combine caramels and water in another microwave-safe bowl; microwave on HIGH 2 to 3 minutes or until melted and bubbling. Pour evenly over cocoa layer in pan; sprinkle with peanuts.
Combine milk chocolate chips and butterscotch chips in another medium-size microwave-safe bowl; microwave on HIGH one to 2 minutes or until melted. Spread evenly over peanut layer in pan. Chill until firm; let stand 15 to 20 minutes at room temperature before cutting into squares. Makes 3 pounds.

Nana's Christmas
Caramels (page 413)

Giftable
goodies

Delight your loved ones with these heartfelt gifts from the kitchen.
We've included whimsical labels with the recipes' preparation directions that
you can copy and attach to many of the mixes like Ginger & Spice &
Everything Nice Muffin Mix. You'll also find creative packing ideas
that will inspire you to share in the spirit of the season.

Munch & Crunch
Snack Mix

MUNCH & CRUNCH SNACK MIX

1 c. mini pretzels
1 c. corn chips
1 c. oyster crackers
1 c. roasted, salted pumpkin seed
   kernels
1 c. honey-roasted peanuts
2 T. butter or margarine, melted

2 T. brown sugar, packed
1 t. chili powder
1 t. Worcestershire sauce
1/2 t. onion salt
1/2 t. ground cumin
1/8 t. ground red pepper

This crunchy snack has a Southwestern kick!

Toss together first 5 ingredients in a large bowl; set aside. Whisk together butter and remaining 6 ingredients in another bowl; pour over snack mix, stirring to coat. Spread mix in a roasting pan; bake at 300 degrees for 25 minutes, stirring after 12 minutes. Cool completely; store in an airtight container. Makes about 5 cups.

CUP OF VEGGIE NOODLE SOUP MIX

1/3 c. dried mixed vegetable flakes
1 T. cracked wheat
2 T. angel hair pasta, coarsely broken
   and uncooked
1/4 t. dried parsley

1/8 t. dried, minced onion
1/4 t. dried basil
1/8 t. garlic powder
1/8 t. onion powder

Process dried mixed vegetables in an electric blender or a food processor until pea-size flakes form; place in a bowl. Add cracked wheat and remaining ingredients; toss to mix well. Divide and place into 2 plastic zip-lock bags; press to make as airtight as possible. Attach instructions. Makes 2 mixes.

Instructions
Pour one package soup mix into a bowl or large mug; pour one cup boiling water, chicken broth or beef broth on top. Stir to mix. Makes one serving.

Make a copy of this label to attach to the soup mix.

Cup of VEGGIE NOODLE Soup Mix

Pour one package soup mix into a bowl or large mug; pour one cup boiling water, chicken broth or beef broth on top. Stir to mix. Makes 1 serving.

1¾ c. all-purpose flour
½ c. sugar
1 T. baking powder
¼ t. baking soda
1 t. vanilla powder

2 t. ground cinnamon
½ t. ground nutmeg
1 t. ground ginger
⅛ t. ground cloves
¼ t. salt

Stir together all ingredients in a bowl; place in an airtight container. Attach instructions. Makes 2 cups.

Instructions
Combine muffin mix with ½ cup melted butter, one egg and one cup milk; stir until just moistened. Fill greased or paper-lined muffin cups ⅔ full with batter; bake at 400 degrees for 15 minutes. Makes one dozen.

Don't forget to include a colored copy of the
label to attach with the muffin mix!

On the label:

Ginger & Spice & Everything Nice

MUFFIN MIX

Combine muffin mix with ½ cup melted butter, 1 egg, and 1 cup milk. Stir until just moistened. Fill greased or paper-lined muffin tins ⅔ full of batter. Bake at 400° for 15 minutes. Makes 12.

GOTTA-HAVE-IT CORNBREAD MIX

6 c. all-purpose flour
6 c. cornmeal
2 c. powdered milk
1 c. sugar

⅓ c. baking powder
1 T. salt
1½ c. shortening

Combine first 6 ingredients together in a large bowl; cut in shortening with a pastry blender or 2 forks until mixture resembles coarse crumbs. Store in an airtight container at room temperature for up to 6 weeks or freeze for up to 6 months. Attach instructions. Makes 16 cups.

Instructions

Combine 2 cups cornbread mix with one teaspoon chili powder in a large mixing bowl; form a well in the center and set aside. Whisk one egg and ¾ cup water together; pour into well. Mix just until combined; spread batter in a greased 8"x8" pan. Bake at 425 degrees for 20 to 25 minutes or until a toothpick inserted in the center comes out clean. Makes 16 servings.

Package Gotta-Have-It Cornbread Mix with a mini cornstick pan and a jar of salsa. Add a line to instructions: "For a quick & easy appetizer, bake batter in pan, then dip tiny cornsticks into salsa." Delicious!

TUXEDO BROWNIES IN A JAR

½ c. walnuts
½ c. white chocolate chips
½ c. semi-sweet chocolate chips
⅔ c. brown sugar, packed

1 c. plus 2 T. all-purpose flour
⅓ c. baking cocoa
⅔ c. granulated sugar
½ t. salt

Layer all ingredients in order listed in a one-quart, wide-mouth jar, being sure to pack down after each addition. Secure lid and attach baking instructions and a gift tag. Makes about 4 cups.

Instructions
Empty brownie mix into a large bowl. Add 3 eggs, ½ cup oil and one teaspoon vanilla extract. Pour into a greased 9"x9" pan. Bake at 350 degrees for 22 to 25 minutes. Cut into squares. Serves 6 to 8.

PRALINE ICE CREAM SYRUP

Make hand-dipped waffle cones to give with Praline Ice Cream Syrup. Dip the top half of cones in melted chocolate chips, then roll in chopped peanuts or colorful sprinkles.

2 c. corn syrup
⅓ c. brown sugar, packed
½ c. water
1¼ c. chopped pecans

½ t. vanilla extract
4 (1-pt.) canning jars and lids, sterilized

Combine syrup, sugar and water in a saucepan. Bring to a boil over medium heat; boil for one minute. Remove from heat; stir in pecans and vanilla.
Pour into hot jars, leaving ¼-inch space at the top. Secure lids; process in a boiling water bath for 10 minutes. Makes 4 pints.

LOTSA PEPPER JELLY

"Attach a festive card to each jar with serving suggestions such as: Spoon over cream cheese-topped crackers or use as a glaze on roast turkey or ham."

Teresa Hill
Lima, NY

2 large green bell peppers, seeded and cut into 2" pieces
4 large jalapeño peppers, halved crosswise
1 c. cider vinegar

6 c. sugar
2 (3-oz.) pkgs. liquid pectin
7 (½-pt.) canning jars and lids, sterilized

Process peppers in a food processor until liquefied; pour into a 6-quart Dutch oven. Stir in vinegar and sugar. Bring mixture to a boil, stirring constantly. Add pectin and stir until well blended. Return mixture to a boil and boil for one minute. Remove from heat and skim off foam.
Pour into hot jars, leaving ¼-inch space at the top. Secure lids; process in a boiling water bath for 5 minutes. Makes 7 (8-ounce) jars.

Tuxedo Brownies
in a Jar

ALMOND-PEAR MUFFINS

1¼ c. all-purpose flour
¾ c. brown sugar, packed
1 T. baking powder
1 t. ground ginger, divided
½ t. salt
1 c. chopped pears
1 c. whole-bran cereal

1 c. milk
1 egg
¼ c. oil
2 T. chopped almonds
8-oz. pkg. cream cheese, softened
1 T. honey

Combine flour, brown sugar, baking powder, ½ teaspoon ginger and salt in a large bowl; stir in pears and set aside. Mix cereal and milk together; set aside for 5 minutes.
Add egg and oil to cereal mixture; mix into pear mixture just until moistened. Fill greased or paper-lined muffin cups ¾ full with batter; sprinkle tops with almonds. Bake at 400 degrees for 18 to 20 minutes; cool.
Mix together cream cheese, honey and remaining ½ teaspoon ginger; serve with muffins as a spread. Serves 12 to 16.

CHOCOLATE-COVERED PEANUT CLUSTERS

2 (12-oz.) pkgs. semi-sweet
    chocolate chips
1 c. creamy peanut butter
16-oz. pkg. mini marshmallows

2½ c. milk chocolate-covered
    peanuts
Powdered sugar

Melt chocolate chips with peanut butter in a heavy saucepan; stir until smooth. Remove from heat; stir in marshmallows and chocolate-covered peanuts. Drop by tablespoonfuls onto a wax paper-lined baking sheet. Chill until firm; sprinkle with powdered sugar before serving. Makes about 4 dozen.

CANDIED NUTS

½ lb. whole nuts, shelled and halved
1 egg white
1 t. water
½ lb. nuts, finely ground

½ c. sugar
½ t. ground cinnamon
½ t. salt

Place halved nuts on a lightly greased baking sheet; set aside. Beat together egg white and water; pour over halved nuts and stir to coat well. Combine ground nuts, sugar, cinnamon and salt; sprinkle over coated nuts; mix well. Bake at 200 degrees for one hour, stirring every 15 minutes. Makes about one pound.

SUGARED PECANS

1 c. sugar
1½ t. salt
1 t. ground cinnamon

1 egg white
1 T. water
1-lb. pkg. pecan halves

Combine first 3 ingredients in a small bowl; set aside. Whisk egg white and water together until frothy; fold in pecan halves. Add sugar mixture; stir to coat pecans. Spread on an aluminum foil-lined baking sheet; bake at 300 degrees for 30 to 35 minutes. Remove from oven; separate pecans using a fork as they cool. Store in an airtight container. Makes about one pound.

NANA'S CHRISTMAS CARAMELS

(pictured on page 404)

1 c. butter
1 c. milk
1 c. whipping cream
2 c. granulated sugar

1 c. brown sugar, packed
1 c. light corn syrup
1 t. vanilla extract

Grease around the inside top of a Dutch oven to prevent boiling over. Melt butter in Dutch oven; use a brush and some of the melted butter to grease a heavy-duty foil-lined 9"x9" pan; set aside.
Add milk and next 4 ingredients to Dutch oven. Cook, stirring constantly, over medium-high heat 35 to 38 minutes until mixture reaches firm-ball stage (250 degrees). Remove from heat and stir in vanilla. Quickly pour caramel into prepared pan. Let stand at room temperature or in the refrigerator until firm. Lift out caramel and invert onto a cutting board; remove foil. Cut into 1"x1" squares; wrap each square with wax paper and twist ends. Makes about 2½ lbs.

Special Section: Holiday

Flip through these pages for helpful hints throughout the holidays. You'll find ideas for seasonal projects, luscious menus, party planning and even journaling suggestions for capturing your memorable events.

Holiday Hints...

For Decorating

- **Turn cookies into yummy edible place markers;** just use frosting to write each guest's name.
- **For a sweet topiary, slide a candy cane stick into the center of a foam ball,** and then cover the ball with peppermint candies. Secure the candy stick in a festive terra-cotta pot filled with florist foam.
- **For a clever and festive tablecloth, cover a table with giftwrap.**
- **Add whimsy to windows** by tying a pine cone onto each end of a ribbon for festive curtain tiebacks.
- **Dress up your mantel** with chunky scented candles that are tied with homespun or sheer ribbon. Arrange the candles among fruit and greenery.
- **Add sparkle to your centerpiece** by using sugared fruit. Brush apples, pears and plums with a thin mixture of meringue powder and water, roll in coarse sugar and let dry.
- **Serve holiday snacks & treats on a peppermint stick tray!** Cut a piece of cardboard into the desired tray size and cover with peppermint sticks using royal icing as the "glue." Allow to harden overnight before use.
- **For tree skirts, use old quilts and blankets from your children's nursery.** Just wrap around the bottom of the tree and you'll have a nostalgic, country touch in no time.

From Gooseberry Patch Crafters

Recipe Magnets

Last Christmas I made ceramic tile recipe magnets for my friends & family. I chose my favorite homestyle recipes, typed them on the computer so they would fit on the tiles and printed them out on decorative paper. I then decoupaged the recipes to square tiles, took them to a well-ventilated area and sprayed each tile with a coat of clear sealer. Once the sealer was dry, I hot-glued a heavy-duty magnet to the back of each tile. Everyone was so happy to get these as gifts because I usually make these tried & true recipes for them once a year...now they can make them whenever they want!

MAILE HELEKAH
HONOLULU, HI

Jar of Thank-Yous

A couple of years ago, I gave my mom a "jar of thank-yous." I decorated a glass canning jar with stickers and ribbons and then filled it with about 100 strips of paper on which I had thanked my mom for all the little things she did to make my life so wonderful. I included things like "Making orange juice Popsicles for me and my friends," "Letting me have slumber parties," "Making snickerdoodles," "Encouraging me when I was away at college," and "Adjusting my veil on my wedding day." Christmas morning, she read a few aloud and was so moved that she saved the rest to read on her own. She told me later that it was the best gift I had ever given her.

MICHELLE KIRK
HAMPTON, VA

Guide

For Gifts

- **Keep your eyes open year-round at tag sales and flea markets** for anything that you might be able to tuck your holiday sweets into. Vintage pie tins, mugs, jelly jars or enamelware pails would all be perfect!

- **Give neighbors a cookie kit.** Fill a basket or holiday tin with ready-made dough, sprinkles, cookie cutters, frosting and a favorite recipe.

- **Package holiday treats** such as fudge, almond brittle, cookies or brownies in airtight containers, and then slip them into gift bags tied with ribbon or raffia. Set them in a basket by your door so there will always be a treat waiting for guests to take home.

- **Give a pail of fun!** Fill an enamelware pail with packets of hot cocoa mix, homemade cookies, bags of microwave popcorn and a classic holiday movie.

- **Be creative when giving holiday gift mixes!** Flavored coffees and teas can be given in a one-of-a-kind teacup; cocoa mix in a nostalgic milk bottle; bread mixes in an ovenproof bread crock; and soup mixes in a speckled stockpot.

- **For a personal gift tag,** string fresh cranberries on wire and shape into the recipient's initial.

- **Purchase holiday cookie cutters and make several batches of fudge in pans the depth of the cookie cutters.** Then cut out the fudge, leaving it inside the cutters, decorate with nuts, cherries or peppermints, if desired, and wrap in transparent gift bags tied with holiday ribbon.

For Kids

- **Count down the 12 Days of Christmas** by baking and decorating 12 different cookies! Slip each one in a plastic bag for each member of the family to enjoy each day.

- **Kids will love finding treats inside old-fashioned paper crackers.** Just fill a cardboard tube with candy and confetti, wrap in tissue paper and secure the ends with ribbon.

- **Pile children's toys in a wagon,** set the toys under the tree or arrange them on a mantel for a warm-hearted, sentimental way to decorate.

- **Hang cheery mittens or Santa hats on the mantel** instead of stockings.

- **Make a mitten wreath out of mittens your children have outgrown.** Attach them to a greenery wreath and add a big bow.

- **Let the kids help make personalized giftwrap.** Just ask them to cut pictures of flowers, animals and holiday images from magazines, and then glue the images onto packages that have been wrapped in solid-color paper.

- **Trace your children's hands on heavy paper** to make charming gift tags.

- **If you're traveling for the holidays,** have the little ones leave Santa a note telling him where you'll be the night before Christmas!

12 Days of Christmas Menus

These menus are based on recipes found within the book.
Recipe Key: *Double recipe   **Triple recipe

1
Appetizer Open House

Serves 12

*Smoky Nuts, page 359

Cheery Cheese Ring, page 300

Black-Eyed Pea Dip, page 291

Crab Rangoon, page 363

Hot Antipasto Squares, page 360

**Grapefruit Margaritas, page 355

2
Just for the Kids

Serves 8

Cheddar Fondue, page 356

Chicken Fingers with Apple Butter-Peanut Sauce, page 362

Cheese Fries, page 387

Giant Chocolate Malt Cookies, page 391

sodas and milk

3
Easy Weeknight Supper

Serves 4 to 6

Jambalaya, page 324

green salad

French bread

7
Holiday Dessert Party

Serves 16

Espresso Biscotti, page 295

Caramel Apple Dip, page 268

Chocolate-Peanut Butter Fudge, page 329

Spiced Eggnog Pound Cake, page 338

**Cranberry Hot Toddies, page 354

coffee

8
Rise & Shine Breakfast

Serves 4

Blueberry-Croissant French Toast, page 369

Crispy Brown Sugar Bacon, page 370

orange juice

9
Christmas Eve Dinner

Serves 6

Christmas Eve Oyster-Corn Chowder, page 379

Cumin Pork Roast with Wild Mushroom Sauce, page 312

Macaroni au Gratin, page 317

*Roasted Asparagus, page 326

dinner rolls

Chocolate Pecan Pie, page 319

4

Shoppers' Lunch

Serves 6

Cranberry-Turkey Wraps,
page 334

tortilla chips

Can't-Leave-Alone Bars,
page 398

5

Make-Ahead Favorites

Serves 8

Ziti with Spinach & Cheese,
page 346

Caesar salad

garlic bread

6

Souper Supper

Serves 10 to 12

White Chicken Chili,
page 382

Gotta-Have-It Cornbread
Mix, page 409

Chocolate Chip
Pudding Cake, page 328

10

Munchies for Santa

Munch & Crunch Snack Mix,
page 407

Moravian Spice Crisps,
page 396

Candy Bar Fudge,
page 403

carrots (for Santa's
reindeer)

milk

11

Christmas Brunch

Serves 8

Savory Ham-and-Swiss
Breakfast Pie, page 372

Warm Spiced Fruit,
page 366

Simple Citrus Coffee Cake,
page 370

*Cinnamon Hot Chocolate,
page 354

12

Christmas Day Feast

Serves 8

Roasted Walnut &
Pear Salad, page 327

Lobster & Chive Bisque,
page 376

Holiday Beef Tenderloin,
page 303

Make-Ahead
Mashed Potatoes, page 314

*Homestyle Green Beans,
page 314

Chocolate-Macadamia Pie,
page 307

Party Planner

Use this chart to coordinate menu items for your holiday celebration, as well as a reminder of who's bringing what.

Guests	What They're Bringing (appetizer, beverage, bread, main dish, side dish, dessert)	Serving Pieces Needed

Party Guest List

....

....

....

....

....

....

....

....

....

....

....

Pantry List   ## Party To-Do List

....

....

....

....

....

....

....

....

....

Favorite Recipes

Use these pages to jot down the recipes you and your family liked best
and those you'd like to prepare another time.

Appetizers & Snacks . . . .   Beverages . . . .   Breakfast Entrées . . . .

Cakes . . . .   Condiments . . . .   Cookies & Candies . . . .

Desserts. . . . . Entrées. . . . .

. . . .

. . . .

. . . .

. . . .

. . . .

. . . .

. . . .

Food Gifts. . . . . Pies & Pastries. . . . .

. . . .

. . . .

. . . .

. . . .

. . . .

. . . .

. . . .

Salads & Side Dishes . . . . Soups & Stews. . . . .

. . . .

. . . .

. . . .

. . . .

. . . .

. . . .

General Instructions

Fig. 1

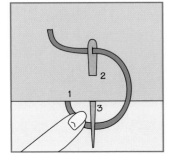

Fig. 2

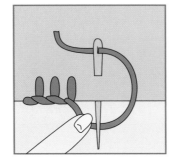

Fig. 3

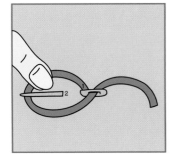

Fig. 4

Fig. 5

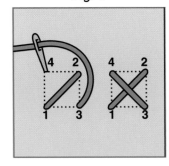

Fig. 6

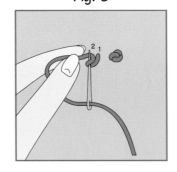

Embroidery Stitches

Blanket Stitch

Referring to Fig. 1, bring the needle up at 1. Keeping the thread below the point of the needle, go down at 2 and come up at 3. Continue working as shown in Fig. 2.

Chain Stitch

Referring to Fig. 3, bring the needle up at 1; take the needle down again at 1 to form a loop. Bring the needle up at 2; take the needle down again at 2 to form a second loop. Bring the needle up at 3 and repeat as in Fig. 4. Anchor the last chain with a small straight stitch.

Cross Stitch

Bring the needle up at 1. Go down at 2. Come up at 3 and go down at 4 (Fig. 5).

French Knot

Referring to Fig. 6, bring the needle up at 1. Wrap the floss once around the needle and insert the needle at 2, holding the floss end with non-stitching fingers. Tighten the knot; then, pull the needle through the fabric, holding the floss until it must be released. For a larger knot, use more strands; wrap only once.

Fig. 7

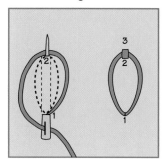

Fig. 8

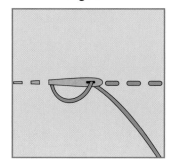

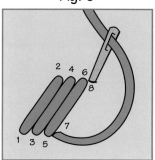

Fig. 9

Fig. 10

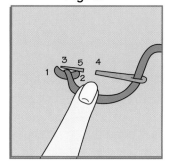

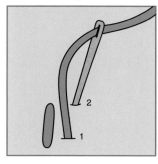

Fig. 11

Fig. 12

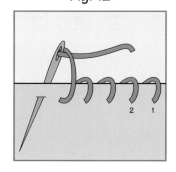

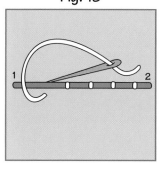

Fig. 13

Fig. 14

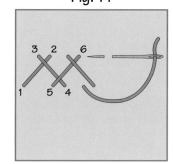

Lazy Daisy Stitch

Bring the needle up at 1; take the needle down again at 1 to form a loop and bring the needle up at 2. Keeping the loop below the point of the needle (Fig. 7), take the needle down at 3 to anchor the loop.

Running Stitch

Referring to Fig. 8, make a series of straight stitches with the stitch length equal to the space between stitches.

Satin Stitch

Referring to Fig. 9, come up at odd numbers and go down at even numbers with the stitches touching but not overlapping.

Stem Stitch

Referring to Fig. 10, come up at 1. Keeping the thread below the stitching line, go down at 2 and come up at 3. Go down at 4 and come up at 5.

Straight Stitch

Referring to Fig. 11, come up at 1 and go down at 2.

Whipstitch

Bring the needle up at 1; take the thread around the edge of the fabric and bring the needle up at 2. Continue stitching along the edge of the fabric (Fig. 12).

Couched Stitch

Referring to Fig. 13, bring needle up at 1 and go down at 2, following line to be couched. Work tiny stitches over threads to secure.

Herringbone Stitch

Referring to Fig. 14, bring the needle up at 1; go down at 2. Bring up at 3 and pull through; go down at 4.

Knit

Abbreviations

cm	centimeters
K	knit
M1	make one
mm	millimeters

P	purl
Rnd(s)	Round(s)
st(s)	stitch(es)
tog	together

★ — work instructions following ★ as many **more** times as indicated in addition to the first time.

( ) or [ ] — work enclosed instructions **as many** times as specified by the number immediately following **or** work all enclosed instructions in the stitch or space indicated **or** contains explanatory remarks.

colon (:) — the number(s) given after a colon at the end of a row or round denote(s) the number of stitches you should have on that row or round.

Fig. 1

Gauge

Exact gauge is essential for proper size. Before beginning your project, make the sample swatch given in the individual instructions in the yarn and needle specified. After completing the swatch, measure it, counting your stitches and rows or rounds carefully. If your swatch is larger or smaller than specified, make another, changing needle size to get the correct gauge. Keep trying until you find the size needles that will give you the specified gauge.

Markers

As a convenience to you, we have used markers to help distinguish the beginning of a pattern or round. Place markers as instructed. You may use purchased markers or tie a length of contrasting color yarn around the needle. When you reach a marker on each round, slip it from the left needle to the right needle; remove it when no longer needed.

Knitting in the Round

Using a circular needle, cast on all stitches as instructed. Untwist and straighten the stitches on the needle before beginning the first round. Place a marker after the last stitch to mark the beginning of a round. Hold the needle so the skein of yarn is attached to the stitch closest to the right-hand point. To begin working in the round, knit the stitches on the left-hand point (Fig. 1).

Fig. 2b

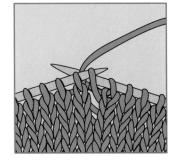

Make One
(abbreviated M1)

Insert the left needle under the horizontal strand between the stitches from the front (Fig. 2a). Then knit into the back of the strand (Fig. 2b).

Knit 2 Together
(abbreviated K2 tog)

Insert the right needle into the **front** of the first 2 stitches on the left needle as if to **knit** (Fig. 3); then, **knit** them together as if they were one stitch.

Purl 2 Together
(abbreviated P2 tog)

Insert the right needle into the **front** of the first 2 stitches on the left needle as if to **purl** (Fig. 4); then, **purl** them together as if they were one stitch.

Slip 1, Knit 1, Pass Slipped Stitch Over
(abbreviated slip 1, K1, PSSO)

Slip one stitch as if to **knit** (Fig. 5a). Knit the next stitch. With the left needle, bring the slipped stitch over the knit stitch (Fig. 5b) and off the needle.

Picking Up Stitches

When instructed to pick up stitches, insert the needle from the **front** to the **back** under 2 strands at the edge of the worked piece (Fig. 6). Put the yarn around the needle as if to **knit**; then, bring the needle with the yarn back through the stitch to the right side, resulting in a stitch on the needle. Repeat this along the edge, picking up the required number of stitches. A crochet hook may be helpful to pull the yarn through.

Weaving Seams

With the **right** side of both pieces facing you and the edges even, sew through both sides once to secure the seam. Insert the needle under the bar **between** the first and second stitches on the row and pull the yarn through (Fig. 7). Insert the needle under the next bar on the second side. Repeat from side to side, being careful to match rows. If the edges are different lengths, it may be necessary to insert the needle under two bars at one edge.

Fig. 3
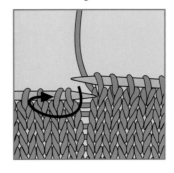

Fig. 4
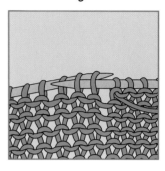

Fig. 5a
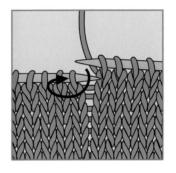

Fig. 5b
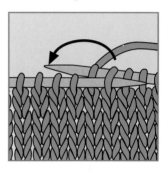

Fig. 6

Fig. 7
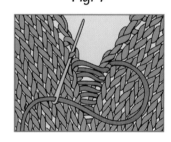

Crochet

Abbreviations

ch(s)	chain(s)	Rnd(s)	Round(s)
cm	centimeters	sc	single crochet(s)
dc	double crochet(s)	sp(s)	space(s)
hdc	half double crochet(s)	st(s)	stitch(es)
mm	millimeters	YO	yarn over

★ — work instructions following ★ as many **more** times as indicated in addition to the first time.

( ) — work all enclosed instructions in the stitch or space indicated **or** contains explanatory remarks.

colon (:) — the number(s) given after a colon at the end of a row or round denote(s) the number of stitches you should have on that row or round.

Fig. 1

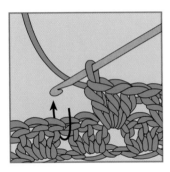

Gauge

Exact gauge is essential for proper size or fit. Before beginning your project, make the sample swatch given in the individual instructions in the yarn and hook specified. After completing the swatch, measure it, counting your stitches and rows or rounds carefully. If your swatch is larger or smaller than specified, make another, changing hook size to get the correct gauge. Keep trying until you find the size hook that will give you the specified gauge.

Joining with Sc

When instructed to join with sc, begin with a slip knot on the hook. Insert the hook in the stitch or space indicated, YO and pull up a loop, YO and draw through both loops on the hook.

Fig. 2

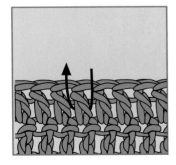

Joining with Dc

When instructed to join with dc, begin with a slip knot on the hook. YO, holding loop on hook, insert hook in loop or space indicated, YO and pull up a loop (3 loops on hook), (YO and draw through 2 loops on hook) twice.

Working in Space Before a Stitch

When instructed to work in a space before a stitch, insert hook in space indicated by arrow (Fig. 1).

Whipstitch

With **wrong** sides together, sew through both pieces once to secure the beginning of the seam, leaving an ample yarn end to weave in later. Insert the needle from **right** to **left** through one strand on each piece (Fig. 2). Bring the needle around and insert it from **right** to **left** through the next strand on both pieces. Repeat along the edge, being careful to match stitches and rows.

Fig. 3

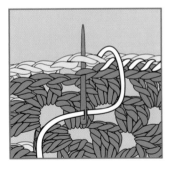

Front Post

Work around post of stitch indicated, inserting hook in direction of arrow (Fig. 3).

Making Patterns

When the entire pattern is shown, place tracing paper over the pattern and draw over the lines. For a more durable pattern, use a permanent marker to draw over the pattern on stencil plastic.

When only half of the pattern is shown (indicated by a solid blue line on the pattern), fold the tracing paper in half. Place the fold along the solid blue line and trace the pattern half. Turn the folded paper over and draw over the traced lines on the remaining side. Unfold the pattern and cut it out.

Fig. 1

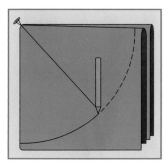

Making a Fabric Circle

Matching right sides, fold the fabric square in half from top to bottom and again from left to right. Tie one end of a length of string to a fabric marking pen; insert a thumbtack through the string at the length indicated in the project instructions. Insert the thumbtack through the folded corner of the fabric. Holding the tack in place and keeping the string taut, mark the cutting line (Fig. 1).

Continuous Bias Binding

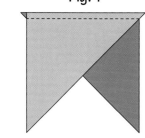

Fig. 1

1. Fold the fabric square in half diagonally; cut on the fold to make 2 triangles.

2. With the right sides together and using a ¼" seam allowance, sew the triangles together (Fig. 1). Press the seam allowances open.

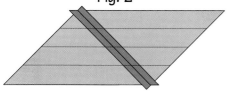

Fig. 2

3. On the wrong side of the fabric, draw lines the width given in the project instructions, parallel to the long edges (Fig. 2). Cut off any remaining fabric less than this width.

Fig. 3

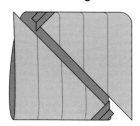

4. With the right sides inside, bring the short edges together to form a tube; match the raw edges so the first drawn line of the top section meets the second drawn line of the bottom section (Fig. 3).

5. Carefully pin the edges together by inserting pins through the drawn lines at the point where the drawn lines intersect, making sure the pins go through the intersections on both sides. Using a ¼" seam allowance, sew the edges together; press the seam allowances open.

Fig. 4

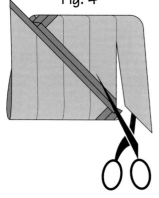

6. To cut a continuous strip, begin cutting along the first drawn line (Fig. 4). Continue cutting along the drawn line around the tube.

7. Trim each end of the bias strip as shown in Fig. 5.

Fig. 5

Latch Hooking

Transferring Patterns

Arrange patterns, print side up, between rug canvas and a piece of cardboard larger than the patterns; tape in place on cardboard. Use permanent marker to outline patterns on canvas. Remove canvas from cardboard.

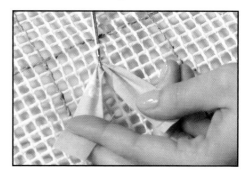
Fig. 1

Using the Latch Hook

1. To hook strip to canvas, slide hook beneath one crossbar in canvas. Wrap one strip around hook with ends even (Fig. 1); slide hook back through canvas until strip is about halfway through.

2. Leaving shaft of hook in loop, catch ends of strip in hook and pull them through the loop (Fig. 2). Pull knot tight (Fig. 3).

Fig. 2

Filling the Canvas

To keep canvas square, begin at one corner on the top or bottom of the canvas. Work across the row, changing strip colors as necessary, before moving to the next row. Yardages given are based on the hooking patterns below. Use this hooking pattern to ensure having enough yardage to complete the project.

Fig. 3

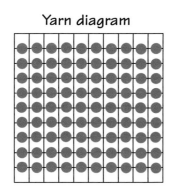

Fleece diagram   **Yarn diagram**

Painting

DRY BRUSHING: Do not dip the brush in water. Dip a stipple brush or old paintbrush in paint; wipe most of the paint off onto a dry paper towel. Lightly rub the brush across the surface. Repeat as needed.

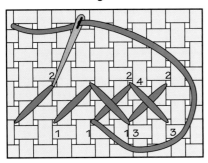

Fig. 1

Cross Stitch

Counted Cross Stitch (X)
Referring to Fig. 1, work one Cross Stitch to correspond to each colored square in chart. For horizontal rows, work stitches in 2 journeys.

For vertical rows, complete stitch as shown in Fig. 2.

Quarter Stitch
Quarter Stitches are shown as triangular shapes of color in chart and color key (Fig. 3).

Backstitch (B'ST)
For outline detail Backstitch (shown in chart by black straight lines) should be worked after all Cross Stitch has been completed (Fig. 4).

French Knot
Referring to Fig. 5, bring needle up at 1. Wrap floss once around needle and insert needle at 2, holding end of floss with non-stitching fingers.

Fig. 2

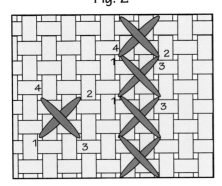

Fig. 3

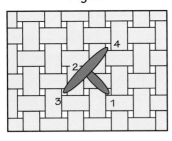

Fig. 4

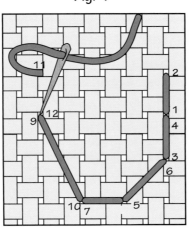

Fig. 5

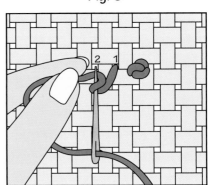

Needlepoint

STITCHING THE DESIGN

Securing the First Stitch
Don't knot the end of your yarn before you begin stitching. Instead, begin each length of yarn by coming up from the wrong side of the canvas and leaving a 1" to 2" tail on the wrong side. Hold this tail against the canvas and work the first few stitches over the tail. When secure, clip the tail close to your stitched piece.

Stitches
Needlepoint is worked in horizontal or vertical rows over one intersection. Stitches slant from lower left to upper right. Referring to Fig. 1, bring needle up at even numbers and down at odd numbers.

Fig. 1

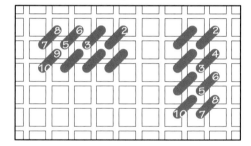

Using Even Tension
Keep your stitching tension consistent, with each stitch lying flat and even on the canvas. Pulling or yanking the yarn causes the tension to be too tight, and you will be able to see through your project. Loose tension is caused by not pulling the yarn firmly enough, and the yarn will not lie flat on the canvas.

Ending Your Stitches
After you've completed all of the stitches of one color in an area, end your stitching by running your needle under several stitches on the back of the stitched piece. To keep the tails of the yarn from showing through or becoming tangled in future stitches, trim the end of the yarn close to the stitched piece.

TIPS
• It is best to begin stitching with a piece of yarn that is approximately one yard long.

• Most stitches tend to twist the yarn. Drop your needle and let the yarn untwist every few stitches or whenever needed.

Working with Polymer Clay

Getting Ready
Always begin by covering your work surface. Clay should not come in contact with surfaces where food is prepared or be used on plastic or wood surfaces. Cover the surface with freezer paper, shiny side up. Tape corners of freezer paper to table or counter to hold in place while working. Designate tools used with polymer clay for use with clay only: do not use them for food preparation.

Conditioning
Although it may feel very soft and workable right out of the package, polymer clay should always be conditioned before use. To condition clay by hand, knead balls of clay that are a comfortable size to work with (about $1/2$ ounce) until warm and pliable.

For the projects in this book, we used a hand-crank pasta machine. This handy tool, with easy-to-adjust settings, can be used to condition clay and make clay sheets of varying thickness. To condition clay using a pasta machine, fold clay over before each pass and work out any air bubbles; simply pass clay, folded edge first, through machine set on #1 setting 10 to 15 times.

Rolling Clay Sheets
To roll a clay sheet using a pasta machine, send conditioned clay through machine at thickest setting (#1).

Baking
Cure clay by baking as directed by manufacturer in a standard home oven or a toaster oven designated for use with clay only. Do not use a microwave oven. Bake in a well-ventilated area. Place project on a piece of parchment paper or an index card on an aluminum pan, baking dish, or heavy-duty cookie sheet to bake.

PROJECT INSTRUCTIONS

FAMILY CALENDAR

(shown on page 78)

Spend memory-making family time together creating this scrapbook-type calendar, then share a photocopy version of it with grandparents or other family members! Use our example here for a December idea, then just use assorted scrapbooking supplies and photos befitting the season to complete pages for the rest of the year.

- assorted colors and textures of cardstock, including 2 full 8¹/₂"x11" sheets for the calendar backgrounds
- photographs (original or photocopied)
- hole punch
- ribbon
- self-adhesive photo mounts
- decorative-edge craft scissors
- 3 silver scrapbooking tags with seasonal wording
- scrapbooking paper fasteners
- craft glue stick
- letter to Santa (original or photocopied)
- dimensional foam dots
- alphabet, numeral and Christmas icon stamps and inkpads
- 1¹/₂" diameter circle punch
- ⁵/₁₆" diameter round letter tags for days of week
- small jute
- three 1" diameter loose-leaf rings

To decorate the top page of the calendar, cut out a cardstock tag large enough to accommodate each photo to be used. Punch a hole in each tag and knot a length of ribbon through each hole; use photo mounts to attach photos to the tags. Use craft scissors to cut rectangle strips to accommodate 2 of the silver tags; use paper fasteners to attach the silver tags to the strips. Glue the letter to a piece of cardstock, then tear the cardstock larger on each side than the letter. Arrange the letter and tags on one of the background sheets. Use glue and foam dots to attach the elements to the page.

For the bottom calendar page, photocopy the calendar layout, page 474, onto the remaining background sheet. Glue a length of ribbon across the top of the page. Stamp "December" onto cardstock; use craft scissors to cut out a rectangle around the month word. Glue the month to another piece of cardstock, then cut out a rectangle around the month piece; glue to the top of the page. Use the circle punch to cut 7 circles from cardstock. Glue one round letter tag to each circle and poke a hole in the circle through the hole in the letter tag; knotting on the backside, tie short lengths of jute through the holes in each letter tag and circle. Use foam dots to attach the circles and paper fasteners to attach the remaining silver tag to the calendar page.

Stamp the dates of the month onto cardstock; cut out a rectangle or square around each date; glue the dates to the calendar. For the holiday "stickers," stamp an icon onto cardstock, then cut out the cardstock just outside the stamped lines. Use foam dots to attach the icons to the calendar. Aligning the holes, punch 3 holes along the bottom of the top calendar piece and 3 holes along the top of the bottom piece; use rings to connect the calendar pieces.

FAMILY PHOTO TREE

(shown on page 80)

The tree is the theme for this time of year, so why not make your tree really personal and unique…your family tree, that is? Let the memory makers in your life shape the branches of this special tree.

Discard the glass and remove the back from a wooden picture frame; cover the back with decorative paper. Cut a piece of cardstock ³/₄" smaller on each side than the frame opening; cut a piece of decorative paper ¹/₂" smaller on each side than the cardstock piece. Center the paper piece on the cardstock piece (this is the mat); sew along the mat edges.

Place the mat on a flat surface centered under the frame opening. Arrange, then trim your photos to stack into a tree shape within the frame opening. Adhere each photo to cardstock; use decorative-edge craft scissors to trim the cardstock just larger than the photo. Arrange and glue the photos on the mat. Arrange a length of ¹/₄"-wide ribbon 1¹/₂" longer than each row of photos below the photos. Attach ribbon lengths to the mat with paper fasteners. Center and adhere the mat to the frame back.

For the nameplate, use paper fasteners to attach a label holder large enough to accommodate tiles spelling out the family name to cardstock, then cut the cardstock into a rectangle just larger than the label holder. Cut a rectangle larger than the nameplate from corrugated cardboard; glue it on the mat for the tree trunk. Center and glue the nameplate to the trunk.

Cut a star from yellow foam; glue to the tree for the topper. For each ornament, poke a tiny paper fastener through the top of a purchased scrapbook-size ornament; spread prongs on the backside. Coil one end of a 2" length of 24-gauge wire; wrap the remaining end around the paper fastener on the backside of the ornament. Hang the ornament by the coil from one of the ribbons on the tree...if you can't find pre-made ornaments, make your own by cutting ornament shapes from foam, then gluing decorative paper to each side.

CARD OR PHOTO ORGANIZER
(shown on page 81)
Hummm? Where'd I put that card I just got . . . or Mary Elizabeth's picture with Santa? Well, never wonder again...the answers will be right at your fingertips with this handy holiday organizer.

Use decorative paper to cover the lid of a white photo storage box gift-wrap style. Glue jumbo rick-rack along the inside bottom edge of the lid; adhere coordinating border stickers (or a strip of vellum) along the edges of the lid. Overlapping, trimming and piecing as necessary, cover the sides of the box with vellum.

For the label on the end of the box, adhere the desired word sticker to cardstock. With the word centered in the opening of a label holder large enough to accommodate the word, draw around the holder on the cardstock; cut out the cardstock just inside the drawn lines. Glue the label holder to the cardstock piece, then glue the cardstock piece to the box.

Select a photograph to go on the lid. Glue the photo to cardstock, then trim the cardstock larger on each side than the photo; attach a small paper fastener to each corner of the photo. Glue the matted photo to 2 more layers of cardstock, trimming or tearing each layer just a bit larger than the previous one. Use photo mounts to attach the matted photo to the lid.

Embellish the lid of the box with glued-on snowflake or word charms, spiraled paper clips and stamped tags. To make the tile letter tags, stamp all but the first letter of the desired word onto cardstock; leaving room for a tile letter, tear the word out and glue it to another piece of cardstock. Glue a tile letter to the tag. Arrange, then glue or use double-sided self-adhesive foam dots to attach the tags to the lid.

KID-MADE CARDS
(shown on page 82)
Let this holiday season be Christmas as seen through the eyes of a child. Hand the kids or grandkids a pack of crayons, markers or watercolors and a piece of cardstock and let them draw and color their favorite thoughts of Christmas...be sure they add their signature and the year to the artwork (or you can add a typed nameplate).

When their masterpiece is complete, trim it to the desired size and glue it to a piece of cardstock; trim the cardstock to fit around the drawing. Trim, layer and stack the artwork as desired, then glue it to the front of a blank card or a piece of folded cardstock. Now, add foam or sticker embellishments, or other scrapbooking accessories and elements to each card. To make dimensional embellishments, simply use a dimensional foam dot to attach cut-out cardstock motifs or

purchased embellishments to the card. To make quick & easy gift package embellishments, cut out squares from foam sheets and wrap one or more squares with narrow decorative ribbon.

CHRISTMAS JOURNAL
(shown on page 83)
• mat board
• assorted cardstock
• craft glue
• patterned vellum
• spray adhesive
• small bell
• 10" length of ribbon
• dimensional foam dots
• 2"tall letters to spell "joy"
• $1/8$" diameter hole punch
• six 4-hole buttons
• embroidery floss

From mat board, cut two $1 1/2$"x6" pieces for hinges and two 6"x9" pieces for covers.

To cover the front, cut an 8"x12" piece from cardstock the color you want the hinge to be. Glue one hinge piece and one cover piece, $1/16$" apart, to the center on the wrong side of the cardstock. Mitering corners, wrap excess paper to back of hinge and cover pieces (inside of cover) and glue to secure in place. Cut an 8"x10" piece each from vellum and cardstock; use spray adhesive to adhere the pieces together. Centering one 8" edge of paper pieces along spacing between hinge and cover and mitering corners, wrap excess paper to inside of cover and glue in place. Repeat step to cover back cover.

(continued on page 434)

3. For the inside cover liners, cut two 5³/₄"x8³/₄" pieces from cardstock. Glue one of the liners inside the front cover. For the bookmark, tie the bell to one end of the ribbon. Gluing the end of the bookmark between the liner and the back cover along the top about 1" from the right edge, glue the remaining liner piece inside the back cover.

4. To decorate the front of the journal, cut a 3"x6" tag and a 2¹/₂"x5¹/₂" tag from cardstock; center and glue the tags together, then arrange and glue them on the front cover. Use foam dots to attach the letters on the tag.

5. For each blank page, cut a 5³/₄"x10¹/₄" piece from cardstock. Refer to **Fig. 1** to make a hole placement template. Punch holes in the covers and blank pages.

Fig. 1

6. Stack the blank pages (or pages you may have already finished) between the covers and align the holes. For each set of holes, place a button on the front cover and one on the back cover; knotting floss on the back, use 6 strands of floss to sew the buttons together through the holes.

MEMORY SHADOW BOX
(shown on page 84)
Gather a collection of those memory-jogging tidbits and trinkets from Christmases past and display them in a timeless shadow box sure to please even Santa himself!

Begin with a wooden shadow box, new or recycled, and paint it to match your Christmastime décor. Next, cut or tear pieces from fabrics (maybe from Granny's favorite apron . . . but not while she's wearing it!) to fit on the back of each section of the box; glue them in place. Layer small swatches of homespun fabrics or strips of braids or twill tape here & there on the background. Now, stamp and cut out holiday sayings, verses or dates from vellum papers; glue them in the shadow box. Lastly, fill the shelves with your treasures…add pictures, buttons, wooden blocks from yesteryears, chunky wooden cutouts, labels, stamped tags or anything you want to use. If you don't have much of a collection yet, use the abundance of scrapbooking supplies and embellishments available to help you start a brand-new collection.

MEMORY WREATH
(shown on page 85)
This wreath is as simple and easy to make as cherished memories are to leave an impression in your heart.

Begin with an 18" evergreen wreath; ours is artificial, but one created from fresh pine boughs and greenery would surely add the perfect aroma to your room.
Gently wrap ribbon around the wreath…use more than one kind and if it overlaps a little bit, it's ok. Select and frame a photograph of your loved one and maybe find a small scarf or hankie belonging to him or her as well. Shape the hankie into a background for the photo to nestle on…wire or glue the hankie, then the photo, to the wreath. Use vintage glass ornaments, buttons and jewelry pieces to fill in empty areas on the wreath. Make a wire hanger on the back of the wreath and you are ready to share your memories with your family & guests.

LATCH-HOOKED RUG
(shown on pages 86 and 87)
• 28" square of rug canvas
• clear tape
• 30" square of cardboard
• permanent markers
• drawing compass
• rotary cutter and cutting mat
• 1¹/₄ yards red fleece
• ³/₄ yards white fleece
• 1 yard light green fleece
• ¹/₄ yard green fleece
• ³/₄ yards dark green fleece
• ¹/₄ yard brown fleece
• latch hook
• non-skid backing material (optional)

Read Latch Hooking, page 429, before beginning project. Finished rug is 24" square.

1. Press each edge of the canvas 2" to the wrong side. Working on the right side, use markers to draw a 4"-wide border along the edges of the canvas; draw seventeen 2"-diameter circles (and a few half circles) randomly on the borders.

2. Enlarge the tree pattern, page 475, by 200% on a photocopier. Transfer the pattern to the center of the canvas.

3. Use the rotary cutter and mat to cut the fleece into $^3/_4$"-wide lengthwise strips. (If cut selvage to selvage, the strips will stretch.) Cut each white strip into $4^1/_2$" lengths; cut remaining long fleece strips into 4"-long lengths.

4. Referring to the photo for color placement, hook the fleece strips into the canvas…when hooking the tree, just scatter strips of green in here & there with the dark green.

5. Follow manufacturer's instructions to apply non-skid backing material to the back of the rug, if desired.

LATCH-HOOKED WREATH
(shown on page 86)
- 30" square of rug canvas
- string, thumbtack and a pencil
- 2$^3/_4$ yards red fleece
- $^3/_4$ yard white fleece
- $^1/_4$ yard green fleece
- latch hook
- hot glue gun
- 24" square of mat board
- staple gun and staples
- 18-gauge floral wire
- wire cutters

Read Latch Hooking, page 429, before beginning project. Finished wreath is 24" in diameter.

1. Refer to *Making a Fabric Circle*, page 427, to mark cutting line on canvas. Insert thumbtack through string 14" from pencil to mark the outside cutting line. Insert tack 5" from the pencil to mark the inner circle. Cut out canvas along the outer cutting line.

2. Mark a 2"-wide border around the canvas piece. Draw 2"-diameter circles randomly around the wreath between the border and inner circle.

3. Use the rotary cutter and mat to cut the red and white fleece into $^3/_4$"-wide lengthwise strips. (If cut selvage to selvage, the strips will stretch.) Cut the red strips into 4" lengths; cut the white felt into 5" lengths. Filling in between the inner circle and outer border, hook the wreath red and the circles white.

4. For the backing, cut a 23"-diameter circle from mat board; cut a 10$^1/_2$"-diameter circle at the center of the backing. Glue the wreath to the backing; wrap the outer canvas border to the back of the backing and staple in place. Cutting from edge to edge, cut the inner circle in the wreath like a pie to make 6 wedge shapes; wrap each wedge to the back of the backing and staple in place.

5. For the bow, cutting selvage to selvage, cut one 5"-wide strip from green fleece. Matching long edges, fold the strip in half, then using a $^1/_4$" seam allowance and leaving a 3" opening at the center, sew the long edges together; sew the ends together at an angle. Turn the strip right-side out through the opening and sew the opening closed. Leaving about 4"-long streamers, tie the bow strip into a bow with 4 loops.

6. For the knot cover, cut one 5" square from green fleece. Press the fleece square in half, then unfold; fold the edges in to the pressed line, then refold along the pressed line and tack the fold together. Thread the center of 20" length of floral wire through the knot cover; wrap the knot cover around the knot in the bow and twist the wire together to hold the cover taut. Spacing evenly between the outer edge of the wreath and the inner circle, poke a hole through the top of the wreath. Thread the wire ends on the knot cover through the hole and twist the wires together to secure the bow snugly on the wreath. Shape the wire ends into a hanging loop, then twist the ends together to secure.

7. Cut four 5" lengths of wire; bend each length in half. With the V in the wire against the knot of the bow, glue the wire on the inside of one loop to help shape the loop. Apply one length of wire to each loop. Cut four $^1/_2$"x5" strips from green fleece. Glue a fleece strip over each wire length. Shape the loops.

NINE POINT TREE SKIRT

(shown on page 90)

- 1 1/4 yards red Christmas fabric
- 7/8 yard green Christmas fabric
- 9 vintage 12"x12" handkerchiefs
- 3 yards fusible interfacing
- 6 1/2 yards 3/8"w ribbon
- assorted buttons
- 2 1/2 yards jumbo red rickrack
- fusible web
- fabric glue
- pinking shears
- cardboard for template

Match right sides and use a 1/2" seam allowance for all sewing unless otherwise indicated.

1. Cut 12" squares of fusible interfacing and iron onto the backs of the hankies.

2. Referring to Fig. 1, draw a triangle template onto cardboard and cut out. Using template, draw 9 triangles onto red fabric; cut out.

Fig. 1

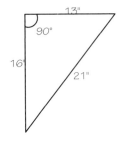

13"
90°
16"
21"

3. Referring to Figs. 2 to 4 for the basic placement of pieces, lay one triangle piece right-side down on top of another triangle piece. Sew triangles together as indicated; press.

Fig. 2

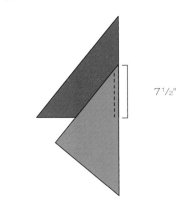

7 1/2"

Fig. 3

Fig. 4

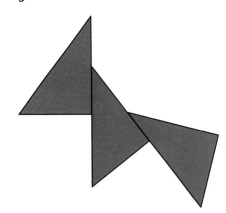

4. Referring to Fig. 5, topstitch hankies to triangles.

Fig. 5

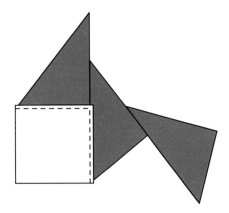

5. Cut a 27" square of green fabric. Center the tree skirt on top of fabric. Insert rickrack between fabrics along the opening; pin together. Topstitch around opening twice for strength. Use pinking shears to trim seam allowance to 1".

6. Enlarge facing pattern, page 478, by 167%; draw pattern onto interfacing. Fuse interfacing onto wrong side of a piece of green fabric and cut out. With right sides facing, pin facing to the center of the green fabric with the tail of the facing pointing to the opening in the tree skirt. Stitch around slit and opening twice. Cut slit open and cut away excess fabric in hole. Clip seam allowance around hole to allow fabric to lay flat. Turn facing to wrong side and press.

7. Glue ribbon over the seams where hankies are joined. Glue a button to the point between hankies.

CROSS STITCHED MONOGRAM ORNAMENTS

(shown on page 95)
- embroidery floss
- 22 ct Zweigart® Antique Mushroom Hardanger
- cardboard
- striped fabric
- fleece
- felt
- 3/8"w wire-edged ribbon
- red baby rickrack and assorted trims
- 24-gauge wire
- assorted beads and charms
- fabric glue

Refer to Cross Stitch, page 430, before beginning project. For all sewing, match right sides and raw edges and use a 1/4-inch seam allowance. For each ornament, use 4 strands of floss for Cross Stitches and Backstitches and work over 2 fabric threads.

Center and cross stitch desired monogram, page 477, on cloth. For each ornament, cut a 5" square of cardboard and fleece. Glue fleece to cardboard.

For each design with circle inset, cut a 6" square of striped fabric. Cut a 3 1/4" dia. circle from center of fabric. Turn raw edges of circle 1/4" to wrong side and press. Center circle over monogram and whipstitch in place. Wrap fabric square around fleece-covered cardboard. Glue raw edges of fabric to back of cardboard.

For each square design, trim stitched piece to 3 1/2" square. Cut two 2"x6" and two 2"x3 1/2" strips of striped fabric. Sew short strips to top and bottom of stitched piece, then long strips to sides; press. Wrap fabric around fleece-covered cardboard. Glue raw edges of fabric to back of cardboard.

For each diamond-shaped design, trim stitched piece diagonally to 3 1/2" square. Cut two 2"x6" and two 2"x3 1/2" strips of striped fabric. Sew short strips to opposite sides of stitched piece and long strips to remaining sides. Wrap fabric around fleece-covered cardboard. Glue raw edges of fabric to back of cardboard.

To finish each ornament, cut an 8" piece of wire-edged ribbon for the hanger. Fold ribbon in half; glue to center back of ornament. Cut a 4 1/2" square of felt. Glue felt to back of ornament. Embellish with beads and charms.

MONOGRAMMED PILLOW

(shown on page 96)
- 14" Graph 'N Latch® pillow cover
- 13 1/2" square of cardboard
- white acrylic paint
- permanent marker
- red chenille yarn
- white chenille yarn
- green chenille yarn
- yarn needle
- 14" pillow form

Read Needlepoint, page 431, before beginning project.

1. Insert cardboard in pillow cover. Paint over blue grid lines with white paint. Allow to dry.

2. Using a computer, pick out your favorite font (we used CurlzMT). Print out your desired letter and enlarge to the size to fit the pillow.

3. Remove cardboard from pillow cover. Center and tape pattern to cardboard. Reinsert cardboard in pillow cover. Use permanent marker to outline pattern on canvas. Remove cardboard.

4. Referring to the photo for color placement, stitch design using 2 strands of yarn.

5. Insert pillow form.

MONOGRAMMED TISSUE BOX COVER

(shown on page 97)
Dress up your plain tissue box with a monogrammed cover created from the vintage napkin you found at the flea market. These covers are so fast & easy to make, you'll want to make more covers as gifts! Trace the desired monogram, page 477, onto tissue paper. Center the tissue paper on an oval of white fabric. Embroider monogram using 3 strands of embroidery floss for *Satin Stitch* and 2 strands for *Backstitch*. Press edges of oval 1/4" to the wrong side and blind stitch to a piece of white felt. Cut felt close to oval and machine stitch at center on edge of your napkin. Fold and overlap the ends of your napkin to the center. Leaving about 6" open at center for tissue, sew ends together. If your napkin isn't large enough to go around a tissue box, cut your napkin in half and add a fabric strip for an extension. Insert tissue box through one open end. With a large-eye darning needle, thread 2 strands of 4mm silk ribbon through each end of napkin and tie into a bow to close. To replace tissue box, untie one end of your tissue box cover.

TABLETOP TOPIARIES AND TOMATO CAGE TREES

(shown on pages 98 and 99)
Transform ordinary wire tomato cages into whimsical Christmas trees to grace your home during the holidays.

TABLETOP TOPIARIES
- 4" dia. clay pots
- masking tape
- plaster of paris
- 9" to 12"h straight sticks for trunks
- sheet moss
- 18" square of green hand-dyed wool
- string, thumbtack and a pencil
- black fusible interfacing
- tracing paper
- dressmaker's chalk
- pinking shears
- hot glue gun
- 4" lengths of twisted wire
- gold felt
- burgundy embroidery floss
- decorative fiber trim for garland

If you want a less full tree, use a larger seam allowance or cut off a portion of your tree body (like a slice of pie…yum…pie!).

1. For each tree, if there is a hole in the bottom of your pot, cover hole with tape. Follow manufacturer's instructions to mix, then fill pot with plaster to within about a half-inch from top; insert stick into pot and let harden. Glue moss over plaster, covering completely.

2. For tree, cut an 18" circle from wool square, following *Making a Fabric Circle*, page 427; cut along folds of wool square to make 4 tree bodies (set 3 aside for additional Tabletop Topiaries). Fuse interfacing to wrong side of wool. Trace scallop pattern, page 483, onto tracing paper; cut out. Use chalk to draw pattern along the curved edge of the interfacing, adjusting pattern as necessary and repeating the pattern as needed. Cut out.

3. Matching right sides, using a ¼" seam allowance, and leaving the top 1" unsewn, sew edges of wool together; pink seam allowance. Leaving the top 1" unturned, turn wool right side out to form tree.

4. For star topper, follow Step 9 of Single-Tier Tree (page 439) to make a star ornament. Cut a smaller star shape for backing. Glue end of wire to back of topper; glue backing star over wire. Bend wire as desired.

5. For garland, wrap trim around tree, gluing or tacking ends as necessary to secure.

6. Insert wire end of star topper into top of tree; glue to secure.

SINGLE-TIER TOMATO CAGE TREE
- large round tomato cage
- 14-gauge wire
- wire cutters
- 4" dia. wire ring (like used in macramé)
- cream felt
- green hand-dyed wool fabric
- cream, gold and burgundy felt
- fiberfill
- black, heavy-duty fusible interfacing
- dressmaker's chalk
- quilting thread for hand basting
- gold and burgundy embroidery floss
- scalloped-edge craft scissors
- pinking shears
- hot glue gun
- tracing paper
- decorative fiber trim for garland

1. For tree, turn tomato cage upside down. Gather and wrap a length of wire 3" from ends of stakes. Trim stake ends just above wrapped wire. Dab a bit of hot glue on the cut ends for safety.

2. Slide wire ring over top of tree until it fits snugly. Cut six 36" wire lengths. Wrap one wire end around

the 4" ring a couple of times, then wrap it around each of the next cage rings (Fig. 1); trim wire end if necessary. Adding 2 wire lengths between each cage stake, repeat with remaining wire lengths.

Fig. 1

4" wire ring

3. Measure the tree height and add 3"; measure around the bottom of the tree and add 3". Cut a piece of cream felt the determined measurement. Overlapping at back and trimming as necessary to fit, wrap excess felt at bottom to inside of tree; secure with glue.

4. For base of tree, measure around the tree bottom and add 2". Use pinking shears to cut a 6"w strip of wool the determined measurement. Work a basting stitch along one long edge of strip. With basted edge 4" from bottom of tree and overlapping ends of strip at back, pull basting thread to fit strip closely to tree; tack in place. Wrap excess felt at bottom to inside of tree; glue to secure.

5. For tree tier, measure the tree height and add 1"; measure around the bottom of the tree and add 3". Use pinking shears to cut a piece of wool the determined measurement. Fuse a 4"w strip of interfacing along the bottom edge on wrong side of tier. Trace scallop pattern, page 483, onto tracing paper; cut out. With scallops along edge of tier, use chalk to trace pattern onto interfacing, repeating the pattern as necessary to fit the length of the tier; cut scallops in tier.

6. Fold the top of the tier 1" to wrong side and with one short edge even with top of tree, wrap and glue felt around tree. Leaving a small opening at top for inserting topper, glue folded edge at top of tree together.

7. For star topper, trace the star topper pattern, page 479, onto tracing paper; cut out. Using pattern, cut 2 stars from gold felt. With wrong sides together and using a $3/8$" seam allowance, sew stars together. Use scalloped-edge scissors to trim edges of topper to $1/4$". Cut a small slit in back of star; stuff star with fiberfill and sew opening closed.

8. For each double penny on star topper (one covers slit in back of topper), use scalloped-edge scissors to cut a $1^{1}/_{2}$" dia. circle from burgundy felt and a $2^{1}/_{4}$" dia. circle from green wool. Work gold *Straight Stitches*, page 423, along the edges of the burgundy circle; repeat with burgundy floss on the green circle. Insert a length of wire through slit in topper and glue to secure; layer and glue double pennies to front and back of topper. Insert topper into hole at top of tree.

9. For each star ornament, trace the star pattern, page 479, onto tracing paper; cut out. Draw around pattern twice on gold felt. Cut out one star just inside the drawn lines and the other star just outside the drawn lines. Work burgundy *Blanket Stitches* along the small star edges. Layer and glue to the larger star.

10. To finish tree, wrap garland trim around tree, gluing or tacking ends as necessary to secure. Glue ornaments to tree.

FOUR-TIER TOMATO CAGE TREE

- small tomato cage
- 14-gauge wire
- wire cutters
- 4" dia. wire ring (like used in macramé)
- cream felt
- green hand-dyed wool fabric
- cream, dark gold and burgundy felt
- batting
- fiberfill
- black, heavy-duty fusible interfacing
- dressmaker's chalk
- quilting thread for hand basting
- dark gold and dark red embroidery floss
- scallop-edged craft scissors
- pinking shears
- assorted small buttons
- hot glue gun
- tracing paper
- decorative fiber trim

1. For tree, use three 24" lengths of wire and follow Steps 1-4 of Single-Tier Tree, page 438.

2. For each scalloped-edge tier, measure around tree where the bottom of your tier will fall. Cut a 9"w piece of wool the determined measurement. Fuse a 3"w strip of interfacing along one long edge on wrong side of wool piece. Trace scallop pattern, page 483, onto tracing paper; cut out. With scallops along edge of tier, use chalk to trace pattern onto interfacing and repeat the pattern as necessary to fit the length of the piece; cut scallops in tier. Work a basting stitch along remaining long edge of tier. Begin with bottom tier and work to the top. With basted edge at top and overlapping ends at back, pull basting thread to fit top of strip snugly to felt; tack in place.

3. For treetop, cutting the fabric circle in half instead of fourths, follow Steps 2 and 3 of Tabletop Topiaries, page 438. Inserting wire through opening in treetop, place treetop over top of tree. Glue in place.

4. For star topper, follow Step 7 of Single-Tier Tree, this page, then work burgundy *Straight Stitches*, page 423, along the edges of the star.

5. For each heart penny for star topper (one to cover slit in back of topper), use scalloped-edge scissors to cut a 2" dia. circle from burgundy felt. Trace heart pattern, page 479, onto tracing paper; cut out. Using pattern, cut heart from wool. Work gold *Straight Stitches* along the edges of the heart, then work gold *Blanket Stitches* along the edges of the circle; sew a button to the heart. Layer and glue heart and circle to topper. Insert a length of wire through slit in topper and glue to secure; attach remaining heart penny over slit in topper.

6. For each single penny ornament, use regular scissors to cut a 1" dia. circle from burgundy felt; work gold *Blanket Stitches* along the edges. Sew a button to ornament, then glue to tree.

7. For each double penny ornament, use scallop-edge scissors to cut a $1^{5}/_{8}$" dia. circle from burgundy felt and regular scissors to cut a 1" dia. circle from cream felt. Work green *Straight Stitches* along the edges of the burgundy circle and gold *Blanket Stitches* along the edges of the cream circle. Layer circles and sew a button to center. Glue ornaments to tree.

8. For each star ornament, follow Step 9 of Single-Tier Tree, this page.

9. For garland, gluing or tacking ends to secure, wrap trim around tree. Glue star ornaments to tree over garland.

DYED WOOL AND EMBROIDERY DRAWSTRING BAG

(shown on page 101)
Complement your holiday wardrobe with this beautifully embroidered drawstring bag or use it as a gift bag and fill it with goodies for a special friend.

For bag, cut one 16"x24" piece each of flannel and green hand-dyed wool. For border, cut one 2"x24" strip of cream felt, one 2¹/₂"x24" strip of burgundy felt, and tear one 3"x24" strip of homespun fabric. Cut out seven ⁷/₈" dia. circles from burgundy felt and seven ⁵/₈" dia. circles from gold felt. Use a ¹/₄" dia. hole punch to punch 7 circles from green wool, 7 circles from light green felt, and 18 circles from burgundy felt. Cut seven 6" lengths of ¹/₈"w variegated green silk ribbon.

Refer to photo, page 101, to overlap the ends of the ribbons and tack ribbon "vines" to the cream felt strip. For large flowers, secure a green wool circle to the center of each gold circle with a *French Knot*. Work green *Blanket Stitches* to attach gold circles to ⁵/₈" dia. burgundy circles. Work gold *Blanket Stitches* to attach flowers to border. Attach light green circles with dark green *French Knots*. Attach sets of 3 burgundy ¹/₄" dia. circles with gold *French Knots*. Work *Lazy Daisy* leaves along ribbon vines.

Working gold *Blanket Stitches* along the edges, attach the cream strip to the burgundy strip. Layer strips on top of fabric strip and machine stitch 6" from top of green wool piece. Match right sides

of green wool piece and machine stitch ends together. Turn right side out. Matching wrong sides, work gold *Blanket Stitches* to join felt circle to bottom of tube.

For lining, press one long edge of flannel ¹/₂" to wrong side. Match right sides of flannel and machine stitch ends together. Do not turn right side out. With right sides together and matching raw edges, sew flannel circle to bottom of tube. Matching seams and wrong sides, slip flannel lining in felt bag. Pin along the top edge and sew together. Using seam line as a guide for the stitch length, work gold *Blanket Stitches* along top and bottom edges of bag.

For drawstring casing, machine stitch around bag 2¹/₂" from top, then 3¹/₂" from top. Clip open seam in felt at casing and insert a 36"-long piece of twisted cording. Tie cording at the ends and loop together with an overhand knot.

DYED WOOL COVERED OTTOMANS

(shown on page 99)
Impress visitors to your home with a classy ottoman dressed up for the holidays. Using ottoman kits and wool felt, you can create your very own unique piece of furniture.

PENNY RUG OTTOMAN

Follow manufacturer's instructions to cut burgundy wool felt to cover ottoman. Position and pin felt to top of ottoman. Trace star pattern, page 478, onto tissue paper. Using pattern, cut 4 stars from gold wool felt. Pin a star to each corner of ottoman cover. For borders, tear 3"-wide strips of homespun fabric to fit

between stars; pin to top between stars. Remove felt from ottoman; work *Blanket Stitches*, page 422, to attach stars and machine stitch fabric strips to felt.

For pennies, cut three 1" circles each from oatmeal, gold and burgundy wool felt, three 2" circles each from burgundy, green and gold wool felt and three 3" circles each from oatmeal, green and gold wool felt. For each penny, alternating colors, layer circles and work *Blanket Stitches* to attach them together. Referring to photo, arrange pennies on top of ottoman to create a diamond shape. Work *Blanket Stitches* to attach pennies to cover. Cover ottoman with decorated felt cover. Use fabric glue to add ¹/₄" burgundy cording between ottoman sections.

TREE OTTOMAN

Follow manufacturer's instructions to cover ottoman with burgundy check homespun and to insert 1" dia. cording covered in burgundy wool felt between sections. For scalloped trim, cut a 4"-wide strip of green wool felt long enough to wrap around the ottoman and overlap slightly at back. Trim one long edge of strip in a scallop pattern; work gold *Blanket Stitches* along scallops. Cover 1¹/₈" buttons with burgundy homespun; sew a button to every scallop. Attach skirt to ottoman below cording. Cut a square of green wool felt approximately 2" smaller than top of ottoman. Using decorative-edged scissors, cut a square of gold wool felt ¹/₂" smaller than green square. Layer squares; work burgundy *Running Stitches* along the edges to join. Cut a piece of burgundy wool felt ¹/₂" smaller than gold piece; center and work green *Blanket Stitches* to attach it to gold felt. Cut a piece of oatmeal felt wool same width as burgundy felt and approximately 5¹/₂" high, then trim one long edge unevenly to form the snow bank. Line up snow bank with bottom of burgundy felt and work *Blanket Stitches* to sew it in place. Trace patterns, page 480, onto tissue paper. Using patterns, cut stars from gold wool felt and trees from green wool felt. Cut ornaments from oatmeal, gold and burgundy wool felt; work *Blanket Stitches* to attach to trees. Refer to photo to work *Blanket Stitches* to attach trees and stars in place. Use green floss to stitch decorated felt to top of ottoman.

Floral Ottoman

Follow manufacturer's instructions to cover top of ottoman with green flannel fabric. For ruffle, measure around ottoman and cut an 8"-wide strip of flannel twice the length of measurement. Matching right sides, sew ends of strip together. Turn one long edge ¹/₂" to wrong side and hem. Sew a gathering stitch along remaining raw edge. Pull gathering stitches until ruffle fits around ottoman. Follow manufacturer's instructions to cover bottom of ottoman with ruffle. Glue a length of twisted cording between top and bottom of ottoman. For embroidered design, cut a piece of oatmeal wool felt 1" smaller on all sides than top of ottoman. Cut lengths of green variegated ribbon; tack it in place as the stem. Trace pattern, page 478, onto tissue paper. Using pattern, cut 11 leaves from green wool felt. Work green *Running Stitches* down center of each leaf for veins. Cut fourteen ³/₄" dia. circles from dark green wool felt, three 4" dia. circles from burgundy wool felt and three 3¹/₄" dia. circles from gold wool felt; layer to form flowers. Arrange flowers and leaves

along ribbon stem; work *Blanket Stitches* to attach. Attach ⁷/₈" dia. burgundy buttons as berries. When design is complete, work *Blanket Stitches* to attach decorated piece to top of ottoman.

QUILT

(continued from page 105)
Place backing wrong side up on a flat surface. Place batting on top of backing fabric. Center quilt top right side up on batting. Begin in center and work toward outer edges to hand baste all layers together. Use long stitches and place basting lines approximately 4" apart. Smooth fullness or wrinkles toward outer edges. Machine quilt using a decorative stitch and sewing along seams.

Cut two 2¹/₂"x55" and two 2¹/₂"x68" lengthwise or crosswise strips of fabric for binding. Piece strips to achieve necessary length. Matching wrong sides and raw edges, press strips in half lengthwise to complete binding. Matching raw edges, sew a length of binding to top and bottom edges on right side of quilt. Trim backing and batting from top and bottom edges ¹/₄" larger than quilt top. Trim ends of top and bottom binding even with edges of quilt top. Fold binding over to quilt backing and pin pressed edges in place, covering stitching line; blindstitch binding to backing. Leaving approximately 1¹/₂" of binding at each end, stitch a length of binding to each side edge of quilt. Trim backing and batting as above. Trim each end of binding ¹/₂" longer than bound edge. Fold each end of binding over to quilt backing; pin in place. Fold binding over to quilt backing and blindstitch in place, taking care not to stitch through to front of quilt.

RIBBON STAR

(shown on page 108)
For each star, cut six 4" lengths of 1¹/₂"-wide ribbon and a 2" dia. circle of felt. Fold ribbon into loops, Fig. 1, and glue to secure. Evenly spacing, glue ribbon loops in place around felt circle. Cover a 2" dia. button with coordinating fabric; sew to center of felt circle, covering ribbon ends. Layer a ³/₈" dia. button and a ⁵/₈" dia. button; sew to center of covered button. For hanger, cut a 10" length of ³/₈"-wide ribbon; tack ends to back of ornament.

Fig. 1

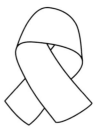

RIBBON CIRCLE

(shown on page 108)
Cut two 10" lengths of 1¹/₂"-wide ribbon. Cut one 10" length of ³/₈" ribbon; sew along center of one 10" ribbon. With right sides together, sew ends of ribbon lengths together. With wrong sides together, sew one side of ribbon lengths together. Work *Running Stitches*, page 423, to sew along remaining edge of one ribbon. Pull threads to gather ribbon into a circle; before tying off, stuff ornament with batting. Layer a ³/₈" button and a ⁵/₈" button; sew to center of ornament. For hanger, cut an 8" length of ribbon. Fold ribbon in half and tack fold to top center of ornament; knot ends.

BRAIDED GARLAND

(shown on page 108)
For each braid, cut 1³/₄"-wide strips of fabric. Wrap a fabric strip around a length of ⁵/₁₆" dia. cording; sew next to cording with zipper foot. Cut off excess fabric with pinking shears. Braid 3 lengths together; sew ends together to secure.

WOVEN BASKET

(shown on page 108)
Beautify a plain, simple basket by tearing strips from your favorite fabric and weaving them through the basket splints. Use a butter knife to help weave the fabric through the splints. If needed, glue the fabric ends in place to secure.

DRAWSTRING GIFT BAG

(shown on page 109)
• green floral flannel
• green cotton fabric
• assorted ribbons
• square buttons

Match right sides and use a ¹/₂" seam allowance for all sewing.

1. Cut 2 pieces of flannel to the desired size for your gift bag. Cut 2 pieces of cotton fabric the same size for lining.

2. Lay one flannel piece on a flat surface; lay lengths of ribbon horizontally across flannel piece and pin in place. Weave additional lengths of ribbon vertically across flannel

piece and pin in place. Sew ribbons in place using decorative stitches. Sew buttons along ribbons.

3. For bag, with right sides together and leaving top open, sew flannel pieces together. To form bottom corners, match side seams to bottom seam; sew across each corner 1" from end.

Fig. 1

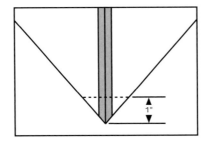

4. Repeat Step 3 for lining.

5. With right sides together, place bag inside lining. Leaving an opening for turning, stitch together along top edge. Turn bag right side out and press. Topstitch ¹/₈" from top edges of bag to close opening.

6. To form the drawstring casing, topstitch the long edges of a length of ribbon across top back of gift bag.

7. For drawstrings, cut 2 lengths of ribbon approximately 2¹/₂ times the width of your gift bag. Beginning and ending on opposite sides of casing, use a safety pin to thread one drawstring through casing, woven ribbon on front and back through casing; knot ends together. Repeat with remaining drawstring.

SNOWFLAKE TOPIARIES

(shown on page 116)
The art of topiary has been practiced for hundreds of years. Topiaries have become popular focal points for landscaping as well as for interior decorating. Try your hand at creating these snowflake topiaries as the focal point of your holiday decorating.

Begin with 3 sizes of clay pots and 3 dowel rods; working in a well-ventilated area, spray paint white. Covering drain holes in pots with tape, follow manufacturer's instructions to mix and fill pots halfway with plaster; insert dowel rods. Allow plaster to set up until firm.

Read *Working with Polymer Clay,* page 431, then follow the polymer clay manufacturer's instructions to condition clay; run clay through a pasta machine (used for clay only) on the #1 setting. Using cookie cutters, cut out snowflakes. Following the instructions on the clay package, bake snowflakes in the oven. Once cooled, spray snowflakes with spray adhesive and sprinkle with mica snow glitter. Repeat on back of snowflake.

Hot glue snowflakes to dowel rods. For largest pot, layer 2 snowflakes. Using dimensional foam dots, adhere a sticker to the center of each snowflake. Tie a length of ribbon into a bow around dowel rod.

Use double-stick tape to adhere torn strips of fabric to the rims of the pots. Stamp words on blue cardstock; insert in metal tags and tie around rims using ribbon. Fill pots to brim with chenille fabric.

ORIGAMI TREE

(shown on page 120)
• red, yellow, blue, brown, light green and green cardstock
• ¹/₄" and ¹/₂" dia. hole punches
• silver earring hooks
• silver jump rings
• 3"x6" foam cone
• 7" length of ¹/₂" dia. dowel rod
• ³/₄" dia. circle punch
• glitter
• craft glue
• straight pins (optional)
• tracing paper

1. Cut 2" from the top of the cone. Cover the cone with brown paper; glue in place or secure with straight pins.

2. Insert 3" of the dowel into the top of the cone.

3. For bottom tree section, start with a 12"x12" piece of light green cardstock. Referring to Figs. 1-4, fold in half diagonally 4 times.

Fig. 1

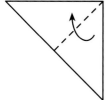

Fig. 2

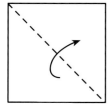

Fig. 3

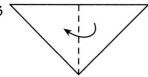

Fig. 4

4. Referring to Fig. 5, cut away ends.

Fig. 5

5. Unfold tree section…refold along original fold lines, accordion style.

6. For middle tree section, repeat Steps 3-5 using a 10"x10" piece of green cardstock.

7. For top tree section, repeat Steps 3-5 using an 8"x8" piece of light green cardstock.

8. Using both hole punches, punch holes randomly along edges of each tree section. Apply glue, then glitter along edges of tree sections. Allow to dry and top off excess glitter.

9. Cut a small hole at center of each tree section. Slide dowel rod in tree base through center of each tree section. Spacing sections evenly and leaving a small section of dowel rod at top for the star, glue tree sections in place along dowel rod.

10. Punch ³/₄" dia. circles from red, yellow, light green and blue cardstock. Punch a ¹/₄" dia. hole near edge of each circle.

11. Apply swirls of glue, then glitter to half of the ornaments. Allow to dry and tap off excess glitter.

12. For hangers, insert a jump ring or an earring hook through the hole in each circle. To decorate tree, insert hangers through holes along edges of tree sections.

13. Using the pattern on page 485, follow *Making Patterns*, page 427, to trace the star pattern onto tracing paper. Using the pattern, cut 2 stars from yellow cardstock. Following the dotted lines on pattern, fold each star.

14. Leaving an opening along bottom, glue the points of the stars together. Apply glue, then glitter along edges of star. Allow to dry and tap off excess glitter.

15. Slip star onto top of dowel rod; glue in place.

PINWHEEL ORNAMENT

(shown on page 120)
For each ornament you will need:
• green and yellow cardstock
• ¹/₂" red foam heart
• 1¹/₂" dia. flower punch
• ¹/₈" and ¹/₁₆" dia. hole punches
• mica snow
• craft glue
• scallop-edged craft scissors
• ¹/₄"w red ribbon

1. Using craft scissors, cut a 1¹/₂"x12" strip of green cardstock.

2. Using both hole punches, punch holes along one long edge of strip.

3. Using approximately ³/₈" wide folds, accordion fold strip.

4. Cut a 2" dia. circle from yellow cardstock. Bend short ends of folded green strip together to form pinwheel; glue together. Glue the center back of pinwheel to the circle.

5. Punch a flower from yellow cardstock; glue to center front of pinwheel.

6. Thin a small amount of craft glue with water; brush over center of ornament. Sprinkle mica snow glitter over glue; allow to dry, then tap off extra glitter.

7. Glue heart to center of ornament.

8. For hanger, thread ribbon through one hole punched in ornament; tie ends together.

BUTTON ORNAMENT
(shown on page 120)
For each ornament you will need:
• Christmas vellum
• red cardstock
• ceramic Christmas button
• 8" length of red trim
• craft glue
• 1/4" dia. hole punch

1. Cut two 4"x10" strips of vellum. Referring to Fig. 1, accordion fold strips, then fold down a triangle between each accordion fold. Fold each strip, then glue one short end of each strip to the short end of the other strip. Fan strips into a circle to form ornament.

Fig. 1

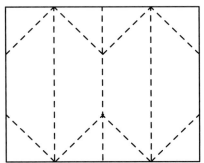

2. Cut a 1 1/2" dia. circle from red cardstock; glue to center front of ornament.

3. Glue button to center of cardstock.

4. For hanger, punch a hole along the top front of ornament; thread trim through hole; tie ends together.

BIRD ORNAMENT
(shown on page 120)
• red and yellow cardstock
• red glitter
• 1/4" dia. wiggle eyes
• 1/3 yard 1/2"w red ribbon
• 1/8" dia. hole punch
• tracing paper

Using the patterns on page 485, follow *Making Patterns*, page 427, to trace the patterns onto tracing paper. Using patterns, cut bird and wings from red cardstock and beak from yellow cardstock. Fold beak in half as indicated by dotted line on pattern; glue to bird. Using approximately 1/3" folds, accordion fold wings; insert through body of bird and glue in place. Glue wiggle eyes to bird's head. Thin a small amount of craft glue with water; brush over sides and wings of bird. Sprinkle glitter over glue; allow to dry, then tap off extra glitter. Punch a hole along center top of bird. For hanger, thread ribbon through hole; tie ends together.

WISH LIST ALBUM
(shown on page 122)
Children will love making this Wish List to proudly show when asked what they want for Christmas. Using the patterns on page 485, follow *Making Patterns*, page 427, to trace the patterns onto tracing paper. Using patterns, cut one small tag from red cardstock and several large tags from red and green corrugated paper. Stamp child's name onto small tag and embellish with a foam snowflake sticker. For hanger, tie a small length of thread through hole and tie ends together. Thread large tags and hanger of small tag onto a shower curtain ring. Use foam alphabet stickers to spell "Wish List" on first large tag. Let the child cut pictures out of a catalog of those special things that they just "have to have," then glue the pictures to the large tags.

NOTEPAD BOOKLET
(shown on page 123)
• 3" square notepad
• mat board
• scrapbook paper
• two 1/2" dia. buttons
• embroidery floss
• craft knife
• craft glue

1. Cut a 3 1/2"x7 1/2" piece of mat board.

2. Referring to Fig. 1, use craft knife to score mat board, then bend board to create folds in booklet. When folded, the short end will overlap the long end by approximately 1/2".

Fig. 1

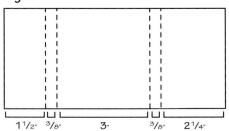

1 1/2"   3/8"   3"   3/8"   2 1/4"

3. Wrapping ends to inside of booklet and securing with glue, cover booklet with paper.

4. Using 6 strands of embroidery floss and poking holes through mat board, sew buttons 1/2" from edge of short end and 1" from edge of long end of booklet. For closure, tie one end of a 10" length of floss to one of the buttons; wrap around both buttons to close booklet.

5. For inside cover, glue a 3"x7" piece of scrapbook paper to inside of booklet. Adhere notepad to inside of booklet.

SANTA DOLL
(shown on pages 125 & 126)
• 1/4 yard red corduroy
• 1/8 yard white chenille fabric
• 1/8 yard white cotton fabric
• peach and black felt
• 5/8 yard 3/8"w plaid ribbon
• gold metallic thread
• white chenille yarn
• polyester fiberfill
• black embroidery floss
• fabric glue

Match right sides and use a 1/4" seam allowance for all sewing unless otherwise indicated.

Bring Santa to life with this

cuddly doll. Enlarging the body pattern by 155% and following *Making Patterns*, page 427, use the patterns on pages 486-488 to trace the patterns onto tracing paper; cut out. Using patterns, cut one beard, one mustache, 2 hat brims and 2 hat tassel pieces from chenille fabric. Cut one beard and one mustache piece from white fabric for backing. Cut face from peach felt. Cut 4 mittens and 4 boots (2 each in reverse) from black felt. Cut 2 bodies and 2 gussets from corduroy. Cut 4 arms and 4 legs (2 each in reverse) from corduroy.

With wrong sides matching, machine satin stitch white fabric to back of beard and mustache. Work *French Knots* on face pieces for eyes.

For front of Santa, glue face piece approximately 2¹/₂" from top of body front piece. Topstitch hat brim to body front along top of face. Sew one tassel to top of body (Fig. 1); press to right side. Repeat to sew beard to bottom of face. Sew mustache in place using red thread and a machine satin stitch for nose. Machine satin stitch a length of ribbon 3¹/₂" from bottom of body piece for belt; machine satin stitch buckle with gold metallic thread. Using 6 strands of floss, work *French Knots* for buttons.

Fig. 1

For back of Santa, sew remaining tassel to top of back body piece; press to right side. Topstitch hat brim to back piece. Machine satin stitch ribbon in place for belt.

Sew one mitten to end of each arm. Leaving top of each arm open,

sew arm pieces together; turn right side out. Stuff each arm with fiberfill; baste in place on body.

Sew one boot to end of each leg. Leaving top of each leg open, sew leg pieces together; turn right side out. Stuff each leg with fiberfill; sew to the straight edge of one gusset piece.

Matching right sides and leaving bottom open, sew body pieces together. Baste straight edges of gusset pieces together. Sew curved edges of gusset piece to bottom edges of body. Beginning at the center, remove enough basting threads in order to turn Santa right side out. Stuff Santa with fiberfill; sew opening closed. Glue yarn along edges of beard, mustache, hat brim, tassel, mittens, boots and bottom of body.

EMBELLISHED SWEATER
(shown on page 127)
Turn an ordinary sweater into a blooming beauty with a few little touches. Use a crewel needle to run a length of yarn along edges of sweater and cuffs. Use a crochet hook to chain stitch flower stems through sweater. For leaves, cut 4" lengths of ⁵/₈"w green ribbon. With right sides together, fold each length of ribbon where the right sides of each end are together; pull ends through sweater and tack in place. For flower, cut a 7" dia. circle from felt. Refer to Fig. 1 and use yarn to cinch felt circle into a flower shape; knot yarn to secure. Use yarn to stitch veins and a *French Knot* on each flower petal. For center of flower, knot a length of 1"w ribbon 3 times; stitch to flower.

Fig. 1

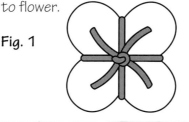

LET IT SNOW SWEATER
(shown on page 127)
When the weather outside is frightful, bundle your little one up in this delightful sweater and "Let It Snow, Let It Snow, Let It Snow." Using the snowman patterns on page 489, follow *Making Patterns*, page 427, to trace the patterns onto tracing paper. Using the patterns, cut the snowman from white felt, the gloves from black felt, the scarf from blue felt and the hat and nose from orange felt. Work *Straight Stitches*, page 423, to attach nose, scarf and buttons to snowman; work *French Knots* for snowman's mouth and work *Cross Stitches* for snowman's eyes. Work *Straight Stitches* to attach snowman to front of sweater. Add *Running Stitches* across brim of hat, then work *Straight Stitches* to attach hat and gloves to snowman. Thread alphabet beads onto a length of embroidery floss and *Couch* in place between mittens. Various sizes of white pom-poms randomly stitched onto sweater provide the finishing touch.

SANTA POCKET ENVELOPE
(shown on page 135)
We used Christmas paper on our Envelope Gift Box but you can change the paper to fit any occasion.

Cut a 10" dia. circle from cardstock and scrapbook paper; in a well-ventilated area, use spray adhesive to adhere paper to cardstock. Score card 3" from top and bottom edges of circle, then score card 3" from each side of circle. Along score marks, fold sides of circle to center. For bottom flap, fold bottom of circle up; for top flap, fold top of circle down. Cut a decorative piece of paper to fit top flap; use spray adhesive to adhere to top of flap. For closure, glue one end of a length of ribbon to back of top flap; sew a button onto bottom flap.

CHRISTMAS MEMORY BOX

(shown on page 188)

• photo box (ours measures
  11"x7¹/₄"x4¹/₂")
• assorted scrapbook papers
• spray adhesive
• typewriter key charms
• twine
• small frame
• craft glue
• color photocopy of a vintage
  postcard
• scrap of fabric
• ¹/₈" dia. hole punch
• ³/₈"w red ribbon
• adhesive foam dots
• small tag sticker
• resin "remember" sticker
• assorted buttons
• beaded snowflake stickers
• small snowflake stickers
• tag alphabet stickers

1. Working in a well-ventilated area,
use spray adhesive to cover the box
sides and lid with scrapbook papers.

2. Thread typewriter keys onto 2
lengths of twine; attach the twine
ends to the sides of the frame
opening. Cover the frame back with
scrapbook paper. Glue the frame to
the lid.

3. Tear the edges of the postcard
photocopy. Tear a fabric piece
slightly larger than the postcard.
Punch holes in the corners and use
ribbon to knot the postcard to
the fabric piece. Use foam dots to
attach the fabric to the lid.

4. Tie a short ribbon length through
the hole in the tag sticker. Apply the
resin sticker to the tag. Use foam
dots to attach the tag to the lid.

5. Apply buttons and stickers
randomly to the box lid.

GIFT TAG ORNAMENTS

(shown on page 189)

For each ornament, cut 2 same-
size felt pieces. Decorate one side
of each piece . . . glue on ribbons or
lace, attach fabric or felt pieces using
embroidery stitches, sew on buttons
or charms or attach pictures. Add
your personalization; then tack fibers
and ribbons to the top for the hanger.
Glue the felt pieces together back to
back.

ACCORDION-FOLD ALBUM

(shown on page 190)

Cut a 6"x25¹/₄" strip of artist's
paper. At one end of the strip, fold
a 1¹/₄" flap. Accordion-fold the rest
of the strip into 6" squares. Add
decorations and photographs to
the pages, cover and flap. Leaving a 6"
tail, attach a 22" ribbon length
to the front cover with foam dots.
Wrap the remaining ribbon end
around the album; tie the ends at
the flap to secure.

FRAMED RECIPE

(shown on page 192)

Cut cardboard to fit inside a frame.
Mount pieces of vintage tea towels
or tablecloths on the cardboard for
a background (if you don't want to
cut your towels or tablecloths, use
a color photocopy of them). Add
the recipe to the background; then
embellish the background with other
memorabilia such as a photo, a doily,
buttons, charms and tags. Insert the
background into the frame.

THE 12 TAGS OF
CHRISTMAS

(continued from page 197)

I Believe

(shown on page 194)

Don't feel comfortable handwriting
on your tag? Just photocopy or
trace the "Believe" pattern on page
505 onto a vellum piece; then use
the vellum to make a pocket on the
tag. The childhood photo framed
with cardstock is sure to remind you
to believe in Santa.

Happy Holidays

(shown on page 195)

Rifle through your stash of
vintage postcards and you're sure
to find just the right background
for this tag. Machine sew a singed
vellum pocket to the tag; then add
brads, embroidered snap tape and a
second tag and you're ready to wish
someone "Happy Holidays."

Ho Ho Ho

(shown on page 195)

Believe it or not, you don't have
to know how to crochet to create
this tag. The cute Santa hat
embellishment is purchased! To
add even more interest, paint a
metal label holder and rough it
up a little with sandpaper before
attaching it to the tag. Use
adhesive foam dots to attach the
snowflake charms to the tag.

Magic Reindeer Mix

(shown on page 195)

Rudolph is sure to stop Santa's
sleigh at your house to snack on
the magical mix included with this
tag. Sew cardstock and cellophane
pieces together to make a pocket
and fill the pocket with Magic
Reindeer Mix (dry oatmeal and
glitter). Print the saying below onto
cardstock and use it to label the
back of the tag. Attach the tag to a
child's gift.

*On Christmas Eve, sprinkle this magic
reindeer mix on your lawn to guide
Santa's reindeer to your rooftop.
While Santa makes his delivery inside,
Rudolph and his friends can have a
snack.*

Santa's Favorites

(shown on page 196)
This tag reminds us that Santa wants us all to be good boys and girls. Spell out some of the message by printing or stamping your words onto cardstock or paper; then adhere them to the tag. "X" and "O" tiles and a "good" sticker complete the message. Finish by chalking the tag edges for an antique look.

Dear Santa

(shown on page 196)
A needle, thread, buttons and a thimble are sure to help Santa mend his suit in case of a rip. For a clever hanger, attach a suspender clip to the top of the tag. Thread ribbon through the clip and sew across the ribbon to secure. Add a small note to Santa using a miniature clothespin.

A Christmas Present

(shown on page 196)
Stamps, stickers and ribbons make this tag a present all by itself. Start by stamping a background on the tag and a Santa figure on white cardstock. Color Santa with colored pencils. Add ribbons and postage stamp stickers and use adhesive foam dots to adhere Santa to the tag.

Wishes

(shown on page 196)
A recycled piece of vintage-look wrapping paper provides the perfect backdrop for this tag. Apply Soft Flock® fibers to Santa's coat and hat to make them look extra soft. Metal embellishments held on with red ribbon and a shiny tinsel hanger make it unique.

Family

(shown on page 196)
Create this tag in honor of your loved ones. Use a label maker to make a red tape that says "Christmas." Add a second tag, stickers and a miniature wreath. (Attach the wreath with craft glue.) Be sure to align the holes in the tags so it's easy to add the ribbon.

Holiday Wishes

(shown on page 196)
Torn fabric pieces turn this tag into a holder for a second tag. How clever! Begin by tearing four 1"x2" pieces of red fabric. Overlapping the long edges of the fabric pieces slightly, arrange the pieces on a cardstock rectangle and machine sew around the outside edges of the strips. Glue the cardstock to the tag. Make and embellish a second tag and weave it through the fabric slits.

FLEECE & CHENILLE STOCKINGS

(shown on page 200)
• ¹/₂ yard of 60"w blue fleece
• assorted cream buttons
• ³/₈ yard white chenille
• ⁷/₈ yard of ¹/₂"w cream twill tape
• ⁵/₈ yard of 60"w cream fleece
• tracing paper
• blue felt
• fabric glue
• ¹/₃ yard of 60"w light blue fleece
• ¹/₂ yard light blue chenille rickrack
• ¹/₂ yard light blue chenille
• ¹/₂ yard cream pom-pom trim
• 3 white chenille stems

Use a ¹/₂" seam allowance for all sewing.

Large Stocking

1. Use a photocopier to enlarge the pattern on page 506 to 197%. Using the enlarged pattern, cut 2 stocking pieces (one in reverse) from blue fleece.

2. Avoiding the seam allowance, sew buttons to the stocking front as desired. Matching the right sides and leaving the top edge open, sew the stocking pieces together and turn right side out.

3. For the cuff, matching the right sides and short edges, fold an 11"x20" white chenille piece in half. Sew the short edges together. Matching the wrong sides and raw edges, fold the cuff in half. Matching the raw edges and the seam in the cuff to the heel-side seam of the stocking, insert the cuff in the stocking. Sew the cuff to the stocking along the raw edges. Turn the cuff to the outside.

4. For the hanger, fold a 10" length of twill tape in half and tack the ends inside the stocking at the heel-side seam.

Medium Stocking

1. Use a photocopier to enlarge the pattern on page 506 to 165%. Using the enlarged pattern, cut 2 stocking pieces (one in reverse) from cream fleece.

2. Matching the right sides and leaving the top edge open, sew the stocking pieces together and turn right side out.

3. Using the pattern on page 503, cut the snowflake pieces from blue felt and glue them to the stocking front.

4. For the cuff, follow Step 3 of the **Large Stocking**, using a 9"x17" piece of light blue fleece. Glue a 16" length of rickrack around the cuff.

5. For the hanger, follow Step 4 of the **Large Stocking**, using a 9" length of twill tape.

(continued on page 448)

SMALL STOCKING

1. Use a photocopier to enlarge the pattern on page 506 to 144%. Using the enlarged pattern, cut 2 stocking pieces (one in reverse) from light blue chenille.

2. Matching the right sides and leaving the top edge open, sew the stocking pieces together and turn right side out.

3. For the cuff, follow Step 3 of the **Large Stocking** (page 447), using an 8"x15" piece of cream fleece; do not turn the cuff to the outside.

4. Pull the cuff out of the stocking. Glue a 14 1/2" length of pom-pom trim along the folded edge and fold the cuff to the outside.

5. For the snowflake on the cuff, twist the chenille stems together at the center and curl the ends. Glue the snowflake to the center of one side of the cuff. Sew buttons to the cuff as desired.

6. For the hanger, follow Step 4 of the **Large Stocking**, using a 9" length of twill tape.

SNOWMAN CHAIRBACK COVER

(shown on page 202)
- 7/8 yard of 60"w white fleece
- cardboard
- polyester fiberfill
- upholstery needle and heavy-duty thread
- two 1/2" dia. black shank buttons
- tracing paper
- scraps of black and orange felt
- fabric glue

- blush and applicator
- 1/4 yard red felt
- three 1" dia. tan pom-poms
- 1/2 yard white pom-pom fringe
- 1/2 yard light blue chenille rickrack
- child's round-back wooden chair
- white decorative yarn
- string
- fabric marking pen
- thumbtack
- 14"x17" watercolor paper
- 14"x17" piece of light blue felt
- stapler
- 1 1/4" dia. foam brush
- tan acrylic paint
- 1 3/4" dia. white pom-pom
- 5/8 yard red chenille rickrack

Our chairback cover was made for a 13 1/2"wx15"h chairback. You may need to adjust the size of your cover to fit your chair.

1. Use a photocopier to enlarge the snowman body pattern on page 497 to 241%. Enlarge the snowman base pattern to 252%. Using the enlarged body pattern, cut the snowman back from white fleece. Extending the bottom edge 5", use the pattern and cut the snowman front from white fleece. Using the enlarged base pattern, cut a base from cardboard.

2. Matching the right sides and top edges and stopping 1/2" from the bottom edge of the snowman back, use a 1/2" seam allowance and sew the snowman front and back together. Sew a 1/2" hem along the raw edges. Turn right side out.

3. Insert the base in the snowman. Stuff the snowman's face. Sewing through both fleece layers and the base, sew the buttons to the face for eyes. Pull the thread tight to tuft the face and knot the ends.

4. Using the patterns, cut eyebrows, a mouth and a nose from felt. Matching the right sides, use a 1/4" seam allowance and sew the sides of the nose together. Turn the nose right side out and stuff. Glue the nose, eyebrows and mouth to the face. Blush the "cheeks."

5. For the snowman's buttons, glue three 1 1/2" diameter red felt circles and the tan pom-poms to the body as shown. Glue a 15 1/2" length each of pom-pom fringe and light blue rickrack to the bottom edge of the snowman front as shown.

6. Place the snowman over the chairback, resting the base on the back of the chair seat. Stuff the snowman's "belly."

7. For the scarf, cut a 3 3/4"x41" red felt piece and make 2 1/2" long cuts, 1/4" apart, along both ends for the fringe. Glue yarn stripes on the scarf. Tie the scarf around the snowman's "neck."

8. For the hat, tie one end of a length of string to the fabric pen. Insert the thumbtack through the string 13" from the pen. Insert the thumbtack in one corner of the watercolor paper. Holding the tack in place and keeping the string taut, mark the cutting line (See Fig. 1 of *Making a Fabric Circle* on page 427). Repeat on the light blue felt with the thumbtack 13 3/4" from the pen. Cut both pieces along the cutting lines.

9. Roll the paper hat into a cone and staple to secure. Overlapping and wrapping to the inside as necessary, use glue to cover the hat with the felt. Paint dots on the hat. Glue the white pom-pom and red rickrack to the hat as shown and place it on the snowman's head.

GIFT TAGS
(shown on page 202)

- small, medium and large tag dies and a die-cutting tool
- light blue, tan and textured cream cardstock
- white and blue polka-dot, red and white polka-dot, blue striped and red and white mesh-print scrapbook papers
- craft glue
- brown ink pad
- red thread
- light blue chipboard monogram
- 1/4"w red ribbon
- snowflake charms
- alphabet rub-ons and stamps
- red staples and stapler
- red jute
- 3/16"w and 1/2"w red rickrack
- black fine-point permanent pen
- white wired pom-pom trim
- silver ball chain with connector

MONOGRAM TAG
Layer and glue die-cut cardstock and paper tags together as desired. Ink, then sew along the tag edges. Decorate the tag with the monogram, ribbon, charm and rub-ons. Cut out each word of a stamped message, ink the edges and staple them along one edge. Knot jute, ribbon and 3/16"w rickrack through the hole in the tag.

TIP: If you don't have red staples, use a red permanent pen to color plain staples.

NOEL TAG
Glue die-cut light blue and cream cardstock tags together. Cut a paper pocket for the tag and glue a paper strip and 1/2"w rickrack along the top. Sew along the tag edges, attaching the pocket to the tag. Decorate the tag with ink, cardstock, rub-ons, jute and a charm. Make one small and one medium layered cardstock and paper tag. Ink the tags and use rub-ons and the pen to add messages. Knot trim and attach the chain through the holes in the tags. Place the smaller tags in the pocket on the large tag.

PEACE ON EARTH CARD
(shown on page 204)

- cream and light blue cardstock
- brown plaid scrapbook paper
- craft knife and cutting mat
- craft glue
- deckle-edged craft scissors
- snowflake punch
- mica flakes
- alphabet rub-ons
- 4" length each of 3/8"w brown velvet ribbon and 3/8"w brown rickrack

1. For the card, matching the short edges, fold a 5 1/2"x8" cream cardstock piece and a 3 7/8"x8" paper piece in half. Cut a 2" square opening in the center front of the paper, 1/2" from the top edge.

2. Matching the folds and top edges, glue the cardstock and paper together; trim the sides with craft scissors. Cut a 1 3/4" square opening in the cardstock at the center of the paper opening on the card front.

3. Punch 3 snowflakes, 5/8" apart, in the center bottom of the card front. Set one punched snowflake aside. Apply glue to the cardstock. Sprinkle with mica flakes, allow to dry and shake off the excess.

4. Matching the short edges, fold a 5 1/2"x8" light blue cardstock piece in half. Matching the folds, glue the cardstock inside the card.

5. Glue the punched snowflake to the cardstock in the center of the front opening. Use rub-ons to spell "peace on earth" in the opening. Glue mica flakes to the snowflake in spots.

6. Glue ribbon and rickrack to the card front over the bottom paper edge.

JOY CARD
(shown on page 204)

- light blue cardstock
- Thinkable Inkable™ Christmas stamp
- silver ink pad
- red and white ticking and polka-dot scrapbook papers
- craft glue
- deckle-edged craft scissors
- craft knife and cutting mat
- sandpaper
- silver wreath and alphabet charms
- red embroidery floss
- adhesive foam dots
- 3/16" dia. silver brads

For the card, matching the short edges, fold a 4 7/8"x6 1/8" cardstock piece in half. Stamp messages on the front. Matching the short edges, fold a 7/8"x6 1/8" strip of ticking paper in half. Matching the folds, glue the strip to the card near one side edge. Trim the bottom front edge with craft scissors.

For the frame, cut a 2 1/2"x2 7/8" polka-dot paper piece with a 1 1/2"x1 7/8" opening at the center. Sand the frame edges. Knot the wreath charm onto the center of a 2" floss length and glue the floss ends to the back of one long frame edge. Attach the frame to the card front with foam dots. Use brads to attach the alphabet charms to the ticking paper.

STAMPED GIFT WRAP

(shown on page 204)
- 1¼" dia. foam brush
- light blue acrylic paint
- plain white gift wrap
- Thinkable Inkable™ Christmas stamp and assorted-sized alphabet stamps
- red ink pad
- red fine-point permanent pen
- light blue cardstock
- double-sided tape
- red and white polka-dot scrapbook paper
- packages
- red wired pom-pom trim
- adhesive foam dot
- large red pom-pom

Paint blue dots on the gift wrap; allow to dry. Stamp and write words and phrases on the gift wrap. Cut a cardstock tag. Tape the tag to the paper and cut the paper slightly larger than the tag. Stamp a message on the tag. Wrap the packages, tape the tag to the top package and tie the packages together with the trim. Use the foam dot to attach the large pom-pom to the top package.

GIFT BOX WITH SNOWFLAKE EMBELLISHMENT

(shown on page 204)
- gift box
- kraft paper
- double-sided tape
- assorted ribbons
- alphabet rub-ons
- black fine-point permanent pen
- tiny tag
- tiny silver bell
- red jute
- spray adhesive
- newsprint scrapbook paper
- 6" square of mat board
- tracing paper
- craft knife and cutting mat
- red wired pom-pom trim
- craft glue

Wrap the box with kraft paper. Tape ribbons around the box as desired. Use rub-ons to spell " 'Tis the Season" on some of the ribbons. Tie wide ribbon into a bow around one end of the box.

Write the recipient's name on the tag and tie the tag and bell onto one of the ribbons on the box with jute and narrow ribbon.

For the snowflake embellishment, working in a well-ventilated area, use spray adhesive to adhere scrapbook paper to the mat board. Using the pattern on page 506, cut the snowflake from the mat board. Cut a length of trim with 8 pom-poms. Remove all but one pom-pom from the trim. Gluing the wired pom-pom to the top, glue the pom-poms to the tips of the snowflake. Use the wire to attach the snowflake to the wide ribbon bow.

CROSSWORD PUZZLE GIFT BAG

(shown on page 205)
- sandpaper
- blue gift bag without handles
- small and large scallop-edged craft scissors
- white paint pen
- white vellum
- vellum tape
- 9" length of ¼"w white ribbon
- craft glue
- white cardstock
- scrapbook paper (optional)
- ⅛" dia. hole punch
- alphabet rub-ons
- black fine-point permanent pen
- ¼" dia. blue brad

For a distressed look, sand the bag and wipe away the dust. Trim the top with the small scallop scissors. Paint dots and snowflakes on the bag. Photocopy the crossword puzzle on page 500 onto vellum; cut it out and tape it to the center of the bag front. Glue a ribbon bow to the corner of the puzzle.

Cut two 2⅜"x4" cardstock tags. If desired, cover one tag with paper. Punch a hole in the top of each tag and trim the bottom edges with the large scallop scissors. Use the rub-ons to spell "ACROSS" and "DOWN" on the tags as shown. Add the clues with the black pen. If desired, write the answers on the back of the tags. Attach the tags to the bag with the brad.

CROSSWORD PUZZLE CLUES

Down

1. December 25th
2. Let there be _____ on Earth
3. ____ log
5. Ebenezer _____
7. Hung by the chimney with care
8. A custom or ritual
12. Red-nosed reindeer
15. Holiday beverage
17. Four-letter word for Christmas

Across

4. Three-letter word for happiness
6. Christmas bread
9. Saint Nick
10. A round door decoration
11. Rejoice, party, enjoy, make merry
13. When you ____ upon a star
14. Christmas flower
16. Famous snowman
18. Rhymes with jolly
19. Newborn king
20. Kiss under this

CROSSWORD PUZZLE ANSWERS

Down

1. Holiday
2. Peace
3. Yule
5. Scrooge
7. Stockings
8. Tradition
12. Rudolph
15. Eggnog
17. Noel

Across

4. Joy
6. Fruitcake
9. Santa
10. Wreath
11. Celebrate
13. Wish
14. Poinsettia
16. Frosty
18. Holly
19. Jesus
20. Mistletoe

HO HO HO CARD

(shown on page 205)
- white and textured red cardstock
- black and red colored pencils
- craft glue
- two $5/8$" dia. black shank buttons with the shanks removed
- $1\,1/4$" square silver buckle
- $1\,1/4$"x6" strip of black faux leather
- awl
- white decorative yarn
- alphabet dies and a die-cutting tool
- iridescent glitter
- adhesive foam dots

For the card, fold a 6"x12" red cardstock piece in half, matching the short edges. For the coat opening, draw a black line down the card front. Shade the front with the red pencil. Glue the buttons to the card front as shown. For the belt, slide the buckle onto the center of the leather strip. Use the awl to punch a hole in the strip for the buckle prong. Glue the belt to the card as shown. Glue yarn along the bottom edge of the card front. Die-cut "ho ho ho" from white cardstock. Apply glue to the letters. Sprinkle with glitter, allow to dry and shake off the excess. Use pieces of foam dots to adhere the letters to the card front.

WISH CARD

(shown on page 205)
- light blue and white cardstock
- blue and green harlequin-print and two-tone green-checked scrapbook papers
- craft glue
- spray adhesive
- mica flakes
- alphabet dies and a die-cutting tool
- iridescent glitter
- adhesive foam dots
- $1/8$" dia. silver brads
- silver snowflake charms
- silver paint pen
- $3/4$ yard of $3/8$"w blue-green ribbon

Use spray adhesive in a well-ventilated area.

For the card, fold a 6"x12" light blue cardstock piece in half, matching the short edges. Tear a $5\,1/2$" white cardstock square and a $5\,1/4$" harlequin-print paper square. Glue the torn pieces together. Spray a torn 3"x4" white cardstock piece with adhesive. Sprinkle with mica flakes, allow to dry and shake off the excess. Glue the flaked cardstock to the center of the torn paper square. Die-cut "WISH" from checked paper. Using glue, apply glitter spots to the letters. Attach the letters to the flaked cardstock with foam dots. Use brads to attach charms to the layered pieces. Paint the edges of the card front. Glue the layered pieces to the card. Wrap ribbon around the card at the fold and tie the ends into a bow.

NATURALS

(shown on page 206)
WINDOW SWAG
Create this swag with real pine and cedar branches and pinecones, or use artificial items for a decoration to use year after year. Use floral wire to join the pine and cedar branches together to form the swag. Accent the greenery with pinecones, white tallow berries, glitter sprays and white mica stars.

PEACE, LOVE AND HARMONY BASKETS
- hot glue gun
- floral foam
- 3 whitewashed baskets
- large pinecones
- 3 small chalkboards and chalk
- matte spray sealer
- copper and green wire
- wire cutters
- cedar and pine branches
- white narcissus
- silver glitter sprays
- white tallow berries
- silver ornaments
- white mica stars

Use spray sealer in a well-ventilated area.

1. Hot glue floral foam inside each basket.

2. Hot glue pinecone scales around the edges of each chalkboard to form frames. Write "peace," "love" and "harmony" on the chalkboards, apply sealer and attach them to the front of each basket with wire and glue.

3. Arrange branches, narcissus and glitter sprays in each basket. Add pinecones, berries, ornaments and stars as shown.

(continued on page 452)

Twig Snowflakes

- twigs
- hot glue gun
- jute
- white acrylic paint
- paintbrush
- craft glue
- mica snow
- clear nylon thread

For each snowflake, cut or break 3 twigs into equal lengths. Arrange 2 of the twigs into an "X" and hot glue them together at the center. Hot glue the third twig across the center of the "X." Wrap jute around the center of the snowflake. For extra detail, hot glue smaller twigs to the snowflake. Brush thinned paint on the snowflake and allow to dry. Brush thinned glue on the snowflake. Sprinkle with mica snow, allow to dry and shake off the excess. Attach a thread hanger.

FROSTY

(continued from page 207)

Luminaries

Never leave burning candles unattended.

Glue glittered buttons on the wire handles of luminary jars. Brush glue over the jar lips and sprinkle with mica snow. Pour mica snow into the bottom of the jars, if you'd like, and add candles. Arrange the luminaries along the porch railing, light the candles and enjoy the glow.

Button Wreath Pillow

A bow of aqua ribbon and a circle of pearl buttons sewn to a plain red pillow add a quick & easy holiday touch to your décor.

Tufted Pillow

Sew a pearl button to the center of an aqua pillow, stitching through the entire pillow. Pull the thread tightly and tie at the back.

TRADITIONAL

(continued from page 211)

Rupert the Snowman

- protective gloves
- wire cutters
- 2 yards of 48"w heavy wire mesh screen
- heavy-duty stapler
- 8-gallon galvanized tub
- newspapers
- queen-size rolled batting
- dental floss
- hot glue gun
- tracing paper
- 7" square of orange felt
- 2 small black buttons
- 2 large black buttons
- spray adhesive
- mica flakes
- 1 yard of 72"w red felt
- 1/4 yard of 72"w white felt
- red embroidery floss
- holly sprig

Use a 1/2" seam allowance unless otherwise indicated.

1. Wearing the gloves, cut 1 1/3 yards from the screen. Spiral the screen into a loose cone shape with an 8" diameter bottom opening. Staple the cone closed at the top. Making sure the cone will fit inside the tub, staple the mesh together where it overlaps. Stuff the cone with crumpled newspapers to form the body and place in the tub.

2. Matching the short edges, shape and staple the remaining 2/3-yard screen into a tube. Place the bottom of the tube over the top of the body and staple in place. Stuff the tube with crumpled newspapers to form a rounded head. Fold the top end of the screen to the inside of the tube.

3. Cut batting long enough to go around the snowman. Wrap the batting around the body and head, stretching the batting slightly. Stitch the ends together at the back using dental floss. Tuck the batting at the bottom into the tub. Tie dental floss around the neck and tighten to emphasize the head.

4. Form 20 to 30 medium and 2 small batting snowballs. Hot glue the small snowballs to the snowman's face for cheeks. Hot glue the medium snowballs to the body, leaving 1" to 2" between snowballs.

5. Stretch a large batting piece until it's thin. Starting at the neck, hot glue the batting over the snowballs, working down and tucking between snowballs for a lumpy effect. Repeat on the face and cheeks, using a smaller piece.

6. Using the pattern on page 501, cut the nose from orange felt. Matching the straight edges, stitch the sides together with a 1/4" seam allowance. Turn the nose right side out, stuff it with batting and hot glue it to the face.

7. For the eyes, hot glue a small button to the center of each large button. Hot glue the eyes to the face.

8. Working in a well-ventilated area, spray adhesive over the snowman and sprinkle with mica flakes. Spray again with adhesive to seal the mica flakes. Allow to dry overnight.

9. For the scarf, cut a 7"x60" red felt piece. Using the small diamond pattern on page 506, cut 6 white felt diamonds and hot glue to the scarf as shown. Using 6 strands of floss, refer to the photo to work *Running Stitches* (page 423) in a diamond pattern across the felt diamonds. Cut 1/2"x3" fringe strips at each end of the scarf before tying it around the snowman's neck.

10. For the hat, cut a 20" red felt square in half diagonally. Sew the pieces together along one long and one short edge; turn right side out.

11. For the brim, sew the short ends of a 6"x39" white felt piece together to form a loop. Matching the raw edges, fold the loop in half. Insert the loop inside the hat and sew the pieces together along the raw edges. Turn the brim to the outside and tack the holly to the edge. Hot glue a batting snowball to the tip of the hat.

ST. NICK
(shown on page 217)
BODY
• drill with $^3/_4$" and $^1/_8$" bits
• $8^1/_2$"x$11^1/_2$"x1" wood base
• 2"x2"x1" wood block
• two 36" lengths of $^3/_4$" dia. dowel rods
• wood tone spray
• craft glue
• 2 pairs of black socks
• polyester fiberfill
• 12 black buttons
• black and white embroidery floss
• 14-gauge galvanized craft wire
• wire cutters
• duct tape
• tissue paper
• XL red sweater
• white bulky weight novelty eyelash yarn
• white bulky weight brushed acrylic yarn
• size 17 (12.75 mm) knitting needles
• kraft paper
• black medium-point permanent marker

HEAD
• tissue paper
• mat board
• $^1/_4$ yard peach cotton fabric
• air-soluble fabric marking pen
• polyester fiberfill
• 3" doll needle
• heavy-duty thread
• transfer paper

• #2 black Pigma® pen
• colored pencils
• white paint pen
• craft glue
• mohair fleece
• doll eyeglasses
• duct tape
• straight pins

Refer to Knit, page 424, before beginning the project, or use purchased trims for the collar, cuffs and hem.

BODY
1. Centering the holes lengthwise, drill two $^3/_4$" holes, 4" apart, in the base. Drill a $^1/_8$" hole through the center of one side of the wood block and through each dowel, 5" from the top (Fig. 1).

Fig. 1

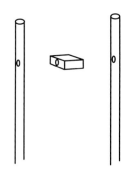

2. In a well-ventilated area, spray wood tone on the base. Securing with glue, insert the dowels in the holes (ends with holes are at the top). For boots, cut small slits in the heels of 2 socks and slip them over the dowels. Stuff the boots. Sew the buttons to the boots. Wrap black floss around the buttons in a crisscross pattern similar to lacing a shoe and tie a bow on each boot. Glue the bottom of the boots to the base.

3. Thread an 84" wire length through one dowel hole, the wood block and the remaining dowel. Even up the wire and bend each end into a "U." Tape the wire at the shoulders (Fig. 2).

Fig. 2

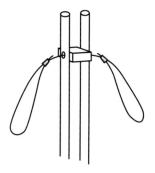

4. Enlarge the coat pattern on page 494, to 304% on a photocopier. Following *Making Patterns* on page 427, trace the pattern onto tissue. Unfold the tissue pattern. Turn the sweater wrong side out. Aligning the bottom pattern edge with the bottom sweater edge, pin the tissue pattern to the sweater through both layers. Machine zigzag along the pattern lines, leaving the bottom, collar and cuffs open. Tear the pattern away, cut $^1/_2$" outside the stitching line and turn the coat right side out.

5. Holding the 2 yarns together, knit the following: a 4-stitch-wide by 15"-long band for the fur collar, a 4-stitch-wide by $10^1/_2$"-long band for each fur sleeve cuff and a 7-stitch-wide by 25"-long band for the bottom coat edge. Use white floss to *Whipstitch* (page 423) the bands to the coat.

6. Slip the coat over the dowel frame. For mittens, put a sock over each hand. Make a kraft paper list and glue it to the mittens.

HEAD
1. Trace the oval and face patterns from pages 494-495 onto tissue paper and cut them out. Using the pattern, cut an oval from mat board. Matching the right sides

(continued on page 454)

and short ends, fold the fabric in half. Use the fabric pen to draw around the face pattern on the fabric. Sew through both fabric layers along the profile line and leave the back open for turning. Cut away the fabric ¼" outside the stitched profile and back lines and turn the face right side out. Sew *Running Stitches* ¼" from the edge along the back opening. Firmly stuff the face, place the mat board in the back opening and pull and knot the threads to secure the opening around the mat board (Fig. 3).

Fig. 3

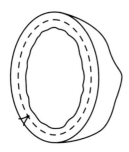

2. To sculpt the nose, follow the Nose Diagram and insert the doll needle through the top of the head, exiting at #1. Insert the needle next to #1. Digging deep into the stuffing and squeezing with your fingers to shape the nose, bring the needle up at #2. Insert the needle next to #2, dig deep and come up at #3. Continue until bringing the needle up at #9, insert diagonally and come up at #10. Insert the needle and come up at #11, gently squeezing the nostril into place. Insert diagonally from #11 to #12; return to #9. Stitch on the outside to #12. Come up at #11, then stitch on the outside to #10. Insert the needle into the fabric, exit through the top of the head and tie a knot.

Nose Diagram

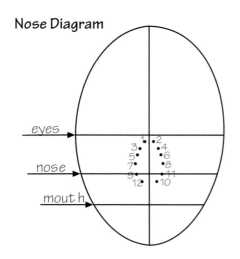

eyes

nose

mouth

3. Transfer the eye patterns from page 494 onto the face. Outline with the Pigma pen. Color the eyes and cheeks with colored pencils. Paint the whites of the eyes and add highlights with the paint pen.

4. Glue mohair to the face as shown for the beard, mustache and eyebrows. Tack the earpieces of the glasses in place.

5. Tape the head to the top of the body and secure with pins. Follow **Santa's Hat Tree Topper** on page 217 to make the hat.

STRIPED KNIT STOCKING
(continued from page 215)
LEFT HEEL
*Note: When instructed to slip a stitch, always slip as if to **purl**, unless otherwise instructed.*

Row 1: Slip 9 sts onto st holder (Right Heel), slip next 18 sts onto second st holder (Top of Foot), slip 1, with Red knit across: 9 sts.

Row 2: Purl across.

Row 3: Slip 1, knit across.

Rows 4-9: Repeat Rows 2 and 3, 3 times.

Heel Turning: P1, P2 tog (Fig. 4, page 425), P1, **turn**; slip 1,

K2, **turn**; P2, P2 tog, P1, **turn**; slip 1, K3, **turn**; P3, P2 tog, P1, **turn**; slip 1, K4, **turn**; P4, P2 tog; cut yarn: 5 sts.

Slip remaining sts onto st holder.

RIGHT HEEL
With **right** side facing, slip 9 sts from Right Heel st holder onto empty needle.

Row 1: Holding 2 strands of Red together, knit across.

Row 2: Slip 1, purl across.

Row 3: Knit across.

Rows 4-8: Repeat Rows 2 and 3 twice, then repeat Row 2 once **more**.

Heel Turning: K1, K2 tog (Fig. 1, page 141), K1, **turn**; slip 1, P2, **turn**; K2, K2 tog, K1, **turn**; slip 1, P3, **turn**; K3, K2 tog, K1, **turn**; slip 1, P4, **turn**; K4, K2 tog: 5 sts.

GUSSET AND INSTEP
Row 1: With **right** side facing, pick up 4 sts along side of Right Heel (Fig. 6, page 425), slip 18 sts from Top of Foot st holder onto an empty needle and knit across, pick up 4 sts along side of Left Heel, knit 5 sts from Left Heel st holder: 36 sts.

Row 2: Purl across.

Row 3: Holding one strand of **each** White together, K8, K2 tog, K 16, slip 1 as if to **knit**, K1, PSSO (Figs. 5a & 5b, page 425), K8: 34 sts.

Row 4: Purl across.

Row 5: K7, K2 tog, K 16, slip 1 as if to **knit**, K1, PSSO, K7: 32 sts.

Row 6: Purl across.

Row 7: Holding 2 strands of Red together, K6, K2 tog, K 16, slip 1 as if to **knit**, K1, PSSO, K6: 30 sts.

Row 8: Purl across.

Row 9: Holding one strand of **each** White together, K5, K2 tog, K 16, slip 1 as if to **knit**, K1, PSSO, K5: 28 sts.

Row 10: Purl across.

Row 11: Knit across.

Row 12: Purl across.

Row 13: Holding 2 strands of Red together, knit across.

Row 14: Purl across.

Row 15: Holding one strand of **each** White together, knit across.

Rows 16-26: Repeat rows 10 to 15 once, Rows 10 to 14 once **more**.

Cut White.

TOE SHAPING

Row 1: Holding 2 strands of Red together, K4, K2 tog, K1, place marker, K1, slip 1 as if to **knit**, K1, PSSO, K8, K2 tog, K1, place marker, K1, slip 1 as if to **knit**, K1, PSSO, K4: 24 sts.

Row 2: Purl across.

Row 3: ★ Knit across to within 3 sts of marker, K2 tog, K2, slip 1 as if to **knit**, K1, PSSO; repeat from ★ once **more**, knit across: 20 sts.

Row 4: Purl across.

Rows 5 and 6: Repeat Rows 3 and 4: 16 sts.

Bind off all sts.

FINISHING

With **right** sides together and beginning at Toe, weave seam to within 3^1/$_2$" (9 cm) from top edge (Fig. 5, page 141); with **wrong** sides together, weave remaining seam. Fold Cuff over.

Hanging Loop: Holding 2 strands of Red together, cast on 12 sts.

Bind off all sts in **knit**.

Sew to seam inside Cuff.

DOTTED KNIT STOCKING
(shown on page 215)
Refer to Knit, page 424, before beginning the project.

Finished Size: 7^1/$_2$"x31" (19x78.5 cm)

MATERIALS
Bulky Weight Yarn
  [5 ounces, 255 yards
  (140 grams, 232 meters)
  per skein]:
  Red - 2 skeins
Bulky Weight Novelty Eyelash Yarn
  [1^3/$_4$ ounces, 47 yards
  (50 grams, 43 meters)
  per skein]:
  White - 2 skeins
Bulky Weight Brushed Acrylic Yarn
  [3^1/$_2$ ounces, 142 yards
  (100 grams, 129 meters)
  per skein]:
  White - 1 skein
Straight knitting needles, size 13
  (9 mm) **or** size needed for gauge
Stitch holders - 3
Yarn needle

GAUGE: Holding 2 strands of Red together, in Stockinette Stitch, 9 sts and 13 rows = 4" (10 cm)

CUFF
Holding one strand of **each** White together, cast on 36 sts.

Work in K1, P1 ribbing for 7" (18 cm).

Cut yarn.

LEG
Row 1 (Right side): Holding 2 strands of Red together, knit across.

Row 2: Purl across.

Row 3: Knit across.

Row 4: Purl across.

Rows 5-64: Repeat Rows 3 and 4, 30 times.

Cut yarn.

LEFT HEEL
Note: When instructed to slip a stitch, always slip as if to **purl**, unless otherwise instructed.

Row 1: Slip 9 sts onto st holder (Right Heel), slip next 18 sts onto second st holder (Top of Foot), slip 1, holding one strand of **each** White together, knit across: 9 sts.

Row 2: Purl across.

Row 3: Slip 1, knit across.

Rows 4-9: Repeat Rows 2 and 3, 3 times.

Heel Turning: P1, P2 tog (Fig. 4, page 425), P1, **turn**; slip 1, K2, **turn**; P2, P2 tog, P1, **turn**; slip 1, K3, **turn**; P3, P2 tog, P1, **turn**; slip 1, K4, **turn**; P4, P2 tog; cut yarn: 5 sts.

Slip remaining sts onto st holder.

RIGHT HEEL
With **right** side facing, slip 9 sts from Right Heel st holder onto empty needle.

Row 1: Holding one strand of **each** White together, knit across.

(continued on page 456)

Row 2: Slip 1, purl across.

Row 3: Knit across.

Rows 4-8: Repeat Rows 2 and 3 twice, then repeat Row 2 once **more**.

Heel Turning: K1, K2 tog (Fig. 3, page 425), K1, **turn**; slip 1, P2, **turn**; K2, K2 tog, K1, **turn**; slip 1, P3, **turn**; K3, K2 tog, K1, **turn**; slip 1, P4, **turn**; K4, K2 tog, cut yarn: 5 sts.

GUSSET AND INSTEP

Row 1: With **right** side facing, slip 5 sts onto left needle, holding 2 strands of Red together, K5, pick up 4 sts along side of Right Heel (Fig. 6, page 425), slip 18 sts from Top of Foot st holder onto an empty needle and knit across, pick up 4 sts along side of Left Heel, knit 5 sts from Left Heel st holder: 36 sts.

Row 2: Purl across.

Row 3: K8, K2 tog, K 16, slip 1 as if to **knit**, K1, PSSO (Figs. 5a & 5b, page 425), K8: 34 sts.

Row 4: Purl across.

Row 5: K7, K2 tog, K 16, slip 1 as if to **knit**, K1, PSSO, K7: 32 sts.

Row 6: Purl across.

Row 7: K6, K2 tog, K 16, slip 1 as if to **knit**, K1, PSSO, K6: 30 sts.

Row 8: Purl across.

Row 9: K5, K2 tog, K 16, slip 1 as if to **knit**, K1, PSSO, K5: 28 sts.

Row 10: Purl across.

Row 11: Knit across.

Row 12: Purl across.

Rows 13-26: Repeat Rows 11 and 12, 7 times.

Cut yarn.

TOE SHAPING

Row 1: Holding one strand of **each** White together, K4, K2 tog, K1, place marker, K1, slip 1 as if to **knit**, K1, PSSO, K8, K2 tog, K1, place marker, K1, slip 1 as if to **knit**, K1, PSSO, K4: 24 sts.

Row 2: Purl across.

Row 3: ★ Knit across to within 3 sts of marker, K2 tog, K2, slip 1 as if to **knit**, K1, PSSO; repeat from ★ once **more**, knit across: 20 sts.

Row 4: Purl across.

Rows 5 and 6: Repeat Rows 3 and 4: 16 sts.

Bind off all sts.

FINISHING

With **right** sides together and beginning at Toe, weave seam to within 3¹/₂" (9 cm) from top edge (Fig. 7, page 425), with **wrong** sides together, weave remaining seam. Fold Cuff over.

Hanging Loop: Holding 2 strands of Red together, cast on 12 sts.

Bind off all sts in **knit**.

Sew to seam inside Cuff.

Dots: Tack spirals of White Eyelash yarn to the stocking.

NEWSPRINT NOEL MANTELSCAPE
(shown on page 218)

MERRY CHRISTMAS BANNER

Use a computer to print "Merry Christmas"; then enlarge the letters to the desired size with a photocopier. Cut out the letters and glue them to newsprint scrapbook paper squares. For the banner, evenly space and glue the squares onto 2 long strips of lightweight cardboard.

Folding between letters, accordion-fold each strip. Brush thinned glue over the banner edges. Sprinkle with mica snow, allow to dry and tap off the excess.

NEWSPRINT STARS

Adhere newsprint scrapbook paper to cardstock. Trace the pattern on page 495 onto tracing paper. Using the pattern, cut 2 stars from the covered cardstock. Refer to the pattern to accordion-fold each star along the dashed lines. Matching the wrong sides, glue the tips of the stars together.

WREATH

Wrap 1¹/₂"-wide ribbon around a plain 20" diameter wreath. Referring to the photo, use floral wire to attach poinsettias, ornaments and flocked branches to the wreath. Tuck a few **Newsprint Stars** into the branches and hang the wreath in front of a mirror.

GARLAND

Swag the garland across the mantel. Insert flocked branches into the garland, add ornaments and attach a bow to each end. Finally, tuck a few **Newsprint Stars** here and there. You can also hang the garland across the top of a doorway or along the top of a china cabinet.

CHRISTMAS GARDEN MANTELSCAPE

(shown on page 219)
Use spray sealer in a well-ventilated area.

Noel Gate Sign

For the chalkboard embellishment, find a chalkboard to fit your gate or paint a wooden plaque with chalkboard paint. Write holiday wishes across the chalkboard with a white colored pencil; then seal the chalkboard with matte spray sealer. Use a computer to print "NOEL"; then enlarge the letters with a photocopier to fit on the chalkboard. Transfer the letters to the chalkboard. Allowing to dry between coats, paint the letters with crackle medium, then ivory acrylic paint. Add a second coat if necessary. Seal the chalkboard again. Wire the chalkboard and a **Distressed Tin Dove** to the gate.

Garland

Embellish a shell garland by dotting glue on the shells and sprinkling them with mica snow. Weave the garland across your mantel along with a beaded-leaf garland, greenery, candles and **Crackled Papier-Mâché Apples**.

Distressed Tin Doves

Refer to *Painting* on page 429 to *Dry Brush* 2 tin doves with ivory acrylic paint. Seal the doves with matte spray sealer. Wire the doves to the **Noel Gate Sign** and a **Distressed Obelisk**.

Crackled Papier-Mâché Apples

Refer to *Painting* on page 429 to *Dry Brush* papier-mâché apples with burnt umber acrylic paint; allow to dry. Allowing to dry between coats, paint the apples with crackle medium, then green acrylic paint. Seal with matte spray sealer.

Distressed Obelisks

Refer to *Painting* on page 429 to *Dry Brush* each metal obelisk topiary form with ivory acrylic paint. Seal with matte spray sealer.

Envelopes

Use caution when placing items near an open flame.

For each envelope, cut a 7"x30" rectangle from textured wallpaper. Fold the rectangle into three 10" sections. Referring to Fig. 1, mark 2¹⁄₄" above the bottom corners of the rectangle. Draw a line from each mark to the top corner of the center section and cut along the marked lines.

Fig. 1

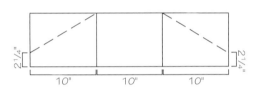

Refer to *Painting* on page 429 to *Dry Brush* burnt umber acrylic paint over the textured side of the wallpaper; allow to dry. Repeat with antique white acrylic paint. Cut an 8"x10" cotton fabric piece. Press one long fabric edge 1" to the back. With the pressed edge at the top, glue the fabric to the smooth side of the center wallpaper section. Fold the outside wallpaper sections to the center and glue along the bottom edge to form the envelope. Punch a hole in the upper right corner. For the hanger, fold an 18" ribbon length in half. Insert the ribbon ends through the hole and knot them together. Punch a hole in the lower left corner and attach a decorative tea ball.

LODGE-INSPIRED MANTELSCAPE

(shown on page 220)
Sock-Like Stockings

A red wool sweater, purchased at a thrift shop and felted, provides the fabric used for the details on these sock-like stockings. Felt could also be used, if desired.

- red wool sweater, felted
- fusible web
- red and grey embroidery floss
- corrugated cardstock
- alphabet stickers
- ¹⁄₄" dia. hole punch
- twine

For each small stocking:
- ¹⁄₄ yard cream textured fabric for stocking
- ¹⁄₄ yard cream fabric for lining

For each large stocking:
- ²⁄₃ yard green plaid flannel for stocking and lining

Use a ¹⁄₄" seam allowance unless otherwise indicated.

Use a photocopier to enlarge the pattern on page 505 to 194% for the small stocking or 243% for the large stocking. For each stocking, cut 2 stocking pieces and 2 lining pieces from fabric (one each in reverse). Cut 2 toes and 2 heels (one each in reverse) and stripes from felted wool. Fuse the wool pieces to the stocking pieces. Referring to *Embroidery Stitches* on page 422, embroider the stocking as desired. Matching the right sides and leaving the top open, stitch the stocking pieces together; turn right side out. Repeat to sew the lining pieces together, leaving an opening for turning; do not turn the lining right side out. Matching the right sides and raw edges, place the stocking in the lining. For the hanger, fold a 2"x6" wool strip in half lengthwise and sew the long edges together. Matching the raw edges, place the

(continued on page 458)

hanger between the stocking and lining at the heel-side seam. Using a $1/2$" seam allowance, sew the pieces together along the top edges. Turn the stocking right side out through the opening in the lining and sew the opening closed. For each stocking, cut a corrugated cardstock tag, add a name with stickers and punch a hole at the top. Tie the tags to the stockings with twine.

Birch Twig-Wrapped Candles
Never leave burning candles unattended.

For each candle, use a rubber band to hold trimmed twigs in place around the candle. Tie twine around the twigs; remove the rubber band. Hang resin snowflakes from the twigs as desired.

Birch-Framed Cabin Art
• 11$1/4$"x18" wooden board
• transfer paper
• wood burning tool
• color blending medium
• white, yellow, green, brown, grey, blue and red acrylic paints
• paintbrushes
• sawtooth picture hanger
• jigsaw
• moss-covered faux birch branches
• hammer & nails
• hot glue gun
• twine

Use caution when working with the wood burning tool. Allow paint to dry after each application.

Use a photocopier to enlarge the pattern on page 496 to 244%. Transfer the pattern to the front of the board. Use the round tip of the wood burning tool to outline the design. To add dots to the spokes of each snowflake, briefly hold the tip straight down. Mix thinned paint with blending medium to make a wash of each color. Paint

the design. Add an additional coat of white to the snow and smoke. Attach the hanger to the back of the board. Cut 2 branches each 18" and 24" long. Nail long branches to the long edges of the board. Glue short branches to the short edges of the board. Use twine to tie the short branches to the long branches at the intersections.

DREAMY MANTELSCAPE
(shown on page 221)
Wish Glitter Letters
• mat board
• craft knife and cutting mat
• silver and champagne-colored metallic acrylic paints
• paintbrushes
• craft glue
• silver and gold glitter
• 14-gauge wire
• wire cutters
• 1" dia. dowel rod
• four 4" square wooden blocks
• drill & small drill bit
• hot glue
• duct tape

Use caution when placing items near an open flame.

Use a computer to print "WISH"; then use a photocopier to enlarge the letters to the desired size. Cut out the letters. Draw around the letters onto mat board; cut out. Alternating colors, paint the letters; allow to dry. Brush thinned glue onto the letters. Sprinkle silver glitter over the silver letters and gold glitter over the champagne-colored letters. Allow to dry; then, shake off the excess glitter. Coil 4 wire lengths around the dowel rod. Drill a hole in one side of each wooden block. Hot glue one end of each wire into a wooden block and duct tape a letter to the opposite wire end.

Glitter Stars
Use spray paint in a well-ventilated area.

Spray 3-dimensional papier-mâché stars with silver and gold spray paints; allow to dry. Brush thinned glue onto the stars. Sprinkle silver glitter over the silver stars and gold glitter over the gold stars. Allow to dry; then shake off the excess glitter. Tuck some of the stars into the greenery on the mantel. Hot glue sheer ribbons to the backs of the remaining stars and hang them from the ceiling.

Mantel Candles
Use caution when placing items near an open flame. Never leave burning candles unattended.

For each candle, using the pattern on page 505, without the seam allowance, and repeating the pattern as necessary to fit around your candle, cut a red felt collar. Wrap the collar around the candle, overlapping the ends at the back and pinning them to the candle with a gold sequin pin. Thread a gold seed bead and sequin onto a gold sequin pin and insert the pin into the center of each scallop to secure the collar to the candle.

Tussie-Mussie "Stockings"
For each "stocking," you will need:
• $1/3$ yard brown linen
• $1/3$ yard cotton print for lining
• $1/8$ yard white felt
• tissue paper
• dark brown embroidery floss
• $1/8$ yard red felt
• fabric glue
• pre-strung silver sequins
• beaded snowflakes
• $3/8$" dia. silver sequins
• silver seed beads

Use a $1/2$" seam allowance for all sewing.

Use a photocopier to enlarge the cone pattern on page 505 to 285%. Using the pattern, cut one cone each from linen and lining fabric. Cut the band from white felt. Trace the embroidery pattern on page 499 onto tissue paper. Center the pattern on the band. Referring to *Embroidery Stitches* on page 422 and stitching through the tissue, follow the stitch key and embroider the design on the band using 3 strands of floss. Carefully tear away the tissue. Referring to the pattern for placement, zigzag the embroidered band to the linen cone piece. Repeating the pattern as needed, use the scallop pattern on page 505 and cut a red felt scallop piece; sew the straight edge to the top of the linen cone piece. Fold each cone piece in half, matching the right sides and side edges. Sew the side edges together, leaving an opening in the side of the lining for turning. Clip the points and turn the linen cone right side out. Matching the right sides and top edges, place the linen cone in the lining cone. Sew the pieces together along the top edges for the stocking. Turn the stocking right side out through the opening in the lining and sew the opening closed. Topstitch around the top of the stocking 1/4" from the edge.

For the hanger, fold a 2"x5" linen strip in half, matching the right sides and long edges; sew the long edges together. Turn the strip right side out and press with the seam at the center back. Turning the ends of the strip 1/2" to the back, sew the hanger to the top back of the stocking. Glue the pre-strung sequins along the edges of the embroidered band. Tack the beaded snowflakes and sequins with seed beads in the center to the stocking.

CHOCOLATE-COVERED CHERRIES RECIPE TAG
(shown on page 225)

For each tag, use a computer to print the recipe on page 225 onto cream cardstock and cut it into a tag (we mixed fonts on our tag). Punch a hole at the top. Stamp "Chocolate-Covered Cherries" on the back and glue rickrack along one long edge. Knot red ribbons and jute through the hole. For the tag holder, cut a red cardstock piece wider than the tag. Arrange ribbon and fabric strips on the cardstock as shown. Sew along the side and bottom edges, securing the strips to the cardstock. Attach crocheted cherries to the corner of the holder with a brad. Insert the tag in the holder.

PERSONALIZED ORNAMENT BOX
(shown on page 226)

- 5/8 yard floral print cotton fabric
- 11"x7 1/2"x4 1/2" photo box with lid
- spray adhesive
- fabric glue
- 2 1/8 yards of 1"w red ribbon
- red, black, green and cream cardstock
- beige striped scrapbook paper
- tracing paper
- 1/4" dia. red plastic snap
- alphabet rub-ons
- black fine-point permanent pen
- green, brown and red chalk
- 1/2" dia. black pom-pom

Use spray adhesive in a well-ventilated area. Yardage is based on fabric with a 40" usable width.

Use spray adhesive to cover the box and lid with fabric. Glue ribbon over any raw edges. Cut a 6 7/8"x10 1/8" red cardstock piece and tear a 6 5/8"x10" black cardstock piece. Use spray adhesive to glue the pieces to the lid. Print the desired letter from a computer. Use a photocopier to enlarge the letter to the desired size and cut it out. Draw around the letter on paper and cut it out. Using the patterns on page 501, cut flower and vine pieces from cardstock. Attach the snap to the top of a small green cardstock tag. Spell a name on the letter with rub-ons. Write "ornaments" on the tag. Chalk the edges of the tag, letter, flower and vine pieces. Glue the pieces on the lid as shown, gluing the flower petals at the center only. Glue the pom-pom to the center of the flower.

SNOWMAN TAG ORNAMENT
(shown on page 227)

- white frosted shrinkable plastic
- colored pencils
- black fine-point permanent pen
- 3/16" and 1/4" dia. hole punches
- wire cutters
- 24-gauge blue wire
- red, green and blue beads
- jewelry pliers
- 7 3/4" length of 1/4"w sheer white ribbon
- craft glue
- white cardstock
- red and white striped scrapbook paper

Trace the patterns on page 495 onto the frosted side of the plastic and color with colored pencils. Draw over the face with the pen. Cut the pieces out and punch 3/16" diameter holes as indicated on the patterns. Follow the manufacturer's instructions to bake. Connect the body and leg pieces with wire. Cut a 13" wire length for the arms and top loop. Attach one end to the snowman and thread one mitten, beads and the remaining mitten onto the wire, using pliers to curl the wire as shown. Attach the remaining end to the opposite side of the body. Glue the ribbon ends to the back of the head for a hanger. Glue 2 5/8"x4 3/4" cardstock and paper tags together; punch a 1/4" diameter hole in the top. Thread the hanger through the hole and spot glue the head to the tag.

SANTA CARD ORNAMENT

(shown on page 227)

Cover a tabbed index card with scrapbook papers and ribbon. Adhere foil tape along the edges. Add a Santa image, vellum messages and a wooden disk with a rub-on initial. Use wire and alphabet beads to spell "Santa" on a "Handmade by" label. Decorate the card with crocheted leaves, buttons, charms and a paperclip. Knot wide ribbon through a suspender clip attached to the tab.

PINK & BROWN CARD SET

(shown on page 228)

- double-sided solid/printed scrapbook papers
- scallop-edged craft scissors
- alphabet rub-ons
- tracing paper
- cream linen-print scrapbook paper
- craft glue
- 1/4"w ribbon
- recycled clear plastic package (ours measures 3 5/8"x1 3/4"x5 3/8")
- paper shreds
- colored pencil
- 1 5/8"w sheer ribbon
- star charm with jump ring
- stem with leaves and berries

For each card, matching the solid side and short edges, fold a 2 5/8"x8" double-sided paper piece in half. Cut away 3/8" of the front short edge with the craft scissors. Use rub-ons to spell a name on the card front.

For each envelope, use the pattern on page 500 and cut an envelope from cream paper. Fold the side and bottom flaps to the back as indicated by the dashed lines on the pattern and glue them together where they overlap. Glue a 5/8"w double-sided paper strip trimmed with the craft scissors along the bottom edge of the envelope flap as shown.

Stack the cards and envelopes and tie 1/4"w ribbon around them. Trim the front and side edges of the package with the craft scissors. Place paper shreds, the cards and envelopes and the colored pencil in the package. Wrap sheer ribbon around the package. Attach the charm to the ribbon and tie the ribbon ends into a bow. Tuck the stem behind the bow.

INITIAL CARD SET

(shown on page 229)

- tan cardstock
- large scallop-edged craft scissors
- tan and black striped and floral scrapbook papers
- craft glue
- 4"x5 1/2" cream cards with pointed-flap envelopes
- black paint pen
- clear dimensional glaze
- 1/4"w black satin ribbon
- large red beads

For each card, use a computer to print a letter on cardstock and trim the cardstock to 2 1/2"x3" with the letter at the center. Using the craft scissors on the long edges, cut a 2"x5 1/2" striped paper strip. Cut a 1 1/2"x5 1/2" floral paper strip. Glue the paper strips and letter to the card as shown. Paint dots on the card front.

For each envelope, print the letter on cardstock at a smaller point size. Cut the cardstock into a 1" diameter circle with the letter at the center. Apply glaze to the circle and allow to dry. Glue the top half of the circle to the point of the envelope flap.

Stack the cards and envelopes and tie ribbon into a bow around them. Being careful not to get glue on the cards, glue beads to the bow.

BOXED GREEN & BROWN STATIONERY SET

(shown on page 231)

- textured green cardstock
- craft glue
- multi-color striped, multi-color dotted, yellow dotted, pink alphabet and brown pin-striped scrapbook papers
- 1/8"w pink and white polka-dot ribbon
- 1 1/2" and 1 1/4" dia. circle punches
- alphabet stamps
- brown ink pad
- 5 1/2" square white envelopes
- 6 3/4"x6 3/4"x5/8" gift box with lid
- die-cutting tool and a 3 1/4"-tall tag die
- vellum quote
- deckle-edged craft scissors
- 1/8" dia. pewter brads
- 7/8 yard of 1"w green grosgrain ribbon

For each note card, cut a 5 1/4" cardstock square. Layer and glue a 3/8"x5 1/4" multi-color striped paper piece, a torn 7/8"x5 1/4" multi-color dotted paper strip and a 5 1/4" polka-dot ribbon length on the note card, 3/8" from the top edge. Punch a 1 1/2" diameter circle from yellow dotted paper and a 1 1/4" diameter circle from alphabet paper. Layer and glue the circles on the center of the layered strips. Stamp a monogram on the circles.

Glue a multi-color striped paper piece to each envelope flap. Stack the envelopes and tie an 18" polka-dot ribbon length around them; repeat for the cards.

Trimming the paper corners as necessary, cover the inside of the box with pin-striped paper, the outside of the box with multi-color striped paper and the outside of the lid with multi-color dotted paper. Glue a 27 1/2" polka-dot ribbon length along the top edges of the box.

Die-cut a tag from pin-striped paper. Trim the vellum quote with the craft scissors and attach it to the tag with brads. Layer and glue a 9¼" length each of grosgrain and polka-dot ribbon together. Tie an 18" length each of grosgrain and polka-dot ribbon into a bow around the center of the layered length. Tie the tag onto the center of the bow with a 4" polka-dot ribbon length. Wrapping the ends to the inside, center and glue the layered length across the lid. Place the envelopes and note cards in the box.

BOXED PERSONALIZED CARD SET
(shown on page 231)
• double-sided floral/light green scrapbook paper
• small scallop-edged craft scissors
• white vellum
• pink cardstock
• double-sided tape
• ⅛" dia. hole punch
• ¼"w green sheer ribbon
• tracing paper
• craft glue
• tissue paper
• 4"x4"x1¼" white gift box with lid
• black fine-point permanent pen
• 1"-tall tag
• white embroidery floss
• ⅜"w green ribbon
• snowflake charms

For each card, matching the light green side and short edges, fold a 3½"x7½" paper piece in half. Trim ¼" from the bottom front edge with the craft scissors.

Using a computer, type a name several times as shown. Print it on vellum and cut the vellum into a 2¾" square. Enlarge and print the first initial. Cut it out and use it as a pattern to cut a monogram from cardstock. Tape the monogram to the vellum square. Center the vellum on the card front. Punch 2 holes, ¾" apart and ¼" from the

top of the vellum, through the vellum and card front. Thread the ends of a 4¾" sheer ribbon length through the holes from front to back. Cross the ends, thread them through the holes again from back to front and trim.

For each envelope, use the pattern on page 499 and cut a paper envelope. Fold the side and bottom flaps to the back as indicated by the dashed lines on the pattern and glue them together where they overlap. Glue a ⅝"w paper strip trimmed with the craft scissors along the bottom edge of the envelope flap as shown.

Arrange the tissue in the box. Stack the cards and envelopes, tie sheer ribbon around the stack and place it in the box. Write a message on the tag. Thread the tag onto the center of a length of floss and knot the ends together. Wrapping the ends to the inside, glue two 9" lengths of ⅜"w ribbon to the lid as shown. Tie a bow with another length and glue it to the lid where the ribbons intersect, securing the floss ends of the tag under the bow. Glue the charms to the lid.

PERSONALIZED TAGS WITH GIFT BOX
(shown on page 230)
• 4¾"-tall scalloped tag die and a die-cutting tool
• leather-textured and tan floral scrapbook paper
• brown ink pad
• pinking shears
• floral fabric scrap
• craft glue
• alphabet stencils and stickers
• metal photo corner
• decorative brad and ⅛" dia. silver brads
• assorted charms
• paper twine
• assorted ribbons and fibers
• 2⅜"x4¼" shipping tags
• deckle-edged craft scissors

• grommet and grommet kit
• jewelry tag
• vellum quote
• round-head pin
• sheet of cork
• 4"x4"x5" paper box with lid
• greenery
• small silver ornament
• paper shreds

SCALLOPED TAG
Die-cut a textured paper tag; ink as desired. Zigzag a pinked floral fabric square to the tag. Add an inked stencil monogram and the photo corner. Use a brad to attach charms tied onto paper twine to the tag. Attach a decorative brad through the hole and tightly wrap ribbon around it on the front.

SHIPPING TAGS
Cover one shipping tag with floral scrapbook paper and ink the other. Trim the bottom of the paper-covered tag with the craft scissors. Attach the grommet through the hole in the tag and add the jewelry tag, charms, ribbon and stickers. Tear the long edges of the vellum quote and trim the short edges with the craft scissors. Attach a charm with the pin. Arrange the vellum on a cork piece, spot gluing to secure. Glue the cork to the inked tag. Knot ribbons and fibers through the holes in the tags.

BOX
Tie two 20" ribbon lengths together into a bow around the center of two 8¾" ribbon lengths. Wrapping the ends to the inside, glue the 8¾" lengths to the lid as shown. Tuck the greenery under the bow and glue the ornament to the center of the bow. Place the paper shreds and tags in the box.

BROOCH WITH GIFT BOX
(shown on page 232)
- tracing paper
- illustration board
- silver leaf
- assorted charms
- 15" length of $^1/_8$"w cream ribbon
- craft glue
- assorted beads
- 1$^1/_8$" dia., two $^1/_4$" dia. and two $^3/_8$" dia. cream buttons
- watch face
- awl
- wire cutters
- needle-nose pliers
- fine-gauge wire
- cream and textured green cardstock
- 1" pin back
- green acrylic paint
- paintbrush
- $^1/_{16}$" dia. hole punch
- $^3/_8$ yard of $^7/_8$"w green variegated wire-edged ribbon
- 3"x3"x2" white box
- Christmas stamps
- black ink pad
- wood excelsior
- 1$^1/_8$ yards of $^3/_{16}$"w green variegated ribbon

1. For the brooch, using the pattern on page 498, cut an oval from illustration board. Follow the manufacturer's instructions to apply silver leaf to the front and sides of the oval.

2. Leaving a streamer on the left back, threading charms onto the ribbon as desired and spot gluing at the back to secure, wrap the cream ribbon around the center of the oval as shown in Fig. 1. Wrap the ribbon to the center back and spot glue, letting the ribbon end dangle for the right streamer. Thread a bead and knot a $^1/_4$" button onto each streamer end; trim the ends.

Fig. 1

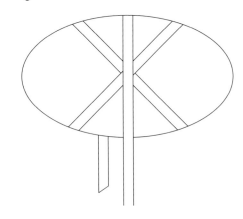

3. Glue the 1$^1/_8$" button to the center of the oval and glue the watch face to the button. Use the awl to punch 2 small holes in the oval on each side of the large button. Bending the wire ends at the back of the oval to secure, thread wire through the holes, attaching a $^3/_8$" button and beads to each side.

4. Cut a cream cardstock piece the same size as the oval and glue it to the back. Glue the pin back to the back of the brooch.

5. Cut a 2$^7/_8$" textured cardstock square. Refer to *Painting* on page 429 to *Dry Brush* the square with green paint; allow to dry. Punch 2 holes in the center of the square, $^1/_2$" apart and $^3/_4$" from the top edge. Knotting the ends at the top, wrap the $^7/_8$"w ribbon around the center of the square. Insert the pin through the holes; close the clasp.

6. *Dry Brush* the entire box with green paint; allow to dry. Stamp messages on the outside of the box. Fill the box with excelsior and place the brooch inside. Close the box and tie a 39" length of $^3/_{16}$" ribbon around it.

REINDEER TOWEL AND BATH MITT
(continued from page 241)
BATH MITT

1. Using a photocopier, enlarge the mitt pattern on page 503 to 130% and cut it out. Fold the remaining hand towel in half, matching the short edges. Aligning the bottom edge of the pattern with the short edges of the towel, cut 2 mitts from the folded towel.

2. Using a photocopier, reduce the antler pattern on page 502 to 55%. Using the reduced pattern, cut 2 antlers (one in reverse) from brown felt. For each eye, use the lower case die to cut an "o" from black and white felt. Avoiding the seam allowance and using the outlines from the white die-cuts and the centers from the black die-cuts, *Whipstitch* (page 423) the antlers and eyes to one mitt as shown.

3. Leaving the bottom edge open, sew the mitt pieces together and turn right side out. Tack the $^3/_4$" pom-pom to the mitt for the nose.

MANICURE GIFT SET
(shown on page 244)
- painter's masking tape
- ivory spray paint for plastic
- manicure set with plastic handles
- green and light green acrylic paints
- paintbrush
- $^1/_4$ yard brown fabric
- pinking shears
- 1 yard of $^5/_8$"w green and white polka-dot grosgrain ribbon
- fabric glue
- vellum tape
- vellum quote
- green scrapbook paper
- decorative-edged craft scissors
- 6$^1/_2$"x3$^5/_8$"x2$^5/_8$" white candy box
- brown cardstock
- alphabet stamps
- brown ink pad
- paper shreds

Allow paint to dry after each application.

Working in a well-ventilated area and masking areas that you don't want painted, spray paint the handles of the manicure tools. Remove the tape after the paint has dried. Paint stripes and use the end of the paintbrush handle to add dots on the tool handles with acrylic paints. Cut four 3¼"x6" fabric pieces. With the bottom fabric piece wrong side up and the remaining pieces right side up, stack and sew the fabric pieces together ⅜" from the edges; pink the edges. Arrange the tools across the fabric. Center a 6¾" ribbon length across the tools and pin the ribbon to the fabric between the tools. Remove the tools and sew down the ribbon at the pins. Remove the pins and glue the ribbon ends to the back.

Tape the vellum quote to the paper, cut it out with craft scissors and glue it to the inside of the box lid. Cut a small paper oval and a large cardstock oval. Glue the ovals together and stamp a message on the center.

Fill the box with paper shreds and place the manicure set inside. Close the lid and wrap a 28" ribbon length around the box, tying a bow at the top. Glue the ovals to the front of the box over the ribbon.

PENNY SACK AND GIFT BOX
(shown on page 246)
• star background and holiday message stamps
• brown ink pad
• penny sack
• 3"x3"x2" brown gift box
• deckle-edged craft scissors
• red, tan, green, red-checked and off-white cardstock
• green chalk
• craft glue
• tracing paper
• red seed beads
• ⅛" dia. hole punch
• red jute

Stamp stars all over the sack and box. Use craft scissors to cut cardstock squares as follows: 2½" red, 2¼" tan, 2" green, 1¾" red-checked and 1½" off-white. Chalk the edges of the off-white square. Layer and glue the squares on the bag front. Cut an off-white cardstock tag for the box. Using the pattern on page 505, cut 2 green holly leaves each for the box and bag. Chalk the tag edges. Glue the tag to red cardstock and cut the cardstock slightly larger than the tag. Stamp a message and glue holly leaves and seed bead "berries" on the tag and bag. Punch 2 holes, ¾" apart, through the top of the bag front and back. Thread jute through the holes and tie into a bow at the front. Punch a hole at the top of the tag, thread jute through the hole and knot the ends together. Tie jute around the box and tuck the tag under the jute.

EARRINGS WITH GIFT TAG
(shown on page 247)
Dress up an ordinary shipping tag with scrapbook paper, ribbon and red zigzag stitches for a classy gift tag for handmade earrings. Stamp Santa on cream cardstock and color with colored pencils. Tear the cardstock and sew it to a torn red cardstock piece. Glue Santa to the tag along with crocheted leaves and red buttons. Cut an arrow-shaped scrapbook paper tag and add red stitches, a stamped message, red seed bead "berries" and leaves colored with a pencil. Stamp the date on the gift tag and attach the paper tag and a knotted ribbon length with a brad. Knot ribbon and fiber through the hole in the gift tag.

For each earring, thread assorted beads onto a 1½" eye pin. Use round-nose pliers to make a tight loop at the end of the pin near the bottom bead. Trim the excess wire with wire cutters. Attach the eye pin to a shank earwire. Punch tiny holes in the tag and attach the earrings to the tag through the holes.

Velvet Jewelry Pouch

(page 30)

Stitching Diagram

—— Ecru Stem Stitch

⟋ Red Lazy Daisy

—— Green Stem Stitch

⟋ Green Lazy Daisy

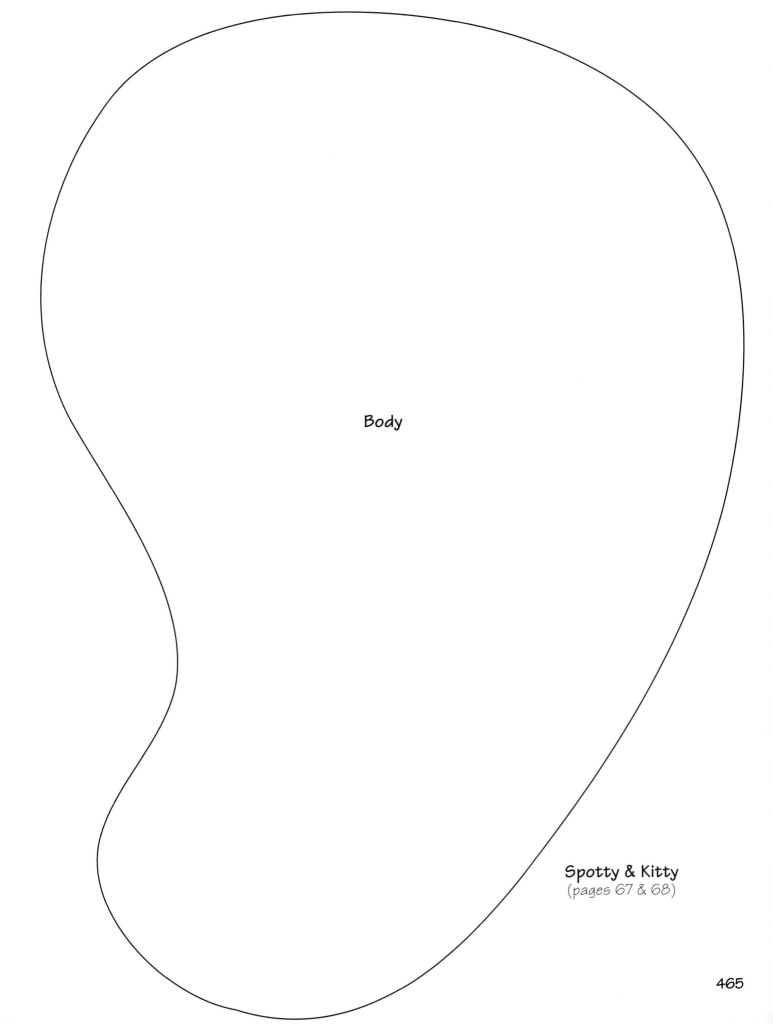

Body

Spotty & Kitty
(pages 67 & 68)

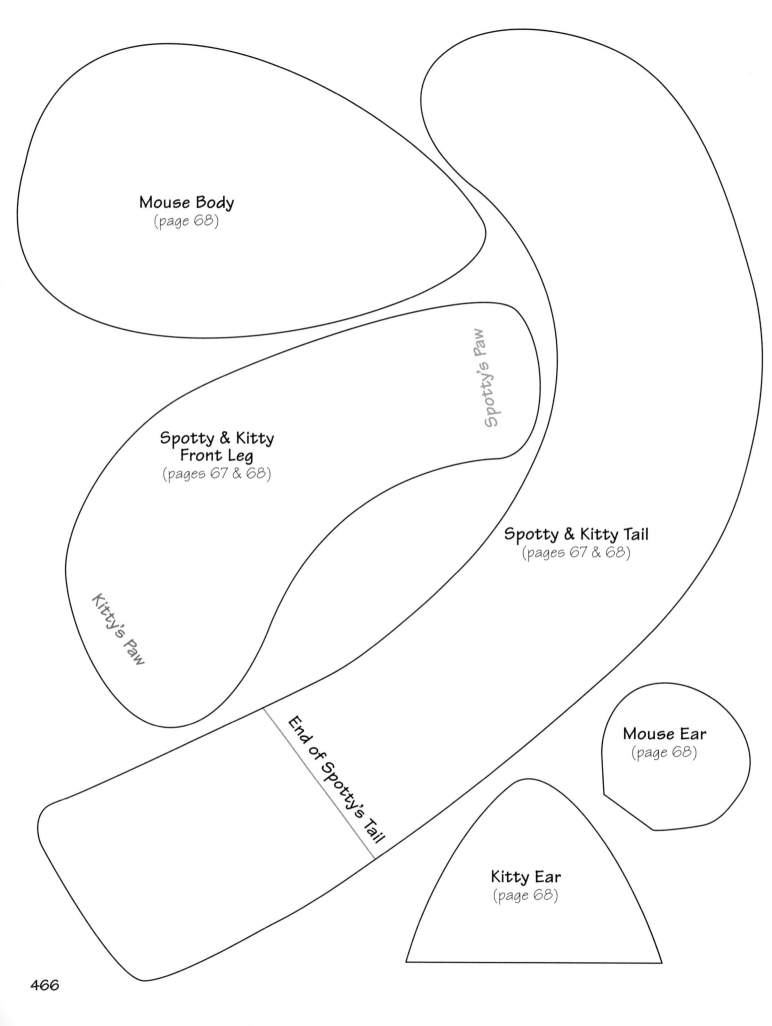

Mouse Body
(page 68)

Spotty & Kitty
Front Leg
(pages 67 & 68)

Spotty's Paw

Kitty's Paw

Spotty & Kitty Tail
(pages 67 & 68)

End of Spotty's Tail

Mouse Ear
(page 68)

Kitty Ear
(page 68)

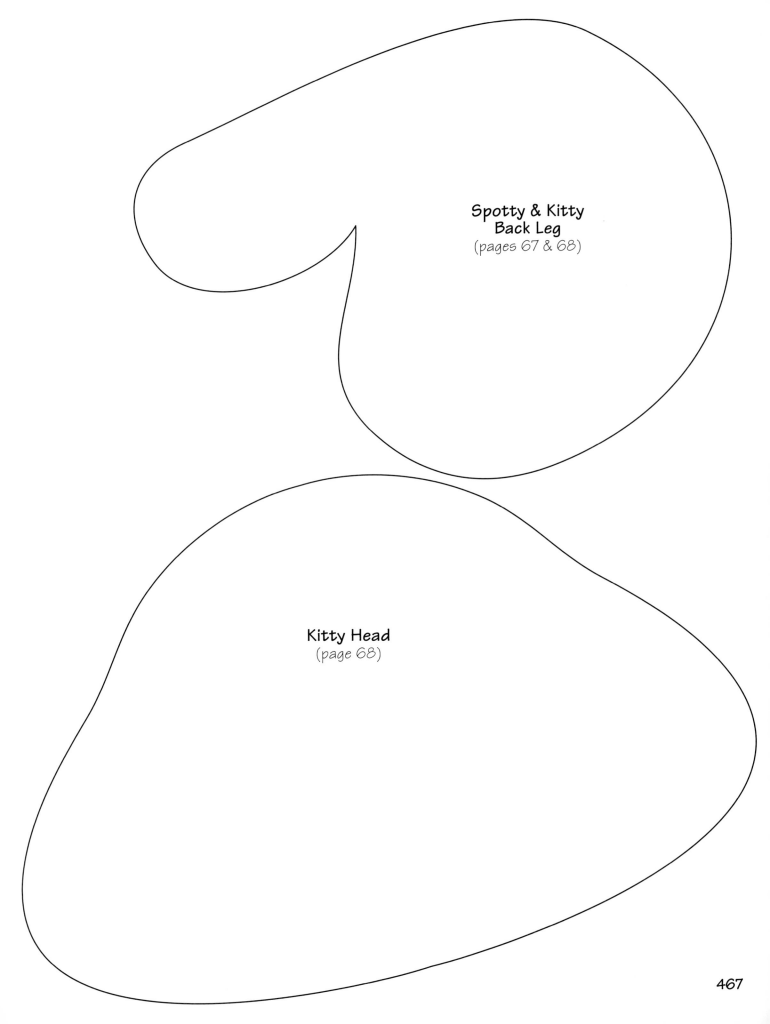

**Spotty & Kitty
Back Leg**
(pages 67 & 68)

Kitty Head
(page 68)

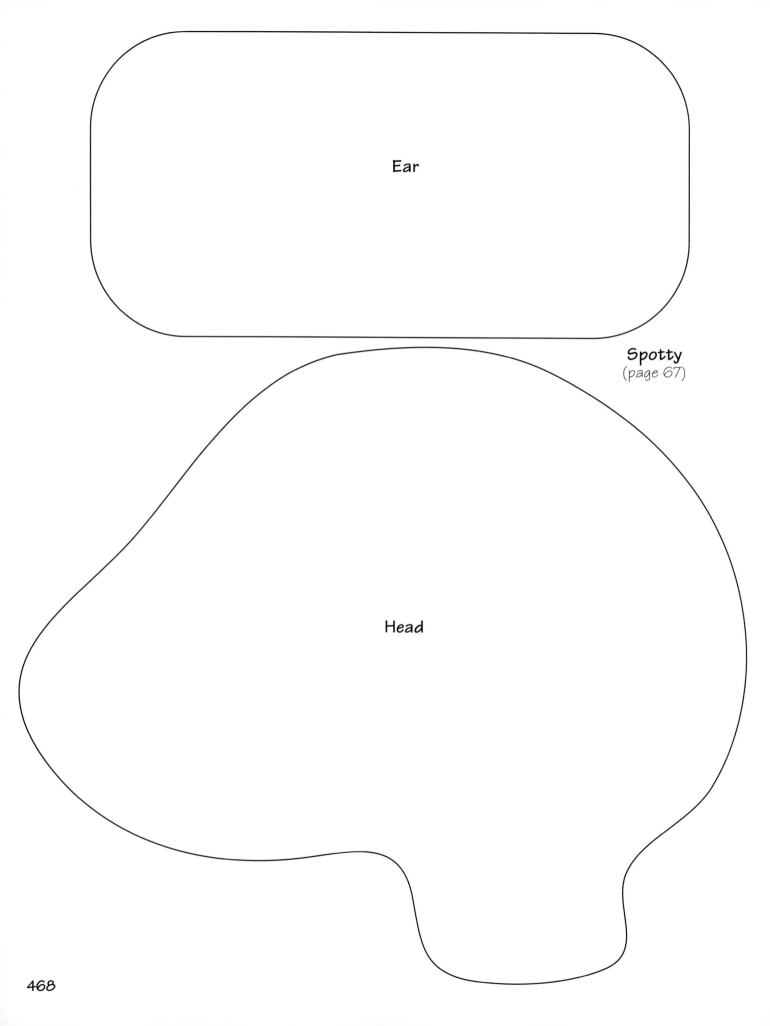

Ear

Spotty
(page 67)

Head

Kitty I.D. Tag Ornaments
(page 23)

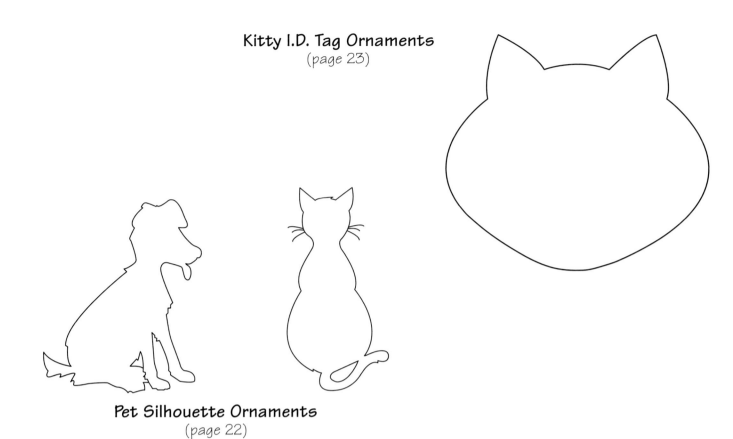

Pet Silhouette Ornaments
(page 22)

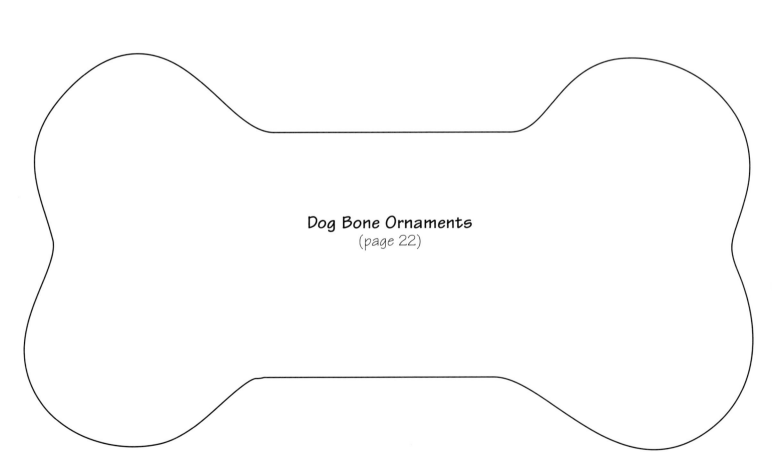

Dog Bone Ornaments
(page 22)

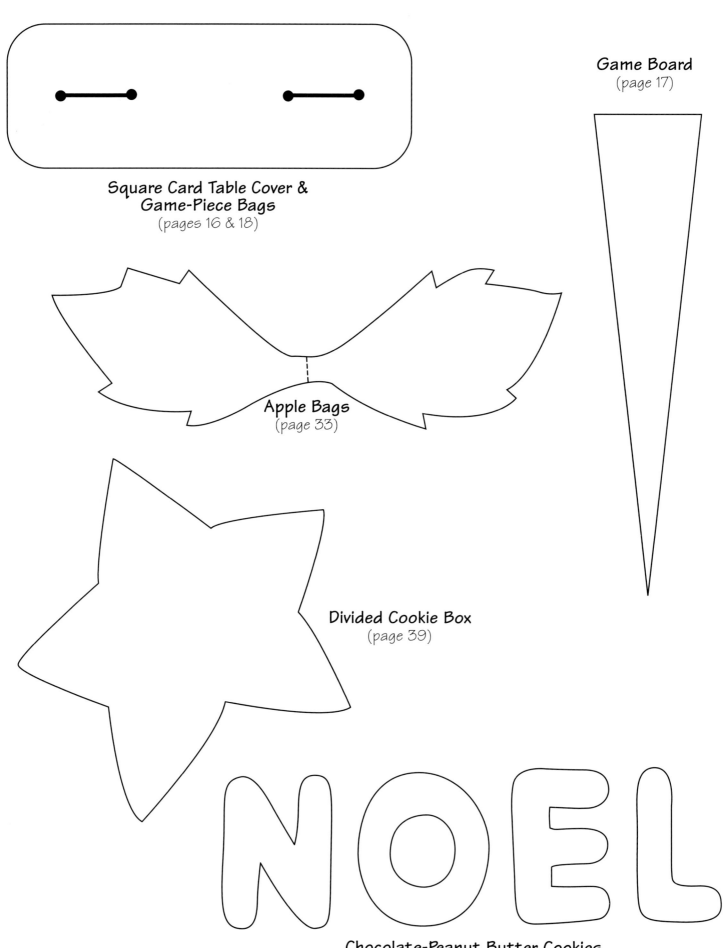

Square Card Table Cover &
Game-Piece Bags
(pages 16 & 18)

Game Board
(page 17)

Apple Bags
(page 33)

Divided Cookie Box
(page 39)

NOEL

Chocolate-Peanut Butter Cookies
(page 39)

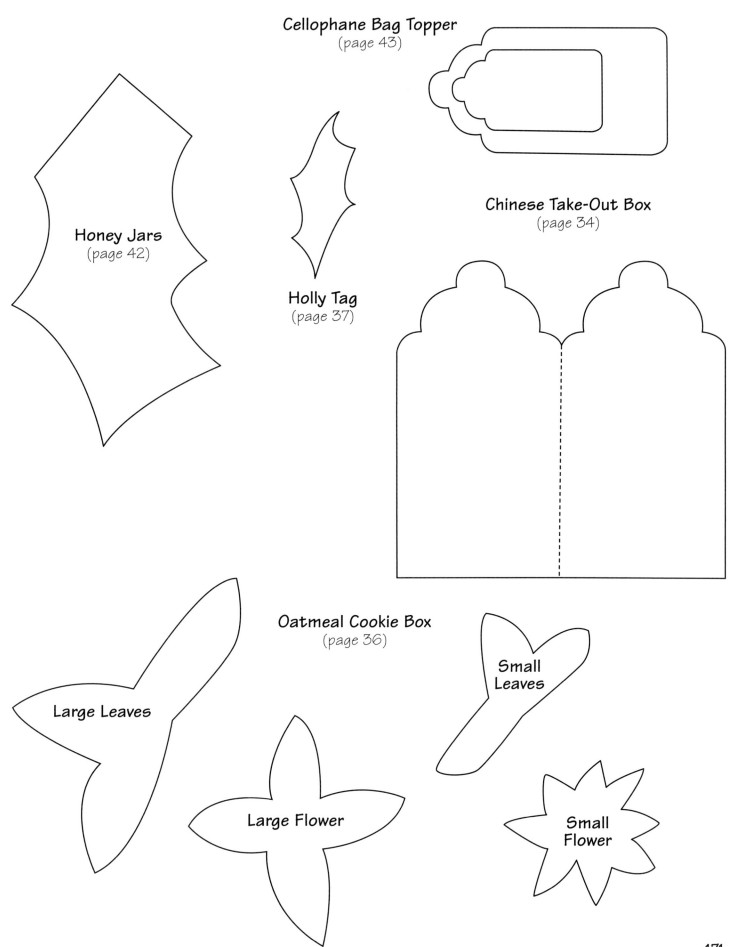

Cellophane Bag Topper
(page 43)

Honey Jars
(page 42)

Holly Tag
(page 37)

Chinese Take-Out Box
(page 34)

Oatmeal Cookie Box
(page 36)

Large Leaves

Large Flower

Small Leaves

Small Flower

Flower Brooch
(page 28)

Appliquéd Bag
(page 31)

Top

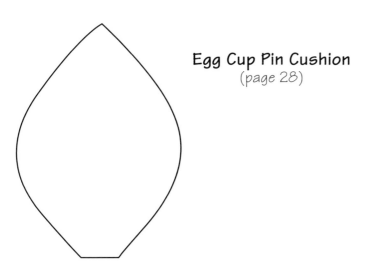

Egg Cup Pin Cushion
(page 28)

Flocked Candle Box
(page 25)

Family Calendar
(page 78)

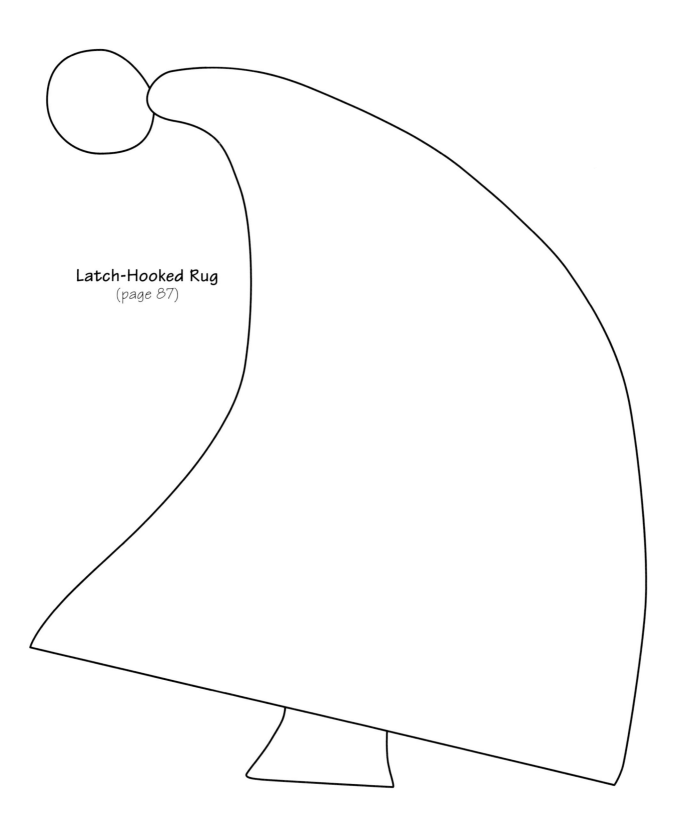

Latch-Hooked Rug
(page 87)

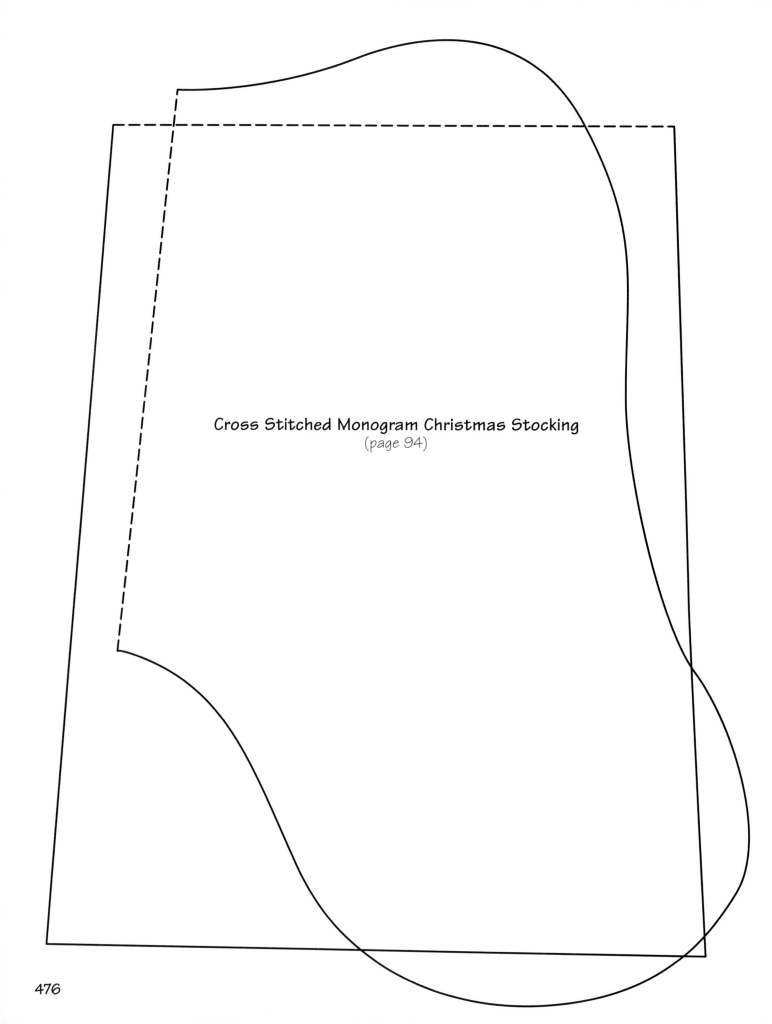

Cross Stitched Monogram Christmas Stocking
(page 94)

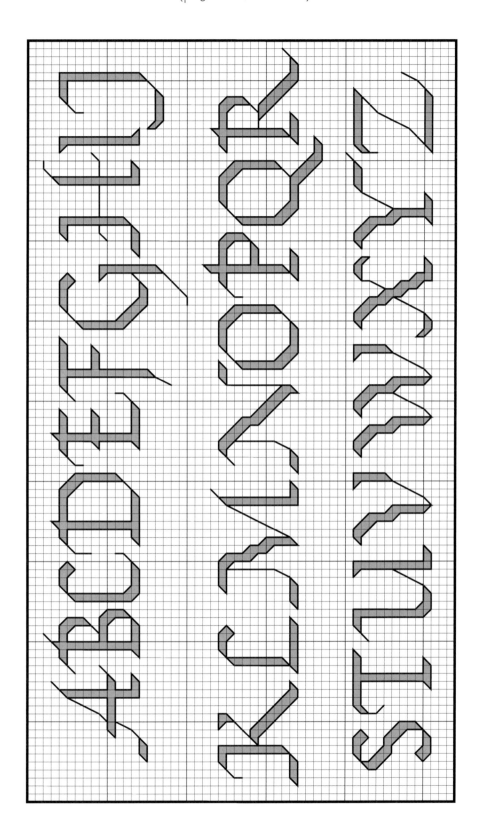

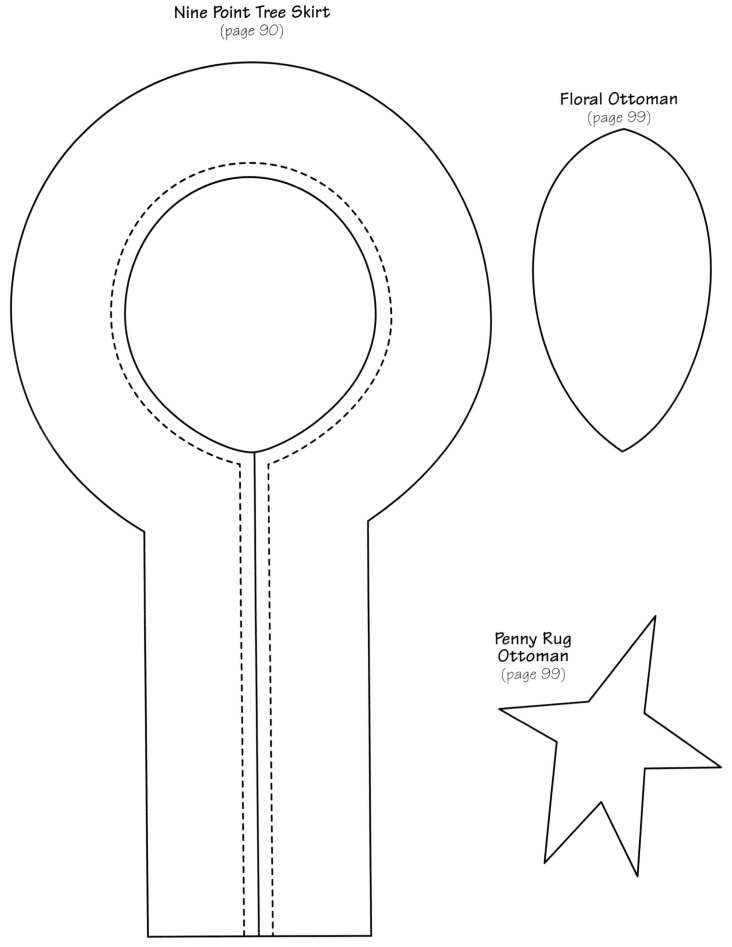

Nine Point Tree Skirt
(page 90)

Floral Ottoman
(page 99)

Penny Rug
Ottoman
(page 99)

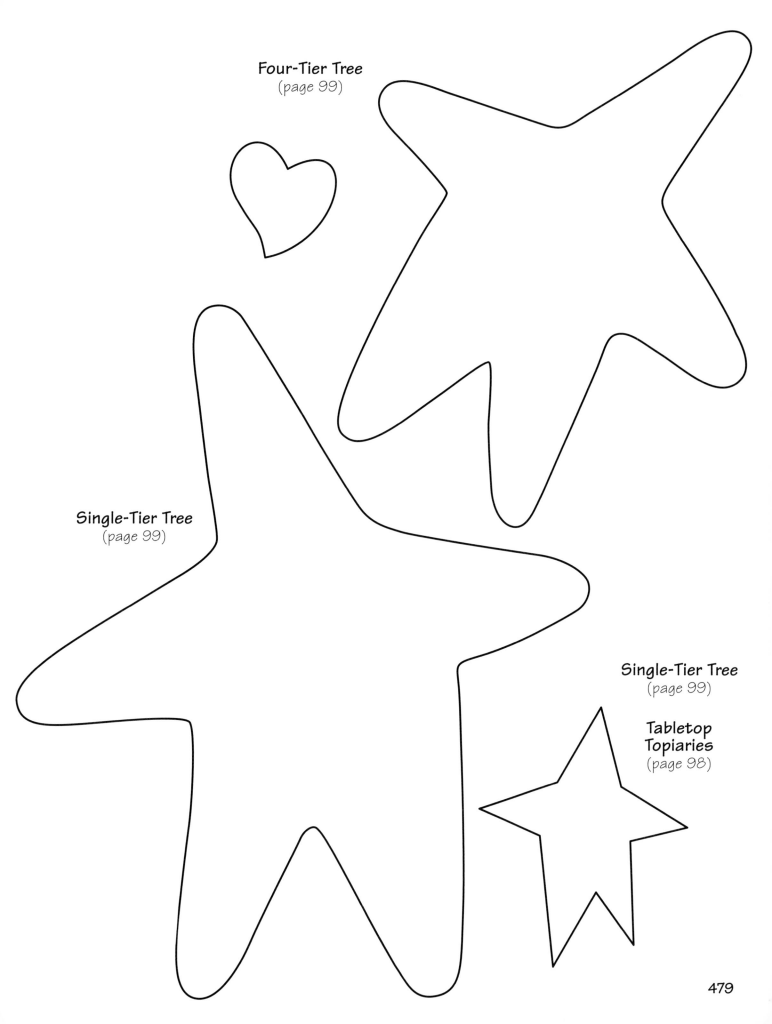

Four-Tier Tree
(page 99)

Single-Tier Tree
(page 99)

Single-Tier Tree
(page 99)

Tabletop Topiaries
(page 98)

479

Tree Ottoman
(page 99)

Embroidered Tote Bag
(page 101)

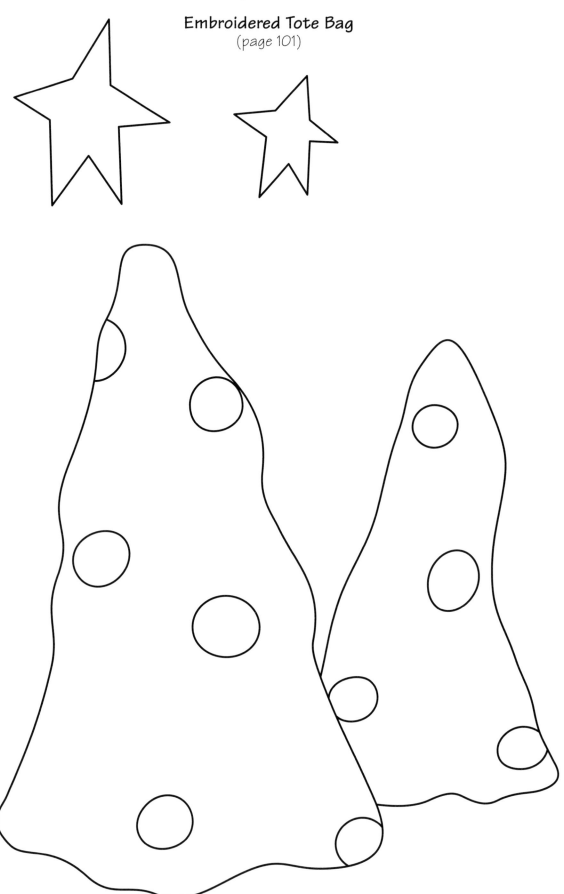

Stitched Wall Hanging

(page 100)

Every gift
though it be
small,
is in reality great
if given with
affection
Liddie Fudim

Flannel Bags
(pages 108 & 109)

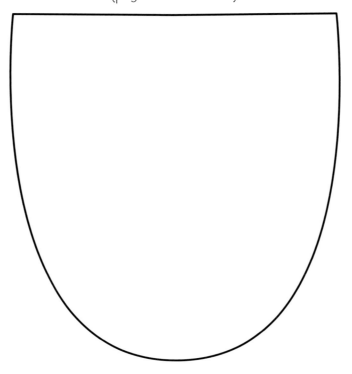

**Round Box Ornaments
and Gift Boxes**
(pages 113 & 118)

Icicle Garland
(page 113)

**Snowflake and Mitten
Wall Hanging**
(page 117)

**Tabletop Topiaries and
Tomato Cage Trees**
(pages 98 & 99)

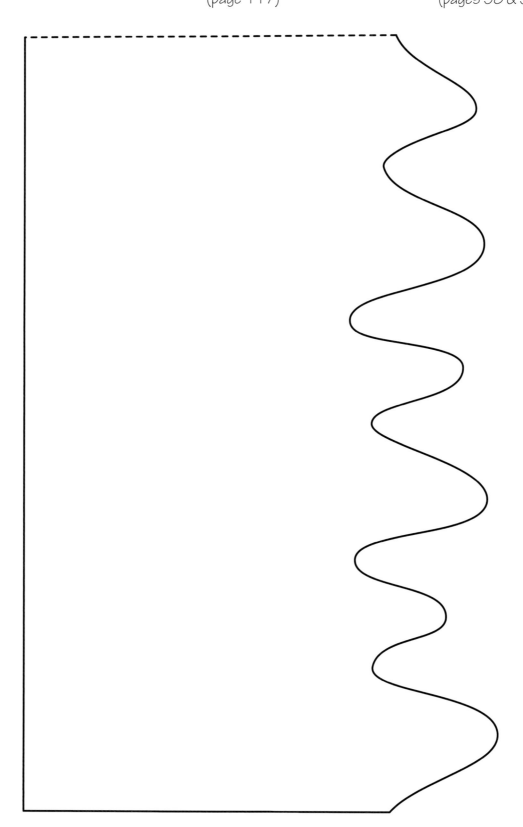

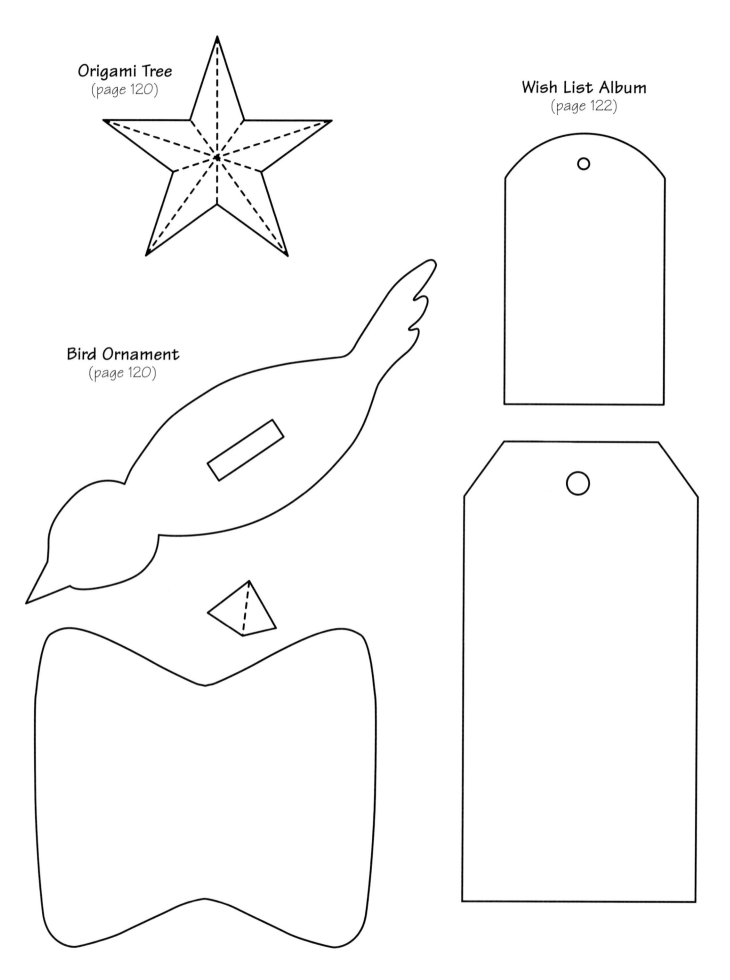

Origami Tree
(page 120)

Wish List Album
(page 122)

Bird Ornament
(page 120)

Santa Doll
(pages 125 & 126)

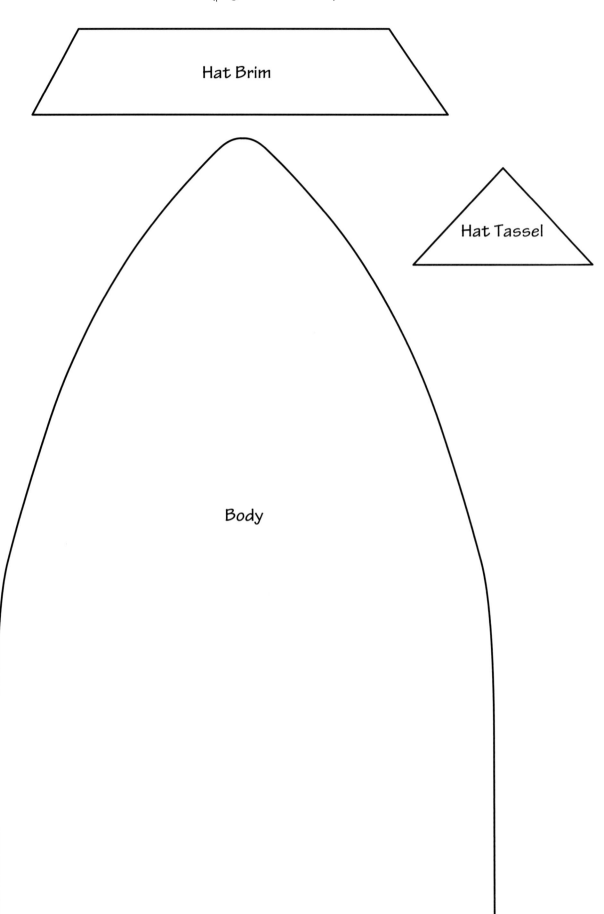

Hat Brim

Hat Tassel

Body

Santa Doll
(pages 125 & 126)

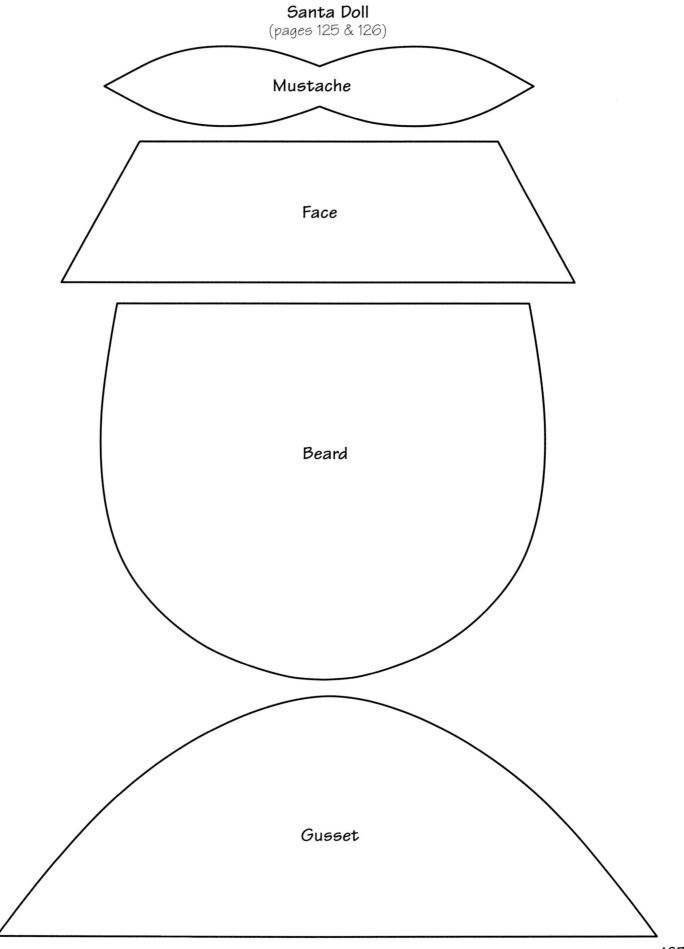

Mustache

Face

Beard

Gusset

Santa Doll
(pages 125 & 126)

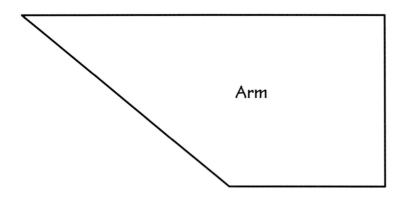

Arm

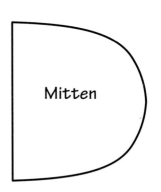

Mitten

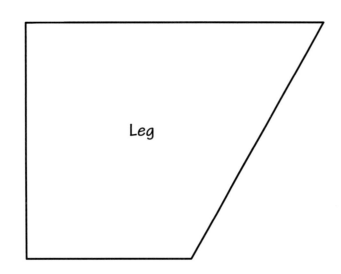

Leg

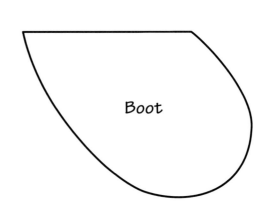

Boot

Let It Snow Sweater

(page 127)

Embellished Gloves
(page 128)

| | green |
| | brown |

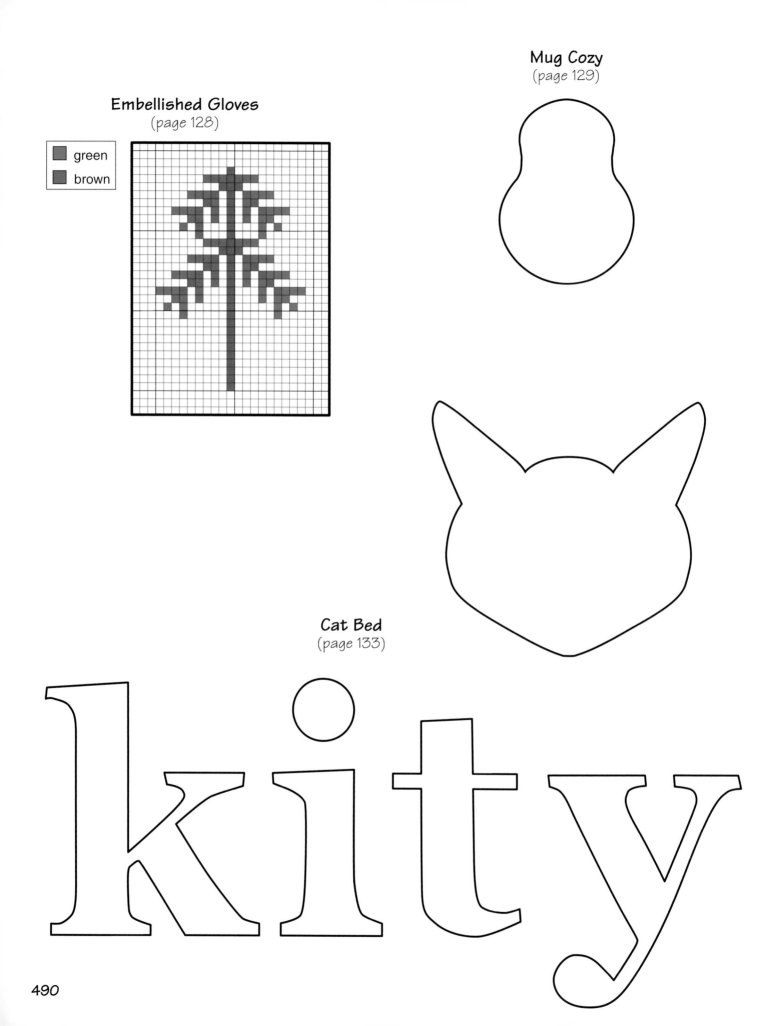

Mug Cozy
(page 129)

Cat Bed
(page 133)

kity

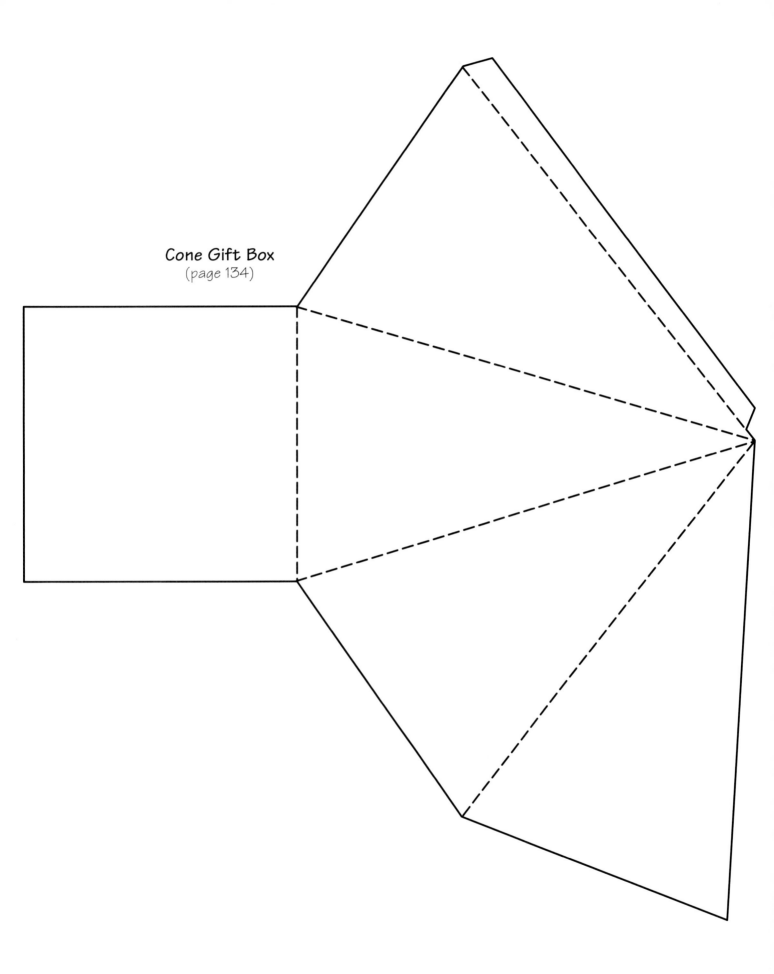

Cone Gift Box
(page 134)

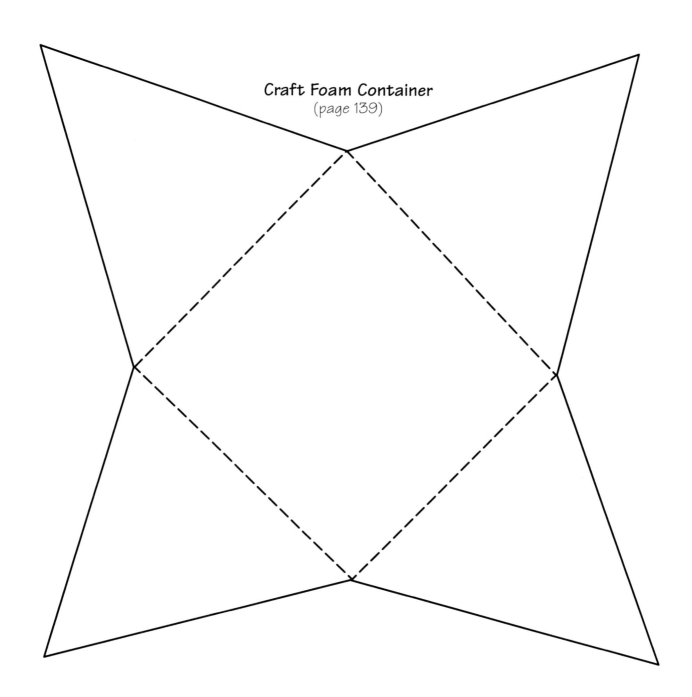

Craft Foam Container
(page 139)

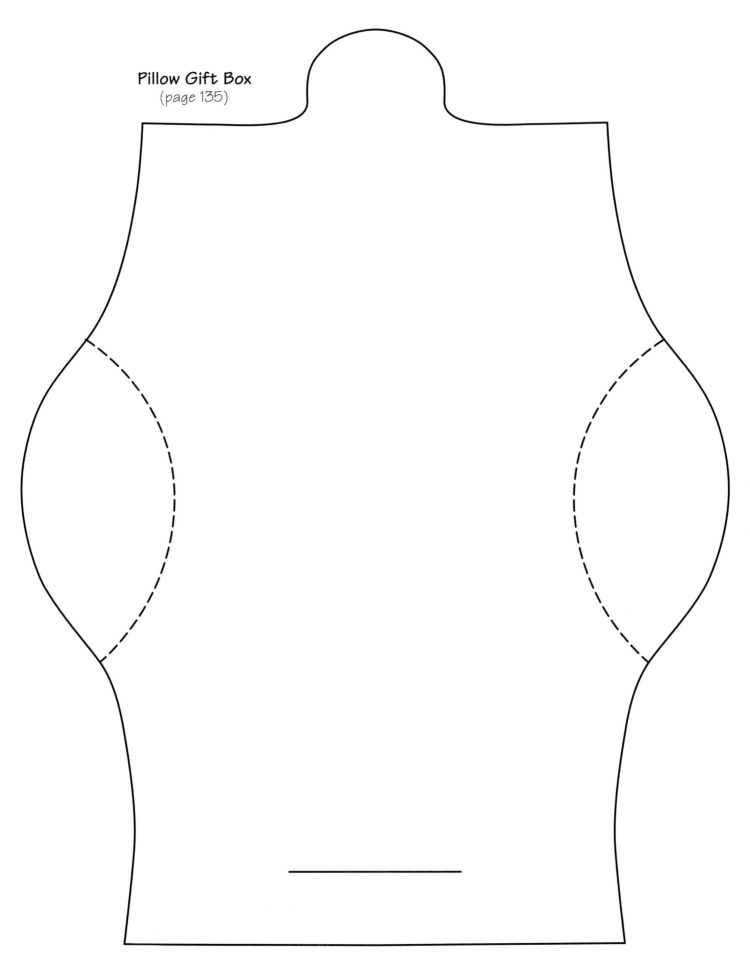

Pillow Gift Box
(page 135)

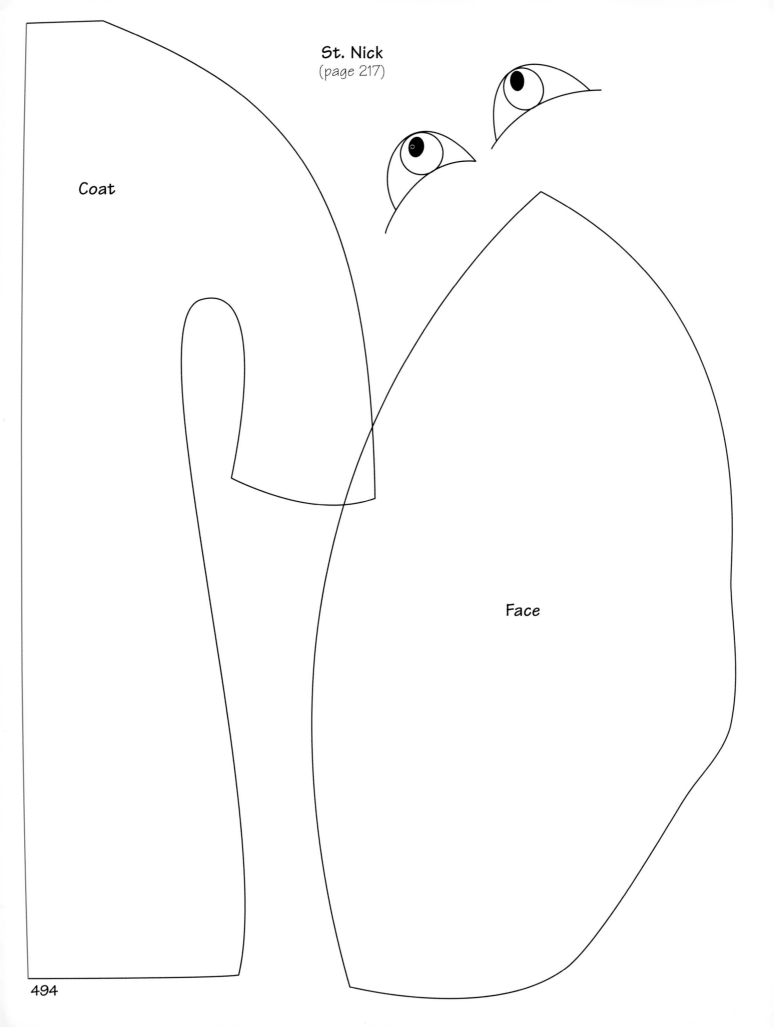

St. Nick
(page 217)

Coat

Face

494

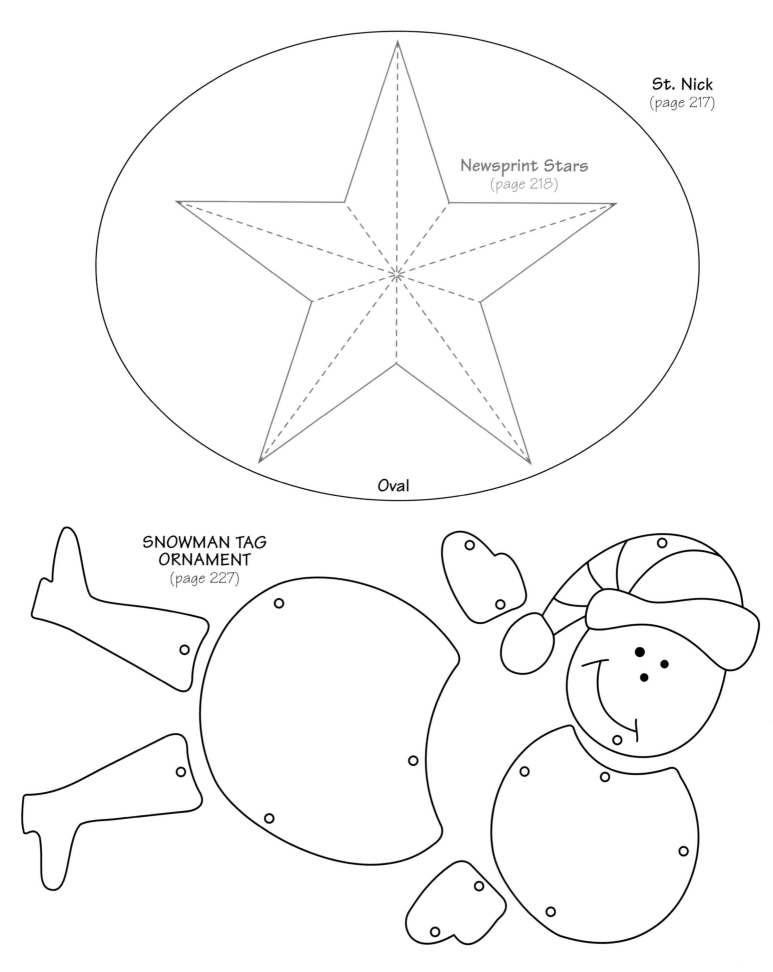

St. Nick
(page 217)

Newsprint Stars
(page 218)

Oval

SNOWMAN TAG
ORNAMENT
(page 227)

Birch-Framed Cabin Art
(page 220)

Santa Doormat
(page 243)

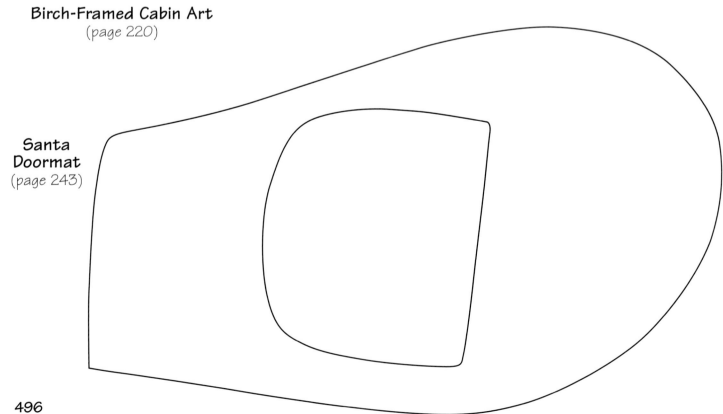

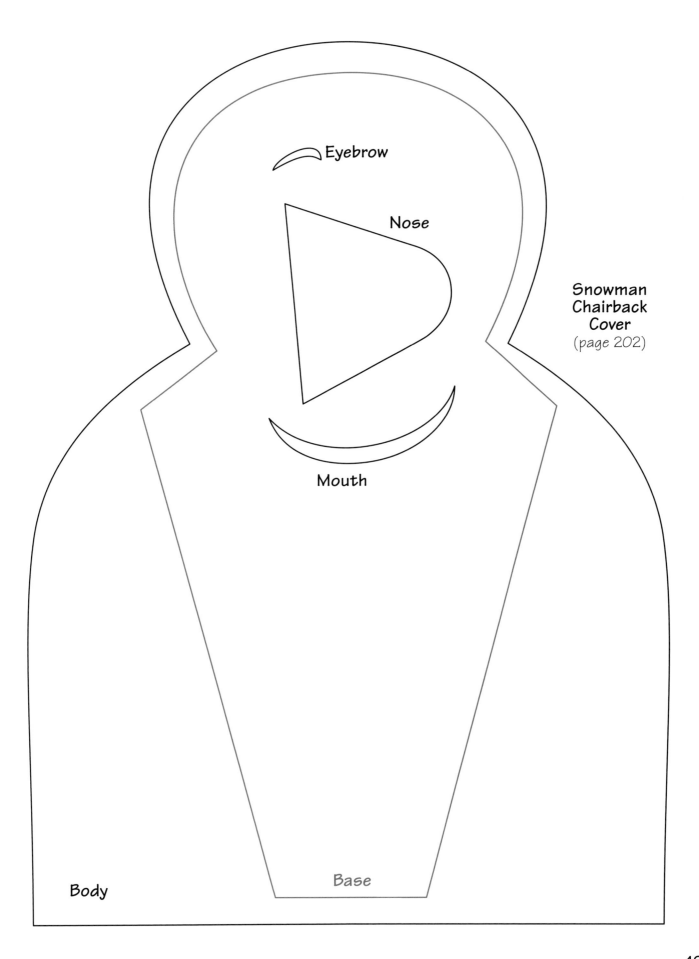

Eyebrow

Nose

Snowman
Chairback
Cover
(page 202)

Mouth

Body

Base

Clown Hat Ornaments
(page 201)

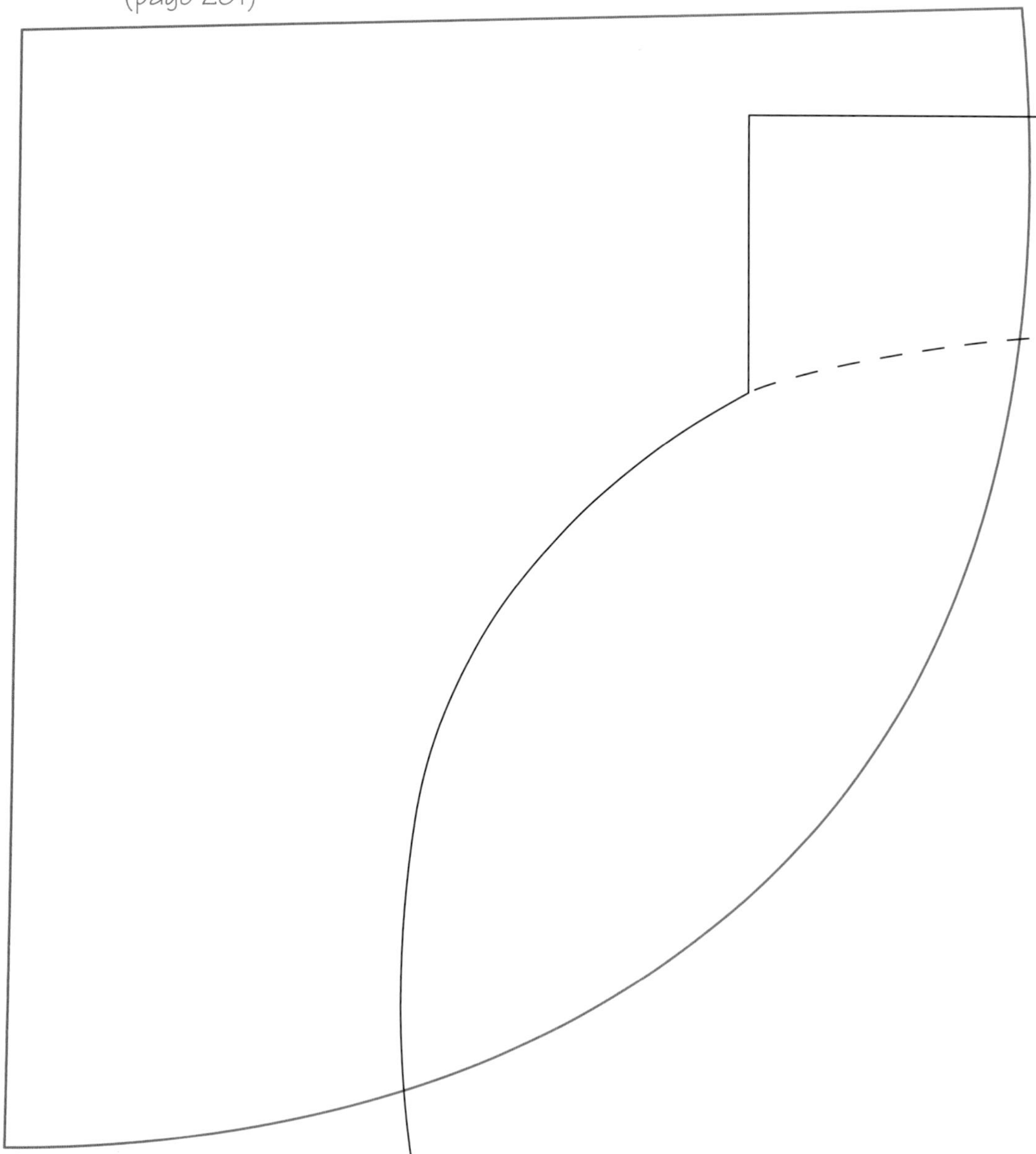

Pedicure Kit
(page 238)

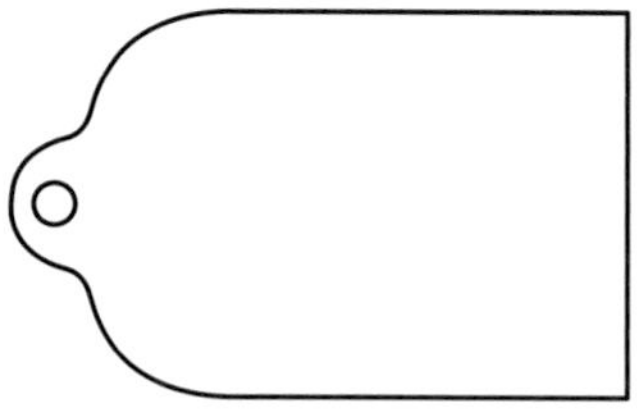

Brooch with Gift Box
(page 232)

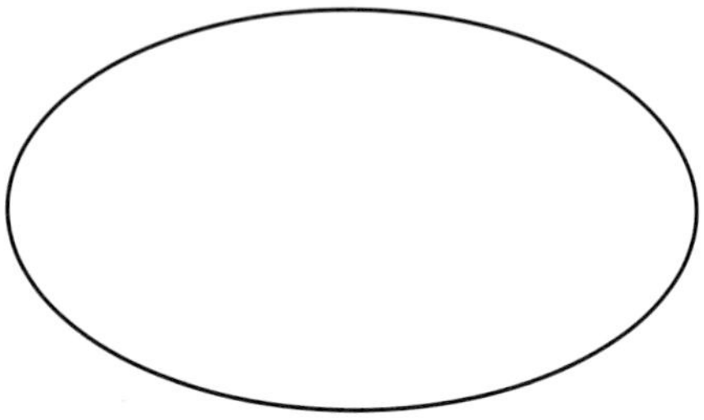

Neck Warmer
(page 235)

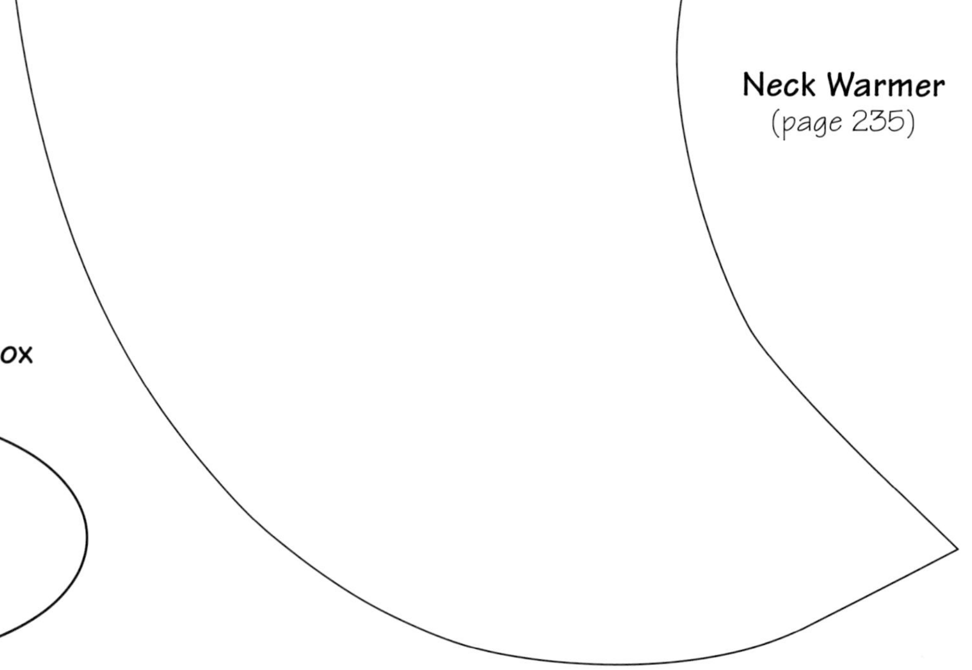

Tussie-Mussie
"Stockings"
(page 221)

Boxed Personalized Card Set
(page 231)

———— Chain Stitch

∅ Lazy Daisies

● French Knots

Pink & Brown Card Set
(page 228)

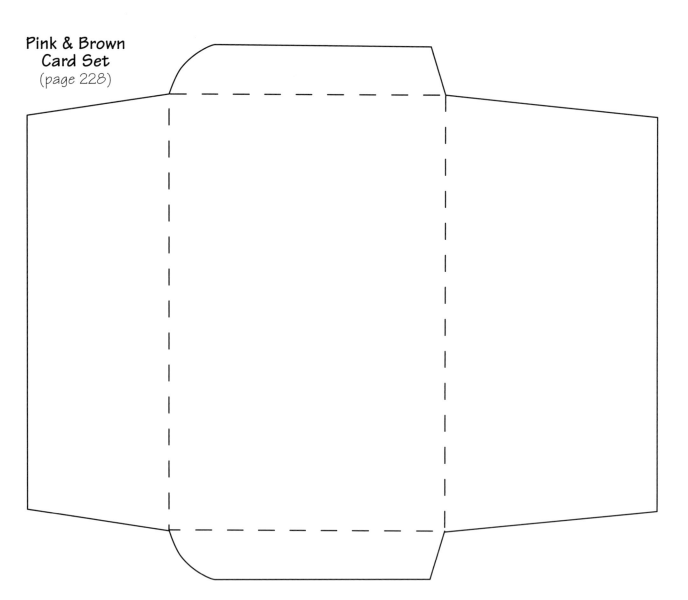

Crossword Puzzle Gift Bag
(page 205)

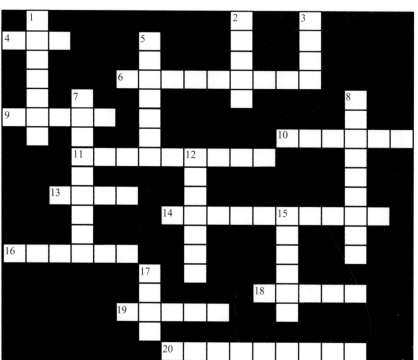

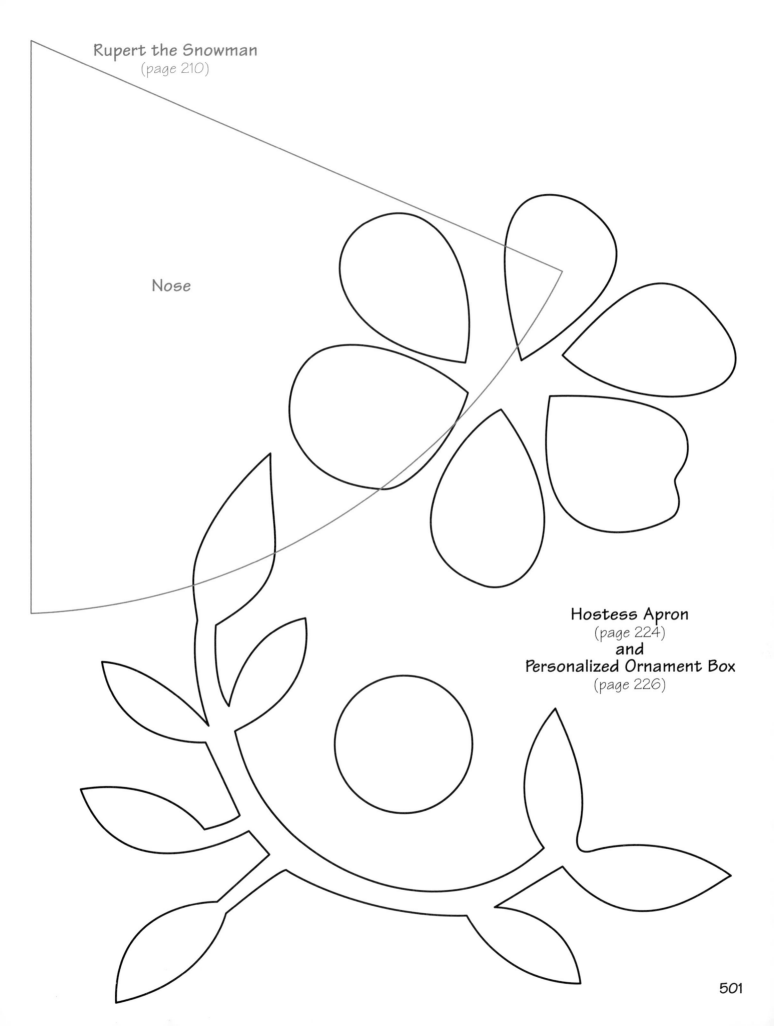

Rupert the Snowman
(page 210)

Nose

Hostess Apron
(page 224)
and
Personalized Ornament Box
(page 226)

**Reindeer Towel
and
Bath Mitt**
(page 241)

Antler

Girl's Fleece Capelet
(page 239)

Collar

Ear

Reindeer Towel
(page 241)

Girl's Fleece Capelet
(page 239)

Reindeer Bath Mitt
(page 241)

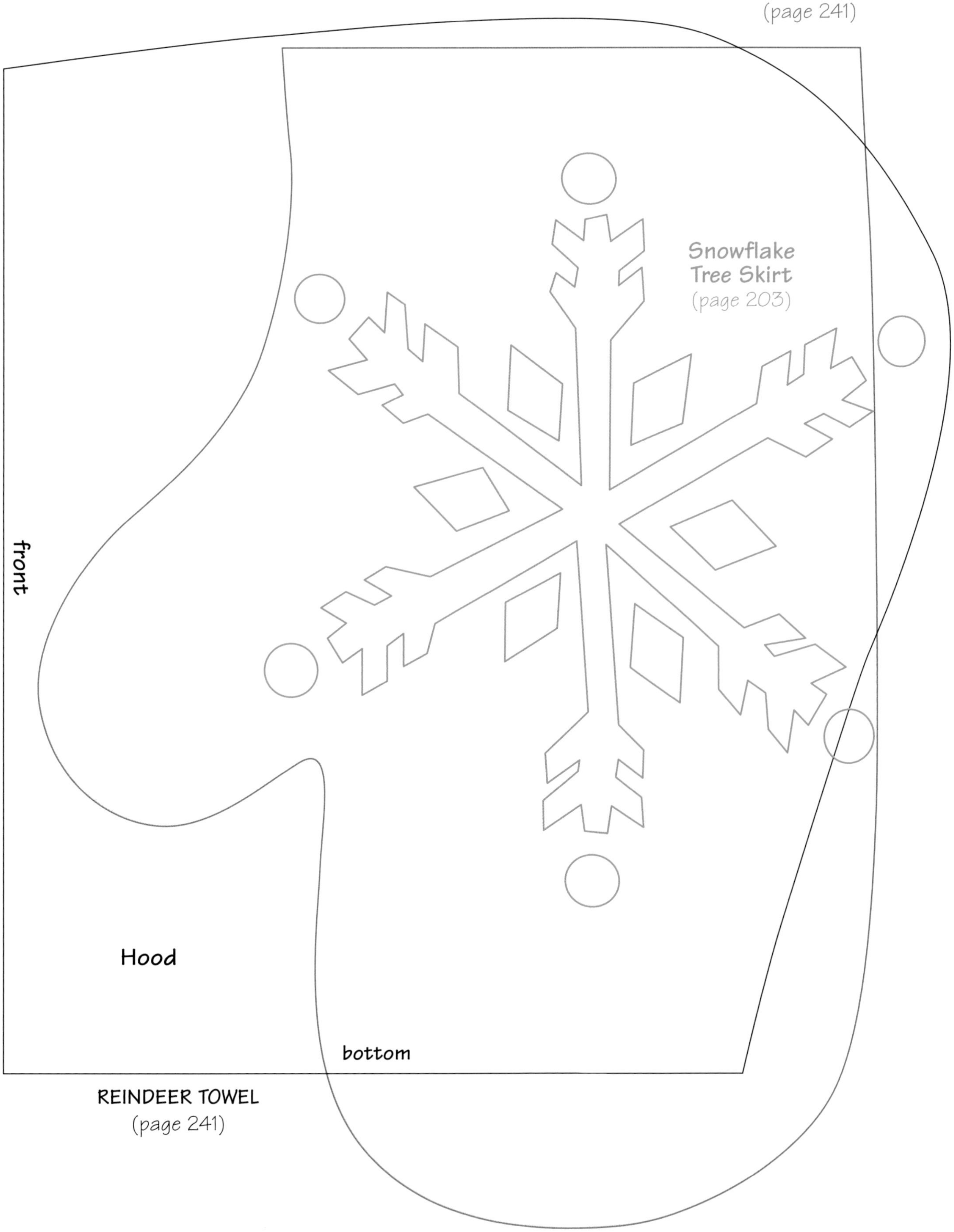

Snowflake
Tree Skirt
(page 203)
front
Hood
bottom
REINDEER TOWEL
(page 241)

Dog Album
(page 243)

M

Merry Tag
(page 197)

Merry Tag
(page 197)

C

Christmas Tag
(page 197)

Cat Album
(page 243)

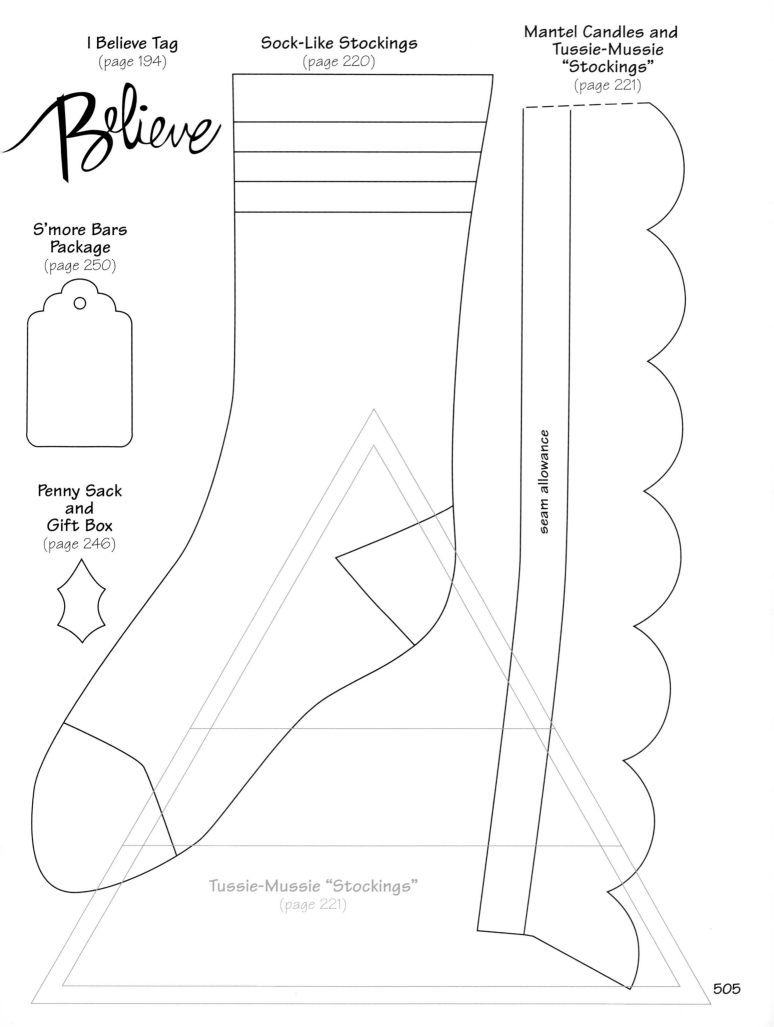

I Believe Tag
(page 194)

Believe

Sock-Like Stockings
(page 220)

Mantel Candles and Tussie-Mussie "Stockings"
(page 221)

S'more Bars Package
(page 250)

Penny Sack and Gift Box
(page 246)

seam allowance

Tussie-Mussie "Stockings"
(page 221)

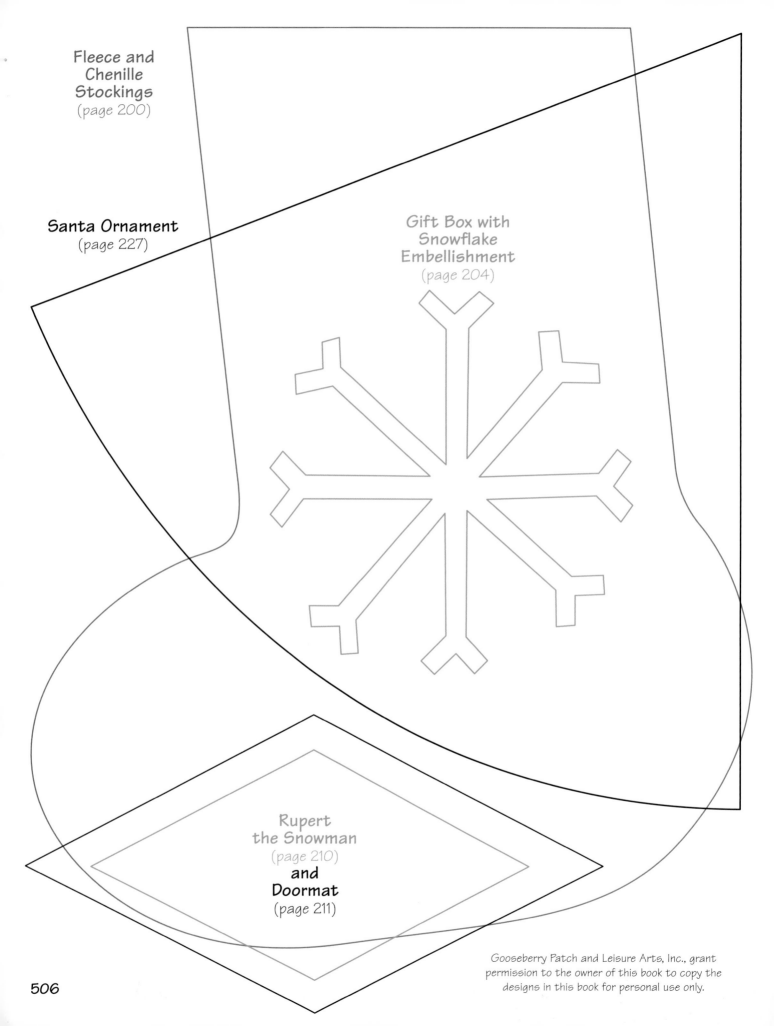

Fleece and
Chenille
Stockings
(page 200)

Santa Ornament
(page 227)

Gift Box with
Snowflake
Embellishment
(page 204)

Rupert
the Snowman
(page 210)
and
Doormat
(page 211)

Project Index

Bath & Beauty
Manicure Gift Set, 244
Monogrammed Hand Towel, 97
Monogrammed Tissue Box Cover, 97
Neck Warmer, 235
Painted Guest Towels, 31
Pedicure Kit, 238
Reindeer Towel & Bath Mitt, 241
Snowflake Soaps, 118
Travel Jewelry Box, 130
Travel Tray, 130

Clothing & Accessories
Appliquéd Bag, 31
Brooch with Gift Box, 232
Card with Earrings, 232
Dyed Wool & Embroidery Drawstring
    Bag, 101
Earrings with Gift Tag, 247
Embellished Gloves, 128
Embellished Sweater, 127
Embroidered Tote Bag, 101
Fleece Scarf, 128
Flower Brooch, 28
Girl's Fleece Capelet, 239
Hostess Apron, 224
Let It Snow Sweater, 127
Padded Hangers, 30
Reader's Scarf, 236
Velvet Jewelry Pouch, 30
Woven Scarf, 233

Gift Packaging
Apple Bags, 74
Celebrate Package Banner, 204
Cellophane Bag Topper, 43
Chinese Take-Out Box, 34
Cone Gift Box, 134
Craft Foam Containers, 139
Crossword Puzzle Gift Bag, 205
Divided Cookie Box, 39
Drawstring Gift Bag, 109
Embellished Brown Bag, 144
Fabric Bag, 150
Flannel Bag, 109
Flocked Candle Box, 69
Gift Bags, 114
Gift Box with Snowflake
    Embellishment, 204

Gift Card Holder, 135
Gingerbread Cookie Canister, 38
Honey Jars, 42
Oatmeal Cookie Box, 74
Painted Gift Tin, 147
Paper Cones, 35
Penny Sack and Gift Box, 246
Photo Wrapping Paper, 138
Pillow Gift Box, 135
Polka Dot Bag, 148
Santa Pocket Envelope, 135
S'more Bars Package, 250
Stamped Bags, 44
Stamped Gift Wrap, 204
Tea Towel Gift Bags, 106
Trimming the Tree Snack Box, 146
Truffle Box, 75

Gift Tags, Cards & Writing Accessories
Boxed Green & Brown Stationery
    Set, 231
Boxed Personalized Card Set, 231
Candy Cane Card, 247
Card Organizer, 81
Cards with Envelopes and Tags, 114
Chocolate-Covered Cherries Recipe
    Tag, 225
Christmas Address Book, 246
Christmas ATC, 248
Dog Tag, 196
Embossing Gift Wrap, Cards and
    Simple-to-Make Projects, 136
Friendship ATC Gift Card, 231
Ho Ho Ho Card, 205
Holly Tag, 75
Initial Card Set, 229
Joy Card, 204
Kid-Made Cards, 82
Monogram Gift Tag, 202
Noel Gift Tag, 202
Ornament Party Invitations, 223
Party Invitations, 40
Peace on Earth Cards, 204
Personalized Tags with Gift Box, 230
Pink & Brown Card Set, 460
Recipe Cards, 45
Sleepy Time Tag, 196
Snowflake Card, 247

The 12 Tags of Christmas, 197
Wish Card, 205

Home Décor & Accessories
Basket Liner, 19
Birch-Framed Cabin Art, 220
Birch Twig-Wrapped Candles, 220
Chairback Covers, 111
Christmas Garden Mantelscape, 219
Christmas Memory Box, 188
Crackled Papier-Maché Apples, 219
Decorative Packages, 201
Distressed Obelisks, 219
Distressed Tin Doves, 219
Dreamy Mantelscape, 221
Dyed Wool Covered Ottomans, 99
Envelopes, 219
Etched Snowflake Candle Holders, 116
Fat Quarter Napkins, 12
Floral Ottoman, 99
Framed Recipe, 192
Game Board, 69
Game-Piece Bags, 18
Glitter Stars, 221
Goody Basket, 214
Handkerchief Mantel Scarf, 91
Handrail Garland, 214
Hanging Basket Arrangement, 14
Hankie Wall Hanging, 93
Hinged Frame with Ornament, 26
Holiday Swag, 110
Kitty, 68
Latch-Hooked Rug, 86
Latch-Hooked Wreath, 86
Lodge-Inspired Mantelscape, 220
Mantel Candles, 221
Merry Christmas Banner, 218
Mouse, 68
Newsprint Noel Mantelscape, 218
Newsprint Stars, 218
Noel Gate Sign, 219
Paperwhite Kit, 251
Penny Rug Ottoman, 99
Place Mats, 12
Playing Card Tray, 66
Score Pad, 18
Snowflake and Mitten Wall Hanging, 117
Snowflake Topiaries, 116
Snowman Chairback Cover, 202

Home Décor & Accessories
(continued)

Spotty, 67
Square Card Table Cover, 18
Stitched Wall Hanging, 100
St. Nick, 217
Table Centerpiece, 12
Table Runner, 111
Tiered Ornament Display, 13
Tree Ottoman, 99
Woven Basket, 108
Yarn Snowballs, 202

Journals, Albums & Photo Displays
Accordion Album, 122
Accordion-Fold Album, 190
ATC Album with Card, 249
Bookmarks, 131
Boxed Photo Albums, 26
Christmas Journal, 83
Family Calendar, 78
Family Photo Tree, 80
Framed Hankie Card Holder, 92
Memory Shadow Box, 84
Notepad Booklet, 123
Pet Albums, 243
Pet Photo Frame, 23
Playing Card Album, 123
Wish List Album, 122

Just for Dad
CD Holder, 234
Valet Tray, 237

Kids' Stuff
Kringles Can, 121
Origami Tree, 120
Paperweight, 131
Santa Doll, 126

Kitchen Décor & Accessories
Gingerbread Man Card and
    Bag, 152
Holly Plates, 151
Kate's Wooden Treat
    Basket, 155
Mug Cozy, 129
Mustard Jar, 149
Syrup Bottle, 143

Pet Accessories
Cat Bed, 133
Doggy Quilt, 132

Pillows & Afghans
Crochet Center Pillow, 105
Monogrammed Pillow, 96
Motif Scrap Afghan, 71
Quilt, 105
Snowman Pillow with Jammie Bag
    Hat, 240
Tea Towel Pillow, 15
Vintage Pillow, 15

Sewing & Knitting Accessories
Egg Cup Pin Cushion, 28
Embellished Knitting Needles, 29

Stockings
Cross Stitched Monogram Christmas
    Stocking, 94
Dotted Knit Stocking, 215
Fleece & Chenille Stockings, 200
Striped Knit Stocking, 215
Tussie-Mussie "Stockings," 221

Trees, Ornaments & Skirts
Already-Knit Ball Ornaments, 216
Beaded Monogram, 96
Bird Ornament, 120
Braided Garland, 108
Button Ornament, 120
Chenille Stem Ornaments, 201
Clown Hat Ornaments, 201
Cross Stitched Monogram
    Ornaments, 95
Dog Bone Ornaments, 22
Flannel Bag Ornament, 109
Flocked Ornament, 226
Four-Patch Ornament, 103

Framed Hankie Ornaments, 90
Gift Tag Ornaments, 189
Hankie Tussy Mussies, 91
Holly's Hankie Garland, 89
Icicle Garland, 113
Kitty I.D. Tag Ornaments, 23
Luggage Tag Ornaments, 22
Nine Point Tree Skirt, 90
Package Ornaments, 217
Personalized Ornament Box, 226
Pet Silhouette Ornaments, 22
Pinwheel Ornament, 120
Ribbon Circle, 108
Ribbon Star, 108
Round Box Ornaments, 119
Santa Card Ornament, 227
Santa Ornament, 227
Santa's Bag, 214
Santa's Hat Ornaments, 216
Santa's Hat Tree Topper, 217
Snowflake Ornament, 113
Snowflake Tree Skirt, 203
Snowman Tag Ornament, 227
Soft Mitten Ornaments, 113
Striped and Dotted Ball
    Ornaments, 216
Tabletop Topiaries, 98
Tabletop Tree Stand, 67
Tea Towel Tree Skirt, 104
Tomato Cage Trees, 99
Vintage Pillow Ornaments, 90

Wreaths & Outdoor Displays
Boxwood Monogram, 209
Button Wreath Pillow, 207
Candle Centerpiece, 207
Chairback Wreaths, 14
Doormat, 211
Door Spray, 211
Luminaries, 207
Memory Wreath, 85
Patch Pillow, 208
Peace, Love and Harmony Baskets, 206
Railing Swag, 207
Reversible Throw, 208
Rupert the Snowman, 210
Santa Doormat, 243
Small Wreath, 209
Snowballs for Sale, 211
Swag with Ornaments, 211
Tree Centerpiece, 209
Tufted Pillow, 207
Twig Snowflakes, 206
Window Swag, 206
Wreath, 218

Recipe Index

Appetizers & Snacks
Aloha Chicken Wings, 276
Black & White Salsa, 268
Black-Eyed Pea Dip, 291
Brie Kisses, 265
Brown Sugar Granola, 144
Brown Sugar Pecans, 65
Burgundy Meatballs, 266
Caramel Apple Dip, 268
Celebration Cheese Balls, 47
Cheddar Fondue, 356
Cheery Cheese Ring, 300
Chewy Graham Popcorn, 44
Chicken Fingers with Apple Butter-Peanut
    Sauce, 362
Christmas Brie, 356
Chunky Gorgonzola Dip, 356
Cinnamon & Ginger Treats, 257
Crab Rangoon, 363
Crab-Stuffed Mushrooms, 268
Cranberry Meatballs, 360
Creamy Olive Spread, 55
Crispy-Crunchy Crouton Sticks, 148
Debbie's Long-Distance Michigan Corn
    Chip Dip, 276
Dipped & Drizzled Pretzels, 43
Florentine Artichoke Dip, 358
Good Honey-Garlic Chicken Wings, 170
Ham-Cream Cheese Croissants, 63
Herb-Marinated Cheese, 64
Herb-Marinated Shrimp, 63
Hot Antipasto Squares, 360
Hot Pecan Dip, 257
Hot Seafood & Artichoke Dip, 64
Italian Cheese Terrine, 162
Mint Chocolate Chip Cheese Ball, 284
Munch & Crunch Snack Mix, 407
Nachos Magnifico, 389
Not-Your-Usual Party Mix, 62
Pickled Mushrooms, 256
Pineapple Ball, 266
Roasted Olives, 64
Roasted Red Pepper Bruschetta, 359
Santa's Snack Mix, 66
Sassy Shrimp, 363
Smoky Nuts, 359
Spicy Vanilla Pecans, 35
Sweet Red Pepper Dip, 268
The Great Disappearing Snack Mix, 107

Toasted Pecans, 257
Trimming-the-Tree Pita Snacks, 146
Wrapped Water Chestnuts, 266
Zesty Mozzarella Cheese Bites, 147

Beverages
Apple-Cinnamon Punch, 355
Apple-Cranberry Sparkler, 175
Candy Cane Cocoa, 172
Christmas Champagne Punch, 258
Christmas Morning Cappuccino Mix, 174
Cinnamon Hot Chocolate, 354
Citrus Mimosa, 267
Comfy Cider, 173
Cranberry Cider Mix, 32
Cranberry Hot Toddies, 354
Creamy Nog Punch, 174
Farmhouse Punch, 50
Grapefruit Margaritas, 355
Homemade Eggnog, 267
Hot Cocoa Mocha, 129
Hot Percolator Punch, 366
Hot Vanilla, 366
Kid's "Champagne," 386
Mom's Cranberry Tea, 175
Montana Winter Spiced Cider, 50
Pineapple Wassail, 173
Snow Cocoa, 173
Spiced Apple Cider, 208
Spiced Cider, 19
Spiced Coffee-Eggnog Punch, 355
Spiced Hot Buttered Rum Punch, 354
Spiced Hot Cocoa Mix, 174
Sunshine in a Glass, 366
Sweet Almond Coffee, 259
The Governor's Hot Buttered Coffee, 65
Victorian Blackberry Punch, 63
Wake-Up Shake, 386
White Hot Chocolate, 59

Breads, Rolls & Muffins
Almond-Pear Muffins, 412
Barley Quick Bread, 142
Can't-Fail Biscuits, 367
Cheese Biscuits, 368
Cinnamon Puffs, 391
Country Corn Cakes, 54
Dakota Bread, 278

Ginger & Spice & Everything Nice Muffin
    Mix, 408
Gotta-Have-It Cornbread Mix, 409
Herbed Fan Dinner Rolls, 162
Lemon-Orange Rolls, 57
Melt-In-Your-Mouth Rolls, 48
Monkey Paw Biscuits, 386
Olliebollen (Doughnuts), 278
Parsley Biscuits, 255
Pecan Mini Muffins, 145
Snowflake Bread, 256
Sour Cream Twists, 368
Sugar-Topped Muffins, 271
Sunday Dinner Potato Rolls, 161
Yummy Garden Bread, 327

Breakfast Entrées
Aunt Ruthie's Breakfast Casserole, 291
Blueberry-Croissant French Toast, 369
Country Breakfast Sandwiches, 292
Cream Cheese Scrambled Eggs, 373
Creamy Crab Bake, 373
Crispy Brown Sugar Bacon, 370
Sausage-Filled Crêpes, 373
Savory Ham & Swiss Breakfast Pie, 372

Cakes
Blueberry-Sour Cream Breakfast
    Cake, 145
Buttermilk Pound Cake, 351
Candied Fruitcake, 294
Chocolate-Cappuccino Cheesecake, 65
Chocolate-Caramel Sheet Cake, 56
Chocolate Chip Pudding Cake, 328
Chocolate Mint Torte, 165
Cinnamon Cake, 154
Cookies & Cream Cake, 177
Cream-Filled Pumpkin Roll, 284
Grandma Gracie's Lemon Cake, 272
Holiday Fruitcake, 154
Hot Cocoa Cake, 60
Lane Cake, 318
Mini Christmas Cheesecakes, 281
Mom's Special Occasion Cherry
    Cake, 269
Nutty Pudding Cake, 348
Old South Pound Cake, 153
Orange Pound Cake, 181

Cakes (continued)

Peppermint Candy Cheesecake, 176
Pistachio Cake, 272
Praline-Cream Cheese Pound Cake, 285
Pumpkin Cake Roll, 51
Pumpkin Crisp, 273
Pumpkin Praline Layer Cake, 178
Quick Italian Cream Cake, 304
Raspberry Upside-Down Cake, 272
Red Velvet Cake, 180
Simple Citrus Coffee Cake, 370
Sour Cream-Streusel Pound Cake, 57
Spiced Eggnog Pound Cake, 338
Triple Chocolate Cake, 59
Warm Turtle Cake, 284

Candies & Confections
Amazing Double Chocolate Truffles, 282
Candied Apples, 193
Candied Nuts, 413
Candy Bar Fudge, 403
Chocolate-Coconut Bonbons, 400
Chocolate-Covered Cherries, 225
Chocolate-Covered Peanut Clusters, 412
Chocolate-Peanut Butter Fudge, 329
Chocolate-Peanut Nuggets, 329
Chocolate-Raspberry Truffles, 37
Chocolate Truffles, 179
Easiest Pecan Pralines, 329
Eggnog Fudge, 339
English Toffee, 182
Grandma's Molasses Popcorn Balls, 153
Holly-Jolly Almond Brittle, 402
Meringue Kisses, 402
Nana's Christmas Caramels, 413
Pan O' Fudge, 59
Peanut Butter-Cocoa Truffles, 400
Sugared Pecans, 413

Condiments & Sauces
Apple Butter-Peanut Sauce, 362
Apple Syrup, 142
Buttery Maple Syrup, 261
Chocolate Gravy for Biscuits, 367
Cinnamon, Pecan & Honey Syrup, 261
Festive Cranberry Honey, 42
Fresh Cranberry Relish, 159
Glaze, 256
Homemade Maple Syrup, 143
Lotsa Pepper Jelly, 410
Mom's Spaghetti Sauce, 169
Nutmeg-Molasses Cream, 300
Orange Butter, 262
Sauce, 360
Sweet & Tangy Mustard, 149
Sweet Hot Mustard, 265

Turkey Gravy, 275
Walnut Cranberry Sauce, 163

Cookies & Bars
Almond Grahams, 391
Amish Sugar Cookies, 182
Buckeye Brownies, 58
Can't-Leave-Alone Bars, 398
Caramel Brownies, 273
Chocolate Chip Cheesecake Squares, 59
Chocolate-Coconut Sweeties, 283
Chocolate Cutouts, 397
Chocolate-Peanut Butter Cookies, 39
Chocolate-Pecan Bars, 56
Chocolate Snappers, 61
Chocolate Snowballs, 398
Chocolate-Wrapped Peppermint
   Cookies, 37
Coffee Hermits, 269
Cranberry-Almond Blondies, 106
Cranberry-Chip Cookie Mix, 150
Danish Spice Cookies, 279
Decorated Gingerbread Cookies, 38
Devil's Food Sandwich Cookies, 271
Espresso Biscotti, 295
Fantasy Fudge Cookies, 61
Frosted Turtle Cookies, 296
Giant Chocolate Malt Cookies, 391
Grace's Bourbon Balls, 50
Graham Cracker Brownies, 153
Holiday Gumdrop Cookies, 398
Holly Jolly Cookies, 151
Holly's Brownie Blast!, 60
Jo Ann's Walnut-Oatmeal Cookie Mix, 36
Kelly's S'more Bars, 250
Luscious Layered Brownies, 259
Merry Munchers, 178
Mexican Wedding Cookies, 282
Mint Brownies, 399
Mom's Gingerbread Cookies, 281
Mom's No-Bake Cookies, 328
Moravian Spice Crisps, 396
Nut Roll Bars, 273
Orange-You-Glad Cookies, 397
Peanutty Caramel Bars, 399
Peppermint Pinwheels, 180
Praline Shortbread Cookies, 282
Raspberry Bars, 269
Rocky Road Fudge Brownies, 181
Snowball Sandwich Cookies, 163
Soft Gingerbread Cookies, 177
Stained Glass Cookies, 396
Sugar Cookies, 258
Sugar-Dusted Pecan Squares, 155
The Easiest Gingerbread Men, 152
Tuxedo Brownies in a Jar, 410

Waffle Cookies, 395
White Chocolate-Cranberry Cookies, 395
White Sugar Cookies, 283

Desserts
Half Dip Tips, 164
Lemon Fondue, 165
Pineapple Sorbet, 164
Snow Ice Cream, 296
Speedy Sorbet, 164
Strawberry Sorbet, 164
Stuffed Strawberries, 64

Entrées
Anytime Enchurritos, 348
Artichoke-Chicken Pasta, 168
BBQ Chicken Pizza, 325
Best-Ever Baked Ham, 311
Cajun Seafood Fettuccine, 344
Cheeseburger & Fries Casserole, 390
Cheesy Chicken & Mac, 386
Cheesy Chicken Curry Casserole, 53
Cheesy Sausage & Tomato Manicotti, 53
Chicken & Green Bean Bake, 170
Cider-Baked Ham, 49
Cranberry-Turkey Wraps, 334
Creamy Beef Stroganoff, 55
Cumin Pork Roast with Wild Mushroom
   Sauce, 312
Easy Turkey Pot Pie, 336
Filet Mignon with Mushrooms, 322
Fruited Pork Loin, 254
Grilled Beef Tenderloin Diablo, 313
Ground Beef-and-Tomato Manicotti, 53
Ham-Stuffed Baked Potatoes, 337
Herb-Roasted Holiday Turkey, 275
Herb-Roasted Turkey, 158
Holiday Beef Tenderloin, 303
Holiday Leftovers Casserole, 334
Juicy Prime Rib, 311
Landslide French Dip, 167
Linguine with Tomato-Clam Sauce, 325
Mandarin Pork Chops, 322
Mexicali Chicken, 294
My Favorite One-Pot Meal, 292
Parmesan Baked Chicken, 322
Pot Roast & Veggies, 170
Quick Salisbury Steak, 323
Ravioli Lasagna, 389
Salsa-Chippy Chicken, 390
Shredded Beef BBQ, 167
Smoky Red Beans & Rice, 54
Smothered Steak, 167
Spaghetti Bake, 389
Stroganoff Skillet, 325

'Taco Pizza, 390
Tried & True MeatLoaf, 166
Turkey, Almond & Wild Rice
    Casserole, 347
Turkey & Wild Rice Casserole, 52
Turkey-Cheddar-Broccoli Strata, 333
Turkey with Maple Glaze, 311
Use-Your-Noodle Casserole, 336
Weekend Beef Burgundy, 347
Whole Baked Ham, 265
Ziti with Spinach & Cheese, 346

Frostings & Dessert Sauces

Butter Frosting, 269
Chocolate Frosting, 296, 395
Coffee Cream, 307
Cream Cheese Filling, 284
Cream Cheese Frosting, 304
Decorated Gingerbread Cookie Royal
    Icing, 38
Frosting, 60, 177, 180, 182, 272, 283
    , 285, 397
Glaze, 272
Icing, 154
Lane Cake Filling, 318
Nutmeg Sauce, 51
Powdered Sugar Frosting, 281
Praline Ice Cream Syrup, 410
Quick Caramel Frosting, 56
Seven-Minute Frosting, 318
Sugar Cookie Frosting, 258
Vanilla Frosting, 283
Vickie's Chocolate Fondue, 61
Walnut Topping, 183

Mixes

Christmas Morning Cappuccino Mix, 174
Cranberry-Chip Cookie Mix, 150
Cranberry Cider Mix, 32
Cup of Veggie Noodle Soup Mix, 407
Ginger & Spice & Everything Nice Muffin
    Mix, 408
Gotta-Have-It Cornbread Mix, 409
Jo Ann's Walnut-Oatmeal Cookie Mix, 36
Munch & Crunch Snack Mix, 407
Not-Your-Usual Party Mix, 62
Santa's Snack Mix, 66
Seasoned Rice Mix, 34
Spiced Hot Cocoa Mix, 174
The Great Disappearing Snack Mix, 107
Tuxedo Brownies in a Jar, 410

Pancakes

Buttermilk Pancakes, 262
Chocolate Chip Pancakes, 263
Country Crunch Pancakes, 261

Dublin Potato Pancake, 263
Ham & Apple Filled Puffed Pancake, 260
Jelly-Roll Pancakes, 262
Santa Face Pancakes, 263

Pet Treats

Here Kitty-Kitty Cookies, 133

Pies & Pastries

Bar Harbor Cranberry Pie, 279
Caramel Pecan Pie, 161
Caramel Pie, 171
Chocolate Chess Pie, 285
Chocolate Ice Box Pie, 329
Chocolate-Macadamia Pie, 307
Chocolate Pecan Pie, 183, 319
Chocolate Silk Pie, 60
Christmas Pie, 285
Favorite Chocolate Pie, 61
Grandma's Peanut Butter Pie, 179
Granny's Sweet Potato Pie, 50
New England Pumpkin Pie, 258
Quick 'n Easy Pie, 163
Walnut Crunch Pumpkin Pie, 183

Salads & Salad Dressings

Ambrosia, 159
Feta & Walnut Salad, 159
Hot Chicken Salad, 343
Italian Bread Salad, 333
"Must-Have-Recipe" Salad, 254
Roasted Walnut & Pear Salad, 327
Salad Dressing, 254
Spinach & Cranberry Salad, 302
Spinach-Pecan Salad, 47
Turkey-Walnut Salad, 333
Warm Chutney Dressing, 302

Side Dishes

Apple & Sausage Stuffing, 315
Asparagus with Mushrooms &
    Bacon, 304
Baked Butternut Squash and
    Apples, 277
Blue Cheese & Cheddar Potato
    Gratin, 303
Broccoli with Orange Sauce, 314
Cheese Fries, 387
Chunky Applesauce, 326
Cornbread Dressing, 313
Cornbread Stuffing, 160
Corn Pudding, 49
Creamed Corn, 326
Creole Green Beans, 277
Dressed-Up Holiday Stuffing, 255
Great-Grandma's Dressing, 275
Green Bean-Corn Casserole, 160

Holiday Apple & Cranberry Casserole, 50
Holiday Yams, 317
Homestyle Green Beans, 48, 314
Leftover Potato Pancakes, 338
Macaroni & Cheese, 171
Macaroni au Gratin, 317
Make-Ahead Mashed Potatoes, 314
Mom's Broccoli Casserole, 343
Old-Fashioned Potato Casserole, 343
Pears with Cranberry Relish, 367
Polenta with Tomato, 276
Roasted Asparagus, 326
Roasted Vegetables, 49
Savory Limas, 326
Seasoned Rice Mix, 34
Shoepeg & Green Bean Casserole, 344
Take-Along Potatoes, 277
Vegetable Bake, 257
Warm Spiced Fruit, 366
Yam Risotto, 257

Soups & Stews

Baked Potato Soup, 378
Bistro Onion Soup, 376
Butternut Squash Soup, 48
Chicken Soup with Wild Rice &
    Mushrooms, 380
Chow-Down Corn Chowder, 168
Christmas Eve Oyster-Corn
    Chowder, 379
Chunky Beef Chili, 55
Cream of Pumpkin Soup, 255
Cream of Tomato Soup, 379
Cup of Veggie Noodle Soup Mix, 407
Farmstyle Beef Stew, 383
Fiesta Turkey Soup, 336
Hearty Ham & Bean Soup, 380
Hearty Winter Pork Stew, 293
Jalapeño-Chicken Chili, 168
Jambalaya, 324
Kathleen's Fabulous Chili, 383
Lobster & Chive Bisque, 376
Slow-Cooker Potato Soup, 169
Sweet Potato-Peanut Soup, 300
Taco Soup, 382
3-Bean Ravioli Minestrone, 381
Tortilla Soup, 382
White Chicken Chili, 382

Credits

We want to extend a warm thank you to the people who allowed us to photograph some of our projects at their homes: Bill & Nancy Appleton, Gary & Jane Bell, Alda Ellis, Cheryl Johnson, August & Christy Myers, Duncan & Nancy Porter, Elizabeth Rice, Scott & Angela Simon, Anne & Randy Stocks and Leighton Weeks.

We want to especially thank photographers Jerry R. Davis of Jerry Davis Photography, Jason Masters, Mark Mathews Photography, Ken West Photography and Larry Pennington Studios, all of Little Rock, Arkansas, for their excellent work.

We would like to recognize the following companies for providing some of the materials and tools we used to make our projects: Meltie Feltie's hand-dyed wool felt; DonJer for flocking adhesive and fibers; Dan River, Inc. for fabric; Saral® Paper Corp. for transfer paper; Lion Brand® Yarn Company and Patons Yarn for yarn; Viking Husqvarna Sewing Machine Company for sewing machines; DIY Furniture Kits and Kirkwood USA, Inc. for ottomans; Midwest of Cannon Falls for props in some of the photographs; Taylor Linens; David Textiles for fleece; Die Cuts with a View for Monogram Stacks; Sizzix for die-cutters and dies; and Delta Technical Coatings for some of the paints used.

Special thanks go to Marianna Crowder for crocheting the Motif Scrap Afghan and Janet Akins & Sue Galucki for crocheting the Granny Square Slippers.

Special thanks to our friends at Leisure Arts in Little Rock, Arkansas, for development of the projects and crafts featured in this book.

If these cozy Christmas ideas have inspired you to look for more Gooseberry Patch® publications, treat yourself to a Gooseberry Patch product catalog, which is filled with cookbooks, enamelware, mixing bowls, gourmet goodies and hundreds of other country collectibles. For a subscription to "A Country Store in Your Mailbox©," visit gooseberrypatch.com.